This book may be kept

FOURTEEN DAYS

A fine will be charged for each day the

S0-AOM-689

GAYLORD 142			PRINTED IN U.S.A.

Salesmanship Fundamentals

Salesmanship

THIRD EDITION

**Creative Selling
for Today's Market**

Fundamentals

John W. Ernest
Associate Professor
Business Administration
Los Angeles City College

George M. DaVall
Supervisor
Business Education Curriculum
Los Angeles City Board of Education

GREGG DIVISION   McGraw-Hill Book Company

New York   Chicago   Dallas   San Francisco   Toronto   London   Sydney

66 — 7644

Design by VOLNEY R. CROSWELL
Drawings by EDWARD MALSBERG

SALESMANSHIP FUNDAMENTALS: Creative Selling for Today's Market,
Third Edition

Preface

We live in a market-oriented economy. One needs only to look around him to appreciate that statement—huge new shopping centers on the outskirts of cities and towns; glittering new stores and renovations of old stores in downtown shopping districts; new products and services being introduced constantly; advertising messages everywhere, pitched to the eye and ear, extolling the merits of these new products and services; and transportation facilities straining to distribute goods that Americans want. Never in the history of our economic growth was marketing such a vital function.

An increasingly important part of the marketing function is selling, and this new third edition of *Salesmanship Fundamentals* recognizes the significant role of selling in our economy. Employers are demanding salesmen not only trained in sales techniques and psychology but thoroughly grounded in the field of distribution. Industrial purchasing has become highly specialized and is being done more and more by professionals. Large business firms are making increasing use of buying committees, in which many people influence the buying decision. Even the consumer is becoming more sophisticated in his buying habits; the annual flood of new and improved products and services has forced him to be more knowledgeable about what he buys.

Specialized buying on the part of industry, business, and consumer demands specialized training of salespeople. No longer is the salesman merely a persuasive talker; he must know his product, his market environment, and his customer. He is expected to be a skilled and knowledgeable consultant.

Features of the Third Edition

Salesmanship has changed dramatically in recent years; it *had* to change in order to adjust to the new demands of today's buyers. *Salesmanship Fundamentals, Third Edition,* takes these changes into account. The content and emphasis of the third edition have been carefully adapted to reflect the dynamics of the field of marketing.

Writing Style and Stress. The writing style is geared to the level of the student's ability and interest. Actual selling practices and procedures in business firms all over the country are illustrated and emphasized. Considerable stress is placed on the personal side of selling and the salesman's responsibility to customer, employer, and fellow worker.

v

Organization. The book is divided into five major parts dealing with (1) the definition of selling and its role in distribution and production, (2) a review of basic knowledge and personality requirements, (3) the various methods and techniques involved in making a sale, (4) the kinds of sales problems that the salesman encounters and ways to solve them, and (5) a step-by-step program for getting and succeeding in a selling position.

Marketing Atmosphere. As mentioned, this new edition presents selling in a marketing atmosphere, where it rightfully belongs. Not only does the student see the salesman's job in its own setting but he understands how it relates to the total marketing area, including marketing research, advertising and promotion, and customer services.

Communication. The salesman's main job is communicating, and communication as a distribution skill is emphasized throughout. A new chapter, "The Salesman Communicates," not only describes the importance of good communication to the salesman but provides valuable suggestions on how to achieve it. This important chapter also offers something unique in salesmanship texts: specific helps to improve a little-known aspect of communication—listening.

Cases. This edition makes effective use of sales cases throughout to illustrate important principles. These cases are situations that the student may have already experienced and in which he can easily picture himself.

Quotations. Quotations of prominent persons that relate to the subject are placed throughout the book where they support the text and make the student aware of the importance of selling in our modern society. The words of well-known successful businessmen and leaders provide authenticity throughout the text.

Student Activities. At the end of each of the twenty-four chapters are questions and projects to stimulate the student's thinking and to apply the principles he has learned. First come review questions covering the material that has been read. Discussion-type questions on related problems follow. Sales problems, paralleling the sales cases in the text, present problems for which there are no absolute answers. These problems do not "test" the student; they encourage creative solutions. There are also short projects to awaken the student's interest in everyday selling situations. In addition, there is a long-term project in Appendix 1 that may be completed over an extended period of time. These projects, either singly or together, provide activities bound to arouse student awareness of selling techniques.

Illustrations. One of the most important features of a book, beyond the text itself, is the illustrations. Photographs were chosen with painstaking care to ensure that each accurately depicts the idea it is meant to illustrate. Particular effort was made to present up-to-date photographs showing mostly young people in interesting situations. Many photographs were taken especially for this text. The drawings are noteworthy because they are characterized by a subtle sophistication and because they frequently introduce a touch of humor that provides a change of pace.

Supporting Materials. The *Student Activity Guide* contains exercises, activities, and projects that enrich and extend the text. It also contains forms required in some of the textbook projects.

The *Teacher's Manual and Key* provides the key to all text and student activity guide exercises and offers helpful suggestions to the teacher.

A set of objective tests is available.

Acknowledgments

The authors gratefully acknowledge the assistance of many individuals, business firms, and organizations in preparing this new edition. They are especially appreciative of the help of Mr. Henry K. Astwood, director of the Sales Manpower Foundation of the Sales Executives Club of New York, who supplied many of the statistics and data concerning career information and the income and duties of salesmen. Mr. Astwood also read portions of the manuscript and made valuable suggestions.

Numerous business organizations supplied illustrations, sales manuals, and sales training literature so that the book might reflect the most modern selling practices. To these firms, the authors express grateful thanks. Also, the authors wish to thank the SCM Corporation for supplying the sales letter at the top of page 369.

Many teachers offered suggestions, and a number of these have been incorporated. This assistance from the "firing line" is appreciated.

A special acknowledgment is due Mrs. Kathleen Langan, of Greenwich, Connecticut, who contributed her vast writing talent and research sources to help produce much of the new material for this book.

JOHN W. ERNEST
GEORGE M. DAVALL

Contents

PART FOUR. Imagination in Selling

PART FIVE. Succeeding in Your Selling Career

A Career in Selling

Part One

The demand for good salesmen and saleswomen never wanes. Anyone who dreams of an exciting career can easily find it in selling. And there is a selling job to suit every taste, whether it is working in a store, calling on buyers in business offices, or visiting with customers in their homes. Selling today doesn't mean forcing people to buy or "glad-handing" them. It is a science—a science that requires a knowledge of products, of customers, of psychology. A career in selling offers many rewards, from job satisfaction to good pay.

Selling in Our
Modern Economy

THE UNITED STATES enjoys the highest level of living of any country in the world.

Americans are better fed. One of the most impressive sights to visitors from foreign lands is the huge supermarket with its vast assortment of attractively packaged and temptingly displayed foods.

Americans are better clothed. We can choose from an almost unlimited selection of wearing apparel fashioned from dozens of different fabrics and materials.

Americans enjoy more leisure time. The housewife's work is made easier, faster, and more pleasant with such conveniences as automatic dishwashers, garbage disposals, clothes dryers, blenders, and electric can openers. The homeowner's lawns and shrubs are easier to maintain with a power mower, power edger, electric hedge clipper, and power leaf rake. Our cars have power steering, power brakes, automatic transmissions, and now air conditioning. Even the farmer's tractor comes equipped with a heater, power steering, and automatic transmission.

1

■ Each year vast amounts of goods are produced in American factories. All these goods must be sold.

Courtesy General Motors Corporation

Americans possess many of the material things to help them to enjoy their leisure time. There are a television set and at least one radio in almost every home. The two-car family is no longer a rarity. And thousands of people own boats, motion-picture cameras, sports cars, stereo sets, swimming pools, and tape recorders.

In order to enjoy such a high level of living, Americans must produce goods and services in vast quantities. And they do. Our industrial and business firms produce over $650 billion in goods and services each year for over 195 million Americans. This tremendous production of goods and services provides the jobs and incomes to give American families the greatest purchasing power ever attained in the history of the world.

Salesmanship Helped Make It Possible

Do you think that consumers rushed headlong into stores to buy power mowers, electric can openers, Polaroid cameras, and color television the moment these products were available? Certainly not. New products often call for new concepts of living; and introducing new concepts of living requires persuasion. The one-car family had to be persuaded that it really needed a second car so that mother would not be stranded when dad had the only car; the owner of a push-type lawn mower had to be persuaded that he should not work so hard and that a power mower (perhaps one he could ride) would give him more leisure time; the person who had always thought a fast motorboat was beyond his reach had to be persuaded that it was not; and so on. In short, the goods produced in the American factories didn't move into our economic stream alone. They had to be *sold*. Without the efforts of many American salesmen, these goods could not have been distributed in the quantity needed to bring the price within reach of so many people.

Let's remember that nothing happens in business and industry until somebody sells something. The salesman is a key man.

—Lynn Surles, "Now Listen to Me," *Sales/Marketing Today*

All Goods Must Be Sold

Not only do luxury items, such as an extra car, a riding power mower, and a fast motorboat, require selling effort, but such necessities as food, clothing, and furniture must also be sold. Of course, people buy some necessities simply because they must have them. The salesman, however, helps them to decide where and from whom to buy. He also helps them to buy more intelligently, in greater variety, and in greater quantity. In this way he performs a needed service to the American consumer and to American business.

Each year thousands of new buyers enter the market. Among them are new residents from foreign countries and young men and women who are just starting to earn an income. Still other buyers change their patterns of purchasing. The young person who gets married may no longer spend as much money on clothing, but he becomes a fresh prospect for household goods. The older person who retires may become a prospect for golf clubs, oil paints, and so on. These people present the salesman with an opportunity to exercise one of his most important functions: to supply information about the products in which potential customers have a buying interest. This includes information about new goods and services that have recently come on the market, as well as established products and services in which improvements have been made or for which new uses have been discovered. Even old customers constantly need product information, not only on new articles but on established products that are unfamiliar to them.

People seldom make up their minds by themselves. They usually make a buying decision only after they have heard the opinions of their friends and relatives, have seen the product demonstrated, and have discussed it with a salesman. They have learned that the well-informed salesman is one of the most competent authorities to advise them on the merits of a product or a service.

The Growth of American Salesmanship

The mass-production system that characterizes American business did not always exist. Only 150 years ago most goods were produced in the home. The family spun its own cloth, made its own clothing, grew its own food, cut down

■ The main floor of a large department store. Many competent, friendly salespeople are needed to handle the great assortment of goods such a store offers.

trees and made its own home, and provided its own entertainment. Each family member became a specialist in one activity. One specialized at spinning cloth; another was an expert at making shoes; still another excelled at carpentry, perhaps making his own nails. There were few businesses to provide these goods for the family. And since there were few products available, there were few salesmen. The salesmen who did exist were mainly merchants in cities and larger towns, and Yankee peddlers who went about the country, their wagons loaded with clocks, kitchen utensils, bolts of cloth, spices, and notions of various kinds. Many of these peddlers followed the wagon trains west and became a familiar sight in villages and mining towns.

By 1860 the Industrial Revolution had started. Machines were invented that made the production of goods on a large scale possible. Railroads were extended in all directions, making it possible to distribute these goods to buyers in cities and towns all over America. Great factories and great cities sprang up. Soon shoes, clothing, furniture, utensils, and farm implements were being produced in large quantities. Later came refrigerators, sewing machines, vacuum cleaners, typewriters, automobiles, radios, cash registers, and thousands of other articles in ever-increasing quantities.

As goods began to flow in greater and greater quantities, the need for salesmanship became more and more important. Manufacturers had to find ways of disposing of their large outputs. They employed thousands of salesmen, whose jobs were to reach out for new markets and develop old ones more intensively. It was the salesman who sold the advantages of the motorcar over the horse and buggy, the vacuum cleaner over the broom, the washing machine over the washtub.

By selling more goods, the salesman encouraged the producer to produce more. As more goods were produced, costs were lowered, so that the producer was able to bring the prices of his products within the reach of average Americans. The result was a higher level of living for all.

And as more and more goods were produced, the demand for competent salesmen increased. The highly intricate technical products that were rolling off America's assembly lines required salesmen that were well informed and thoroughly trained. The Yankee-peddler type of salesman could not do the job.

The New Concept of Creative Salesmanship

Many years ago the average American's idea of a salesman was a fast-talking, backslapping "city slicker," and he was depicted in this light in numerous cartoons that appeared in newspapers and magazines. This characterization was fairly accurate 100 years ago. The term "natural-born salesman" was widely used to describe anyone who was eloquent of speech and aggressive in manner.

Today that picture has changed. We know that there is no such thing as a natural-born salesman. A good salesman today must be intelligent, knowledgeable, articulate, imaginative, and well trained. Of course, there are many people who use the title "salesman" when they do not actually deserve it. This type of "salesman" merely stands by while the customer makes up his mind to purchase a particular product. The salesman simply goes through the mechanical function of exhibiting his stock and, once the customer arrives at a buying decision, of making out the sales slip or ringing it up on the cash register. This type of person makes little or no effort to understand the buyer's needs, to give him product information, or to help him reach a purchasing decision.

Businessmen call this form of salesmanship *order taking* to emphasize the lack of creative planning and persuasion in the sales presentation. Of course, many of our staple products, such as grocery, drug, and hardware items, require little

■ The fast-talking, backslapping salesman of the nineteenth century has been replaced by the modern salesman on the right. In addition to filling current demand, the successful salesman of today must be able to create demand for new products and for new concepts of living.

or no selling effort. The extreme example of *nonselling* is in self-service stores where articles are placed within the reach of customers who merely help themselves. Information about the products is obtained from display signs and labels or price tags on the merchandise.

In most selling, however, the art of salesmanship has advanced far beyond the order-taking or backslapping routine. And it consists of more than merely meeting current demand and filling obvious needs. Today's expert salesman is creative. He creates wants and needs that never existed before. In order to achieve effective distribution of our enormous output of goods, it is essential that salesmanship progress beyond the level of merely filling current demand; it must *create demand*—demand for new products, new brands, new methods, new concepts of living. Creative selling requires imagination in developing new ideas both in planning the sales presentations and in making the presentations. It involves persuading people to do something that they had not contemplated doing. Creative selling arouses desires that can be satisfied only by possession of the product or service. Our economy can prosper only when demand is consistent for both new and old products, and creative selling plays a vital role in building a higher level of living for all Americans.

Today's salesman is more than a salesman; he is a merchandising consultant. In serving the customer, the salesman may go far beyond persuasive talking. He must know his product better than anyone else and perform many extra services for his customers. The restaurant owner may expect the coffee salesman to show him how to make good coffee. The retail paint dealer may expect the paint salesman to set up effective displays for his line. The salesman who calls on the retail appliance dealer may pitch in and sell for the dealer or help to develop local tie-in advertising. The business-machines salesman may make a thorough study of the customer's accounting system in order to determine the type of equipment that would work best. He may even revise the entire system. One drug salesman remarked that he sets up counter displays, advises on remodeling store fronts, trains soda-fountain clerks, takes inventory in the stock room, replenishes shelf stock on the selling floor, and offers ideas on how to promote new business and handle complaints.

What Is Selling?

There are many definitions of selling. The dictionary tells us that selling is "the transfer of property from one person to another for a valuable consideration" or that selling is "to dispose of something for money." But such definitions are inadequate, because they imply that if there is no exchange of goods or money, there is no selling. Selling takes place when people are motivated to buy whether

SELLING IS UNIVERSAL

■ Travelers purchasing airline tickets in Rome.

■ A girl looking at material for a silk kimono in Tokyo.

■ Housewives shopping for kitchenware in Melbourne.

■ Shoppers buying items in a department store in Mexico City.

they buy now or not. If a salesman spends an hour with a prospect demonstrating the merits of his product and departs without an order, would you say that there is no selling since no transfer of money or goods takes place? People drive by many billboards and look at hundreds of advertisements each week; yet they don't always buy the products advertised. Would you say that selling is absent because of this fact? Probably not.

The Definitions Committee of the American Marketing Association made a thorough study of the various terms used in the field of marketing. This committee defines selling as "the personal or impersonal process of persuading a prospective customer to buy a commodity or service, or to act favorably upon an idea that has commercial significance to the seller."

Notice that this definition tells us that selling is "impersonal" as well as "personal." We may have always thought of selling as involving a face-to-face presentation. The committee's definition provides for two types of selling: direct, individual contact with the prospect (*personal selling*) and indirect, mass contact (*impersonal selling*). Impersonal selling (also called nonpersonal selling) includes advertising, display, and sales promotion. In this book we will concern ourselves primarily with personal selling. But we should not forget that both forms of selling require a mastery of common principles of salesmanship; success in advertising, promotion, and display comes faster to those who have mastered the principles of personal selling.

Selling Is Providing Service. The Definitions Committee of the American Marketing Association suggests in its definition that selling also involves assisting the prospect. People have basic needs or wants, and the sales process must include ascertaining these needs or wants if it is to function effectively. The salesman who is not interested in a customer's needs and problems is not likely to be a success in the selling field. Providing customer service is the cornerstone on which American business is built. The salesman must learn what customers want and provide the products or services that satisfy those wants.

Selling Is Using Persuasion, Not Compulsion. The successful salesman knows that people cannot be forced to buy. He leads the customer to a favorable buying decision by (1) imaginatively presenting the merits of his product, (2) encouraging the customer to participate in the sales process, (3) suggesting favorable courses of action for the customer, and (4) allowing the customer to exercise complete freedom of choice.

Selling Is Educating. People need and want certain things, but they are not always aware of these needs and wants. It is the job of the salesman to find out what they are. Many products on the market are too technical for the average customer to understand, and the help of a good salesman is needed. A product may contain hidden qualities that are not apparent on casual inspection, such as a vacuum cleaner that may also be used as a paint sprayer. The good salesman knows these hidden qualities and makes the customer aware of them. Often a feature that is not apparent in a product is the one that will satisfy a need. The salesman, then, is a teacher. He explains, demonstrates, compares, enlightens, educates.

We can now formulate a simple and practical definition of selling that we can use from here on: *Selling is the process of determining the needs and wants of a prospective customer and of presenting a product or service in such a way that the customer is motivated to make a favorable buying decision.*

How does this definition fit a typical selling situation? Let's look at the following case example in which a customer has just entered a retail furniture store:

CUSTOMER: I'd like to look at those marble-top lamp tables you have on sale.

SALESMAN (*pointing them out*): **They're right over here.**

(The customer looks at the price tags on the different styles of tables while the salesman waits. Finally she makes her selection.)

CUSTOMER: I'll take this one which is priced at $59.95.

SALESMAN: **OK, that will be $61.75 with the 3 percent sales tax.**

(The salesman writes the sales slip and accepts the customer's check. Then the customer walks out.)

This type of sale takes place thousands of times during the day. Was salesmanship used by the salesman? You might reply, "Well, a sale was made." Yes, a sale was made, if we are willing to accept the dictionary definition of a sale;

■ The successful salesperson is aware of her customer's needs and wants. She may present a product in such a way that the customer will make a favorable buying decision, but she must never force the customer to buy.

■ Every day thousands of Americans shop for groceries in huge supermarkets. Because supermarkets provide self-service rather than face-to-face selling, they depend on a vast array of attractively displayed items to attract the shopper's attention.

after all a transfer of title took place. But did the salesman practice salesmanship, or did he merely fill a request? Don't you feel that the customer was already sold when she entered the store? The salesman did not *persuade* the customer to buy the table; he only took an order. Even though a sale had taken place, salesmanship was not used if we accept the premise that salesmanship is the art of persuading people to buy something that will benefit them.

Now let's return to the case example and see how a good salesman might have handled this same sales situation. The customer has just chosen the table she wants.

SALESMAN (*reaching for sales book*): You have made a very wise choice. It is a beautiful table, isn't it? By the way, are you doing some redecorating?

CUSTOMER: Yes, I am. We plan on getting rid of some of our old Early American pieces and replacing them with something more contemporary and colorful.

SALESMAN: What colors are you thinking of adding, Mrs.—uh, Mrs.—uh—?

CUSTOMER: Mrs. Seagraves. I would like to add some turquoise.

SALESMAN: In that case let me show you how one of our new lamps would look on this table. We have one in turquoise.

(*He picks up a lamp from a nearby table and places it on the table the customer has just purchased.*)

CUSTOMER: Oh, it's beautiful. (*Looks at the price tag.*) But $79 seems like so much to spend on a lamp.

SALESMAN: **How often have you had to buy a lamp, Mrs. Seagraves? This lamp will enhance the attractiveness of your home for years to come. A small cost when you consider the long period of time you will enjoy it, wouldn't you say?**

(*The customer stands looking at the lamp, obviously thinking about what the salesman has said.*)

CUSTOMER: Yes, you are right. This lamp is surely beautiful, and it's just the color I had in mind.

(*The salesman begins to write up the order.*)

SALESMAN: **With the fine-quality brass fittings and the easy-to-clean shade, you'll get a maximum amount of use and enjoyment out of this lamp. Its large size and three-way switch will distribute lots of light when you need it, and the light can be cut down for a more subdued effect when you want it. (Demonstrates.)**

(*After the salesman finishes writing up the order, he turns the sales book around to face the customer and goes over the figures with her, so that she knows they were added correctly.*)

SALESMAN: **Will that be cash or charge, Mrs. Seagraves?**

CUSTOMER: I'll write a check.

(*The salesman accepts the check and hands her a receipt.*)

SALESMAN: **Your lamp and table should be delivered next Tuesday, Mrs. Seagraves. Here is my card, and please drop in soon and let me know how you are enjoying your new purchases.**

Was the art of salesmanship practiced? If you will refer back to the definition on page 9, you will arrive at the conclusion that it was.

Five Steps to a Sale

There are five steps through which the salesman must lead the prospective customer in making a sale: (1) gaining attention, (2) arousing interest, (3) building desire, (4) winning conviction, and (5) getting action.

1. *Gaining attention.* It is obvious that you cannot begin selling until you have the attention of your prospect. The door-to-door salesman appreciates this fact most, since in many cases he cannot finish his opening sentence before the door closes! Attention is gained when a prospective customer is aware that he needs something. The prospect's attention may already have been drawn to the product through an advertisement while the prospect was leisurely reading a

THE FIVE STEPS TO A SALE

1 GAIN ATTENTION OF PROSPECTIVE CUSTOMER.

2 AROUSE INTEREST IN PRODUCT OR SERVICE.

3 BUILD DESIRE TO OWN PRODUCT.

4 WIN CONVICTION OF THE PROSPECT.

5 GET ACTION FROM THE PROSPECT.

magazine, watching a television program, or listening to the radio. Often, however, the salesman must win attention; and he can do so by using a prompt approach, giving a friendly introduction, or having a courteous and businesslike manner. Or he can win attention by doing or saying something unusual.

2. *Arousing interest.* Interest is aroused by getting the prospect to appreciate fully his need for the product. This step in the sales process, like gaining attention, may have taken place already in the prospect's home or at some time before he has even seen a salesman. If not, it will be necessary for the salesman to arouse the prospect's interest. To accomplish this, the salesman may need to try several different approaches.

For example, if the safety features and smart styling of an electric range are being demonstrated and the prospect seems obviously unmoved, the salesman has failed as yet to arouse interest. At this point, he might mention the automatic controls that turn off the heat at a designated time, leaving the customer free to go shopping while the dinner is cooking; or he might mention the even-temperature cooking that lessens the danger of scorching food (a feature he knows many older stoves lack). He watches for signs of interest and proceeds from one feature to another until he is sure he has that interest.

3. *Building desire.* The salesman must build a desire for the prospect to own the product before he can hope to make a sale. The desire may be built by stressing such qualities as beauty, timesaving features, smartness of design, durability, or economy. The prospect must want to own the product, or he will not buy it no matter how much he may be interested in what the salesman tells him about it. If a man has become interested in a salesman's presentation of a riding-type power lawn mower, he will purchase it only if the salesman can pinpoint the features that will make him want to own it. It may be the laborsaving features, the fact that his neighbor has one, or merely an interest in mechanical things.

4. *Winning conviction.* The prospect may have a desire to own the product, but often he still needs to be convinced that yours will fit his needs best. At the "conviction stage" the salesman must be prepared to back up his statements with facts—facts about the advantages claimed for the product, how it measures up to other products, why it is a smart buy, how easy it is to own, and so on. This is where the salesman emphasizes the features that aroused the prospect's desire in the first place.

5. *Getting action.* Even though the prospect may be convinced that a product will suit him perfectly and he has the desire to own it, he still may not act. The salesman must help him make the decision to buy. He may say, "Shall I have it wrapped for you?" or "We can deliver this tomorrow morning," or "What color did you decide on?"

The sales process may be considered as a series of links in a chain, each link representing a sales proposition. These links should be put together so smoothly

■ Before this man purchased his riding power mower, he went through the five steps to a sale even though he may have taken several of the steps by himself before he ever visited a store.

that neither the prospect nor the salesman is aware that they have been separate parts.

It will not help the salesman to stop and ponder over whether the prospect is in step 2 or 3. If he makes an effective approach, conducts a "live" demonstration, and uses a strong close, he will find that the prospect will pass through these five steps subconsciously. Consider, for example, the sales presentation for the lamp on pages 10 and 11. Can you distinctly separate the five steps?

It is not essential that the five sales steps be in the order presented. If, for example, Mrs. Ernest wants a new automatic washer and she shops around, talking to different salesmen, it would be a waste of time to start with step 1 or 2, since she is already interested. Start out with step 3—building desire. Give reasons why she will want to have your particular automatic washer rather than one of the competing washers.

Retail-store customers often have taken all the steps by themselves, except closing, before they visit the store. All the retail salesperson has to do is to fill the order. Of course, if he is a good salesperson, he will call the customer's attention to a better-quality, higher-priced article. Or he will mention related articles in the department and endeavor to sell something additional.

These five steps are the heart of this book. Learn them well, because you will use them throughout this course and over and over again in all forms of selling.

SUMMING UP

Salesmanship plays a vital role in our economy and has helped to make possible the high level of living we enjoy today in the United States. Our system of mass production depends on the sales efforts of hundreds of thousands of salesmen, who educate consumers in the uses and benefits of new products.

Ordinarily, products are not merely bought; they have to be sold. Selling involves providing service, using persuasion as opposed to compulsion, and educating people.

The salesman today is a different type of person from that of his nineteenth-century counterpart. Modern industry demands good salesmen who are intelligent, knowledgeable, articulate, imaginative, and well trained.

In making a sale, there are five fundamental steps through which the salesman must lead the prospective customer:

1. Gaining attention   3. Building desire   5. Getting action
2. Arousing interest   4. Winning conviction

1. Define selling.
2. Explain the statement, "If America is to produce goods in large quantities, it must have good salesmen."
3. Distinguish between order taking and selling.
4. How does the salesman contribute to the present high level of living in this country?
5. Give examples of activities a salesman may perform for a retail store.
6. Contrast the Yankee-peddler type of salesman with today's creative salesman.
7. What is the difference between filling current demand and creating demand?
8. Distinguish between impersonal selling and personal selling.
9. What are the five basic steps to a sale?

For Discussion

1. Goods and services are not bought voluntarily without influence of any kind. Why do you think this is so?
2. Give an example from your own experience of a salesman who merely fills an order and of another who uses creative selling.
3. Do you think salesmen could study psychology to their advantage? Why?
4. Can you think of anyone who does not have to use any of the principles of salesmanship? Defend your answer.
5. "Salesmanship is getting the customer's point of view and then making him see yours." What is your opinion of this definition of salesmanship?
6. Why do you want to sell? If you had your choice, what would you prefer to sell?
7. Why is the United States the richest nation in the world, and why does it have the highest level of living?

Sales Problem

The case problem that follows illustrates the basic steps to a sale as mentioned in this chapter. Can you recognize which sales step the customer is going through at any particular time? Read the case carefully and answer the questions following it.

Scene: The men's suit department in a large store. The customer is looking at a suit displayed on a manikin. He is approached by a salesperson who has been watching his actions since he entered the department.

SALESPERSON: This is one of our new worsted cheviots. It just came in. It's good looking, isn't it?

CUSTOMER: Yes, it is sort of good looking.

SALESPERSON: Cheviot is one of the most popular materials for suits this season. It combines beauty and luster with exceptionally long wear.

CUSTOMER: It's a beautiful fabric all right, but why should it wear better?

SALESPERSON: The secret lies in the yarn. It is carefully selected in the first place for its long-wearing qualities. Then it is twisted very tightly before it is woven into a fabric. Just feel this material.

CUSTOMER: That may be OK, but I understand that a tightly woven material soon gets extremely shiny. I'm not going to buy a suit that gets shiny.

SALESPERSON: I can certainly go along with you on that; but one of the characteristics of cheviot is that it will retain its luster, yet never shine. This is because the luster is woven into the fabric. I happen to be wearing a cheviot now. This suit has had a lot of hard wear, but you will notice that it doesn't shine.

CUSTOMER: Yes, it looks all right. How about the style, though? Is this style of coat popular now?

SALESPERSON: Oh, yes. We're selling about twice as many of these this season as any other style. They're especially popular with well-proportioned men. This suit would look well on you. Let's just try on the coat.

CUSTOMER (*trying on coat*): I didn't really intend to look at suits. I came in to buy a shirt and tie.

SALESPERSON: I don't blame you for being interested in this particular suit. It's one of our better suit values. It does look good on you, doesn't it?

CUSTOMER: How about the color? I'd prefer blue.

SALESPERSON: I can offer you this same suit in blue. If you'll pardon my saying so, brown is more youthful and there's no reason for your not wearing it.

CUSTOMER: Do you really think so? What is the price?

SALESPERSON: It's $79.50. As long as I've been here, I've never seen a suit of this quality sold at such a price. It's a suit you will be proud to wear.

CUSTOMER: It looks like a real value.

SALESPERSON: Just step over here, and we'll have the tailor measure you for the trousers. The coat fits you almost perfectly, except possibly for a slight alteration in the sleeve length.

CUSTOMER (*walking over to the tailor*): I think it's just what I've been looking for.

QUESTIONS

1. When was the customer's attention gained?
2. When and in what way was the customer's interest aroused?
3. When and how did the salesperson create desire?
4. Was conviction necessary?
5. How did the salesperson get action?

Salesmanship in Action

1. Assume that you are a salesman in the candy department of a drugstore. A customer enters your department and asks for a package of gum.
   a. Write a brief paragraph describing how an order taker would handle this situation. You may use the dialogue form illustrated in the sales case example on pages 10 and 11 in this chapter if you wish.
   b. Next, write a brief paragraph or dramatization illustrating how a creative salesman would handle the same situation. Make certain your creative sales example fits all the requirements of the definition of salesmanship given on page 9.
   c. Be prepared to discuss your examples in class.
2. Make a list of the ways in which salesmanship should help you in your personal life both in and out of school. Be prepared to discuss the items on your list and to defend your views as to why they require salesmanship ability.
3. Make a list of five commodities sold in your community that you believe require a great deal of selling effort. Give your reasons for including each item on your list.
4. Make a list of five commodities that you believe require little sales effort. Give your reasons.

The Salesman's Market Environment

THE ENORMOUS QUANTITY of goods manufactured in the United States will serve little use if these goods are not made available to prospective buyers in a convenient place. When a housewife in Ohio needs a box of laundry detergent, she obviously cannot be expected to go to a soap factory in New Jersey to pick it up. That box of detergent must be made available to her right in her home town, preferably only a few blocks from her home. The farmer who wants to buy a new tractor should not have to travel far from home to obtain it. A hardware dealer who must restock his supply of nails for his customers must be able to obtain the nails quickly and easily, perhaps by telephone.

The process of getting goods from the place where they are made or grown to the place where they are to be used is called *distribution*, or *marketing*. The marketing function is one of the most important functions in any economic system, and the salesman plays a vital part in it. The term marketing covers everything that happens to a product from the time it leaves the producer until it is bought by the user—transportation, packaging, storing, advertising, and selling, all are a part of the marketing process.

How are goods distributed by the producer (manufacturer) to the user? The procedure varies greatly by product and by producer. One manufacturer may sell his product direct to the consumer; another may sell to retail stores, which sell to the consumer; still another may sell to a wholesaler, who in turn sells to retail stores, which sell to the consumer; and so on. Many manufacturers use a combination of these marketing methods.

The marketing function is an enormously intricate one; and the discussion here will be limited to some of the more common marketing methods and procedures and to the new role of marketing.

Types of Goods Marketed

Goods to be marketed are of two main types: (1) industrial goods and (2) consumer goods.

Industrial Goods. Industrial goods are those goods used in producing other goods or in rendering services. Some examples of industrial goods are as follows:

Equipment: Printing presses for a publisher, bottling equipment for a soft-drink manufacturer, hydraulic lifts for a filling station
Parts: Bearings for an automobile manufacturer, motors for an automatic-washer manufacturer, diamond needles for a phonograph manufacturer

THE FIVE FUNCTIONS OF MARKETING

TRANSPORTATION

PACKAGING

ADVERTISING

STORING

SELLING

Raw materials: Chemicals for a soap manufacturer, plywood sheets for a furniture maker, aluminum for an aircraft manufacturer

Supplies: Stationery for a business office, paper towels for a factory washroom, oil for a machine shop

Consumer Goods. Goods that are bought for use by individual consumers are called consumer goods. The things you and your family buy are consumer goods —toothpaste, furniture, clothing, phonograph records, shoes, and so on.

Some articles may be both industrial goods and consumer goods. For example, the factory buys towels for use in wiping greasy machinery (industrial); the housewife buys towels for use in the kitchen (consumer). The use to which the article is to be put, then, determines whether it is classified as an industrial good or a consumer good.

Direct Marketing

The simplest form of marketing of any kind of good is that in which the producer sells his product direct to the user. It is called direct marketing. Here are two examples:

1. A farmer sets up a roadside stand alongside a main highway and sells fruits and vegetables to passing motorists. Some farmers load their produce on a truck and take them direct to homes for sale.
2. A manufacturer sells direct to the consumer by mail. Such things as neckties, garden seeds, and shrubs are sold in this manner.

■ The salesman selling automobile parts to a factory handles industrial goods. Here the salesman is discussing a new product with the plant manager.

■ **The notions section of a department store carries a wide variety of consumer goods.**

These two examples of direct marketing pertain to consumer-type goods. In terms of dollars the value of goods sold by the producer direct to the consumer is relatively small. However, many industrial goods are distributed in this manner. For example, a company that bottles and sells soft drinks would probably order bottling equipment direct from the manufacturer of that machinery. The owner's need is highly specialized—the machine he wants may be made especially for his plant and cost thousands of dollars—and sources of supply are limited. Tire manufacturers often sell their tires direct to automobile manufacturers. Paper manufacturers often sell direct to publishers. In general, however, most goods are not distributed by direct-marketing methods.

Indirect Marketing

About 75 percent of all goods sold in this country pass through the hands of one or more people on their way from producer to ultimate user. This is called indirect marketing; and it is in this type of marketing that the salesman is most interested, because he plays a significant role in the process.

Those through whom goods pass between the producer and user in the marketing of goods are called *middlemen*. There are two main types of middlemen: (1) merchant middlemen and (2) agent middlemen.

■ The farmer's son who sells melons direct to the consumer is using the simplest form of marketing—direct marketing.

Merchant Middlemen. Merchant middlemen own the goods they sell. They may be either (1) wholesalers (sometimes called jobbers) or (2) retailers.

W*holesalers.* The wholesalers buy goods in large quantities from producers and sell them in smaller lots to retailers; institutions such as hotels, hospitals, and schools; and industrial and commercial users. In the industrial-goods market, the wholesaler is more commonly referred to as an industrial distributor.

Wholesalers are independent business firms that own the merchandise they seek to sell. They carry this merchandise in the form of inventories; and in the course of selling these inventories, they hope to make a profit. Wholesalers perform a valuable service to their customers. Usually they are located near the retailers or industrial users who buy their products and thus can make quick delivery. They often offer credit privileges, delivery services, and other assistance to their customers. Many wholesalers employ salesmen who call upon stores and various institutions regularly.

There are several types of wholesalers. *General-line wholesalers* handle a complete line of merchandise in one general field. Examples are wholesale grocers who handle all types of food and other products from canned pineapple to cigars, and wholesale hardware dealers who stock a wide variety of merchandise from power lawn mowers to paint. *Specialty wholesalers* specialize in handling a part of a line, such as sports clothing, millinery, cotton fabrics, or spices. They attempt to carry complete and fresh stock in the items they handle. *Wagon wholesalers* maintain regular routes and specialize in selling to such customers as restaurants and delicatessens. Some wholesalers are described as *cash-and-carry wholesalers;* they keep a stock of fast-moving staple goods (food or clothing, for example) and require customers to call in person for their needs and to pay cash. *Drop shippers* are a special type of wholesaler. They keep no stock on hand but take orders and arrange for goods to be shipped direct from the manufacturer to the customer.

Retailers. The merchant middlemen more familiar to you are the retailers—those who own and operate department stores, drugstores, service stations, appliance stores, and so on. Retailers buy most of their needs from wholesalers, although they may buy direct from the producer. Generally speaking, however, retailers function between wholesalers and consumer. Retail stores account for over 55 percent of the total number of business firms in the United States.

There are three main classes of retail stores: chain, independent, and multi-independent. *Chain stores* are in every community and carry such famous names as A & P, Safeway, J. C. Penney, Woolworth, and Kroger. The designation "chain" comes from the fact that there are several stores—four or more—under the same ownership, or "in the chain." Chain stores are usually managed and operated by local people who have no ownership in the stores. Although only about one out of ten of the total retail stores in the country are chain stores, they account for approximately $3 out of every $10 worth of retail business done in the United States.

The *independent* retailers, on the other hand, own and operate a *single* store or establishment. Furniture stores, hardware stores, barbershops, restaurants, small drugstores, and gift shops are examples. Over 92 percent of retailers are independents. Retailers who operate from two to four stores are called *multi-independents.* Many large department stores fit in this group.

Agent Middlemen. The merchant middlemen discussed above buy goods, physically take possession of them, and assume ownership. Agent middlemen are another important type of middleman. The main difference between the two types is that agent middlemen do not assume ownership of the goods in which

■ The busy loading dock of a wholesaler who specializes in handling fruit. The wholesaler is a merchant middleman and he owns the goods he sells.

■ A group of retail stores located in a large modern shopping center. The retailer is also a merchant middleman.

they deal; in some cases they do not even take possession of them. The function of agent middlemen is to bring seller and buyer together. For this service they receive a fee or commission.

There are three common types of agent middlemen: (1) commission merchants, (2) brokers, and (3) manufacturers' agents. Each of these agent middlemen usually employs one or more salesmen who call upon prospective buyers.

Commission Merchants. Commission merchants take goods on consignment from a supplier or an agent and sell them to buyers. To explain the term *consignment,* let's assume that a friend of yours leaves his radio at your home and asks you to sell it for him. For this help he promises to give you a portion of the price you get for the radio. You do not actually buy the radio; you merely take it with the understanding that if you sell it, you will turn the money—less your "cut"—over to him. If you don't sell the radio, you return it to the owner. This is a simplified form of consignment. In this case you are the consignee; he is the consignor. When commission merchants collect the money for the merchandise from the buyers, they deduct their fee and send the money (and possibly any unsold goods) to the consignor. Commission merchants deal in many types of goods—fresh fruit, vegetables, textiles, wool, and similar goods. They sell to wholesalers, retailers, and other buyers. Many commission merchants *auction* goods, placing them on display and selling them to the highest bidder. Tobacco is sold in this manner.

Brokers. Brokers, like commission merchants, handle various goods, such as cotton, grain, and fruits and vegetables, for a fee. They can represent either the buyer or the seller but there is no continuing relationship. Unlike commission merchants, however, they do not take physical possession of the goods.

Manufacturers' Agents. Manufacturers' agents are independent representatives who act in behalf of one or more clients. Like commission merchants and brokers, they receive a fee for their distribution services.

The Producer's Choice

In deciding which marketing channel to use, the producer must decide which one will serve his needs most efficiently. He may choose to:

1. Distribute all his goods direct to the consumer, using no middlemen.
2. Distribute all his goods direct to the retailer, bypassing the wholesaler.
3. Distribute all his goods through a wholesaler, who will sell them to the retailer.
4. Distribute all his goods through an agent, who will distribute them to the wholesaler, who in turn will sell them to the retailer.
5. Use a combination of these methods.

Few producers stick to one method of distribution. Too, the method chosen often varies with the product. As you can see, there is a great deal of flexibility within the distribution system.

■ The producer must choose which method of distribution he will use to market his goods. Often he uses more than one method of distribution.

The New Role of Marketing

Regardless of the method used in marketing goods, the aim of the producer is simple: to produce goods that the consumer will want to buy. Competition is keen for the consumer's dollar, and in order to survive, the producer must direct all his efforts toward consumer acceptance of his product. "The consumer is king" is his motto. This is why today it is said that we have a "market-oriented" economy. Producers cannot afford to manufacture goods with the hope consumers will want them. They must find out in advance what consumers want and produce the goods that will satisfy those wants.

This relatively new concept of marketing has greatly affected sales and distribution techniques. In recent years large companies have reorganized their sales and advertising departments to accomplish these objectives. The emphasis has become so heavily oriented toward the market that the former title of Vice-President—Sales has now become Vice-President—Marketing; the title of Sales Manager has become Marketing Manager or Marketing Director. Two of the topics of vital interest to marketing managers today are (1) marketing research and (2) product planning.

Marketing Research. A continuing study and evaluation of present and potential markets and of company policies, methods, and performance related to these markets is called marketing research. Businessmen depend on this research to answer many questions. The following are some of the areas in which marketing research helps to provide vital information needed to make intelligent marketing decisions: consumer preferences, package design, pricing policies, distribution methods, plant location, analysis of salesmen's activities, store location, and effectiveness of advertising and promotion. Most salesmen take part in a marketing-research study at one time or another; for example, they may be asked to answer questions about customer reaction to prices, to tell why certain sales were lost, to give estimates of future sales volume, and so on.

Product Planning. The modern manufacturer cannot afford to produce products that do not sell, no matter how well he makes them. He has come to rely on product planning—that is he asks his marketing department to find out in advance about the size of the market for such a product, specific needs and preferences of consumers, and the price that can be charged. After the manufacturer has this information, he can instruct the engineering department to design a product that will fit these requirements. Today, then, the marketing role is not confined to distribution; it begins long before the product is even manufactured.

The Sales Pattern in Distribution

When the salesman in a retail dress shop sells a dress to a customer, he may not realize how many previous sales have taken place on the article before the dress is finally wrapped and handed to the customer. In the first place, the cotton from which the dress was made had to be sold to a spinner; the material was then sold by the spinner to a weaver; the woven fabric was sold by the weaver to a printer; the printed fabric was sold by the printer to a garmentmaker; the garmentmaker fashioned a dress and sold it to a wholesaler; the dress was sold by the wholesaler to a retailer; finally, the retailer put the dress on display and made the sale to a consumer. Along the way many other sales occurred, including a pattern for the dress and such accessories as buttons and zipper. Do you see why selling is such an important part of every distribution system?

Courtesy Association of American Railroads

SOME PEOPLE GROW THINGS

SOME PEOPLE MINE THINGS

SOME PEOPLE MAKE THINGS

ALL PEOPLE USE THINGS

...BUT IT TAKES SELLING TO BRING PEOPLE AND THINGS TOGETHER

SUMMING UP

The important link between production and consumption is distribution, or marketing. The salesman plays a vital part in this process. Goods may be distributed directly from producer to consumer, or they may be distributed indirectly through one or more middlemen.

When distributing his goods, the producer may choose from any of several channels, depending upon his specific needs.

Goods to be marketed are of two main types: (1) industrial and (2) consumer. The ultimate use of the article determines whether the goods are classified as industrial or consumer goods.

To survive in a highly competitive economy, business firms are becoming market-oriented and are placing greater emphasis on marketing research and product planning.

Reviewing Your Reading

1. Define marketing.
2. Distinguish between industrial goods and consumer goods.
3. What determines whether an article is an industrial or a consumer good?
4. Give three examples of both industrial goods and consumer goods.
5. Describe how certain goods can be classified as either industrial or consumer.
6. What is the simplest form of marketing?
7. Give three examples of manufacturers that sell direct to the consumer.
8. Define middleman.
9. Describe the functions of wholesalers.
10. List three types of wholesalers.
11. Distinguish between commission merchants and wholesalers.
12. What are the three types of retailers?

For Discussion

1. Examine your textbook closely. What kinds of marketing do you think took place during the process of its manufacture and delivery to your school?
2. In this chapter it was mentioned that packaging, storing, and advertising goods are all a part of the marketing process. Discuss each of these functions and give examples of products that must be packaged, stored, and advertised. Can you think of any products that bypass one or more of these functions?

3. Selling industrial goods is often very different from selling consumer goods. Discuss some of the factors that account for this difference.
4. Some people maintain that middlemen are unnecessary in distributing goods and that they should be abolished. What do you think? Why?
5. List some of the chain stores in your community. What benefits do you think have been derived from the establishment of these chains in your community?

Sales Problem

The Brecker Company sells $20 million worth of household cleanser throughout the United States. The company's sales organization consists of three divisional sales offices—New York, Chicago, and Los Angeles; these are divided into seventeen districts. The divisions and districts are staffed by three division managers, seventeen district managers, eight supervisors, and sixty salesmen. In the sparser markets, such as the Rocky Mountain region and Great Plains states, Brecker uses approximately sixty brokers at a commission rate of about 5 percent of sales. The sales cost of the Brecker Company each year is $2,400,000.

The vice-president of marketing, Mr. Michael Lawrence, is not satisfied with this high cost of distribution. He figures that sales costs should be brought within 10 percent of sales in order to improve the net-profit position of the company. The profit objective of the company is 4 percent of sales. Mr. Lawrence feels that the present organization is too costly and complex. He also feels that communication is not too effective under the present set-up.

QUESTIONS
1. What is the Brecker Company's present sales cost percentage?
2. How can the company overhaul its organization so as to achieve more effective distribution at less cost?

Salesmanship in Action

1. List four ways that a salesman can contribute to the marketing-research studies conducted by his employer.
2. List products grown or manufactured in your community that are sold by direct-marketing methods.
3. Make a list of retail firms in your community that use salesmen outside the store. Discuss how effective you think their sales organizations are.
4. Find out from a retail-store manager in your community what types of salespeople he employs and what job titles are used. Does he employ outside salespeople? If so, for what types of products?

Types of Selling Jobs

YOU HAVE SEEN how many different sales must be made in order to bring a product from the raw-material stage to the finished-product stage and ultimately into the hands of the consumer. Behind every one of these many sales there is a salesman. All these salesmen have one thing in common: they sell.

Selling has been defined as *the process of determining the needs and wants of a prospective customer and of presenting the product or service in such a way that the customer is motivated to make a favorable buying decision.* This definition explains clearly what every salesman must do—he must sell—but it doesn't say *how* he is going to do it. Giving the "how" of every sale would be impossible, since every sales job is different from every other. Each requires not only different methods of selling but even different qualifications in the salesman.

Have you ever heard the slogan, "The right man in the right job"? Personnel managers use it frequently, because they are concerned daily with the problem of obtaining the best-qualified person for each job that is to be filled; and they know that the effectiveness of each individual hired depends directly upon placing him in the particular job for which his skills, experience, education, background, aptitudes, and interests best fit him.

30

What does this mean to you? It means that it is not enough to decide on a career in selling. You must also study carefully the different types of selling jobs and try to choose the one for which you are best qualified and in which you would do best.

The Three Fields of Personal Selling

There are three general fields of personal selling: (1) industrial salesmanship, (2) merchant salesmanship, and (3) consumer salesmanship. These three fields correspond to the three types of buyers in the chain of sales in the distribution system—industry, middleman, and consumer.

Industrial Salesmanship. In industrial salesmanship, the salesman's customers are industrial and commercial firms. The products sold by industrial salesmen are used either to manufacture other products or to equip factories, mills, public utilities, banks, stores, and offices so that the manufacturing or commercial process can be carried on there. These products include:

1. Raw materials, such as wood, cotton, wool, tobacco, crude oil, coal, and ore
2. Semi-finished goods, such as lumber, fibers, plastics, aluminum ingots, pig iron, and steel
3. Finished parts, such as bearings, gears, locks, valves, filters, nuts, and bolts
4. Installed equipment, such as conveyors, cranes, machine tools, and heating and cooling systems
5. Equipment used in manufacturing offices and commercial offices, such as desks, typewriters, adding machines, time clocks, and drinking fountains
6. Operating supplies, such as fuel, electricity, stationery, light bulbs, and paper cups
7. Services, such as hospitalization and accident insurance and pension plans

Three types of salesmen service the industrial field: (1) the general industrial salesman, (2) the sales engineer, and (3) the service salesman.

The General Industrial Salesman. Not so many years ago the general industrial salesman was thought of as a person who simply made a sales presentation to a customer in his plant or office and walked away with an order. He needed no special training, because he was not expected to render services to the customer beyond showing the product and praising its advantages. But in the past few years this concept has changed drastically. Because the cost of labor and materials has increased steadily, management must continually search for new ways of making the best product the easiest way possible for the least amount of money. Small manufacturers, especially, cannot afford the research that is

■ The industrial sales-
man calls on industrial
and commercial firms.
He must be able to give
his customers service as
well as fill their orders.

Courtesy *Steelways*

carried on by larger corporations to find these new ways. They turn, therefore, to their suppliers for expert guidance on everything from manufacturing proc-esses to advertising and promotion. The suppliers, in turn, find that their own sales volume takes a sharp turn upward in proportion to the help they can offer their customers. Complete customer service, then, has become a real factor in industrial salesmanship. This fact is demonstrated by United States Steel Corpo-ration's new slogan, "Service is our most important product." Another example is the new ten-point program that the Polymer Division of W. R. Grace and Company has developed as a sales tool. It is called "The Extra Touch of Grace," and it includes counsel in distribution, product and mold design, merchandising, market research and development, materials handling, finance, and technical operations.

Complete service to the customer has understandably made some changes in the general industrial salesman's job. He is a prime example of the merchandis-ing consultant that was referred to in Chapter 1. Of course, he has the whole research staff of his company behind him if problems come up that he can't handle; but he, too, must be armed with more information than ever before. For this reason, companies are beginning to favor college graduates, preferably with some technical training, for this type of work, although a college degree is not an absolute requirement. Most companies, however, do make an intensive train-ing program mandatory for all their salesmen, not only when they begin their careers but also at periodic intervals along the way. This program is designed to teach the salesmen all that they need to know about the technical details of the product, its uses, and all relevant facts about the company making the product and the potential buyers for it.

The necessity for this training program and its scope, as well as the necessity for a college degree or a technical background, will vary with the complexity of the product to be sold. A man who is selling office supplies for a factory will obviously not need the special training that the man will need who sells industrial fastenings, such as the bolts that hold bridges together. But the point is that the salesman's success depends on his ability to relate his product, whether it is simple or complex, to a particular company's needs and to explain this relation to a highly trained buyer.

The general industrial salesman may represent manufacturers; wholesalers or jobbers; or agent middlemen, such as commission merchants, brokers, or manufacturers' agents. He will sell to purchasing agents, plant foremen and superintendents, engineers, office managers, and general administrators. Depending on the type of product that he is selling, and the importance and amount of the order, he may have to sell to the entire top management in the firm rather than just one individual. Again depending on the type of product, the general industrial salesman may have a relatively small number of customers. Even so, his sales volume is likely to be large because of the high cost of the goods.

The general industrial salesman must be patient; he can't expect quick results on every call. Sometimes he has to call on prospects for several years before a sale is made; but with the large orders that are typical in this field, this kind of patience pays off. The general industrial salesman should be ambitious, intelligent, alert, self-reliant, and self-generating. In return, not only can he earn large financial rewards, but he can also have the satisfaction of knowing that he plays a big role in our industrial economy.

The Sales Engineer. The general climate in which the sales engineer works is somewhat like that of the general industrial salesman. But to explain the difference between them, let's borrow an analogy from medicine. The general industrial salesman is the general practitioner; the sales engineer is the specialist.

The sales engineer is highly trained. At the least he has a college education and perhaps even an advanced degree in the field in which he is selling. He may be a chemical, metallurgical, mechanical, civil, or aeronautical engineer or other highly specialized technologist. In addition, he has probably had an apprenticeship in the factories and laboratories of his company. He must be the most knowledgeable of all the types of salesmen.

The sales engineer usually works for a company that makes intricate and expensive factory machinery or materials which are sold for fabrication and remanufacture. For instance, he may sell for a company like Ametek, which makes all kinds of ingenious motors for such complicated equipment as computers in the Lamb Electric Division; or he may sell for a company like the Celanese Corporation of America, which makes chemicals, fibers, plastics, and polymers to be used in the manufacture of other products.

The sales engineer is as much an inventor as he is a salesman. Sometimes he has to figure out new ways of utilizing old equipment to suit new processes and products. Sometimes he has to invent new pieces of equipment and then train the buyer's employees to use them. Then again, he may have to iron out a kink in the manufacturing process of a particular plant, both analyzing the problem and finding the remedy. These are only a few examples of the work that the sales engineer may do; but they illustrate the main point: whatever the particular job of the sales engineer is, he must have a highly inventive mind that thrives on solving problems. Also, he must have a special degree of enthusiasm, articulateness, and persuasive power, because many times he is selling the most difficult product of all—a new idea.

The Service Salesman. This type of industrial salesman does not have to have any advanced education, but he must have a high mechanical aptitude and some technical training along with a great deal of technical experience. His principal job is to sell a product with the understanding that he will service it afterward. He must know every nut and bolt in his product. He must be able to take it apart and put it back together again, and to keep it running at maximum efficiency.

Not only does the service salesman sell the product to the prospect in the first place, but he must persuade him to replace his equipment at the right time. However, the service salesman is not likely to be a high-pressure type. He must be reliable, competent, and pleasant and sure of his ability in handling machines so that he can gain his customer's complete confidence. The service salesman cannot expect to earn as much money as the other types of industrial salesmen, but he will have a steady job with less pressure.

An example of the service salesman is the refrigeration salesman, who sells to warehouses, butcher shops, hotels, restaurants, supermarkets, and hospitals. Once the equipment has been sold, the service salesman continues to call regularly on the client to see if the equipment is in good condition and to provide needed parts and accessories.

Merchant Salesmanship. The merchant salesman sells his products to middlemen, who will in turn resell the products to consumers. These middlemen include wholesalers or distributors, chain-store organizations, mail-order retailers, and independent retailers. The merchant salesman may sell any of a great variety of goods, for instance, necessities, such as foods, drugs, hardware, and clothing; specialties, such as electrical appliances, automobiles, and sporting goods; or luxuries, such as jewelry and furs. But whatever his product, the merchant salesman's common denominator is that he is selling his product to a customer who is not going to use the product and who has to make money on its resale.

There are four types of merchant salesmen: (1) the pioneer salesman, (2) the dealer-service salesman, (3) the wholesale or jobber salesman, and (4) the detail salesman.

The Pioneer Salesman. The pioneer salesman, who represents a manufacturing firm, is so named because he goes into uncharted territories to convince wholesalers, distributors, and retailers that they should take a chance on buying from a brand new company or on buying a brand new product for resale. The pioneer salesman has to be positive, quick-thinking, imaginative, and facile with words to be able to make his prospects see what they have to gain by taking the risk of trying to sell an unproven product. This kind of salesman is well paid and is very much in demand.

The Dealer-Service Salesman. After the pioneer salesman has made the initial sale, the manufacturer will turn the account over to a dealer-service salesman. At regular intervals, he calls on the trade which has been established for him, and his chief purpose is to obtain a constant flow of reorders for the manufacturer who hires him. If the dealer-service salesman represents a well-known manufacturer, especially one that consistently has a large advertising campaign, the company does not have to bother with a pioneer salesman. Instead the company lets the dealer-service salesman get the new accounts himself and also makes it part of his job to persuade established dealers to include new products in their line.

In either case, in order to increase constantly his own sales volume and his company's profits, the dealer-service salesman must help his established dealers

■ The merchant salesman sells his products to middlemen. Here the salesman for a large manufacturer of grocery products calls on the wholesaler at his warehouse to obtain reorders.

increase their sales volume and their profits. This is another proof of how true it is that the modern salesman has turned into a merchandising consultant. The dealer-service salesman fulfills this job by seeing that (1) the dealer's inventory of the salesman's line of products is always complete, (2) the products are advantageously and attractively displayed, and (3) the dealer's salesclerks know how to sell the product.

Examples of the dealer-service salesman are the cigarette and cigar salesman, the greeting-card salesman, and the scotch-tape and fountain-pen salesman. The dealer-service salesman does not lead an adventurous life that calls for a great deal of imagination and spirit, but he can have great security and a steady income with a minimum of wear on his nervous system. He does need physical energy, for he must make many calls during a day; and he should have the type of warm, friendly personality that would make his customers glad to see him every time he calls.

The Wholesale or Jobber Salesman. The job of the wholesale or jobber salesman is similar to that of the dealer-service salesman except that instead of representing a single manufacturer, he represents a wholesaler or jobber who is the middleman for many manufacturing concerns. Here is an excellent description of the work of the wholesale salesman:

> The average druggist carries several thousand items, made by several hundred manufacturers, in his stock. He would have no time left for serving his customers if he had to deal direct with each of these manufacturers. His favorite drug wholesaler, however, carries most of these several thousand items in stock, and the druggist will probably purchase 80 to 90 percent of his supplies from one house.
>
> The salesman for this drug wholesaler—or hardware, or grocery, or electrical supplies, or any other type of wholesale business—calls on his customers at regular intervals. He cannot do very much selling on any particular item because his catalog may contain anywhere from 1,000 to 10,000 items. Usually, he is so well known to the store proprietor that he walks in and makes up his own order from the "want book."
>
> It is the wholesale salesman's responsibility to see that his company is prompt and accurate in filling orders and that his customers get fair and equitable treatment in all other respects. He may act as a collection agent for his company, or he may merely keep the company accurately informed about the credit rating and responsibility of his customers.[1]

Although the wholesale salesman cannot do any really creative selling, he does not have to be just an order taker. He can build sales volume by making the customer aware of new products, of promotion aids offered by the manufacturer, and of profit possibilities. But it is unlikely that an aggressive, highly

[1] *Opportunities in Selling*, U.S. Department of Commerce, p. 15.

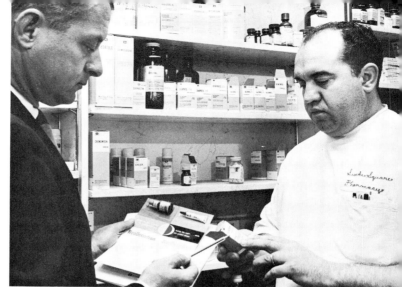

The medical salesman introducing a new product to the pharmacist. He must be able to acquaint the pharmacist with all the essential facts about the product.

Courtesy Merck Sharp & Dohme

ambitious man would be content with this job. The low-pressure type, who is friendly, reliable, and punctual, would make the best wholesale salesman.

The Detail Salesman. The job of the detail salesman requires a completely different type of approach from that of the other merchant salesmen. The detail salesman is not actually making sales. His job is sales promotion. He is a specialist in a selected field, such as pharmaceuticals, advertising, printing, display, packaging, or merchandising methods. He must have complete knowledge about his product, and he must also have absolute faith in it. Some companies call this type of salesman a missionary salesman, because his job is to spread the good word about the product. This does not mean that he should be a high-pressure type, but he should be intelligent and a clear thinker who can be counted on to come up with the right answers in a tactful and businesslike manner.

The best example of the detail salesman is the representative of the pharmaceutical manufacturer, who visits doctors and pharmacists to introduce his company's new products. He must know the ingredients of each product and how they are put together, what illnesses the product is designed to combat, how it should be administered, and what its side effects might be on individuals with chronic diseases. The detail salesman is not trying to sell the doctor and pharmacist the product. He just wants to acquaint them with it and to try to persuade the doctor to prescribe it for his patients rather than a competitor's product.

The detail salesman represents his company to the professional man. He must therefore be as diplomatic, honest, and personable as possible to make the right image for the company.

Courtesy Dayton's, Minneapolis

■ Retail selling is a creative field for the salesman who applies the principles of salesmanship.

Consumer Salesmanship. The consumer salesman sells to an individual who is going to use the product or service to satisfy his own needs or desires. There are over 180 million people in the United States today; and according to a recent study made by the Stanford Research Institute and reported in *Nation's Business*, the annual per capita personal consumption amounts to more than $1,900. By 1975 the Institute expects the figure to be $2,600, and by then the population will be about 215 million. Behind these statistics are the consumer salesmen, who keep this tremendous flow of consumer goods moving.

In consumer salesmanship there are four types of salesmen: (1) the retail salesman, (2) the specialty salesman, (3) the door-to-door salesman, and (4) the route salesman. The retail salesman does inside consumer selling, or retail selling, in a store. The other three types of salesmen do outside consumer selling—that is, they seek out the prospect in the prospect's home or office.

The Retail Salesman. The retail salesperson may work in a drug, hardware, department, or specialty store. There is one major difference between his job and that of other salesmen: the customer comes to the salesman rather than his seeking out the customer. However, this does not alter the fact that all the principles and techniques of salesmanship apply to inside consumer selling, or retail selling. Retail selling can and should be a creative field.

Unfortunately, in recent years, retail selling has often deteriorated into retail clerking. Many retail salesmen are not salesmen at all but simply order takers. They find the item that the customer asks for, write out a sales slip, and make change and wrap the package. (Some cannot even manage to stay pleasant while they are performing these simple tasks!)

This situation probably came about because retail salesmen are in great demand and because salaries in retail stores are not always high at the start. But the young person who is planning a career in selling can find excellent opportunities in retail selling. This is especially true for those who are eager to learn, who like people and have a knack for getting along well with them, and who are willing to work and anxious to get ahead.

Since the retail salesman is on a salary, the store requires him to fill his time when he is not waiting on customers by arranging and replenishing the stock and keeping it neat and clean. These duties can also be turned to the salesman's advantage, for he can thus increase his product knowledge. It should be noted that most stores offer a percentage of the sale as a commission to the salesman, in addition to his salary, so that the salesman can figure on immediate rewards for hard work, as well as long-range ones. The time spent trying to analyze the customer's needs and attempting to sell not only the best product to satisfy those needs, but also related products, will not be lost.

Some retail stores require their salesmen to spend a part of their time in outside selling—that is, calling on customers in their homes or places of business. Appliance dealers, furniture stores, and automobile dealers are examples. Retail salesmen employed in this way fall into the next category of consumer salesmanship, the specialty or direct-selling salesman.

The Specialty Salesman. The specialty salesman sells a particular product or service or a limited line of products direct to the ultimate consumer in his own home or office. This product, service, or product line may be any one of the thousands of items that are available to fill the needs and desires of American families today. The range goes from wearing apparel, publications, cosmetics, household supplies, vacuum cleaners, furniture, and air conditioners to sports and hobby equipment, life insurance, and investments.

■ **This woman selling cosmetics to the customer in her home is a specialty saleswoman. She must be able to help her customers select makeup that is appropriate for them.**

The specialty salesman practices a highly creative type of selling; and the rewards for it can be great, especially if the product is a new one. Generally speaking, the more difficult a product is to sell, the higher the rewards are for selling it. Television sets have now become a necessity to most American families, but the specialty salesmen who sold the first hundred sets had to be very ingenious men.

Even if the specialty salesman is selling a product that is well advertised and easily understood by his customers, he still has to be a creative salesman to think of ways of finding the prospect in the first place. Then he must, no doubt, carry the prospect through the five steps to the sale of a product that the prospect may not have even suspected he would ever want.

The specialty salesman must be hard-working, ambitious, energetic, enthusiastic, and likable. Like the general industrial salesman, the degree of education or training that the specialty salesman needs will vary with the complexity of the product or service that he sells, but here again the salesman's company will see that he has the training and information that he needs through a training program. The specialty salesman may represent the manufacturer who markets direct to the consumer; he may represent the franchised dealer, such as the life insurance agent or the home-appliance dealer; or he may represent the retail store, which has already been discussed above.

The Door-to-Door Salesman. While the door-to-door salesman also sells direct to the consumer, he does not pick his prospects or work by appointment. He simply rings doorbells in his territory and tries to sell the householder on the spot. Usually the door-to-door salesman sells products of comparatively low dollar value. He sells on commission and this commission must be high enough to compensate him for the many fruitless calls that he will make between sales. The average commission is about 25 percent of the price of the product.

Selling door to door can be very difficult; and it should not be considered by anyone who is thin-skinned, self-conscious, or easily discouraged. On the other hand, an outgoing type of person who is convinced of the value of his product and who feels that he is doing the householder a favor by making the product so easily available can make a big success of this job. In addition, it can be a good way for students, housewives with time on their hands, and retired people to supplement their incomes.

The Route Salesman. The route salesman combines the duties of delivery with that of sales. The company he works for usually provides a truck or other form of transportation. This salesman has a regular route and delivers to the same accounts on a prescribed basis. He wants to (1) keep his accounts by satisfying his customers, (2) get new customers, and (3) persuade his regular customers to buy more. Examples of route salesmen are milkmen and those who deliver bakery goods from house to house.

The route salesman must possess good health and stamina. Usually he must check in at the plant at 5 or 6 A.M. to load his truck and sign out. He puts in a full eight-hour day or more of physical work. He must keep moving at a crisp pace to finish all his calls. At the same time he has to be always cheerful, friendly, courteous, and anxious to be of service. But he does not need any of the aggressive or imaginative qualities that real creative selling demands.

Tangibles Versus Intangibles

The salesman may sell a product or a service. A product is tangible, something that the customer can see and feel. A service is intangible; it is just an idea and cannot be seen or felt or physically examined. When you are considering which selling job is the right one for you, not only should you consider the field of salesmanship in which you want to work, but also you should think about whether you can best sell tangibles or intangibles.

As a general rule, it's easier to sell tangibles than intangibles. The salesman of tangibles has the advantage of being able to appeal directly to the prospect's senses of sight, hearing, smell, touch, or taste. Small items can be placed right in the customer's hand, to be felt, held, and examined during the sales talk. Large items such as refrigerators and cars can also be carefully examined in a sales-

■ Combining delivery with sales, the route salesman calls at his customers' homes on a regularly scheduled basis.

■ The insurance salesman sells intangible goods; the vacuum-cleaner salesman sells tangible goods.

room setup. Of course, the specialty salesman would not carry a refrigerator into the prospect's house with him any more than the industrial salesman would carry a diesel engine with him on his call at the factory; but nevertheless, either salesman can carry brochures, photographs, and technical literature so that the prospect can see exactly what he is buying.

Intangibles are another story. Here there is nothing that can be touched or seen. There is only the salesman's ability to describe how the service will benefit the prospect. The salesman of intangibles obviously needs a vivid imagination, a high degree of intelligence, and the ability to communicate his thoughts clearly and persuasively. Selling intangibles can represent the most creative type of selling of all, and the rewards are commensurate with the challenge. The insurance salesman who is able to make the prospect understand that he is buying protection, happiness, and financial security for his family can earn one of the highest incomes of any type of salesman, sometimes as much as $100,000 a year.

Nonpersonal Selling

The emphasis of this book, as has already been stated, is on personal selling. But the student who is analyzing the kinds of selling jobs in terms of the right job for himself should be reminded that there are also opportunities for successful careers in the nonpersonal areas of selling—advertising, display, packaging, and public relations.

The men who work in these fields are also salesmen, but they sell to groups rather than to individuals. They must understand all the principles of salesman-

■ In the nonpersonal area of selling are those who prepare newspaper and magazine ads. They must know the principles of salesmanship also.

Good Value!

Pile-lined

campus

coat

40.⁰⁰

Rugged wool tweed with warm lining and zip-off collar of alpaca pile. 36" split-shoulder model with patch pockets. Brown plaid or brown and blue plaid. The Bailiwick Shop, sixth floor, Fifth Avenue and at White Plains, Manhasset and Short Hills.

ship; indeed, many of them start as personal salesmen. In addition, to be successful, they should have an above-average degree of specialized talent—in art, creative writing, or imaginative thinking. They also need a working knowledge of psychology and human motivation. These fields are highly competitive and demanding, but the rewards can be very great.

The work of these group salesmen does not now, and probably never will, replace the role of the personal salesman. All that they can do is to set the stage for the man who will meet the customer face to face.

SUMMING UP

It is not enough to decide on a career in selling. You have to try to figure out exactly which job is the right one for you by studying carefully the different types of selling jobs. To begin with, there are three general fields of personal selling; and within each of these fields, there are opportunities for men with quite different qualifications.

In industrial salesmanship, the salesman sells his product to an industrial or commercial firm. The product will be used either in the manufacture of other products or to equip factories, mills, public utilities, banks, stores, and offices so that the manufacturing or commercial process can be carried on there. Servicing the industrial field is the general industrial salesman, the sales engineer, and the service salesman. In merchant salesmanship, the salesman sells his product to middlemen, who will in turn resell the product. Working in this field are the pioneer salesman, the dealer-service salesman, the wholesale or jobber salesman, and the detail salesman. In consumer salesmanship, the salesman sells direct to an individual who is going to use the product or service to satisfy his own needs or desires. Consumer selling is done in a retail store by the retail salesman or in the customer's home or office by the specialty salesman, the door-to-door salesman, and the route salesman.

It is also necessary to make a choice between selling tangibles and intangibles. A tangible is a product, and it can be physically examined. An intangible is an idea, without any physical dimension at all. As a rule, it is harder to sell intangibles than tangibles and the rewards are commensurately greater.

The nonpersonal areas of selling—advertising, display, packaging, and public relations—are other possibilities for anyone who wants a career in selling. The men who work in these fields are also salesmen, but they sell to groups rather than to individuals. They cannot replace the personal salesman.

1. What does the slogan "The right man in the right job" have to do with you?
2. In industrial salesmanship, who is the salesman's customer? How would the products that are being sold be used?
3. Why has the idea of service to the customer become important to the general industrial salesman?
4. What is the main difference between a general industrial salesman and a sales engineer?
5. To whom does the merchant salesman sell? What will the merchant salesman's customer do with the product that he buys?
6. What special characteristics does the pioneer salesman need?
7. How does the dealer-service salesman prove that he is really a merchandising consultant?
8. Why is it better for a druggist to buy from a wholesale salesman instead of buying from each manufacturer?
9. How does the detail salesman's job differ from the jobs of the other merchant salesmen?
10. Is the consumer salesman important to our national economy? Explain your answer.
11. What is the major difference between the retail salesman's job and that of all other salesmen?
12. What duties does the retail salesman have besides waiting on the customer?
13. Is the job of the specialty salesman a creative one? Why?
14. What are the three main objectives of the route salesman?
15. Why is it harder to sell intangibles than tangibles?
16. Can nonpersonal selling replace the personal salesman in our economy?

1. On page 31 there is a list of seven kinds of products that industrial salesmen sell. Several examples of each kind of product are given. Give one more example for each of the seven kinds of products.
2. What type of salesman would handle each of the following products?
   a. New type of filing cabinet
   b. New shampoo
   c. New water-softener device for the home
   d. New water-softener device for the factory
   e. Intricate machine tool

3. Which fields of salesmanship make the greatest use of creative sales ability? Why?

4. Suppose that you are the manufacturer of a new type of potato chip called "Chipsies." What kind of salesman would you choose to sell your product? Why? Could you have made any other choice?

5. What personal characteristics are needed to sell automobiles? Computers? Life insurance?

6. Do you think that the specialty salesman should be paid on a straight-salary basis? Why? What do you think of the salary-plus-commission method of payment for the retail salesman?

7. What college courses would help you prepare for selling?

Salesmanship in Action

1. Make a list of ten specific products that a general industrial salesman might sell. To whom would he sell each product?

2. Describe three men who have entirely different personalities, but who you think could be successful salesmen. Which selling position would be best for each of the three men?

3. Look up the words *profession* and *professional* in the dictionary. Then write a one-page paper on the topic, "What Is a Professional Salesman?" Consider all aspects of selling, including the salesman's personality, relationship with customers, knowledge of the product, and use of sales techniques.

Opportunities in Selling

SELLING OFFERS big opportunities to young men and women who want to start their careers in this field. Unlike many of the other fields of endeavor, selling is seldom overcrowded with well-trained people. Careers in selling are always open; and as was pointed out in Chapter 3, there are many different types of sales jobs that require many different types of people. You have merely to turn to the help-wanted section of a large city newspaper to see the evidence of opportunities existing for people who possess the capabilities of selling.

But think also of the large number of people now engaged in the sales field. Undoubtedly, a great many of these people have found sales work satisfying and rewarding.

Advantages of a Career in Selling

What are the advantages of selling as a career? There are many, and they will be discussed under four headings: (1) job security, (2) job satisfactions, (3) remuneration, and (4) opportunities for advancement.

Job Security. A good salesman actually enjoys more security in his job than any other employee. In the American economy today, selling is the most important part of every business. In some countries the problem faced by the economy is that of producing goods in sufficient quantities to satisfy the needs of people. In the United States the problem is just the opposite—that of selling all the goods that American know-how can produce.

The salesman, then, is the spark plug of American industry. There is an old saying that "nothing happens until a sale is made." This means that all the forces of production and distribution go into gear *after* the salesman has done his job. Thus, all the jobs in a company are dependent upon the salesman. The office force, engineers, production workers, shipping personnel, and managers of a firm will be needed only as long as the salesman is selling its product.

So the salesman has direct responsibility for the survival and growth of his own firm. He plays an equally important part in the economic health of the whole country. By keeping the production lines moving, the salesman is responsible for an increase in employment, a reduction of costs through increased production and distribution, and the development of new and better products. The result is a higher standard of living for everyone.

With this picture of the salesman's importance in mind, you can readily understand why the good salesman will always have a job. This is true in bad times as well as good, for during a depression sales are more important than ever. In fact, as long as a company is in business, it will need the salesman.

■ Many sales jobs can be found in the want-ad section of the daily newspaper.

Courtesy Consolidated Papers, Inc.

■ There is an ever-increasing demand for creative salesmen in industry.

But the salesman's own prosperity does not depend on any one firm. If he is a good salesman, he can get a job anywhere, as the want ads in newspapers throughout the country will attest. In most large newspapers there are so many want ads for salesmen that the columns and columns of ads have to be put together in a special section. These ads are for every kind of salesman.

The ever-increasing demand for salesmen has also been pointed up by a nationwide survey made in January, 1964, by the Sales Manpower Foundation

Division of the Sales Executives Club of New York, Inc. According to this survey, 267,000 additional salesmen would need to be hired in 1964 to market new products, to expand territories, and to take care of normal turnover. The firms polled said that they would need a 15.2 percent increase over their 1963 sales force to handle the 1964 demands.

The survey also found that 74.8 percent of the new salesmen would be trainees and that it would cost an average of $8,731 to find, select, train, and supervise each salesman until he became productive.[1]

This fact is another strong plus for the salesman's job security. A company that has so much invested in a man will make every effort to hold on to him.

Any consideration of security would be incomplete if it did not include the question of how much displacement there will be in the future because of automation. Just a few years ago it was thought that there was no possible way that a computer could replace a salesman. Recent trends in the computer field, however, make it obvious that in another ten years purchasing computers will "talk" to selling computers to handle the buying and selling of industrial staples and standard items, and to process reorders. But all that this means is that the order takers will have been automated out of their jobs. All the recent articles on this subject are agreed that the *creative* selling work will still have to be done by human beings, just as it always has. In fact, most authorities feel that in the automated future, the salesman who sees himself as a merchandising consultant will be more essential to the economy than ever.

Job Satisfactions. The average person wants more from his job than just money. He wants to feel that what he is doing is important and that it is benefiting society; he wants the respect of his neighbors; and he wants to contribute his share to the general economy. With these as criteria, the salesman is fully entitled to be proud of what he does. As has been shown, the salesman is in large measure responsible for the prosperity of our country. In addition, he makes a real contribution to the safety, comfort, health, and happiness of others. Selling represents the chance to serve people and to help them to live their lives more fully by satisfying their needs and wants. Thus the salesman's job is a high-status one, important and valuable to the community.

Selling can also be satisfying because it is challenging and stimulating. Each selling job is new and different; each day brings fresh problems to be solved that

[1] *A Nationwide Survey of the 1964 Sales Manpower Requirements of American Manufacturing and Service Companies,* conducted by the Sales Manpower Foundation Division of the Sales Executives Club of New York, Inc.

■ The salesman who travels enjoys the comforts of first-class accommodations.

Courtesy Hilton Hotels

the salesman has never met before. The salesman need never worry about getting in a rut or about his work becoming monotonous.

In addition, the salesman has a special opportunity for self-expression and for liberty of thought and action. The salesman is free to plan his time and his work methods to suit his own personality and needs. He is also free to use all his intelligence, energy, and talents in his attempt to find new uses, new wants, and new markets for the product that he is selling. In other words, the salesman can be an individual. For many men, this is the greatest satisfaction of all.

Remuneration. It is very difficult to be specific about the earnings of salesmen, but it is safe to say that selling is noted for its high financial rewards. Income varies widely among the different types of salesmen and even among salesmen in the same field because of the wide range of knowledge, experience, and ability that different individuals have. But in general the rewards are greatest where the greatest amount of creative selling is necessary, so that specialty salesmen, industrial salesmen, and pioneer salesmen will do better than retail salesmen, dealer-service salesmen, and wholesale salesmen. Also, selling intangibles is generally very rewarding financially.

The Sales Executives Club of New York found recently that its member firms paid their salesmen from $4,500 to $25,000 per annum, with the average figure being $9,612.[1] There are also many salesmen in the country who earn far more than the $25,000 top in this survey, so there is no doubt that the salesman can aspire to a relatively high income.

[1] *Top Problems in Sales Management in 1962*, The Results of a Special Questionnaire Survey, Sales Executives Club of New York, Inc.

Courtesy Genesco

■ The young executive often begins his career as a salesman.

A salesman is usually compensated on a straight-commission basis or on a salary-plus-commission basis. Where a salesman works on commission alone, he may be allowed a weekly or monthly "draw" against the commissions he can be expected to earn annually. This "draw" provides him with a steady income, regardless of how his sales fluctuate from month to month. In addition, most companies offer the salesman fringe benefits in the form of paid vacations of from two to four weeks, life insurance, accident and hospitalization insurance, and retirement annuities. A salesman also has the advantage of being able to buy merchandise at discount prices. In retail stores this can be a real factor in increasing the buying power of the salesperson's earnings, for the usual discount is from 10 to 20 percent and may even be extended to members of the sales-person's family.

If the salesman travels, he may be provided with a car or an allowance if he uses his own car. He may also have an expense account to cover the cost of hotels, meals, tips, entertaining clients, and so on.

There are two especially significant facts about the earnings of a salesman. One is that the salesman earns while he learns. As an average trainee, he can begin earning from $4,000 to $9,000 a year,[1] so that he does not have to make the financial sacrifices to learn the job that doctors and other professional men have to make. The other significant fact is that the salesman does not have to wait until he is an old man to achieve real financial rewards. His earning power has nothing to do with his age or with seniority; he can go as far and as quickly as his ability will take him. In fact, it is not at all uncommon for fairly young

[1] *Nationwide Spot Survey of the 1963 Sales Manpower Requirements of American Manufacturing and Service Companies,* conducted by the Sales Manpower Foundation Division of the Sales Executives Club of New York, Inc.

salesmen to be earning more than their supervisors—some salesmen have turned down promotions to management because they would lose money by doing so.

Opportunities for Advancement. The achievement of the salesman is very easy to measure. The number of new accounts obtained and the sales volume provide an exact picture of the salesman's ability very early in his career. In many fields it is possible to do an excellent job and still go unnoticed, but this is not so in selling.

The pamphlet *Opportunities in Selling* points out that there has been a definite trend in the last ten years toward selecting company presidents from sales departments and that this has come about because getting more customers is far more important to the growth of most firms than any other phase of the business. The pamphlet quotes a study made by a Chicago consulting firm, Heidrick and Struggles, in which it was established that 26 percent of the presidents of 500 leading corporations had a marketing background.[1]

Obviously not every salesman is going to wind up as the president of a large corporation. But according to *Opportunities in Selling:*

> In the middle-to-high echelons of management there are many interesting and highly paid jobs where experience in selling is a prime requisite for advancement. . . . Obviously the necessary expansion of sales forces in the approximate ratio of one manager for every ten salesmen requires an increased number of branch sales managers, general sales managers, directors of marketing, [and] vice-presidents of sales and marketing. It is only in this field of business that advancement is independent of the usual requirement of seniority and may be gained through the successful selling of the company's products or the ability to assume managerial responsibility.[2]

The salesman's advancement may also be in the form of a move into the nonpersonal areas of selling—advertising, public relations, display, and packaging. Many of the most successful and best-paid men in these fields have a sales background. These men are selling to groups rather than to individuals, but all the techniques and principles of selling still apply.

As a specific example of the normal opportunities for advancement available to young people going into selling careers, consider the ad shown above, which recently ran in the *New York Times.*

[1] *Opportunities in Selling,* The Council on Opportunities in Selling, Inc., New York, 1963, pp. 15–16.
[2] *Ibid.,* p. 17.

This group of sales trainees are receiving instruction about the technical background of the products they are going to sell.

The Steps That Lead to the Top

What is the exact route that a salesman will take to advance himself? There is no precise answer to this question, because (1) jobs vary so much by company, (2) different companies have different routes of advancement, and (3) job titles in selling vary widely from company to company. But for the purpose of clarifying the opportunities for advancement in selling, let's assume that you have become a specialty or a general industrial salesman with a well-known and reputable firm. This is the way that your advancement could proceed.

Trainee. Many companies hire new sales personnel as trainees (see illustration above). The time that a salesman remains a trainee varies greatly. For some it means only a short course at the factory followed by intensive training in a branch office under the supervision of field sales supervisors. For others it involves a much longer period during which the trainee learns about all phases of the production and distribution of the product by spending time in the various departments of the company. In industrial selling the training program may be as long as two years. Your whole future will depend on how much you are willing and able to learn while you are a trainee.

Junior Salesman. When you have graduated from your position as a trainee, you will be assigned to a selling territory. However, your work will still be closely supervised either by a senior salesman with whom you may travel or by a sales supervisor. In any event, you will still be looked upon as a trainee, and you will be expected to ask for help when you need it. The length of time that you will spend as a junior salesman will depend directly upon your production—the number of new accounts that you receive, your sales volume, and your need for direct supervision.

Senior Salesman. When you reach the status of senior salesman, you have become a proven producer. You are thoroughly familiar with your product, your company, and your prospective buyers; and you are a master of sales techniques. You have also learned how to organize and budget your time. You will have to report to your sales supervisor, of course, but you will enjoy a great deal of independence and freedom of action.

It is interesting to note that for many men the job of senior salesman is an end in itself. They are so satisfied with their earnings and with the challenge of their jobs that they don't even aspire to any other promotion and will turn down a managerial job if it is offered to them.

Sales Supervisor. For the men who are interested in management, the next step above the senior salesman is sales supervisor. The sales supervisor is in charge of a sales territory for the company. In this job you may continue to do some selling, but it will mostly take the form of "clinching" sales for your trainees and junior salesmen—that is, you will step in when the junior men are having trouble closing their sales. Teaching these junior men will be a major part of your job. Also, you will be responsible for keeping up the morale of the senior salesmen and encouraging them to do their best work. You will have to translate the company's policies and procedures to the men under you and in turn report back to the divisional sales manager, who is your boss. You will be responsible for the sales volume and for the company's public relations in your territory.

Divisional Sales Manager. Large companies find it necessary to divide their market into regions or areas, such as New England, Mid-Atlantic, Southeastern, Midwest, Pacific Coast, and so on. As a divisional sales manager you will be in charge of a region, and the sales supervisors whose territories lie within that region will be answerable to you. It will be your job to transmit company policies to the sales supervisors and to see that the policies are carried out. You will work closely with your sales supervisors in the division of sales territories, the establishment of sales quotas for each salesman, the administration of training programs, and the planning of divisional sales meetings.

Marketing Manager. When you advance to the position of marketing manager, you have demonstrated that you are an able administrator as well as a top-notch

VICE-PRESIDENT IN CHARGE
OF MARKETING

MARKETING
MANAGER

DIVISIONAL
SALES MANAGER

SALES
SUPERVISOR

SENIOR SALESMAN

JUNIOR SALESMAN

TRAINEE

■ The road up for the general industrial salesman.

salesman. You have also proved that not only can you handle people but you can also lead them; you are the right-hand man of the vice-president in charge of marketing, who is your boss. The area of your responsibility is now the entire marketing organization of your company. All the divisional sales managers will report to you, and you will make the top-level decisions on recruiting, hiring, and training new salesmen; keeping senior salesmen productive and happy; setting price levels and discounts for quantity purchases; establishing sales quotas; and maintaining sales volume. You will either be in overall charge of advertising and promotion or work closely with those who are. You will also have to be aware of all the responsibilities of your boss so that you can assist him as much as possible.

Vice-President in Charge of Marketing. The vice-president in charge of marketing is the top sales executive in the company. Those who reach this top rung have proved that they can "think big." Not only does this executive have the ultimate responsibility for all the aspects of selling, but he must also work closely with the other executives of the company to coordinate the marketing program with every other phase of the company's activities.

The magazine *Industrial Marketing* asked 649 top sales executives in companies throughout the country to describe their duties. This summary of the answers to the survey will give you an idea of the tremendous scope of the job.

In addition to sales management, advertising, sales promotion, public relations, market research, and new-product planning, the marketing bosses wrote in a number of other activities in which they participate:

> Acquisition, customer service, personnel development, warehousing, packaging, traffic, trade relations, puchasing, exporting, sales training, government and civic affairs, product and package design, financial planning, distribution, agent selection and relations, salary administration, inventory planning, applications development, capital spending planning.[1]

With this kind of knowledge of the company's whole picture, it is no wonder that so many of these men ultimately become president of the company.

The Road Up in Retailing

The retail salesperson can work his way toward the top by demonstrating an ability for selling and a capacity for assuming managerial functions.

The retail salesperson also begins as a *trainee*. There is usually a brief course of instruction on store policies and procedures and the basic principles of selling. The trainee receives the rest of his instruction from the buyer and assistant buyer in the department to which he is assigned. The retail salesperson will be considered a trainee for a very brief period of time; but if he is interested in promotion, he should continue to learn all that he can about the products in his department and the principles of retail selling.

As a retail salesperson, your first promotion will usually be to transfer to a department where your selling ability will bring in more money for the store and increase your own income through your commissions. For example, you can earn more selling men's suits than selling notions, and still more selling furniture.

From the position of salesman, you may move up to being an *assistant buyer* and then a *buyer*. The buyer is in charge of a department and must not only supervise all the salespeople in it, but must also make the purchasing decisions for the department, selecting the lines of merchandise that will be carried. The

---

[1] Bud Reese, "The Marketing Boss—Does He or Doesn't He?" *Industrial Marketing*, Aug. 13, 1963, p. 77.

GENERAL MANAGER

MERCHANDISE MANAGER

DIVISION MERCHANDISE MANAGER

BUYER

ASSISTANT BUYER

SALESMAN

TRAINEE

The road up in retailing.

buyer is responsible for the sales volume in the department and probably will have duties in connection with advertising the goods to be sold in the department. The buyer's job is an interesting and stimulating one in any store. In very large department stores the job can also be one of tremendous responsibility. The buyer for the Miss Bonwit Department of Bonwit Teller's in New York City is responsible for a million-dollar-a-year business.

Above the buyer is the *division merchandise manager,* who is in charge of coordinating the activities of a group of buyers. He acts as a liaison between the buyers and the top management, taking the buyers' problems to the top if he can't settle them himself and transmitting the management's decisions back to the buyers.

Above the division merchandise manager is the *merchandise manager,* who is in complete charge of all merchandising activities. Finally there is the *general manager,* who is at the top.

Is Selling the Career for You?

The opportunities in selling that have been discussed in this chapter make it clear that selling can be an interesting and rewarding career. However, it must also be pointed out that selling is not for everyone. An extremely introverted person could hardly expect to succeed as a salesman. But the salesman needs another important quality besides liking to be with people. He needs a high degree of emotional stamina—that is, he needs to be able to take rebuffs and refusals as part of the game. It is highly unlikely that any salesman anywhere has a perfect score in selling. The salesman needs to keep his successes and failures in perspective. The beginning salesman in particular must remember the old adages that "Rome wasn't built in a day" and "practice makes perfect." Success in selling, like success in any other field, comes through hard work and perseverance.

If you would like to know whether you have a chance to succeed in sales work, try taking the Self-Evaluation Test for Prospective Salesmen on page 60, prepared by the Psychological Corporation. Tests such as these are not devised to give a definite indication of your capacity; but if you are honest in your answers, you can obtain a fairly sound evaluation of yourself. If you find your score reasonably high on the favorable side, you are justified in seriously considering selling as a career.

Prepare Now for Selling

If you are interested in a selling career, you can start preparing yourself for it right now, while you are still in school. A good idea would be to take a part-time job and discover for yourself whether you can sell. If you do well with part-time selling, you will be earning an income while you are building for your future.

■ The buyer's job in a retail store is a busy but interesting one. In addition to her other duties, she is responsible for the selection of the lines of merchandise carried in her department as well as for the sales volume.

SELF-EVALUATION TEST FOR PROSPECTIVE SALESMEN

Which of these statements describes you? On a separate sheet of paper, write the number of each statement and "yes" or "no," whichever is your answer. It is to your interest to be fair to yourself and as accurate in your opinions as possible. When you have completed this test, check your answers with the key given in Appendix 2.

STATEMENTS	YES	NO
1. I would rather deal with things than people.		
2. I think chemistry is a very interesting subject.		
3. I like talking to strangers.		
4. I would like to be a college teacher.		
5. People find it easy to approach me.		
6. I would like to do research in science.		
7. I enjoy raising money for a charity.		
8. I would like to teach in a school.		
9. I like fashionably dressed people.		
10. I would like to be a watchmaker.		
11. I like to attend conventions.		
12. I have more-than-average mechanical ingenuity.		
13. I dislike people who borrow things.		
14. I would like to be a mechanical engineer.		
15. I like blind people.		
16. I like to have regular work hours.		
17. I would enjoy making speeches.		
18. I would like to be head of a research department.		
19. I like to keep meeting new people.		
20. I enjoy bargaining when I'm buying something.		
21. I would like to develop some new scientific theories.		
22. I like to have a definite salary.		
23. I would rather have only a few really intimate friends.		
24. I am better than average in judging values.		
25. I like to play cards.		

Make yourself conscious of good and bad forms of selling. Practice good selling principles and make them a part of yourself. As evidence of your progress, keep a record of your sales and income and try to better your performance each week.

If you are planning a selling career, a good source of information are the many sales executives clubs throughout the country. They sponsor essay contests, rallies, forums, and similar activities to arouse the interest of students in high schools and colleges. They also have up-to-date data on selling jobs and the requirements for these jobs. Your vocational counselor or business teacher will be able to help you find the address of the sales executives club that is nearest you.

SUMMING UP

The salesman actually enjoys more security in his job than any other employee. As the spark plug of American industry, he keeps the production lines moving and thus is responsible for the prosperity of his own firm and the entire economy. The good salesman is very much in demand, as the want ads throughout the country prove. This is true in bad times as well as good, and will be true even in the automated future.

Selling provides the salesman with the satisfaction of knowing that his job is important to the public welfare. Selling gives the salesman the chance to serve people and to help them to live their lives more fully by satisfying their needs and wants. Selling is also satisfying because it is challenging and stimulating and gives the salesman a special opportunity for self-expression and for liberty of thought and action.

In selling there are wide variations of income, so that it is difficult to be specific about the earnings of a salesman. But it is safe to say that selling is noted for its high financial rewards. The salesman can earn while he learns, and there are no seniority restrictions to keep him from earning as much and as quickly as his ability will allow.

Although the routes to advancement are not the same in every company, the specialty or general industrial salesman's advancement might go in this order: trainee, junior salesman, senior salesman, sales supervisor, divisional sales manager, marketing manager, and vice-president in charge of marketing.

In retail selling the salesman's line of advancement will usually be trainee, salesman, assistant buyer, buyer, division merchandise manager, merchandise manager, and general manager.

Not everyone can be a success in selling, of course, but if you like people, have emotional stamina, and are willing to work hard, selling may be the right career for you.

1. Why is the salesman so important to the prosperity of his firm?
2. How does the national economy benefit when the salesman keeps the production lines moving?
3. The costs to find, select, train, and supervise each salesman until he becomes productive are high. Why is this significant?
4. How will computers affect the jobs of the order takers in the next ten years? Will the creative salesman be replaced by the computers?
5. List four satisfactions that the salesman gets from his job.
6. Does the salesman have to wait until he is an older man to achieve real financial rewards? Explain your answer.
7. Is advancement in selling dependent upon seniority?
8. Is there a definite length of time that each salesman will spend as a trainee?
9. Why are some men completely satisfied with the job of senior salesman?
10. Explain the difference between a sales supervisor and a divisional sales manager.
11. What will the retail salesperson's first promotion probably be?
12. What are the duties of a buyer in a department store?
13. Why does a salesman need emotional stamina?
14. What are the sources of information for aspiring salesmen?

For Discussion

1. In this chapter it has been said that the salesman is the spark plug of American industry. Do you think this is so? Give specific reasons for your answer.
2. Why do so many men with a background in selling become company presidents?
3. What do you think of the statement that "there is no limit to a salesman's possible earnings"?
4. Can you explain why men in the nonpersonal areas of selling are better off if they have had selling experience?

Sales Problem

Bill Jones and a group of his classmates were discussing what they thought they would like to do after they had graduated. Bill felt that selling would be challenging and stimulating and that there would be an excellent future in it.

Tom, whose father was an accountant, felt that a fellow had "to knock himself out" to earn a fair income in selling. He said, "Take those door-to-door salesmen, for instance. They're out all day ringing doorbells and getting doors slammed in their faces. They have too many lean, dry periods in which they get no income. Life insurance salesmen work all day long and all night, too. They don't have any home life."

Harold, whose father was a doctor, said, "Anyone can be a salesman. You don't have to go to college to be able to sell. I want to get a college education, and I'm certainly not going to waste it on selling."

George, whose father was a top-notch salesman for a life insurance company, said, "Selling is the greatest profession in the world. Anyone is foolish not to consider it, especially when you can make big money so easily."

QUESTIONS

1. Criticize the reasoning of each of these boys.
2. Make a list of the advantages of a selling career.
3. Make a list of the disadvantages of a selling career.

Personal Project

People are often sidetracked from their goals. To avoid this yourself, make a list of your present plans in connection with your education, your future career, and your personal objectives.

Salesmanship in Action

1. Interview a life insurance salesman and write a one-page paper on the duties and obligations and the advantages and disadvantages of a career in this type of selling.
2. Interview a retail salesperson who you feel has achieved success in his or her work. Write a brief paper on the specific job duties and the advantages and disadvantages of retail selling.

Preparing for Selling

Part Two

The salesman's personality has a lot more to do with the customer's interest in buying than most people realize. The way he looks, acts, and speaks can sharpen the customer's desire or kill it entirely. Our whole economy revolves around the customer; he is king. The wise salesman finds out all he can about him—why he buys, his likes and dislikes, the appeals that will stir him into action. And there is no substitute for product knowledge. By knowing his product, the salesman is in fact helping rather than persuading people to buy.

Your Sales Personality

NO MATTER how well you know your market, your product, and your customer, you cannot sell successfully until you have sold yourself. What makes one salesman succeed and another salesman fail? Everything else being equal, the difference is usually found in the personalities of the two individuals. It has been said that personality counts 80 percent toward the sale. While this may be exaggerated, there is no debating the fact that personality is highly important. What qualities make up an effective sales personality? In general, they are no different from those qualities that attract you to your personal friends and associates. The effective salesperson is:

1. *Friendly.* He likes people and he shows it by his willingness to wear a pleasant expression, to be cooperative, and to go out of his way to put people at ease. In short, he meets people easily and enjoys being with them.

2. *Interested.* He is interested in his job, and he constantly tries to find ways of doing it better. More important, he is interested in the customer he serves—the customer's wants, needs, and problems.

3. *Tolerant.* The effective salesperson is tolerant of others. He respects them as human beings—their religious and political beliefs, their pride in their racial heritage, their likes and dislikes, their individuality.

4. *Helpful and cooperative.* The salesperson goes the extra distance necessary to be of maximum help to those whom he serves. A retail-store salesman doesn't mind a trip to the stock room for an article of merchandise that is not on hand on the shelves. In fact, he volunteers to do so. He believes that the customer's wants are more important than his own convenience.

5. *Clean, neat, and well groomed.* The salesperson who looks his best sells his best. Grooming is so important to the salesman that all the next chapter is devoted to the subject.

Character Traits That Customers Appreciate

Customers appreciate the following qualities in salesmen:

1. Courtesy and consideration
2. Cheerfulness and cooperativeness
3. Sincerity
4. Genuine liking for people and enthusiasm
5. Tact
6. Genuine interest
7. Honesty
8. Poise and self-control

Let's discuss these qualities separately.

Courtesy and Consideration. Courtesy and consideration are basic qualities for successful selling. You must be considerate of other people and their feelings, problems, thoughts, and opinions. If you are considerate, you will also be courteous. Courtesy is politeness plus good breeding. It is a mark of refinement, culture, and training.

If you are a retail salesperson, courtesy means treating the customer as if he were a guest in your home. If you are a salesman calling on a customer, courtesy means treating the customer as if you were a guest in his home.

If a retail salesperson ignores a customer, fails to approach promptly, laughs or sneers at a customer, rushes a customer, or talks about the customer behind the scenes, he is being discourteous. He cannot expect to be successful in selling.

A salesman shows a lack of courtesy that will lose sales if he enters a prospect's office or home with his hat on or while smoking, if he speaks loudly or roughly to a receptionist, if he fails to keep his appointment or arrives late, or if he fails to apologize for an unintended breach of business etiquette.

Lack of Courtesy Loses Sales. A customer enters the hosiery department of a department store five minutes before closing time. She wants a pair of hose in an unusual shade. She approaches a salesperson who is covering the counter.

Customers appreciate the salesperson who is courteous, friendly, and helpful.

Courtesy Tanners' Council of America, Inc.

CUSTOMER: Do you have any sheer blue hose?

SALESPERSON (*does not turn around and keeps working*): **We're closing now. You'll have to come back tomorrow.**

CUSTOMER (*persistently*): But I need them today, and I've been looking all over town for them.

SALESPERSON: **We have something like it in a mesh stocking. I'm in a hurry; but if you want a pair, I'll wrap them up for you.**

CUSTOMER (*hesitating*): Are they sheer enough?

SALESPERSON: **Of course they are. (*Gives a curt laugh.*) They're a new fashion.**

CUSTOMER (*embarrassed*): May I see them?

(*The salesperson finishes covering the counter and then displays the stockings. The customer examines them for a moment.*)

CUSTOMER: Well, they aren't what I want. I'll have to let it go. Thank you just the same.

SALESPERSON (*in a haughty manner*): **Sorry.**

Courtesy in Action. A young woman holding a newspaper advertisement in her hand enters the blouse department of a department store. She approaches a salesperson who is covering the stock.

CUSTOMER (*pointing to picture in ad*): Miss, do you have this blouse in size 34?

SALESPERSON (*looking at photograph*): **We have only a few of these left; but if you'll step this way, I'll check to see if we have your size.**

(*The salesperson searches through the blouses in stock.*)

SALESPERSON: **I'm sorry, we don't seem to have it.**

CUSTOMER: Oh, dear! It's just exactly what I want.

SALESPERSON: **If you're not in a hurry for the blouse, I'd be happy to check our branch stores. It's possible they may still have one.**

CUSTOMER: Would you, please? I'm very anxious to have it.

SALESPERSON: **Certainly. Will you be seated while I make the calls?**

(*The customer sits down while the salesperson goes to the service desk to telephone. After a brief interval, she returns.*)

SALESPERSON: **I've located the size blouse you need in our Beverly Hills store, and they can ship it out to you tomorrow.**

CUSTOMER: Wonderful! I certainly appreciate your helpfulness. You can be sure I'll remember you the next time I need a blouse.

Cheerfulness and Cooperativeness. Customers like to do business with salespeople who are cheerful and cooperative. Cheerfulness is contagious. When the salesperson is cheerful, the customer is likely to be cheerful, too. Very quickly the atmosphere is friendly, and feelings of suspicion or distrust quickly vanish. Cheerfulness comes from feeling well, liking your job, liking the people with whom you work, and enjoying helping customers. If you are guilty of disliking your job and the people you deal with, you should change jobs—perhaps get out of selling altogether. Everyone has worries—financial problems, family worries, personal disappointments. Don't feel, therefore, that you have them all! Try to submerge your worries and unpleasant thoughts when you are on the job —don't let them dominate your attitude.

Cooperativeness—willingness to go more than halfway to be of help—is another valuable quality appreciated by the customer. Be willing to give the little extra time to the customer, to be patient with an undecided customer, to

■ If the customer has difficulty making up her mind, the salesgirl should remain patient and pleasant.

be helpful to all customers. After all, it is the customer who is your real boss. Your job and the success of the business for which you work depend on the customer's attitude toward the store or organization.

Cooperativeness is also a valuable trait in working with fellow employees. Often salespeople work closely with other employees, such as engineers and servicemen, to solve a problem; and cooperativeness is vital to the final outcome of the effort. Salespeople must cooperate, too, with receiving clerks, stock boys, wrappers, and office personnel. Opinions and prejudices about a plan or procedure often must give way to the procedures and plans that are best for the entire group.

Sincerity. No one likes a "phony"; he cannot be trusted. The opposite of phoniness is sincerity. The sincere salesman has the customer's best interests in mind when he attempts to serve him. He does not "puff" the merchandise out of all proportions to its real value; he does not use high-pressure tactics or oversell. He bases his sales talk on facts and on the benefits the customer will derive from purchasing his product or service—not on exaggeration or deception. The sincere person does not try to make a sale at the risk of customer dissatisfaction. He wants satisfied customers, because he knows that they will purchase from him again and again.

Genuine Liking for People and Enthusiasm. You cannot be successful in selling and at the same time dislike and mistrust people. You must have a *genuine liking* for the other fellow if you expect to sell him anything. As far as you are concerned, there should be no difficult people, only difficult selling situations.

One of the biggest assets you can bring to any kind of job is enthusiasm, and selling is no exception. Enthusiasm breeds enthusiasm. If you are enthusiastic, your prospect is likely to feel the same way. This makes selling an interesting and exciting job.

Enthusiasm cannot be forced. When you display your product to a customer, show genuine enthusiasm for it. You cannot get up in the morning and say, "Well, today I'm going to be enthusiastic." To be enthusiastic about your work, you have to like it and know, or want to know, everything about it.

Tact. Tact is another good quality for the salesman to possess. Tact means saying and doing the right thing at the right time. The basis of tact is good judgment and consideration for others. Tact helps you to handle difficult situations, such as the following, with finesse:

A woman enters a shoe store. In comparison with her build, her feet are unusually large, and she seems sensitive to drawing attention to what, in her mind, is a physical defect.

CUSTOMER (*apologetically*): I don't know whether you can fit me because I have rather large feet. I always have a hard time finding shoes I like in my size.

SALESMAN: **We have many customers who require larger-than-average sizes, and I'm sure we can fit you. Did you want walking shoes or dress?**

Note that the salesman did not agree with the customer that she has large feet. He merely said that many people *require larger-than-average sizes*. Tact is especially important in serving customers who are sensitive about weight, complexion, height, plainness, and the amount of money they can afford to spend.

Genuine Interest. The ability to take a genuine interest in others—in their problems, their happiness, their worries, and fears—will help you to win friends as well as sales. There are many people who are so self-centered that nothing matters to them but their own personal welfare. While they possess interest, it is the wrong type of interest.

A good rule to follow in winning friends and getting along with people is: *Find out the other person's interests, and talk about those interests.* Good salesmen make use of this rule in their sales work, and it is one reason why they get repeat orders.

How can you let a customer know that you are interested in him and in his personal needs? Here are eight suggestions:

1. Be pleasant, cheerful, friendly.
2. Learn the customer's name and use it often.
3. Show appreciation for the customer's time.

■ **One way that the salesgirl can show an interest in each of her customers is to smile and say "Thank you" as she hands the customer her package.**

■ The effective salesman is honest and sincere. He gives the customer accurate information about his merchandise and wants to sell her only those items that actually fill her needs.

4. Listen when the customer is talking.
5. Don't argue with the customer.
6. Get the customer's point of view.
7. Talk in terms of the customer's interests.
8. Thank the customer when he buys from you.

Honesty. Probably no trait of personality is appreciated more by people than honesty. Business is built on honesty. Customers are not familiar with the technical aspects of the merchandise, and they must rely on the honesty and integrity of the salesman. Once they catch the salesman in a dishonest act or statement, they quickly lose confidence and doubt all the statements made about the merchandise. Dishonesty on the part of one salesman causes the customer to become suspicious of other salesmen.

Vincent Riggio, president of the American Tobacco Company, has said that the prime requisites of a good salesman are honesty, knowledge of product, and work. The following story illustrates how honesty played an important role early in his own selling career:

Mr. Riggio was being trained by an older, more experienced salesman who was fond of using high-pressure methods of selling. The older man would enter a cigar store, start his sales talk, and then start to fill out his order book without bothering to make a detailed check of the dealer's stock. When the dealer objected to the size of the order, the salesman promised advertising support. If the order still was not authorized, he promised new window-display material. If that did not work, he promised new counter cards. Finally he would promise new metal signs for the storefront, which generally appealed to the dealer. The salesman would lead the dealer to believe that he was getting a bigger sign than any other store.

Vincent Riggio, who was to take over this territory, asked the senior salesman, "How are you going to get all that promotional material okayed by the sales manager?"

"I'm not. I only promised it. I never intended to send them all that stuff," replied the salesman. "If they are foolish enough to believe all that, they deserve to be stuck."

This did not fit in with Mr. Riggio's code of ethics. That afternoon, the senior salesman went to a ball game. Riggio went over the route, backtracking on the calls that had been made that morning. He asked each dealer for the duplicate of the order and destroyed it, explaining that he was there to serve the dealer, not to load him with a lot of nonsalable merchandise. He hoped to have that territory for a long time and wanted the dealer to feel that he was doing business with a friend. A new order was made out after he discussed the dealer's actual needs with him.

Honesty involves giving the customer accurate information about the product that you sell. It involves persuading the customer only if the product actually fills a need. The salesman who sells an inferior product to a customer who wants and needs a better quality is not being honest with the customer.

Honesty in selling also involves being honest with yourself. Be willing to admit that you do not know all the answers and that there is room for improvement in your selling methods. Ask yourself these questions:

Do I know as much about the product I am selling as I should know?
Do I try to see the customer's point of view before influencing him toward the sale?
When I meet a difficult situation, do I seek an honorable way out of it?

Poise and Self-Control. Poise in handling a difficult situation comes from self-control. Self-control helps you to master your emotions and to appear calm and in command of a situation at all times. It helps you to restrain all those tendencies that may cause you to act in an extreme way and helps you to control a

TYPES OF CUSTOMERS AND HOW TO SERVE THEM

Nervous Customers

For customers who are:	You will need:
Tired and cross ⟵——————⟶	Patience
Fussy and nervous ⟵——————⟶	Consideration
Excitable ⟵——————⟶	Quiet manner
Impatient ⟵——————⟶	Dispatch
Unreasonable ⟵——————⟶	Calmness

Dependent Customers

For customers who are:	You will need:
Timid and sensitive ⟵——————⟶	Gentleness
Undecided ⟵——————⟶	Decision
Old and deaf people ⟵——————⟶	Sympathy
Children ⟵——————⟶	Power to think for them
Foreigners ⟵——————⟶	Helpfulness

Disagreeable Customers

For customers who are:	You will need:
Skeptical ⟵——————⟶	Candid manner
Inquisitive ⟵——————⟶	Knowledge
Talkative ⟵——————⟶	Courteous brevity
Insulting ⟵——————⟶	Self-control

Trying Customers

For customers who are:	You will need:
Critical ⟵——————⟶	Knowledge of goods
Indifferent ⟵——————⟶	Tact
Silent ⟵——————⟶	Perseverance
Bargain hunters ⟵——————⟶	Convincing manner

Common-Sense Customers

For customers who are:	You will need:
Courteous ⟵——————⟶	Courtesy and intelligence
Intelligent ⟵——————⟶	Efficiency

From *Retail Salesmanship*, Merchants Service, The National Cash Register Company, Dayton, Ohio, pp. 4–5.

sharp word or a quick temper. Poise is defined as "the act of raising the eyebrows instead of the roof!"

Sales work is hard work. Meeting all types of customers day after day can be very trying. Occasionally you may feel like speaking harshly to the next customer who seems to ask a foolish question or otherwise takes up valuable time. Consider the following case, for example:

A salesman in a men's apparel store, who has had an unusually poor day, is waiting for a sale. A customer enters the store and starts looking at some shirts. The salesman smiles as he approaches the woman.

SALESMAN: **May I help you?**

CUSTOMER: Aren't you the young man who helped me yesterday?

SALESMAN (*still smiling*): **Oh, yes. I remember you. What can I do for you?**

CUSTOMER: Well, I'd like to return these shirts I purchased. My husband tried them on last night, and the sleeves are too long.

(*The salesman's smile disappears, and his manner becomes gruff, showing his disappointment at not making an additional sale.*)

SALESMAN: **Well, you were quite certain they were the right size yesterday, madam. I'm not sure whether we can refund your money, but we might be able to give you an exchange.**

CUSTOMER: My husband's sleeve length is 31 inches. Can you do anything about that?

SALESMAN (*icily*): **Of course not. You ought to know shirts don't come so short.**

CUSTOMER (*angrily*): I know nothing of the kind, and I expect an adjustment.

SALESMAN (*shouting*): **Don't shout at me, madam. I'm not a dog.**

CUSTOMER (*almost in tears*): I want to see the manager. I'm going to talk to him about this matter.

Notice that in this case the matter became steadily worse. A little heat on the part of the salesman created an argument that resulted explosively for both parties. The salesman lacked self-control. Had he possessed poise, he would not have allowed the situation to develop and certainly not to get beyond his control.

Self-control and poise will help you to subdue any tendency to argue with others. A salesman may win an argument but lose the sale. There is a saying, "Steel that loses its temper is useless; the same applies to people."

What the Employer Expects

What personal qualities does a manager consider when he hires salespeople? Surveys among sales managers, personnel directors, and department heads of industrial firms and department stores reveal that they look for the following:

Accuracy	Honesty
Alertness	Imagination
Ambition	Industriousness
Arithmetic ability	Interest in other people
Cheerfulness	Loyalty
Cooperation	Persistence
Courtesy	Responsibleness
Dependability	"Sales sense"
Enthusiasm	Self-control
Friendliness	Sense of humor
Good judgment	Sincerity
Good memory	Sympathy
Good personal appearance	Tact

You will recognize in this list many of the qualities discussed on the preceding pages as those that customers expect to find in salesmen. Of course, they are just as important to the employer as to the customer. Several qualities in the list above are worthy of special mention. Let's examine some of them.

Alertness. Selling demands the ability to think clearly and quickly. You do not need the analytical mind of a scientist or technician, but you do need a good deal of common sense. You must be very observant and be able to make accurate decisions quickly; in short, you must be alert.

The alert salesman studies human nature daily and is quick and accurate in sizing up a prospect and a sales situation. He notes all the details in the personal

■ The alert salesperson will realize when a customer is perplexed about an item and quickly come to his aid with helpful suggestions.

appearance of a prospect and in the appearance of his home or office that will help him to foresee the prospect's possible reaction to the sales proposition. The salesman listens attentively and quickly determines the possible needs and wants of the prospect without asking needless questions.

"Sales Sense." The successful salesman has "sales sense" in organizing and arranging his selling facts in such a way that a prospect can understand them quickly and easily. He concentrates on the customer's problems and avoids jumping to conclusions.

Here is a scientific way to organize a logical point-by-point sales talk:

1. Get all possible facts about the customer's problem or need.
2. Review the features of the product in relation to the customer's problem.
3. Decide how the product fits the customer's need.
4. Prepare a point-by-point sales presentation.
5. Deliver the sales talk so effectively that the customer will be convinced to buy.

The following case shows how a good salesman organized his selling points in a logical manner and tied them in with the customer's interests. Notice how this salesman, by reviewing the major features that appeal to the customer, closes the sale.

SALESMAN: **You say you are looking for a tire that will give you longer wear, Mr. Andrews?**

CUSTOMER: That's right.

SALESMAN: **That's what you'll get with our Rough Weather brand. We have tested our tires against competitive brands for over three years, and our Rough Weathers averaged 20 percent more service than any other brand.** (*The salesman brings out a cutaway sample.*)

SALESMAN: **Mr. Andrews, this is a section of the tire that I was telling you about. I'm going to show you how it came out on top in all those tests. In the first place, notice how firmly these twin beads are set in. They can't rock and get loose and cause heat. You are, no doubt, also interested in safe tires. Here is a special safety feature, the crisscross diamond tread. No other tire gives you this.**

Notice also how it is designed so that the tread, breaker, cushioning, and cord all form one unit. That does away with friction and means freedom from blowouts.

Then, too, these tires are made of the finest grade of rubber, and they have a cord of the highest tensile strength. After subjecting our tire to a

test in which all the tread was worn off, we found that the cord lost only 10 percent of its tensile strength. That means longer and rougher wear.

(*The salesman shows a brochure illustrating the test.*)

SALESMAN: Mr. Andrews, you can save half a cent a mile over any other tire with our Rough Weathers. Here's the proof.

(*The salesman shows further laboratory test results.*)

SALESMAN: I can quote you a price of $30 a tire on our heavy duties, less your 10 percent fleet discount.

CUSTOMER (*thinking*): Hm-m-m-m.

SALESMAN: Think about what you get, Mr. Andrews. First, these tires will cost you less per mile as the records show. Second, they will give you longer wear, due to grade A-1 rubber and special bead construction.

(*Points to cutaway sample again.*)

Third, they're safe because of the scientifically designed diamond criss-cross tread. You can make quick nonskid stops, even on wet pavement. Now, isn't that all worth having, Mr. Andrews?

CUSTOMER: It sounds pretty convincing. How soon can you make delivery?

Imagination. Imagination is the mental process by which a person recalls his past experiences and uses them to help him develop new ideas to solve present problems. A constructive imagination is a powerful selling tool. In selling, it helps to:

1. Foresee the possible results of a sales talk.
2. Foresee a possible problem for the prospect and suggests how to avoid or solve it.
3. Visualize solutions for problems that arise in connection with a sale.
4. Visualize how the product being sold will harmonize with other articles.

Good Memory. No doubt you know people who can remember the names and faces of almost everyone they meet. You may have wondered how they do it. The answer is that their minds have been trained to remember. People who have good memory ability usually have been called on frequently to remember persons and things. Their daily work may have required a good memory, so that they developed memory power through constant use.

James A. Farley, former postmaster general of the United States and prominent political leader, was well known for his excellent memory. He never forgot a name or a face. Mr. Farley was not specially gifted in this way; he conscientiously practiced the principles of memorization until he was expert.

Are you interested in improving your memory? If so, follow these simple rules:

1. Concentrate often on the thing that you want to remember. Pay close attention. The more attention you give, the better you will remember.
2. Associate the thing to be remembered with some familiar idea or object that will make an impression on your mind. For example, to remember a list of prices (*a*) associate each price with the item to which it applies, or (*b*) arrange and learn the prices in ascending or descending order, forming a chain of thought from the least expensive item to the most expensive, or vice versa.
3. Recall the thing to be remembered from time to time so that it will remain fixed in your mind.
4. Know what to forget. You can remember important things more easily if your mind is not burdened with nonessentials.
5. Cultivate an interest in the things you want to remember. When you lack interest, your mind does not absorb a fact or a face and, consequently, cannot reproduce it clearly when you want it.

Make a game out of improving your memory, as in the following case:

Nancy Penny is a star salesgirl in a chain dress shop. Many of her customers are willing to wait, even on busy days, until she can serve them. What is the secret of Nancy's success? The following incident may give you a clue:

On a particularly busy day, a customer walks into the shop and is approached by one of the salesgirls.

SALESGIRL: **May I help you, madam?**
CUSTOMER: Thank you, but no. I'll wait until Miss Penny is free.

Courtesy Merck Sharp & Dohme

■ Remembering people's names and faces is very important to the salesman. By following a few simple rules, you can improve your memory to recall names and remember faces.

SALESGIRL: She may be busy for quite some time. Couldn't I show you something while you're waiting?

CUSTOMER: Thank you, but I'd rather wait.

(The customer sits down and waits about fifteen minutes for Nancy Penny to finish a sale.)

MISS PENNY *(approaching with a smile)*: How are you, Mrs. Zipolowinski? It's nice to see you after your long trip. Did you have a good time?

Nancy Penny is able to call not only Mrs. Zipolowinski by name but almost all of her other customers. This flattering appeal to the customers' pride makes them always request the services of this exceptional salesgirl.

Whenever Nancy waits on a new customer, whether a charge or cash transaction, she asks the customer's name, repeating it to herself and at the same time noticing distinguishing characteristics of the customer. This helps her to link names with faces and general appearance.

Nancy keeps a record of her customers on index cards. After she has acquired a new customer, she writes the name on one side of the card and the customer's distinguishing characteristics on the reverse side. For example: Mrs. Gray; tall and thin, heavy eyebrows, sharp nose, rapid talker, black suit with sequins.

When not busy selling, Nancy takes out her cards, reads a name, and tries to guess the characteristics. She varies this procedure by reading the characteristics first, then trying to guess the name. Each time she makes a mistake she lays the card aside. She estimates her success by the ratio of mistakes to the total number of card in her file.

With hundreds of cards in her file, Nancy remembers over 90 percent of her customers!

Arithmetic Ability. One of the most important skills the salesman can possess is arithmetic ability. He should be especially skillful in the fundamentals of subtraction, addition, multiplication, division, percentage, and fractions. Moreover, he should be able to perform these processes quickly and easily. Even a simple and common process like making change can build a customer's confidence if the salesman performs this function in an efficient manner. This skill can be highly developed through persistent practice. If you have allowed your arithmetic to become rusty through disuse, then you should consult some basic arithmetic textbooks and review your knowledge.

Dependability. The person who is dependable is reliable, trustworthy, resourceful, and responsible—he can be counted on at all times to do the job assigned.

The dependable person will give up part of his lunch hour or will work over-time, if necessary, in order to meet an obligation.

Loyalty. Loyalty means sticking to your work and upholding your firm, the employees, and the products of your firm. The loyal person wants the company to succeed and does everything possible to make it successful.

Industriousness. Industriousness means working hard and keeping at it consistently. The industrious person is not afraid to "roll up his sleeves" and pitch in on any task that needs to be done.

Developing Your Sales Personality

Personality is largely acquired; very little is inherited. Just as developing sales ability is a matter of practice, so is developing your personality. Since personality is fundamental in selling, you cannot neglect it. Here are three steps in developing a desirable personality for successful selling:

1. *Realize the need for improvement.* The person who feels that he is perfect never even takes the first step. Many people say, "Oh, I realize I need to improve, but so do many other people. Besides, it takes too much time and effort." If you (*a*) want to be attractive to people, (*b*) desire recognition and social fame, (*c*) are interested in power, prestige, and influence, (*d*) desire to have many friends, and (*e*) want financial security, you will want to improve your personality and will plan to do it.

2. *Make a survey of your personality.* A survey will be based on:

a. Self-analysis. You should seriously rate yourself on all the desirable personality factors in the Personality Rating Scale found on pages 86 and 87. You will find the key in Appendix 2.

b. Comparison of your self-analysis with ratings of others. If there is any disagreement, consider your rating as the one in error. Watch for agreement among others who rate you. This is a sign of a particular strength or weakness in your personality.

3. *Develop a systematic plan for improvement.* Benjamin Franklin, in his autobiography, described an excellent plan for developing a desirable personality:

I made a little book in which I allotted a page for each of the virtues. I rul'd each page with red ink, so as to have seven columns, one for each day of the week, marking each column with a letter for the day. I cross'd these columns with thirteen red lines, marking the beginning of each line with the first letter of one of the virtues on which

No doubt this salesman had to develop his sales personality before he began to sell, for personality is largely acquired.

Ewing Galloway

line, and in its proper column, I might mark by a little black spot, every fault I found upon examination to have been committed respecting that virtue upon that day.

I was determined to give a week's strict attention to each of the virtues successively. Thus in the first week my great guard was to avoid every day the least offence against *Temperance*, leaving the other virtues to their ordinary chance, only marking every evening the faults of the day. Thus, if in the first week I could keep my first line, marked T, clear of spots, I suppos'd the habit of that virtue so much strengthen'd and its opposite weaken'd, that I might venture extending my attention to include the next, and for the following week keep both lines clear of spots. Proceeding thus to the last, I could go thro' a course compleat in thirteen weeks, and four courses in a year. And like him who, having a garden to weed, does not attempt to eradicate all the bad herbs at once, which would exceed his reach and strength, but works on one of the beds at a time.[1]

Thus it is seen how Benjamin Franklin worked on developing good traits by concentrating on a few for a definite period of time. Why not try the same method or a similar one?

[1] *The Autobiography of Benjamin Franklin*, chapter entitled, "Continuation of the Account of My Life, Begun at Passy," Random House, Inc., New York, 1950.

SUMMING UP

To develop the ability to get along with customers of all types, the salesperson should enjoy his work and have a real desire to serve others. He must develop a genuine liking for the other fellow and be willing to adapt himself to all kinds of people. Some of the important qualities for maintaining the right attitude are enthusiasm, cheerfulness, courtesy, honesty, and tact. Other qualities include consideration of other people, interest, friendliness, cooperativeness, and sincerity. The salesman must be poised and use self-control at all times.

If the salesman is to rise to the top of his profession, he must be able to think clearly, accurately, and quickly. He must know how to organize his ideas and his selling points for clear presentation. He must have a constructive imagination and a good memory. He must be dependable, loyal, and industrious.

Personality is largely acquired. To develop a desirable personality, the salesman must realize the need for improvement, make a survey of his personality, and then work out a systematic plan for improvement.

Reviewing Your Reading

1. Discuss the statement, "The salesman's job is people."
2. If a person is considerate of others, he is also courteous. Explain.
3. What is meant by cooperativeness?
4. Describe the quality of sincerity. Why is it important to the salesman?
5. What is tact? How does it win sales?
6. List at least five ways of showing genuine interest in a prospect.
7. Why is it said that business is built on honesty?
8. What is the effect on a customer of dishonest statements made by the salesman?
9. How did Vincent Riggio demonstrate the principle of honesty in salesmanship?
10. How can poise and self-control help you in selling?
11. What is meant by mental alertness?
12. What five factors are involved in the scientific organization of a sales talk?
13. Give five rules for developing a good memory.
14. Why is arithmetic ability important to the salesman?

15. Define dependability, loyalty, industriousness.
16. What was Benjamin Franklin's plan for personality development? Could such a plan be used today?

For Discussion

1. What opportunities does the salesman have to demonstrate honesty?
2. Can you prove that enthusiasm comes from knowledge by using an example from sports or student government?
3. What makes a salesman dependable?
4. How can you recognize a loyal salesman? An industrious salesman?
5. Discuss the statement, "It is possible for one to change his personality."
6. How can a salesman acquire enthusiasm on the job?
7. How can you overcome indifference?
8. What part does friendship play in selling? Could a salesman be too friendly with his prospects and customers?
9. How do you think a salesperson's overfamiliarity would affect a customer?
10. In what ways is it possible for salespeople to cooperate with one another?
11. How do you think a salesman's tendency to argue would affect a customer?
12. What are some of the problems in selling that demand clear and effective thinking?
13. What are some of the ways in which a salesman shows that he is alert?
14. Should you try to copy the personality of others?
15. Some employers place *resourcefulness* high on the list of qualities needed by the salesman. Look up the term and give examples as it applies to selling.

Sales Problem I

A sales manager is having difficulty in getting a salesman to take over a certain territory where the previous salesman used high-pressure salesmanship and over-loaded dealers with the company's product. The dealers are angry and are refusing to see any of the company's other salesmen. Moreover, the other salesmen do not want to take on this territory, even though it means promotion.

A new man is hired and told the situation. He knows that it will be difficult to undo the results of the poor selling tactics of the previous salesman. But before going into the territory, he plans how he can handle this problem.

QUESTION

How would you handle the problem?

A customer enters a sporting-goods department. He is smartly dressed in slacks and sport jacket and is carrying a number of packages.

CUSTOMER: I'd like to see some tents. Something large and roomy with a floor.

SALESMAN: **Certainly, right over here. Now here is a smart number. It's 9 by 12 feet, one of our best buys.**

CUSTOMER: But this one doesn't have a floor. Is this the best you have?

SALESMAN: **We have some over here with floors, but they're higher priced.**

CUSTOMER: Is this good strong material?

SALESMAN: **Oh, yes, it should last for years with proper care.**

CUSTOMER: Well, I guess this will do. I don't know much about camping. I hope it will work all right.

(The salesman picks up his sales book and begins to write the order.)

SALESMAN: **Now, what is your name?**

CUSTOMER: Robert J. Courtwell.

(The order is written, and the salesman gives the receipt to the customer.)

SALESMAN: **Thank you, Mr. Courtland. Come back again.**

CUSTOMER: The name is Courtwell. Say, are you sure you spelled it right on the delivery tag?

(The salesman pulls out the sales book again.)

SALESMAN: **Oh, I'm sorry. I'll change it right away.**

QUESTIONS

1. In what ways did this salesman fail in his selling job?
2. Could this salesman have increased his sale in this case? If so, how?

1. Some ways in which retail salespeople and salesmen who call on customers show lack of courtesy are given at the beginning of this chapter. What additional examples of discourtesy can you describe?
2. In the sales example given under the heading "Lack of Courtesy Loses Sales," name the specific words or actions that showed lack of courtesy on the part of the salesperson. How would you have handled this case?
3. In the sales example given under the heading "Courtesy in Action," select the particular ways in which the salesman showed consideration for the customer.

4. In the example of the salesman selling tires on pages 76 and 77, how did he back up his statements? How did he close the sale? What is the advantage of closing in this manner?

5. In giving the correct amount of change for a cash sale, the clerk will start with the amount of purchase and add until the amount received has been reached. For example, if a $5 bill is received for a $1.40 cash sale, the clerk will give the customer one dime and say "$1.50," one 50-cent piece and say "$2," and three $1 bills and say "$5."

Make a change sheet similar to the one shown below, and using the fewest number of coins and bills, record the correct amount of change for each sale listed.

Find the totals for each column, and make the proof as shown at the top of page 86.

CHANGE SHEET

Sale No.	Amount of Sale	Amount Re-ceived	Coins					Bills		
			1¢	5¢	10¢	25¢	50¢	$1	$5	$10
1	$ 2.33	$ 5.00								
2	7.88	20.00								
3	3.07	10.00								
4	3.00	5.00								
5	7.14	20.00								
6	8.12	10.00								
7	.78	10.00								
8	12.40	20.00								
9	9.15	20.00								
10	4.31	5.00								
11	.08	1.00								
12	1.19	10.00								
13	5.06	10.00								
14	3.20	5.00								
15	2.14	5.00								
16	1.23	5.00								
17	7.00	10.00								
18	4.09	10.00								
19	16.67	20.00								
20	1.02	5.00								
Totals										

PROOF

Total sales	$_____
1¢	_____
5¢	_____
10¢	_____
25¢	_____
50¢	_____
$1	_____
$5	_____
$10	_____

Total

Amount received

6. Rate yourself on personality by answering the questions in the Personality Rating Scale below. Twelve important qualities of an effective salesman are given in this rating scale. To rate yourself, select the answer below each question that best describes you. Then write your answer on a separate sheet of paper. When you have answered all the questions, check your answers with the key given in Appendix 2.

PERSONALITY RATING SCALE

1. CONFIDENCE
   To what extent do you succeed in winning the confidence, respect, and good-will of your friends and classmates?

   ☐ Exceptional ☐ Usually successful ☐ About 50-50 ☐ Seldom ☐ Never

2. PERSEVERANCE
   To what extent are you capable of sustained effort (staying at a task until it is finished)?

   ☐ Always stick with it ☐ Usually stick with it ☐ About 50-50 ☐ Seldom ☐ Never

3. COMPREHENSION
   How alert are you at grasping an idea or situation ("catching on")?

   ☐ Always ☐ Most of the time ☐ About half of the time ☐ Seldom ☐ Never

4. RELIABILITY
   How reliable (dependable) are you in performing your work?

   ☐ Thoroughly reliable ☐ Ordinarily reliable ☐ About half the time ☐ Seldom ☐ Never

5. TACT

To what extent do you say or do things without hurting the feelings or incurring the ill opinion of others?

☐ Always tactful ☐ Generally tactful ☐ About 50-50 ☐ Seldom tactful ☐ Offend others constantly

6. LOYALTY

Do you stand behind your employer and stick up for what you believe is right?

☐ Always loyal ☐ Usually loyal ☐ Hesitant ☐ Give up easily ☐ Never stand firm

7. ENTHUSIASM

How enthusiastic are you in undertaking a task or an assignment?

☐ Exceedingly enthusiastic ☐ Mildly enthusiastic ☐ So-so ☐ Often resentful ☐ Always resentful

8. LEADERSHIP

How well can you lead, direct, or influence others?

☐ Can lead forcefully ☐ Lead most of the time ☐ About 50-50 ☐ Usually avoid leadership ☐ Always avoid leadership

9. CONVERSATIONAL ABILITY

To what extent do you participate in conversations with others?

☐ Wholeheartedly ☐ Quite a bit ☐ To a certain extent ☐ Scarcely at all ☐ Never

10. ORAL EXPRESSION

How well do you use the English language?

☐ Exceptionally well ☐ Better than average ☐ About average ☐ Poorly—make many errors ☐ Very poorly—hard to understand

11. POISE

To what extent are you poised (maintain self-control)?

☐ Exceptionally well poised ☐ Usually well poised ☐ About average ☐ Lose control frequently ☐ Rarely poised

12. GROOMING

To what extent do you maintain a neat and well-groomed appearance?

☐ Always ☐ Usually ☐ About half the time ☐ Careless—often sloppy ☐ Don't care

Looking Your Best

MOST CUSTOMERS judge a product first by its appearance. Whether they are aware of it or not, they also judge the product by the appearance of the salesperson. If the salesperson is shabby, dirty, or distastefully dressed, the customer will find him offensive. And even though the product the salesman is selling may be the finest on the market or the retail store he works for the best in the area, the customer is likely to be hard to convince that he should buy. Lacking confidence in the salesperson, the customer will lack confidence in the product. Thus there is more truth than fiction to the saying, "You can't sell your product until you first sell yourself."

The Importance of Good Grooming

Good grooming, which means cleanliness of body and clothing and general sharpness in appearance, is one of the most important facets of one's personality. In fact, your grooming expresses your personality. Your attitude toward your job, toward your employer, and toward the people you serve is revealed by the way you look. When you are careless about your hair, your shoes, your clothing, or your personal cleanliness, you show that you don't really care what others think or how they react to you. The "don't-care" attitude is fatal for the salesman. He *must* care, because it is his business to impress people favorably and to gain their confidence.

Your grooming is important not only because of its effect on others, but because of its effect on *you*. When you know you look your best, you have more confidence, more poise. And because you are not fretting about your appearance, you can devote your full attention to the customer and to your sales presentation. How do you feel when you are all dressed up in a new outfit? Springy? Proud? Of course. You should get this feeling every day when you're meeting the public.

Few professions outrank salesmanship in the importance it attaches to physical appearance. The salesman is on a plane with the actor and the politician as a "public figure." He is on daily display before a critical audience of customers, prospects, competitors. No wonder, then, good appearance is so important to the salesman. He is the image of his company, and he must project an image that will inspire both confidence and respect.

—Jean E. Clohesey, "Dress Right—'Package Yourself' for Success," *Sales Memos,* Dartnell Press

Cleanliness—The Most Important Factor in Grooming

The most important factor in grooming is cleanliness. There is no substitute for soap! Bathe daily and immediately after strenuous exercise. If you have worked all day and are planning an important engagement in the evening, make another trip to the shower. Not only will you feel better physically, but you will feel more secure about your appearance. Always use a deodorant after you bathe. Men who feel that a deodorant is only for women are badly out of date. This precaution is accepted as a natural thing for all adults in our modern society.

It goes without saying that the teeth should be brushed carefully at least twice daily. Use a good mouthwash after each brushing. If your breath offends (an unforgivable sin for the salesman), get the advice of your dentist or physician.

In selling, your hands are on constant display. Make sure that they are always clean when you're on the job—never grimy with grease or stains. Keep nails neatly trimmed and free from stains.

Shampoo your hair at least once a week, or oftener if your hair is oily or if you have a scalp problem. Men should not plaster down their hair with a thick goo —hair that is clean and natural-looking is always preferable to the slick, oily look.

Of course, your clothing should be spotlessly clean—through and through. Get in the habit of changing your clothing every day. Men should wear a clean shirt every day, never trying to "get by" with yesterday's shirt. Both men and women should change to fresh underclothing and hose each day. It is assumed that you will have several changes of outer clothing and that you will not wear the same dress or suit two days in a row. This doesn't mean, of course, that you must have the garment cleaned every time you wear it. But give your outer clothing a rest; hang it up neatly between wearings so that the wrinkles will have a chance to disappear. Even when you buy a new dress or suit, don't wear it every day just because it is new. This is a common mistake. Switch to another garment at least twice a week. If you have only one change of outer garments, brush and press them frequently so that they will present the best possible appearance.

Cleanliness and neatness of clothing are a "must" regardless of what type of clothing your job demands. Even if your job requires a uniform or work clothes, such as are worn by a service-station attendant or a refrigeration serviceman (both of whom are also salesmen), these should be as clean and neat as possible. To a large extent, customers judge the salesman's pride in his product or service by the clothing he wears.

Men should be especially watchful of frayed collars and cuffs on shirts and of missing buttons. Inspect your shirt as you remove it each evening and, before sending it to the laundry, note its condition so that repairs can be made in advance of an otherwise embarrassing moment. Women should watch for ripped seams, tattered lace, and loose threads.

Selection of Clothing for Men

In selecting clothing, men should follow this simple rule: Be in style but avoid the extreme.

Suits. Your most important article of clothing is your suit. Select your suits with great care and thought. Suits that are tight-fitting (especially at the cuff) and dashingly cut may impress some of your friends, but they are not suitable for business wear. The trouser cuffs should touch the top of your shoes, not ride several inches above or fall in folds at the shoe tops. Choose conservative patterns in your suits. Remember, when you are on the job you want the customer to keep his attention on the product, not on the way you are dressed. The customer will be distracted by loud colors and patterns. Choose solid colors or soft plaids and stripes. If you cannot afford more than a couple of suits, buy good ones; two well-tailored suits of good material are better than four cheaply made ones. If you have only two suits, one of them should be dark—say, a dark blue or gray—for evening wear. There are many semiformal occasions when a dark suit is necessary; and, of course, dark suits are always fine for day wear. *Caution:* Don't load your coat and trouser pockets with large objects. Keep your pockets free of articles that make you look bulgy.

■ Good grooming is essential for the salesman. Not only will the well-dressed salesman have more confidence and poise during his sales presentation, but often the customer will judge the salesman's product by his appearance.

Generally speaking, it is best not to wear a sports jacket and slacks when you are at work. Of course, you have seen salesmen dressed in this manner; but this does not mean it is the most appropriate. You should eventually invest in a good-looking sports outfit for casual wear off the job. Here is where you can express your taste for "wild" colors if you wish—but not in your business suits!

Shoes. Buy conservative shoes. While lace-up oxfords are best for business wear, dressy loafers are acceptable, too. Black is the best all-round color. Don't try to get by with sporty loafers in a loud color such as yellow. They are fine for sportswear, but they are too casual for business. Never wear moccasin-type loafers on the job. Of course, your shoes should be kept shined and free of scuff marks. When the heels start to wear down, replace them. Hardly anything spoils a man's appearance more quickly than run-down heels. Incidentally, rubber heels are best for the businessman (they make less noise when a person walks), but there is no hard-and-fast rule here.

Of course, you should own at least two pairs of shoes for business wear so that you can change off frequently. The color of your shoes should harmonize with your suit. Have at least one pair of black shoes, because black can be worn with almost any color of suit. If you can afford only one pair of shoes for business wear, a dark brown cordovan (horsehide) is a good all-purpose color that can be worn with any color of suit. (Men who own brown cordovan shoes usually use black polish so that the color is between a black and a brown.) Don't wear light brown or tan shoes with a black or dark blue suit. Always wear black on formal occasions, such as a banquet.

Be conservative in your choice of shoe style—avoid sharply pointed toes, crepe soles, higher-than-average heels, and so on. *Hint:* Invest in shoe trees. They will keep your shoes in shape, and your shoes will look better for a longer period of time.

Hose. Too many men give no consideration whatsoever to the hose they wear, yet hose are a very important part of one's total grooming impression. Most executives dislike "shortie" hose on their salesmen. Ankle hose are usually at half mast, and bare flesh is exposed when the wearer sits. Longer hose that come at least halfway up the calf are accepted by businessmen as appropriate (some companies insist that their salesmen wear knee-length hose). The newer hose of longer length don't require garters, and they are very dressy and comfortable. In choosing hose, solid colors are best. Make sure the color harmonizes with your suit—and especially your tie. In fact, it is a good idea to match your socks with the predominant color in your tie, unless, of course, the predominant color is very loud. Don't wear bright red or yellow socks on the job. Black, dark brown,

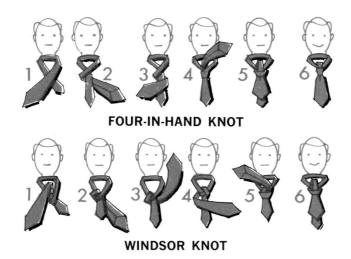

FOUR-IN-HAND KNOT

WINDSOR KNOT

How to tie the four-in-hand and windsor knots.

maroon, dark gray, and dark blue are appropriate colors, depending on the shade of your suit and tie.

Ties. Of course, you should always wear a necktie on the job. The only rule for selecting a necktie is that it should be *tasteful.* This is open to personal preference, to be sure. Extremely loud-colored ties should be avoided, though some striking color in the tie is certainly appropriate if it does not dominate. Colorful ties can be very smart-looking; the trick is in selecting colors that blend, that do not scream. Buy your ties at a reputable men's store. The ties will probably cost you more than if you buy them at a cut-rate store, but at a good men's store you can get advice from alert salesmen concerning colors that will be right for you and your suits.

In any event, choose conservative patterns—stripes, solids, or subdued patterns. Designs that include likenesses of animals, fishing lures, sports scenes, or other depictions are considered "corny" by the well-dressed man for business wear.

It does not matter whether you choose a regular tie (four-in-hand) or a bow tie; in either case, tie your own. Pre-tied ties usually look stiff—they never look as well as those you have tied yourself. Tie the knot neatly, either a four-in-hand or a windsor knot as illustrated.

Make sure that your tie knot fits snugly in your shirt collar—that your shirt is not showing between the knot and the top button.

WRONG   **RIGHT**

■ The tie knot should fit tightly against the shirt collar. Never should the top button of the shirt be exposed.

Have an adequate selection of ties. Even if you have only a couple of suits, a good choice of ties can make your wardrobe seem larger. Always untie your tie when you remove it in the evening; it will look better longer.

Shirts. A white shirt is always in good taste for either day or evening wear. Three collar styles are shown on page 95. While all are suitable for business, the regular and button-down collars are more conservative and are therefore somewhat more appropriate for business wear. Colored shirts may also be worn during the day (but not for evening) as long as they are not loud. Blue, gray, green, and tan are popular colors in light pastel shades. Stripes are also excellent, but the stripe should be subdued and thin. Cuffs may be barrel (with button), convertible (with button and extra buttonhole for use with cuff links), or french (these require cuff links). Shirts that are worn with cuff links are considered dressier.

Hats. Probably you don't wear a hat at this stage of your life. However, when you are employed as a salesman, it is a mark of maturity and good taste to wear a hat. While it is no sin to go hatless—many men do—the well-dressed man does not. A good men's clothing store will advise you on the best color and shape of hat for you.

Accessories. Choose accessories, such as cuff links, tie bars, and belts, with care. Most men do not need to be told that too much "jewelry" is offensive. Don't wear large gaudy rings, tie bars, or belt buckles. Even your wristwatch should be fairly conservative. Again, remember that you want your customer to keep his mind on what you are selling, not on how flashy you are.

Personal Grooming Hints for Men

If you are like most men, you need a haircut at least every two weeks. Don't allow your hair to become shaggy. Even though you may like it that way, your customer may mistake your preference for poverty—and the successful salesman *looks* successful. Avoid extremes in hair styles. Hair that is too long or too "arty" will surely give the impression that you are not mature in your judgment. Long sideburns are definitely out! Regular crew cuts and "Ivy League" or "Princeton" styles are always acceptable for younger men.

Shave daily. If your beard is heavy, shave each morning—don't try to get by shaving the night before; otherwise, your "five-o'clock shadow" is likely to make its appearance much earlier in the afternoon! If you are going out in the evening, it is well to shave again. Many men keep an extra razor in their office desk for such emergencies. The traveling man usually keeps a battery-operated shaver in the glove compartment of his car.

Grooming Chart for Men

Some of the important aspects of good grooming for men are given in the Good-Grooming Chart for Men on page 96. How would you rate if you were being surveyed by a stranger? In answering the questions in the chart, try to look

Three types of shirt collar styles. The button-down and regular shirt collars are more conservative and therefore are considered more appropriate for business wear.

TAB   BUTTON-DOWN   REGULAR

GOOD-GROOMING CHART FOR MEN

YES   NO

Hair

1. Is your hair neatly combed and brushed?

2. Do you wash your hair at least once a week?

Hands

1. Are your hands and nails clean?

2. Are your nails short and neatly shaped?

Cleanliness

1. Do you bathe at least once a day?

2. Do you use a body deodorant?

3. Do you brush your teeth at least twice a day, especially on arising and before going to bed?

Outer Dress

1. Is your suit clean and pressed?

2. Are your clothes conservative and businesslike?

Shoes and Hosiery

1. Do your socks harmonize with your tie?

2. Are your socks long enough to avoid exposing bare shins?

3. Are your business shoes polished at all times?

4. Are the heels neat (not worn down)?

5. Do your shoes harmonize with your suits (e.g., you would not wear tan shoes with a black suit)?

Accessories

1. Does your tie harmonize with your suit?

2. Is your tie neatly knotted?

3. Do you carry a clean handkerchief?

at yourself as a stranger would. Write your "yes" and "no" replies on a separate sheet of paper. Then count the total number of your yes and of your no replies. Any no replies indicate that you should strive to improve those aspects of your grooming.

Good Grooming for Women

All the suggestions for cleanliness and neatness given on the preceding pages apply to women, of course. Women are expected to be even more attentive to appearance and neatness than men.

The following list contains some special "do's" and "don'ts" for women on personal grooming:

1. Avoid hair styles that are too showy. While you don't have to look like a country cousin, neither should you try to look like a nightclub entertainer. In other words, don't try to strive for high fashion in your hairdo for work; achieve the natural look.

2. Use makeup sparingly and tastefully. Avoid extreme colors (iridescent tones, for example). Too much makeup is always in poor taste. Save eye makeup, such as eye shadow and mascara, for evening wear to help to avoid the glamour-girl look during the day. In business most people don't take glamour girls seriously. Of course, there are exceptions. If you work at the perfume counter or in the cosmetic section of an exclusive department store or if you work in a chic women's dress shop, the glamorous look is fine. But observe the appearance of these salespeople the next time you visit your favorite apparel shop or department store. Even though these salespeople may look glamorous, they generally use good taste in their makeup.

3. Dresses should be conservative in style. Avoid those with fancy trimmings, bare shoulders, or low-cut backs. Often retail stores require their salespeople to wear neutral colors, such as black, navy, gray, wine, or beige, but some retail stores now allow more colorful dresses to be worn. Tailored suits are always appropriate, and the well-dressed business girl usually has one or two of them in her wardrobe.

4. Be careful of jewelry. Too much jewelry is worse than none at all. Extra-long earrings, jangling bracelets, too many strands of beads, large rings, and the like are generally to be avoided in the sales atmosphere. Excesses are always bad, and the woman who is otherwise well groomed can easily detract from her appearance if she exceeds good taste in the matter of her use of either makeup or jewelry.

5. Use scents sparingly. Buy a *good* perfume and apply it with restraint. If you have ever been on a crowded bus on a hot summer day and found yourself

The well-groomed salesgirl dresses conservatively and avoids using too much makeup or loud shades of nail polish. She must have an appearance of neatness at all times.

seated next to a girl who has doused herself in cheap perfume, you know how offensive this practice can be.

6. Keep your hands clean and well groomed. Your nails should be short and well shaped. Clawlike fingernails are out of place in a business situation. Use nail polish that is tasteful—not loud. Clear polish or a light tint is most appropriate for business; reserve the "wild" shades for special social occasions. When you do use polish, be sure it is never chipped. It is better to remove the polish entirely than to allow the polish to become chipped.

7. The following suggestions on grooming for secretaries are also appropriate for the saleswoman:[1]

a. Hat veils must be crisp. Pressing between sheets of wax paper will restore crispness.

b. Flower accessories should be fresh-looking. Discard flowers that show repeated wear.

c. Earrings are a part of a costume. Keep them on your ears!

d. Keep clothes in needle-and-thread repair. Don't depend on pins to do the job.

e. Scarves, collars, and cuffs are to be clean and pressed.

f. Dress shields must be kept clean.

g. Hemlines must be even.

h. Slips should never show below the dressline, or through slits in skirts.

i. Lingerie should always be fresh.

j. If your hose have seams, keep them straight.

k. Gloves are a must. Black leather gloves are perfect for fall and winter, white cotton gloves are fresh and summery-looking.

l. Your purse should be kept polished or brushed—it should never bulge!

Grooming Chart for Women

Some of the important aspects of good grooming for women are given in the Good-Grooming Chart for Women on page 100. How would you rate if you were being surveyed by a stranger? In answering the questions in the chart, try to look at yourself as a stranger would. Write your "yes" and "no" replies on a separate sheet of paper. Then count the total number of your yes and of your no replies. Any no replies indicate that you should strive to improve those aspects of your grooming.

[1] John Robert Gregg, Albert C. Fries, Margaret Rowe, and Dorothy L. Travis, *Applied Secretarial Practice,* 5th ed., McGraw-Hill Book Company, New York, 1962, p. 41.

GOOD-GROOMING CHART FOR WOMEN

YES NO

Hair

1. Is your hair style in good taste (not extreme in style)? ☐☐
2. Does your hair show evidence of frequent brushing? ☐☐
3. Do you shampoo your hair at least once a week? ☐☐

Hands

1. Are your hands and nails clean? ☐☐
2. Are your nails of conservative length and neatly manicured? ☐☐
3. Is the nail polish you use in good taste, and does it always look fresh? ☐☐

Cleanliness

1. Do you bathe at least once a day? ☐☐
2. Do you use a body deodorant? ☐☐
3. Do you brush your teeth at least twice a day, especially on arising and before going to bed? ☐☐

Outer Dress

1. Is your dress or suit clean and pressed? ☐☐
2. Are your clothes stylish, yet appropriate for business wear? ☐☐

Shoes and Hosiery

1. Are your hose straight at the seams? ☐☐
2. Are your hose without runs, snags, or pulls? ☐☐
3. Do your shoes harmonize with your dress? ☐☐
4. Are your shoes clean and/or polished at all times? ☐☐
5. Are the heels neat (not worn down)? ☐☐

Accessories

1. Do you wear gloves on appropriate occasions? ☐☐
2. Do gloves and handbag complement your costume? ☐☐
3. Is your jewelry conservative and in good taste? ☐☐

SUMMING UP

Your customers will judge your product, service, or store by your appearance; therefore, you should always look your best on the job. If the customer lacks confidence in you, he will lack confidence in what you have to sell.

The most important factor in grooming is cleanliness. Good grooming also includes appropriate selection of clothing as to color and style, neatness, and general physical attractiveness.

In selecting clothing and accessories, it is well to remember that you should be in style but avoid the extremes. You want your customers to keep their attention on what you are selling, not on what you are wearing. For this reason, flashy clothing and accessories should be avoided.

Reviewing Your Reading

1. What is meant by good grooming? Why is it important to the salesperson?
2. What does careless grooming reveal about your personality?
3. List three important "do's" in observing cleanliness.
4. Why should you avoid extreme styles in clothing and personal grooming?
5. Why are loud colors generally to be avoided in business dress?
6. Why is it important to buy your clothing and accessories at a reputable store? What does your answer reveal about the importance of the salesman?
7. Howard Hancock works as a service-station attendant; Mildred Denton works as a cashier in a discount department store. Neither feels that good grooming is important in his job. List reasons why you think they are both wrong.
8. Why is it important to change outer clothing each day?

For Discussion

1. Discuss the meaning of the statement, "Customers judge the worth of a product by the appearance of the salesman."
2. Recall an effective salesperson whose grooming impressed you and another whose grooming offended you. Discuss.
3. It is said that your grooming has just as important an effect on you as it does on the customer you are serving. What does this mean?

4. When criticized by her supervisor for her sloppy grooming habits, Sally Mason offered the excuse, "I don't have time." Make some suggestions that will help Sally overcome this problem.

5. Phil Parsons was overheard to make this statement: "I don't think it's the customer's business as to how I dress. He dresses the way he wants to, and I do the same." Discuss.

6. Do you agree or disagree that sports jackets and slacks for men are out of place in business? State your point of view and be able to defend it.

7. Can you think of selling positions where good grooming is especially important and others where it is not quite so important?

8. *For men:* List ten "do's" and ten "don'ts" in good grooming for men.

9. *For women:* List ten "do's" and ten "don'ts" in good grooming for women.

Salesmanship in Action

1. Plan a basic business wardrobe for yourself, including probable costs. Assume that you are just starting to work as a salesperson in a large retail department store.

2. Organize two panel discussions on the topic, "What Is Required for a Good Personal Appearance?"

3. Choose an article of clothing, such as a suit, tie, dress, or hat, and find out all you can about current styles and colors. Write a report on the topic you have chosen.

4. Health is extremely important to good grooming. Prepare a report or conduct a panel discussion on "Rules of Good Health for the Young Salesperson."

5. *For men:* Invite a representative of a local men's clothing store to discuss "How to Look Your Best on a Limited Budget."

6. *For women:* Invite a representative of a local cosmetic firm to discuss how to apply makeup.

The Salesman Communicates

EVERY EFFECTIVE SALESMAN is an effective communicator, because selling is essentially communicating. Before you can persuade a person to accept a point of view, a new idea, or your product, you must be able to communicate your ideas and information convincingly. The major communication skills for the salesman on the job are listening and speaking.

Listening as a Communication Skill

Most of us are inclined to think that selling is chiefly a process in which the salesman does all the talking and the prospect merely listens. While this happens occasionally, it should be the exception—not the rule. In selling situations it is advantageous for the salesman to get the prospect to express his opinions, to ask questions, and to react to the presentation or demonstration. And, of course, when the prospect is encouraged to talk, what he says should be given a courteous and thoughtful hearing.

The Problem of Listening. The average person speaks at the rate of about 150 words a minute, but the average listener thinks at a speed of 400 to 500 words

Not only is the successful salesman a skillful speaker, but he is a good listener as well. He knows that he must listen carefully to what the prospect says.

a minute. These different rates of speaking and listening pose problems for both the listener and the speaker. The temptation is for the listener to think far ahead of the speaker; and when he is not challenged by what the speaker is saying, he engages in daydreaming or dwelling on personal thoughts, such as how heavy the traffic will be when he drives home, what to have for dinner, or his appointment with the dentist at four o'clock.

Most people are "lazy listeners"—that is, their minds are so full of their own thoughts that they find it hard to concentrate on what someone else is saying. This probably accounts for the fact that people forget over half of what they hear within a couple of days after they hear it!

Most of what you hear is, of course, not worth remembering down to the last detail. For example, **if** you are discussing your favorite football team with a friend, it isn't very **imp**ortant to remember every single play he describes. You can listen just hard enough to keep the conversation going, but you don't have to be able to react to everything you heard. There is nothing especially wrong with this kind of passive listening—everyone engages in it to some extent. In fact, in some social situations a person may not even want his listeners to remember everything that he said!

But this is where people sometimes get into difficulty—deciding when to listen and when to "half listen." Often it is very important to know exactly what was said. An important review in class just before a big test or an important message given by a prominent speaker are but two examples that call for *careful* listening. For the salesman who is talking with a customer, careful listening is a *must*. He must be able to reconstruct in his own mind what the other person is saying.

If he fails to listen carefully, he may miss an important reaction, excuse, or objection the customer has voiced. The prospect may even be ready to make a favorable buying decision; and if the salesman has not listened, he will miss that golden moment when he should reach for his order pad.

How to Become an Effective Listener. Listening is an art, but anyone can develop the art. There are two requirements to good listening: (1) You must care enough about what the other person is saying to want to remember it and (2) you must practice good listening habits constantly. Following are some of the rules you should practice in order to become an effective listener:

1. *Take an interest in what the prospect is saying.* If you are genuinely interested in giving your prospects and customers the best service you can possibly render, you will be interested in what they have to say. Show this interest as you listen. Give the speaker your undivided attention. Face him when he is talking, and by the expression on your face indicate your interest. If you will really concentrate on what is being said and think of it as providing a clue as to how you can be of better service, you will "get" his message and remember it.

Don't relax too much. Listening is hard work; you must be alert and on your toes. The sloucher is rarely a good listener.

2. *Hold your fire.* Some listeners allow themselves to become aroused, perhaps even angry, at what the other person is saying; and they begin to think of a suitable retort. While they are thinking of how they are going to respond, the rest of what the speaker has said goes in one ear and out the other. Keep calm and be patient—even if the prospect or customer is saying things that are uncomplimentary of your product or your company. Hear him out. Often a person who voices loud criticism eventually talks himself into a positive frame of mind without any help from his listener. Certainly listening carefully to the other person is a lot better than interrupting him to offer a sharp comeback. Someone has said that patient listening solves more problems than talking, and this is a very good rule for the salesman to observe. Keep an open mind; try to listen with objective detachment.

3. *Listen for ideas.* Good listeners focus on central ideas, usually prefaced by such statements as, "My main point is," "What I would really like to know is," or "My chief criticism is." Many listeners who have good intentions fail to discriminate between what is and is not truly important in a speaker's remarks. They try to remember everything. This is very difficult—and it is not even desirable. Listen for the main ideas, sifting the grain from the chaff.

4. *Avoid distractions.* The careful listener doesn't let background noises, movements of people, or other activities interfere with his listening. When the listener allows himself to be distracted by nearby conversations, sounds of

traffic, a loud radio, children at play, or the passing of people, he is not really giving his undivided attention to the speaker. It is a great temptation when, during a conversation, you hear a siren to stop listening to the speaker and concentrate on "where the fire is." When noises or movements of people become annoying, find a quieter place to talk. If this is not possible, try to shut out all extraneous noises and work doubly hard to concentrate on what the speaker is saying.

5. *Participate mentally with the speaker.* As mentioned, most people talk at a speed of about 150 words a minute, and they think about four times that rate. This makes it very difficult to "stay with" the speaker when the mind wants to travel faster than he is talking. The temptation is to think of other things while the speaker is talking, returning your attention to the speaker just often enough to appear absorbed in his remarks. Learn to participate mentally with the speaker as he talks. Repeat to yourself, in your own words, the gist of his remarks. Try to anticipate what the speaker is going to say next. Summarize in your own mind what the speaker has already said. Participate actively in the "conversation" even though you are not doing the talking.

Speaking as a Communication Skill

You have known instances when a smartly dressed person impressed you very favorably—until he spoke. In that instant, all the care given to grooming was wasted, ruined by sloppy speech habits. Can you express yourself effec-

■ **Whether the salesman is talking to a prospect or making a presentation at a sales meeting, he must be able to express himself effectively and to speak distinctly and persuasively.**

Courtesy The Du Pont Company

tively when you speak? The salesman should remember that his voice can be one of his most important assets. The person who speaks distinctly and persuasively and uses correct grammar invariably commands respect and influences others.

Words should be used as tools of communication and not as substitutes for action.

—William A. Ward, Texas Wesleyan College, *Polytechnic Herald*, Fort Worth, Texas, 3/12/64

Words—Basic Tools of Communication

Words are basic tools for the salesman. The more words he understands and is able to apply, the greater will be his ability to express ideas, selling features, and sales facts. Words help the salesman paint mental pictures to give prospects a feeling for the salesman's proposition. A good salesman can, by using words creatively, get the prospect literally to feel that he already owns the product. The salesman uses words with the same pride and satisfaction that a skilled craftsman uses tools.

If the salesman lacks the ability to use words, he has put a serious limitation on his thinking. You can think only with words. If you run out of words, you come to the end of your thinking, and all you can do is to repeat yourself. A large vocabulary and the ability to use it enables the salesman to find specific, practical ways of expressing ideas about his product. Salesmen with limited vocabularies are often forced to generalize about their product. All they can tell the prospect is, "It's wonderful," "It's a mighty fine buy," or "It's the best bargain ever."

Study the following statements used by advertising copywriters about their products. Note the descriptive words.

To sell fresh oysters: Savory oyster stew with plump, pampered oysters.

To sell oranges: Big, plump wedges.

To sell hardwood paneling: The soft beauty and warmth of fine hardwoods.

To sell small cars: The man who is fed up with bigger, thirstier cars switches to _____ .

To sell floor wax: It's a bright shine, a tough shine, an easy-to-wipe-up shine.

To sell a station wagon: From a frisky, sturdy little workhorse to the jauntiest little sedan of them all!

To sell a soft drink: You'll really welcome the cold crisp taste that so deeply satisfies—the cheerful lift that's bright and lively.

To sell fruit punch: The circus-red color, the candy-and-ice-cream taste.

To sell golf balls: The sweet click at the tee is the music of the finest ball in golf.

In describing his product, the salesman tries to choose words that are pleasant and dramatic. A saleswoman in a department store will prefer words such as *lovely, flattering, smart, chic,* and *stunning* in describing a blouse or a hat. She would not say to a customer, "That looks OK on you." In selling a power mower to a man, the salesman would use such words as *sturdy, of light yet durable construction, easy to handle, close-cutting, heavy-duty,* and so on. He would not be satisfied with, "That's a fine mower there."

Choosing Words Carefully

During the business career of J. Pierpont Morgan, one of the country's best-known financiers, a caller approached him with a sales proposition involving many hundreds of thousands of dollars. After a very convincing presentation, the man concluded his conversation with the statement, "So you see, Mr. Morgan, this is a very good gamble." To this Mr. Morgan replied icily, "I'm sorry, young man. I never gamble. Good day." What the salesman really meant to say was, "This is a good *opportunity*"; and using the wrong word probably cost him a great deal of money.

Unfortunately many people feel that any communication that gets the *idea* across is good communication. The salesman should remember, however, that not only must he get the idea across, but he must leave a favorable impression as well. Let's put it this way: A war-surplus army overcoat and heavy boots would keep a person just as warm as a stylish, tasteful topcoat and smart dress shoes. But as a salesman his appearance would be pretty shabby, wouldn't it? The salesman chooses appropriate clothing because he knows that his "image" and that of his company will be judged by what he wears. This is also true of the vocabulary he "wears."

In choosing words, the salesperson must avoid words that sound offensive. The word *deal,* for example, is offensive to many people. "I have just the deal for you," says a used-car salesman; and the customer immediately thinks he is being fast-talked into something he doesn't want. The word *cheap* should never be used to describe merchandise. Cheap suggests inferior quality. *Inexpensive* is a much better word. Even the word *bargain* may offend, as indicated by the trend to call former "bargain basements" by the better title of "thrift floors."

Enlarging Your Vocabulary

The dictionary contains about 400,000 words; the average businessman knows approximately 15,000 words. Why not be above average and try for 20,000 words or more? The larger your vocabulary, the better variety you can achieve in your communications. The best way in which you can increase your vocabulary is to read a great deal. Read books and magazines that are considered good literature. Read with a dictionary within reach, and look up the meaning and pronunciation of any words that you do not know or any that are vague in meaning. In fact, write them down, build up a word list, and review it frequently. In this way, your vocabulary will become larger, giving you self-confidence and poise in business and social life.

On Being Understood

Can people understand you when you speak? Many people have speech faults that make them hard to understand—speech faults that are easily corrected. Are you guilty, for example, of running your words together like this:

Wadjuhavinmind?	(What did you have in mind?)
Werjasit?	(Where did you see it?)
Wenullyouknow?	(When will you know?)
Jalikeitsent?	(Would you like to have it sent?)
Sagoodbrand	(It's a good brand.)

Many young people (and older ones, too) are guilty of these careless speech habits, yet with just a little practice they can overcome them. Be sure to make your speech crystal clear by using properly a "hinged" jaw, "limber" lips, and an "active" tongue. Speak slowly. The following suggestions, adapted from *Business English and Communications*,[1] are excellent pointers for the salesperson:

Hinged Jaw. A rigid jaw is a common fault with those who muffle their speech. All sounds issue through the mouth; and sounds forced through a locked jaw are bound to be hard to understand. Try this: Lock your jaw tight and pronounce these words—*open, able, ideal, bound.* You probably had difficulty understanding yourself!

Move your jaw freely between an open and a closed position as the various vowels are sounded. Unhinge your jaw to the utmost on such sounds as *ow*, but move the jaw almost shut when you sound the *oo* in *room.* To get the free-moving feeling of a relaxed jaw, practice is necessary. First, try out individually or in a group the following words to be sure you have unlocked your jaw:

open	mine	able	round
dough	responsible	ideal	brown

[1] Marie M. Stewart, E. Lillian Hutchinson, Frank W. Lanham, and Kenneth Zimmer, *Business English and Communication*, 2d ed., McGraw-Hill Book Company, New York, 1961, pp. 86–88.

You usually talk in complete thoughts, so the best way to learn this free-moving jaw action is to practice phrases and sentences. Try these.

down and out	Name the day to harvest the hay.
high in the sky	The dime is mine to find a blind for his yacht.
out of bounds	The honest Yankee yelled for help.
yelps and yells	The quality of mine determines its power.
around the house	Round and round he goes in honest confusion.
pot of gold	The long shadows fade into darkness.
down the hatch	The cake dough was baked and baked and baked.
going home	Home is where the heart is.

Limber Lips. Lazy lips are frequently the cause of unintelligible speech. Poor speakers use only one lip position, but good speakers use a variety of lip positions called for by the different spoken words. For instance, *who, lose,* and *shoe* should be said with rounded lips. *Key, see,* and *cat* must be said with the lips widely stretched. *Few, boys, use,* and *how* require two different lip positions. The lips jut out for *shoe* and *church.*

Practice the following phrases and sentences, using maximum lip movement.

friend in need	Peter Piper picked a peck of pickled peppers.
office merger	She sells seashells by the seashore.
triumphant march	How now, brown cow?
British viewpoint	The bond of friendship was broken.
mimeograph stencil	Which was the witch?
rapidly weighed	For the sake of safety, sound your horn.
passive resistance	The whistling west wind whipped the whispering trees.

■ It is just as important to speak slowly and to pronounce your words clearly when talking to a customer over the telephone as it is when talking to him face to face. A cheerful-sounding voice is helpful, too.

Active Tongue. The tongue must be active if you are to be clearly understood. Effective use of the tongue depends to a great extent on the teeth, which act as a backstop or baffle for the tongue. For example, keep your tongue away from your teeth and say "this." Hard, isn't it? Now repeat the word, this time pressing your tongue against your teeth, and notice the improved clarity. To get the feel of an active tongue, say "the tip of the tongue, the tip of the tongue, the tip of the tongue." Your tongue moved very rapidly, didn't it?

> Selling is more of an art than a science. It deals more with people than with things. It traffics in ideas, not absolutes. It is . . . nothing less than dynamic communication.
>
> —Mary Louise McGowan, "Are Salesmen More Professional Than Plumbers? *Sales Management*

Now that you know what a free-moving tongue feels like, practice the following phrases and sentences. Be sure that you use an active tongue.

actually colder	Nothing was lost but a delightful time.
attempted assault and battery	Needles, pins, spools of thread, and lovely linen laces were his stock-in-trade.
automobile battery	Her tale was not strictly factual; yet not fictional either.
loose-fitting clothes	Thirty thousand thermos bottles were auctioned.
zest of children	The sixth letter was smoothly dictated.
through thick and thin	It was a delightful time to be alone at home.
thirty thick thistles	Linger a little longer, lovely lady.

Speaking Slowly. The general tendency among many people is to try to talk as fast as they think. This, of course, is not only impossible but is a major threat to intelligible speech. Prove it to yourself by saying the following three sentences at top speed.

We do not have three-ply thread in stock.
Mr. Melvin is forever talking about health and wealth.
A postscript is needed for the sixth letter you transcribed.

Grammar and Speech

No matter how clearly you speak or how varied your word usage, you will make a very poor impression on your customers if you do not use correct grammar. Are you guilty of such statements as these:

1. We don't have no size 38's in stock.
2. Will you please help Jane and I?
3. Someone left their coat on the counter.
4. I would just as leave not go today.

5. You are much quicker at adding your sales slips than us.
6. Our salesmen works much harder than them.
7. Everyone should look their best.
8. Do you know where the wrapping twine is at?
9. Mr. Brown, some people was asking for you.
10. I don't appreciate him saying those things.

If good grammar is a problem for you (and you know whether it is or not), get busy now to improve it. Nothing brands you as uneducated so quickly as poor grammar. There are several good programmed books on grammar that you can use for individual study. One is *English 2600*, Revised Edition, by Joseph C. Blumenthal, published by Harcourt, Brace, and World, Inc., New York, 1962.

Developing a Pleasant Speaking Voice

What is a pleasant speaking voice? A very practical answer is found in the training ideas of the Bell Telephone System. A pleasant speaking voice is one that is (1) correctly modulated and properly controlled, (2) neither too high nor too low, (3) neither inarticulate nor shrill and sharp, (4) not too feeble or too loud, and (5) not monotonous.

Talk to your customer in a natural conversational manner, not like an orator or an actor. Pretend that your customer is your next-door neighbor or your class-mate across the aisle.

Try to keep those annoying "ers" and "ahs" out of your speech. Have you ever had to listen to someone give a talk that was full of unnecessary expressions? Poor salesmen often do the same thing. For example:

> You see, Mr. Davis—er—the reason for—er—the different sizes—er—is—er—be-cause we have found—ah—that is—ah—our customers—each make a special—er—problem.

Would you feel like listening to a half hour of that? Of course you wouldn't. Talk at a natural brisk speed; and if you pause to think, keep it silent. Talk so that the customer can hear every word you say. Don't mumble. Your customer is not forced to listen to you, and he will not do so if he has to make an effort to hear or to understand you.

By all means, avoid a monotone. Vary your voice up and down the scale—sometimes loud (but don't shout), sometimes soft (but not too soft)—to empha-size the important parts of your sales talk. Speed up and slow down for emphasis.

The salesman, like the actor on the stage, has to strive to keep monotony out

■ A pleasant voice and an animated expression on the salesman's face go a long way toward putting the prospect in the proper frame of mind.

of his voice. He can do so by learning to *dramatize his speech*. For example, try reading the following two sentences aloud without varying your speed or placing emphasis on any particular word:

Naturally, Mrs. Eggleston, you will want a cleaner that will do the job with the most efficient possible action. But above all, you will want a machine that will hold up, even under the heaviest possible work.

Sounds pretty drab doesn't it? Now try it again and see if you can give it more meaning through dramatization. Remember, the salesman tries to sell quality above cost. He tries to "put across" the important fact that his machine will hold up even with the heaviest type of work. Keeping the word emphasis and pitch the same, try to increase the selling effectiveness of these sentences by changing the pace.

Naturally, Mrs. Eggleston, / you will want a cleaner that will do the job with the most efficient possible action. But / above all, / you will want a machine / that will hold up, / even under the heaviest possible work.

Now add a change of emphasis. Try emphasizing the underlined parts.

Naturally, <u>Mrs. Eggleston,</u> / you will want a cleaner that will do the job with the most efficient possible action. But / <u>above all,</u> / you will want a machine / that <u>will hold up,</u> / even under the heaviest possible work.

Now let yourself go. Experiment with different speeds, change your voice emphasis, speak loudly, try whispering, raise your voice at the end of a sentence, drop your voice at the end of a sentence. Get the opinions of others as to how it sounds. Soon you will discover that it's really easy to train your voice so that your words are spoken more meaningfully.

Your Poise and Facial Expression "Speak"

The way you walk, your posture, and the gestures you use are also important in communicating with customers. Having good posture means carrying the body in a manner that commands the respect and confidence of others. One's posture should say, "I believe in myself." This means not stooping, slumping, or slouching. Of course, one's posture should not be rigid; one should appear relaxed, though not casual. Many a salesman has impressed the office receptionist or secretary and won an interview with an important prospect simply because his posture gave him an air of importance. The retail salesperson whose posture suggests alertness quickly wins the confidence of a shopper. The salesman who shuffles into the office of a prospect and immediately slouches down in a chair is in no way prepared to deliver a forceful and enthusiastic sales talk. His action will contradict whatever he says. To register alertness in the mind of the customer, the salesman should sit up straight and lean slightly forward as he talks. If he is standing, he should not lean against a chair or table, rock back and forth on his heels, or display other signs of nervousness.

■ Three types of posture to avoid. Poor posture can make a sales presentation ineffective.

SLOUCHING   LEANING   HUMPING

Good posture when sitting or standing commands the respect and confidence of others.

The expression on the salesman's face goes a long way toward putting a prospect in the proper frame of mind. If the salesman is grouchy and uncommunicative, the response of the prospect is bound to be something less than enthusiastic. If, on the other hand, the salesman smiles frequently and looks the customer in the eye as he talks, the customer is likely to be responsive and cooperative. A single smile will often "say" more than a volume of words. Develop the habit of smiling frequently; the very act of smiling will put you in a more positive mood, and it will put the customer at ease, too.

A Voice-Development Program

It is possible to train your voice to be pleasing to hear, but a pleasant speaking voice does not result overnight. Certain fundamental rules must be followed, and these rules must be practiced constantly. Here are a few suggestions for improving your voice and speech:

1. *Listen to your own voice.* The best way to do this is to make a recording of your voice and study it. An excellent means for reproducing your voice is by tape recorder. Study the tone and pitch of your voice to determine whether you have a voice that is pleasing to hear.

2. *Get the opinion of others.* Voice Rating Scales are provided on pages 122 and 123 to help you discover what others think about your voice. You will use them also to rate your classmates. The Negative Voice Score and the Positive

Voice Score will give you an idea of what causes an unpleasant voice and what produces the pleasing voice that you will want to cultivate for social life as well as for selling. Become familiar with both the negative and positive sides of the rating, and judge yourself as much as possible before the rating scales are used in class. The key to these rating scales is given in Appendix 2.

3. *Learn to relax.* Practice relaxing your whole body. Breathe deeply. You will find that you speak more easily when relaxed this way. Practice making full, round tones. It is easy if you are completely relaxed.

4. *Read aloud as much as possible.* Read both poetry and prose. Allow your voice to express the thought and feeling that the words cause in your mind and emotions. This will help you put feeling into your conversation, and people will be more inclined to listen and to be impressed by what you have to say.

5. *Read and study good books on speech.*

SUMMING UP

You cannot expect to be a successful salesperson unless you can communicate effectively. The major communication skills for the salesman are listening and speaking.

To be an effective listener, you must be a careful listener—that is, think with the speaker as he is talking and repeat to yourself in your own words what is being said. Rules for effective listening include (1) take a genuine interest in what the speaker is saying, (2) don't allow anger or prejudice to interfere with your listening, (3) concentrate on the ideas the speaker is giving, (4) avoid distractions, and (5) participate mentally with the speaker.

Effective speech is one of the salesman's greatest assets. In order to speak effectively, the salesman must have a good vocabulary—a vocabulary that permits him to achieve variety and interest in his speech. He should choose words very carefully, making sure not to use words that offend others. The effective speaker speaks clearly, using a hinged jaw, limber lips, and active tongue; and he speaks slowly. Good grammar is an important part of one's communication skill. The winning speaker has a pleasant speaking voice, varying the tone and pitch so that it is not monotonous. Poise and facial expression also communicate.

The speaking voice can be improved. The person interested in improving his speech should listen to his own voice, get the opinion of others, learn to relax, read aloud as much as possible, and read good books on speech.

1. Why are listening and speaking called the salesman's most important communicating tools?
2. What is the main problem in listening?
3. Distinguish between careful listening and passive listening.
4. List and discuss five rules for effective listening.
5. Why is it important to have a broad vocabulary? Give some of the negative results of a poor vocabulary.
6. Give examples of words that may be offensive to others and then supply more suitable substitutes.
7. How many words are in the average businessman's vocabulary?
8. Discuss the terms *hinged jaw*, *limber lips*, and an *active tongue* as they relate to clear speech.
9. What does poor grammar in your speech reveal about you?
10. What is meant by varying the tone and pitch of your voice to avoid monotony? Give examples.
11. Why are poise and facial expression considered communication skills?
12. What steps can you take to improve your speech?

For Discussion

1. "Listening is the most neglected of the communication skills," according to one authority. What did he mean? Why do you think this is so?
2. There are four basic communication skills—listening, speaking, reading, and writing. Discuss the importance of each to the salesman.
3. Some sales authorities say that your voice will do what your words alone cannot accomplish. What does this statement mean to you?
4. One of the chief obstacles to good communication is semantics. Look up the meaning of the word *semantics* and be prepared to discuss it in class.
5. Choose a product that you would like to sell. Then form committees and list as many dramatic words and phrases as your group can think of to make the products selected by each member of your group sound appealing.
6. Turn to the list of grammatical errors on pages 111 and 112 and supply the correct statement for each.
7. The average dictionary contains much more than a mere list of words and definitions. List six other types of information contained in the dictionary.
8. Prepare a description of a wristwatch you are selling, writing your statement so the customer wants to own it. Give your statement orally in class.

9. Posture is very important in the total impression a salesperson makes when he is communicating with customers. Discuss poor posture habits to avoid.

Sales Problem I

For several months George Smith has been trying to see a difficult prospect who is a purchasing agent for a construction firm. George feels that if he can get permission to make a study of the present job methods of the prospect's firm he will be able to offer the firm a better product than they are now buying at the same price. The study would probably take about two weeks to complete. Finally after persistent telephone calls, talks, and personal visits to the prospect's firm, George is granted an interview with the prospect.

George is prompt in keeping his appointment and makes a good presentation of his proposition. When he thinks he has aroused the prospect's interest, he introduces his request for a study:

SALESMAN: **Mr. Prospect, in order to compute accurately the savings in costs that we were talking about, it will be necessary for me to make a study of your present methods of handling plywood. May I have your permission to start that study now?**

PROSPECT: Well, I don't know. We already have some A-1 companies interested in doing the same thing. I don't want too many people getting in our way.

SALESMAN: **It will take me only two weeks, Mr. Prospect, and it will give me the chance to make up a complete bid for you.**

PROSPECT: Well OK, go ahead; but I want that bid in my hands in five days.

George immediately gets under way with a crash program to provide a bid. Five days later he presents his bid to Mr. Prospect but is told that it is too high. George, a very dejected salesman, returns to his office and tells his sales manager the bad news.

SALES MANAGER: George, we're sorry you lost out on that bid. However, you lost that business on the day your prospect told you to go ahead and make the study. You, like other salesmen, George, must learn to tell when you are losing the sale.

QUESTIONS
1. What does the sales manager mean when he tells George that George lost the business at the time he was given permission to make the study?
2. What other clues in a sales presentation may help to tell the salesman that he is in danger of losing a sale?

A salesman for a men's clothing manufacturer calls on the owner of a new men's clothing store and shows the customer his line of ties. The salesman's presentation goes something like this:

SALESMAN: **Mr. Blake, ties for the new season will be shorter and narrower. Our new lines are right up with the style as you can see. Figure patterns are out in favor of stripes. Your customers will like these new colors. They're conservative for your older trade, and there is a good selection of styles for the high school and college crowd. Now, Mr. Blake, I want you to notice the wonderful workmanship in these ties.**

CUSTOMER: I can see all that, and I'm not interested. Drop in again sometime when you are in this neighborhood.

QUESTIONS

1. Evidently the salesman has failed to get the buyer's interest. Which of the following is most likely to be the trouble?
   a. The salesman was stressing the wrong benefits.
   b. The salesman talked too much.
   c. The buyer wanted to visit, but the salesman didn't take time to spend a little while in chitchat.
2. What questions do you suppose were running through the buyer's mind while the salesman was showing his line? Make a list of at least three.

1. Suppose a speaker made the following statement to you about the progress of manufacturing. How would you summarize his statement in your own words (be brief but clear)?

   Although all areas of business operation and management have made great strides in the past fifty to seventy-five years, none has seen more tremendous growth nor undergone such startling changes in methods and practices than has the important function of manufacturing. The key to this stupendous development has been the introduction of mass production. Where one man used to labor for hours making one pair of shoes, performing all the operations himself and using hand tools, today in the same elapsed time hundreds of pairs of shoes are turned out by almost entirely automatic machines requiring few men, with each man handling one specialized operation that comprises a minor segment in the manufacture of the shoes. Mechanization, specialization, and scientific organization and management are the factors that have made such mass production possible.

2. See how many descriptive adjectives you can supply for each of the following:
   a. A *pretty* fur stole
   b. A *good* hammer
   c. A *nice* party
   d. An *interesting* talk
   e. A *beautiful* steam-and-dry iron
3. Effective words are usually those that are easiest to understand. For each of the following words and phrases, supply a simpler word or shorter phrase:

   a. endeavor   g. utilize   m. at the present time
   b. retain   h. forwarded   n. five in number
   c. difficult   i. ascertain   o. held a meeting
   d. selection   j. consummate   p. in a manner similar to
   e. concluded   k. subsequently   q. in this day and age
   f. initiate   l. cognizant

4. Suppose you are preparing an advertisement for the newspaper on a special sale of apples in a certain grocery store. What could you say about the apples that would be more appealing to customers than simply "big, firm apples"? See how appetizing you can make these apples sound.
5. Sometimes in our speech we omit letters that should be sounded. Which letters in the following words are often omitted? Pronounce the words correctly.

   quantity   gentlemen   recognize
   government   hundred   clothes
   February   Indian   let her
   candidate   library   give me
   didn't   perhaps   general
   accidentally family   sophomore

6. Following are words that are often mispronounced. Can you pronounce them correctly?

   tremendous   bona fide   drowned   superfluous
   mischievous   athletics   data   finance
   maintenance   often   hospitable   research
   extraordinary film   precedence   police
   column   accurate   indisputable adult

7. In the following sentences there are certain words and phrases that are commonly misused. Can you provide the correct statement for each?
   a. This is all the farther I can go.
   b. Did you read where our company is giving a bonus this year?
   c. Try and do as you are told.
   d. Between the three of them, they made many sales last month.

e. Pretend like you don't see him.

f. Where is she going to?

g. Don't leave the store without you have your work finished.

h. I don't know as I like that color.

i. This saw is equally as good as the other one.

j. I can't help but feeling that I'm going to be late.

8. Use the Voice Rating Scales on pages 122 and 123 to find out what your class thinks about your voice. The rating scales should be used in class in conjunction with a tape recorder so that a recording can be made of your voice. After a recording has been taped, copies of these rating scales (in mimeographed form) may be handed out to the other class members by the instructor and the recording played back. The class will rate your voice on these forms by placing a check mark in the correct column following each question. Then they will hand these forms back to the instructor, who will note areas of agreement and will consult with you concerning your weakness or strength. The key to these rating scales is given in Appendix 2.

9. Using a tape recorder, practice saying the following paragraph taken from a sales manual. Make certain you pronounce each word distinctly and strive for emphasis whenever you feel it is needed. Rate yourself using the Positive Voice Score of the Voice Rating Scale on page 123.

> Mrs. Smith, this liquid blender is an electrical appliance that makes meal preparation and entertaining less work and more fun. You'll be amazed and delighted to discover how many different things the liquid blender can do for you. It will take the nuisance and clutter out of chopping, grating, grinding, pureeing, pulverizing, and mincing. It will mix or whip foods in just a few seconds; and it does some things no other appliance can do . . . it liquefies fruits, vegetables, and other solid foods, thus opening up for you an entirely new world of cooking.

10. The expert salesperson does not rely on words alone. He knows that his manner, enthusiasm, and voice inflections go a long way in making sales for him. Using a tape recorder, practice the following sales approach. Assume that you work in the furniture department of a large department store and a customer has stopped to admire a coffee table.

> Good morning. May I help you? (*Pause.*) Isn't that a beautiful table? It's a Cushman maple. You probably know the name Cushman. They're one of the oldest and most highly respected manufacturers of fine maple. (*Pause.*) You'll notice that this is the new Heritage pattern—very popular with young people who like maple but in modern design. (*Pause.*) These tables are stain-resistant. You know, every Cushman piece has seven finishes, each hand-rubbed, so that you get the most possible wear and beauty from the wood. (*Pause.*) Yes, maple has a lot of character, but it's also extremely practical.

VOICE RATING SCALE

Negative Voice Score

	YES	SOME-TIMES	NO
1. Voice too high or shrill			
2. Talks too loudly or too noisily			
3. Tones are muffled and indistinct			
4. Voice has a nasal twang			
5. Speech is artificial and affected			
6. Hesitates, stammers, or stutters			
7. Has the "uh" habit			
8. Has a whining voice			
9. Has a domineering, dictatorial tone of voice			
10. Speech is jerky			
11. Talks too fast			
12. Has a tendency to choke off vowel sounds			
13. Skips over consonants or fails to pronounce them			
14. Commonly mispronounces words			
15. Runs words together			
16. Has a monotonous voice			
17. Has a breathy type of voice			
18. Voice fades out at end of phrases or sentences			
19. Voice is flat, dull, and colorless			
20. Laugh is unpleasant			
Total score			

VOICE RATING SCALE

Positive Voice Score

	YES	SOME-TIMES	NO
1. Speaks fluently; words flow out evenly, clearly			
2. Voice is pleasing to hear			
3. Is easily understood			
4. Has a cordial and friendly voice			
5. Voice is free from monotone			
6. Distinctly pronounces every word and syllable			
7. Voice is resonant (has carrying power)			
8. Has a melodious voice			
9. Voice is natural and unaffected			
10. Has a forceful voice			
11. Has a good level pitch (high enough to be heard)			
12. Tones are clear (no twang or muffled sound)			
13. Voice rises and falls naturally			
14. Maintains a normal rate of speed when talking			
15. Correctly pronounces each word			
16. Controls voice at all times (not too loud or noisy)			
17. Emphasizes the thought rather than the words			
18. Speech is free from colloquialisms or accent			
19. Has a good vocabulary			
20. Voice is agreeable when laughing			
Total score			

Why People Buy

WHAT IS behind every purchase you make? That is, what do you want from the things you buy? Do you buy only because the color, price, or general appearance of an article pleases you? Suppose you purchase a new umbrella, taking a little time to select the one that pleases you the most. You consider the size, the type of handle, and the color. But what are your basic reasons for purchasing the umbrella?

Your immediate reason is to keep dry. But why do you want to keep dry? You don't want to catch cold? You don't want the uncomfortable feeling of water-soaked hair and skin? You don't want to lose your well-groomed appearance? Your basic reasons, then, for this purchase are:

1. Protection of health
2. Comfort
3. Personal pride

A man decides to spend $100 on a correspondence course. What makes him decide to take this course? Because he wants more education? Why does he want more education? His reasoning may run like this: he wants to improve his personal worth; he is dissatisfied with his present job and wants to earn a higher income. His basic reasons, therefore, are:

1. Desire for economic security. He wants to make himself more valuable in his present job and perhaps win promotion.
2. Desire for social approval. He feels that he needs to earn more money so that he can acquire more property, power, and prestige in the eyes of friends and relatives. A new car, a television set, or a new home would help to accomplish this purpose.

Satisfying Needs and Desires

When making purchases, all people have one thing in common, even though they may have different personalities, buying problems, and habits: they are trying to satisfy their needs or wants. Sometimes it is difficult to understand the difference between a need and a want. A need usually means something that is required, such as groceries or a warm blanket. A want is something that is not actually needed but that would satisfy a craving or desire. Ordinarily, needs are satisfied first; wants (desires) are satisfied to the extent that the purchaser's income will allow.

People buy goods, not for their inward value, but for the satisfaction of owning them or of using them. People buy things that represent advantages for themselves or for their families, relatives, or friends. The advantages that people want, and the reasons that cause them to buy, are called *buying motives*.

Mary may buy a new dress because she wants to make an impression on her friends. Jim buys a popular style of sports jacket because he wants to dress like the other fellows. Mother buys a gallon of enamel because she wants to have a gay, colorful kitchen to work in. Father is willing to buy a television set because of the family enjoyment and pride of ownership that such a purchase provides.

Courtesy The National Cash Register Company

■ The housewife buying food is satisfying a need.

Thus we see that, when people decide to make a purchase, it is not primarily because of price, quality, or appearance; it is because they want, first of all, to satisfy a need or a desire.

The need or desire for a product exists within the prospect. It may be either active or dormant. If it is active, the prospect is aware of the need or desire and takes steps to satisfy it. If it is dormant, the prospect is unaware of the need or desire. The salesman, however, can help the prospect to become aware of a dormant need or desire and persuade him to act on it. Therefore, the salesman's job is to locate a buying motive and build his sales presentation around it.

The salesman who sold the first washing machine no doubt found his prospects unaware of a desire to own such a product. Women had been getting along without washing machines for hundreds of years. But the dormant desire for a machine to take over the drudgery of the scrubbing board and to free women from such heavy work was always present. Thus it was the salesman's job to awaken in each prospect the desire to possess the washing machine he was selling.

Classifying Buying Motives

Buying motives are often classified as either emotional motives or rational motives. *Emotional buying motives* are those that prompt the prospect to act because of the appeal to love, fear, vanity, pride, prestige, desire for comfort, and desire to be envied. A glance at the advertisements in any magazine will make you aware of the important role played by emotional appeal.

When the advantages of buying a product appeal to a person's reason and judgment, they are called *rational buying motives*. Examples are economy,

The housewife shopping for an air conditioner is satisfying a want, or desire.

profit, dependability in use, and efficiency of operation. These motives are particularly useful where the prospect carefully analyzes the advantages and disadvantages of buying and weighs the plus features against the minus features.

Emotional Buying Motives. Advertising experts and sales authorities who have studied the buying patterns of people suggest that people buy most articles offered for sale because of one or more of the following emotional buying motives:

1. Better health
2. Poise and social approval
3. Making or saving money
4. Distinction
5. Popularity
6. Comfort
7. Avoidance of effort
8. Romance
9. Companionship
10. Protection of family
11. Curiosity
12. Pleasure and amusement
13. More leisure time
14. Desire to be like others
15. Variety
16. Security
17. Adventure
18. Convenience
19. Pride of ownership

The salesman's task is to determine which motives are more likely to play a dominant role in creating sales for his particular product. Most companies select from such a list as the one given here the buying motives that apply to their products and emphasize them in the sales literature provided for their salesmen. An appliance company, for example, might concentrate on the following motives for people who buy such household appliances as ranges, refrigerators, automatic washers, home freezers, and dishwashers:

1. Protection of health and family
2. Avoidance of effort
3. Pleasure and more leisure time
4. Convenience
5. Pride of ownership

A life insurance company reminds its agents that prospects buy life insurance to:

1. Help save money
2. Provide security in later years
3. Provide protection for loved ones

■ The travel agent in describing European tours appeals to such emotional buying motives as pleasure and adventure.

The experienced life insurance salesman finds out in advance the possible needs of his prospect. For instance, a certain prospect may have a wife, two small children, and a home with a mortgage on it. In the interview the salesman emphasizes these facts and the prospect's resulting needs by asking questions such as these:

How could you keep up the payments on your home if your income stopped?
Could your family keep the home and take care of living expenses in the event of your death or complete disability?
How much insurance do you have now?
Have you provided enough to ensure that your children have a college education?

This affects the prospect where he feels it the most—his family, his home, his old age. Each of these thoughtful questions is based on a desire, a need, or an emotion and is designed to discover the buying motive that will influence the prospect to buy insurance.

Rational Buying Motives. The purchaser of industrial goods usually is moved to buy because of rational buying motives as opposed to the emotional motives that influence the purchaser of personal goods. The salesman who sells heavy machinery, chemicals, and manufacturing supplies, therefore, will appeal to different buying motives from those used by the salesman who sells washing machines, insurance, and men's wear. The industrial purchaser has specific requirements and usually has planned his purchases in advance. Often he knows more about a product and its uses than the salesman. However, that does not mean that the salesman is limited in his selection of buying motives or in his power to direct and guide the sales interview. Following is a list of rational buying motives that play a dominant role in the industrial-goods market:

1. Efficiency
2. Economy
3. Good workmanship and materials
4. Durability and dependability
5. Accuracy
6. Increased profits
7. Low maintenance cost
8. Saving of time
9. Uniformity—all items alike
10. Simplicity in construction and operation
11. Adaptability to many uses
12. Saving of space
13. Automatic operation
14. Ease of repair
15. Ease of installation
16. Increased production
17. Greater power
18. Purity
19. Availability
20. Completeness of stock
21. High-level research and testing
22. Continuous supply
23. Complete servicing

Here is an example of how an expert salesman uses rational buying motives in selling office equipment:

SALESMAN (*seated in the office of a prospective account*): **Mr. McGregor, we have found that our customers are interested in our voice-recording method as a means of cutting costs and increasing profits.**

■ The prospective customer who is considering the purchase of an office copying machine for his company is influenced by such rational buying motives as increased production and economy.

PROSPECT: Our firm is interested in keeping costs down these days.

SALESMAN: **You could give your executives improved service and still cut your costs of writing letters in half. Do you mind telling me what you pay a stenographer a week?** (*From here on, the salesman figures each step with paper and pencil.*)

PROSPECT: Stenographers receive about $80 a week, or $16 a day.

SALESMAN: **And about how many letters a day do your stenographers average?**

PROSPECT: Thirty letters a day is considered a good day's work for a full-time stenographer.

SALESMAN: **At that rate, you pay 53 cents a letter. The same girl with a transcribing machine will do at least sixty letters a day, so that your cost comes down to less than 27 cents. You save 26 cents a letter. About how many letters do all your stenographers complete in a day?**

PROSPECT: I'd say about a hundred.

SALESMAN: **Saving about 26 cents each on 100 letters is $26 a day. That amounts to $6,500 a year.**

As you no doubt have noted, the salesman in this example cleverly utilized three rational buying motives in promoting his equipment. He appealed to the customer's motives for larger profits, economy, and increased production. This does not necessarily mean that the industrial buyer is not influenced by emotional buying motives. Often the industrial buyer may be influenced by the desire to imitate a successful competitor.

Other Buying Motives. Buying motives also may be classified as product motives and patronage motives. *Product motives* lead the prospect to buy one specific product in preference to another and are concerned with the sales appeals based on the product itself. *Patronage motives* make the prospect prefer one company or store over another. Typical patronage motives are dependability, friendship, reliability, and large assortments of merchandise to choose from.

Basic Buying Motives

People always are needing or wanting something. They obtain satisfaction of their needs or desires when they buy. However, all the buying motives are not present at the same time, and it is up to the salesman to find the dominant desire or need in each case and to show how his product will satisfy it.

Now that the various classifications of buying motives have been reviewed, it is possible to condense them into this basic list, which is easier to remember:

1. Self-preservation
2. Gain
3. Social approval
4. Convenience
5. Love
6. Pleasure
7. Variety
8. Curiosity
9. Fear

Behind every decision to buy there always lies a specific buying motive.

—Paul W. Ivey and Walter Horvath, *Successful Salesmanship*, Prentice-Hall

Self-Preservation. Self-preservation is the desire to earn a living and maintain an adequate level of living, to protect personal and family health, to satisfy appetite, and to be secure from unforeseen emergencies and danger. Automobile tires and seat belts, for example, may be sold on the basis of making the family car safer to ride in. A vacuum-cleaner salesman tells Mrs. Jones that, since her small children play on the floor, her rugs should be kept free from dirt and disease-carrying dust; and he points out why his product is the most efficient for accomplishing this purpose. Many foods and medicinal preparations are sold through the motive of self-preservation.

Gain. Gain includes the desire to make a profit, to amass or possess wealth, to save money, or to make possessions last longer. Gain is often a primary buying motive in the mind of the homemaker when she purchases household appliances. She buys a home freezer to save money through buying and storing food in quantity. She buys a vacuum cleaner to protect her rugs from the wear caused by ground-in dirt, and thus make them last longer. She buys an automatic washer to save laundry bills and wear and tear on the family clothing. Of course, gain is the chief buying motive for business firms.

Social Approval. Social approval involves pride of personal appearance, the desire to be distinctive, the desire to attain prestige or power, and the desire to imitate others.

Automobiles often are sold because the customer thinks of the impression that he will make driving a particular model. People want correctly styled furniture and luxurious rugs for the same reason. Distinctively styled clothing is bought so that the purchaser will win the admiration and respect of other people. After a prospect has decided to buy a television set, the particular brand or model will be selected on the basis of the beauty of the cabinet and the air of distinction that it lends to the living room.

Many products are purchased because people want to be like others. Mrs. Smith gets a new automatic washer, so Mrs. Davis wants to buy one. Millions of cakes of soap are sold each year because women, both young and old, want to have skin like the actress whose testimonial appears in the advertisement.

■ The woman shopping for a new hat usually receives pleasure in making her purchase.

Convenience. Convenience includes handiness; saving of labor and time; dependability in use; long service; and easy operation, installation, and repair.

Love. Love includes the love of parents for their children, love of children for their parents, love for the opposite sex (romance), and desire for companionship.

Pleasure. Pleasure includes the desire for amusement, for leisure time, for tasty foods, and for comfort. Television sets, radios, toys, games, and cameras are not the only things that provide pleasure, and a smart salesman knows it. The new dishwasher provides pleasure for the family, too, not only because it is a time-saving device, but because it is easy to operate and fun to watch. Clothing is not purchased solely for the comfort and protection it provides. New hats, coats, suits, dresses, and shoes, all give a great deal of pleasure. Gift buying certainly is based on the motive of the pleasure of giving.

Variety. Variety includes the desire for something different, for adventure, for travel, for change of apparel, and for redecoration in the home. Advertisements are continually appealing to this motive. Breakfast cereals appeal to the idea of trying something new or different. The clever retail ready-to-wear salesperson uses this motive to persuade Mrs. Customer to purchase a completely new wardrobe or to buy fashionable accessories.

Curiosity. Curiosity is the desire to investigate the unknown. This motive can be used in a number of ways. For example, a salesman can use it effectively in an opening remark to a prospect: "Mr. Dealer, you will want to know about our maximatic profit-making plan. Our company is the only one that offers it." By such an approach the salesman is appealing to the customer's desire to make more money as well as to his curiosity.

Fear. Fear is a negative, rather than a positive, buying motive. The other motives considered were based on the search or desire for pleasurable results. Fear is simply being afraid of losing one's health, life, friends, job, money, comfort, or anything else which one prizes.

The feeling of fear is natural. It is found, to some extent, in everyone. Fear is usually closely associated with caution and the desire for security. People buy life insurance, bonds, and stocks, or put money in the bank to gain security for their old age or for a rainy day. They buy locks for doors and windows, rubber mats for bathtubs, and fire extinguishers and sprinkler systems because they fear what may happen if they do not have them. They prefer to take precautions against mishaps rather than chance a catastrophe.

Discovering the Dominant Buying Motive

People buy with different wants in mind. Buying motives differ even for the same product. Mr. Jones may buy a certain automobile because of its economical performance. Mr. Smith will want the same car not because of its economy but because of its distinctive styling and because of a certain amount of prestige he feels he will gain through owning it. A salesman may sell a dozen typewriters to an office manager who is convinced that the new model will outlast other types. Another manager may purchase a dozen of the same machines to get more production out of the office staff.

Customers buy because of certain primary, or dominant, wants. There may be several minor, or secondary, wants, but usually there is one impelling dominant motive. If the salesman tries to close a sale without basing his appeal on the dominant want of that particular prospect, he is wasting his time.

It is easy to discover the dominant buying motive of the prospect. Get him to talk, and then sit back and listen carefully to what he says. If you let people talk, they will actually tell you how to sell them. People like to talk about the things that interest them, as in the following case:

SALESMAN: **I heard your speech before the Downtown Businessmen's Association yesterday noon, Mr. Brown. I never realized that there were so many headaches in the machine-tool industry.**

PROSPECT: There are plenty of problems. Many develop right in our own plant.

SALESMAN: **Are office appliances included in your list, Mr. Brown? If so, I'd like to hear about them.**

Courtesy The Du Pont Company

By listening carefully to the prospect's views and problems, the salesman can easily discover the prospect's dominant buying motive.

PROSPECT: Our present typewriter setup is OK, but our calculators are a headache to the statistical department. Breakdowns interfere constantly with our production schedule. That's why I'm so stubborn about long-lasting equipment.

SALESMAN (*listening attentively*): I see.

In this sales interview the salesman was able to get the prospect to talk by appealing to his pride as a public speaker and to his interest in the problems of the industry. You may talk to a prospect about some trade problems, or you can often "start the ball rolling" by discussing some competitor's problem, provided you do not violate a confidence.

A successful salesman generally spends the first few minutes of an interview getting the prospect's views and problems. He is then in a better position to know what sales features to emphasize and what particular objections he will have to meet.

If the product is highly technical or can be used in different ways, the salesman usually arranges for a special survey of the prospect's needs and technical problems before he attempts to make a sale. If he is not a sales engineer, his company usually employs specialists or engineers for such surveys. Armed with the facts resulting from the survey, the salesman is well equipped to demonstrate how his product will satisfy the needs and solve the problems of the prospect.

What Will the Product Do for Me?

Because all products are purchased in response to different buying motives, the salesman must know the motives that will cause his prospects to purchase the product that he is selling. A good salesman makes a list of the possible motives for buying his product. For example, in selling a high-priced automobile, a list of customers' motives would include dependability, pride of ownership, safety, appearance, comfort, prestige, and performance.

Since the salesman's chief job is to sell satisfaction, he must relate the facts about his product to the wants of the customer. A product may be made of fine materials, put together with great skill and workmanship, and manufactured by the best-known firm in America; however, these facts alone will not make the customer want that product. Such facts are important, of course, when showing the customer how a certain product will satisfy his wants better than a competing product, but first a desire must be aroused by showing him *what the product will do for him.*

The salesman must see the product through the eyes of the customer. He must discover what the customer wants from the product that he is selling and then group his facts around these motives. When facts about the product are converted into reasons for buying, they become *selling points.* For example, if the salesman is selling a refrigerator, he will want to emphasize what the new model does for the homemaker:

Large freezer compartment holds 70 pounds.
Aluminum rustproof shelves revolve and can be cleaned easily.
Fruits and vegetables keep crisp and fresh in extra-deep hydrators.
Beverages chill quickly in the plastic chill drawer.
Food keeps colder as refrigerant circulates around the entire box.
Automatic defrosting maintains even temperature and does not require watching.

Consider how an advertisement for foam rubber cushions relates the following facts to its reader's comfort:

Gives you a resilient, restful support.
Is cooler in summer.
Keeps its shape—wears for years.

In an advertisement for a magnetic toolholder containing three tools, these verbs are related to what the home mechanic needs to do when making repairs around the home. He can:

Grip	Push	Loosen	Fasten
Turn	Pull	Cut	Tighten
Hold	Bend	Squeeze	
Twist	Join	Straighten	

Or consider this selling message of a hair shampoo for women:

Washes more shine into your hair.
Cream-conditions your hair.
Gives a quick, rich lather.
Rinses freely—no soap drag.
Keeps short hair glamorous.
Makes your hair want to curl.

In each of these cases the buyer is told what the product will do. The seller or advertiser is answering the buyer's question, "What will the product do for me?"

The Five Buying Decisions

It is interesting to study the way that people think and act when they are considering a purchase and the reasons why they finally buy. When considering any purchase, the prospect must make five buying decisions, indicated by the following questions:

1. Why should I buy? (The need)
2. What type, brand, or style should I buy?
3. Where should I buy?
4. How much should I pay?
5. When should I buy?

Whether the prospect is buying apples or automobiles, he will not decide to buy until these five questions have been answered in his mind. In some cases the prospect goes to a store with these five questions already answered; consequently, the selling job is simplified. In most cases, however, the prospect must be helped to make these five decisions. This is what lifts the salesman out of the order-taker class.

To show how the five buying decisions are made, consider the following case:

Why Should I Buy? The Browns own a five-year-old automobile, which is still in good condition. One evening they visit friends who have just bought a new car and are shown all the features of the new purchase. Driving home that eve-

What type, brand, or style should I buy? The alert salesperson realizes which buying decisions her customer is trying to make and gives him helpful suggestions.

ning, Mr. Brown is thinking, "The old car is getting to look pretty shabby. I wonder how long it will hold up. It will have to have some expensive repairs soon."

Mrs. Brown is thinking, "The Jones's new car is certainly attractive. If we had a new car like that, our neighbors would surely take notice. It would be fun driving the girls to bridge parties in the new car. Henry has an important job. He needs a new car to keep up appearances."

In other words, the Browns have made the first decision: Why should I buy? They have convinced themselves of a need.

What Type, Brand, or Style Should I Buy? Whenever Mr. Brown passes an automobile dealer's showroom, he stops to look at the cars. He reads advertisements in magazines and newspapers and gathers facts about the new models from friends, neighbors, and relatives. He talks to salesmen and dealers, listens to their sales stories, watches their demonstrations.

The Browns discuss the facts about the various cars and decide on the model they want, thus making the second buying decision: What type, brand, or style should I buy?

Where Should I Buy? Mr. Brown was particularly impressed with a certain salesman, so he and his wife go back to that dealer for a second look. They have made the third buying decision: Where should I buy?

How Much Should I Pay? But Mr. Brown is thinking, "The price is quite high. Should I buy this car or leave the money in the bank? The house needs painting. The children need clothes. Is this car a good buy for the money?"

If the salesman is capable, he helps Mr. Brown to decide that the car is worth the price by demonstrating its outstanding features and explaining how they are adapted to his family needs. If Mr. Brown is convinced, the fourth buying decision is made: How much should I pay?

When Should I Buy? Now the Browns have to decide whether this is the proper time to buy, considering the high cost. In view of the fact that they will have to paint the house and buy fall clothes for the children, wouldn't it be wise to wait awhile? Shouldn't they take a little more time to talk it over? After all, a large sum of money is involved.

The salesman proceeds to sell them on the advantages of owning the car now. He shows them how easy it is to have the car immediately by taking advantage of the firm's easy-payment plan, and he stresses the generous trade-in allowance for the old car. He reminds them that these advantages may not be obtained if they wait. Then he resells them on their needs. He paints a vivid picture of owning the car now, of enjoying it now, and having it paid for that much sooner. The Browns finally arrive at the fifth buying decision: When should I buy?

Differences to Be Considered in Making Buying Decisions

Although customers must make each of the five buying decisions before they buy, they will not arrive at their decisions in exactly the same way. Any of the following situations may occur: (1) the time in making decisions may differ, (2) the need for aid of salesman may differ, and (3) the order of buying decisions may differ.

Time in Making Decisions May Differ. People walk through a store or along the street and suddenly decide to buy something that appeals to them. All this happens in a matter of minutes. You ask, did they pass through the five buying decisions? They certainly did. It makes no difference whether it takes one minute, one hour, or weeks to decide. The customer must make those five basic decisions, or the sale is not made.

Need for Aid of Salesman May Differ. There are times when the customer makes the decisions to buy without the aid of a salesman. Or the customer has a need fixed firmly in mind before he even sees a salesman. However, this is not the usual situation. More often the salesman must first sell the need to help the customer make the first buying decision. For example, it would be useless for an upholsterer to talk first about the features and price of upholstering if his prospect is not convinced that he needs to redecorate. Or, as another example, there may not be many people who feel the need of owning an electric dishwasher. The salesman must make the prospect appreciate its advantages and sell the need for this laborsaving and timesaving appliance before he tries to convince the prospect to buy his particular model.

Order of Buying Decisions May Differ. The five buying decisions are not necessarily made in the order given on page 136. For example, Mrs. Davidson's old refrigerator stops working one morning. Parts are so expensive and the unit is so old that it would not be feasible to repair it. Mrs. Davidson immediately decides to buy a new refrigerator. She made two of the five buying decisions in this order:

1. Why should I buy?
5. When should I buy?

A customer is looking at some rugs. She tells the salesman, "I certainly want to get rugs on the bare floors of my new house right away. These seem to be reasonably priced. Still I'm not sure they're exactly what I want. Perhaps I'd better look around a little more." This customer has made her buying decision in this order:

1. Why should I buy?
4. How much should I pay?
5. When should I buy?

The salesman must help her to make the remaining decisions:

2. What type, brand, or style should I buy?
3. Where should I buy?

Discovering the Missing Buying Decisions

The alert salesman must be able to sense just what buying decisions are missing. Does the customer have the need? Is it the time element that causes the customer to hesitate? Is it the price? By carefully noting which buying decisions the customer has made, the salesman can eliminate those and concentrate on the decisions still to be made. By helping the customer with these, the salesman is providing a useful service and increasing his own ability and value in his field.

SUMMING UP

People have one thing in common when they make a buying decision: they are all trying to satisfy their needs or desires. These needs or desires are called motives. The salesman should not always assume that the prospect is aware of his needs or desires. Often it is up to the salesman to awaken the prospect to his needs or desires by making him realize how much better his position would be by taking the action the salesman suggests.

Motives may be classified as emotional and rational. They may also be classified according to whether the prospect prefers to use a specific product (product motive) or whether the prospect trades with a particular company (patronage motive). Emotional motives account for the majority of favorable buying decisions in the consumer-goods market. Rational motives predominate in the sale of industrial goods.

People buy with different wants in mind. What appeals to Mrs. Mack may have little or no effect on Mrs. Thomas. Usually customers are more interested in motives than they are in technical points about the product. The big question in the mind of every customer is, "What will it do for me?"

Reviewing Your Reading

1. What is a buying motive?
2. What is an emotional buying motive? Give some examples.
3. What is a rational buying motive? Give some examples.
4. What are product motives?
5. What are patronage motives?
6. How do buying motives for consumer goods differ from those for industrial goods?
7. Do the same buying motives always apply to the same product? Why or why not?
8. Do all people have the same dominant buying motives? Explain your answer.
9. How can you discover a customer's dominant buying motive?
10. What is the chief interest of a person whenever he considers buying any product?
11. What are the five buying decisions that a prospect must make before a sale is completed?

1. Give some reasons why a prospect is unable to make the second buying decision: What type, brand, or style should I buy?
2. Give some reasons why a prospect is unable to make the fourth buying decision: How much should I pay?
3. Is it always necessary to expend time and energy to make all five buying decisions?
4. What would be the most effective basic buying motive for each of the following products?

   a. Vitamins   h. New house
   b. Toilet soap   i. Deck of cards
   c. Piano   j. Dancing lessons
   d. Vacuum cleaner   k. Expensive automobile
   e. Mattress   l. Camera for amateur
   f. Best-selling book   m. Camera for professional
   g. Christmas gift   n. Brake lining

5. If you were selling electric ranges, how would you apply the buying motives of protection and safety?
6. Why should a salesman classify buying motives?
7. What buying motives would you use in selling a typewriter to a college student? To a purchasing agent of a large industrial firm?
8. What product would be most adaptable to each of these buying motives?

   a. Pride of ownership   e. Dependability
   b. Love of family   f. Variety
   c. Desire for profit   g. Pleasure
   d. Efficiency

9. As the purchasing agent for a large industrial firm, you are requested to purchase a number of adding machines for the accounting office. What motives would probably influence you most?
10. Name the buying motives that are being used in each of these selling statements:

    a. "You'll enjoy walking in these shoes, because they are built for walking and fit your foot perfectly."
    b. "This refrigerator makes plenty of ice cubes and freezes them quickly."
    c. "And whatever tire you buy, Mr. Prospect, you want the one that will give you the best protection, isn't that so?"
    d. "With a fine home such as you have, you naturally want the furnishings to be of equal quality."

e. "The color of this tie harmonizes especially well with that suit you are wearing."

f. "The beauty of these new draperies will be a constant joy to you."

g. "The health of your children is important to you, isn't it, Mrs. Brown?"

Scene: Household-appliance store. Customer enters and strolls around looking at refrigerators. A particular model catches her eye, and she stops to look at it. At this point, the salesman approaches.

SALESMAN: **Good morning! You are looking at our new kitchen-tested model. It's really good-looking, isn't it?**

CUSTOMER: Yes, it is. I've been looking forward to the time when we could have a fine new refrigerator in our home.

SALESMAN: **Have you been looking around?**

CUSTOMER: Oh, yes, I've been in a number of stores. I like the style of this model.

SALESMAN: **Yes, you can see how the distinctive beauty of this new refrigerator will improve the modern appearance of your kitchen. (*Opens door.*) And here is an interior that is even more beautiful. Notice the abundant storage space throughout. It has aluminum shelves, two crispers, and a big freezer designed for people who use large amounts of frozen foods. Do you use frozen foods?**

CUSTOMER: Very little. Our present refrigerator doesn't have a large enough freezer chest for frozen foods.

SALESMAN: **This chest has ample space for frozen foods and provides plenty of ice cubes. With this feature in your refrigerator, you won't be making many trips to the market for small purchases.**

CUSTOMER: We seem to throw out so much leftover food because it won't keep.

SALESMAN: **You won't have that worry any longer with this new model in your kitchen, Mrs. ___, Mrs. ___ .**

CUSTOMER: Mrs. Jamison.

SALESMAN: **You see, Mrs. Jamison, this refrigerator has our patented temperature control, which automatically starts and stops the unit to maintain the proper temperature in the frozen-food chest and general storage area. And you can select the degree of cold you want. (*Demonstrates.*) This also means low-cost operation for you, Mrs. Jamison.**

CUSTOMER: Well, that is *something*. Our present refrigerator is getting old and needs servicing often. It's getting to be quite a bother.

SALESMAN: This will free you of all that bother and inconvenience, Mrs. Jamison. This refrigerator is your silent servant in the kitchen. It stores an abundance of food for you at a minimum cost. Its beautiful appearance plus the fine service it will give will be a source of great pleasure to you, I'm sure.

QUESTIONS

1. List the buying motives that this salesman used.
2. What cues of the customer provided the salesman with the right buying motives to emphasize?

Salesmanship in Action

1. Study the advertisements in magazines and newspapers, and make a list of buying motives that would sell television sets. Be prepared to classify your motives in class discussion.
2. Select any product, and list all possible reasons why prospects should buy it.
3. For the following products, study advertisements in magazines and newspapers, and list the main buying motives. Classify them as emotional or rational.
   a. Tires (automobile) *d.* Adding machines
   b. Chocolates *e.* Liability insurance
   c. Floor coverings *f.* Paint
4. Make a study of two types of heating appliances—gas burners and oil burners—to determine the buying motives used. Study magazines and newspaper advertisements. Visit a local dealer, and examine each type of equipment. Obtain sales literature about each type.
5. Make a study similar to the one in question 4 of an electric range and a gas range.
6. A salesman, in talking to a dealer, made this statement: "This is a mighty fine product, Mr. Dale. It's just been added to our line, and we expect it to go over big. Why don't you try a few and see how they move?"
   a. Write a brief criticism of the salesman's statement.
   b. Rewrite the statement to make it more effective.

Using Your Product
Knowledge

NOTHING IS more important to the salesman than knowing his product. He may have all the personal qualities required for successful selling, his personal appearance may be outstanding, and his knowledge of customers and their buying motives may be unexcelled. Yet if he does not know his product, he cannot give the customer the sales assistance he expects and to which he is entitled. If a prospect asks only one question about a product that the salesman cannot answer, the prospect loses confidence. Even if the prospect does decide to buy, he will not be convinced that he has made a wise purchase when the salesman is hazy about the merits of the product.

For example, consider the following difficult situation that a salesman recently employed by a retail furniture store finds himself in because he lacks product knowledge:

CUSTOMER: I'm furnishing my dining room in red maple, and I need one piece to fill it out. I am looking for a hutch.

144

SALESMAN: Let's see now, a hutch—that's a type of table, isn't it?

CUSTOMER: No, it's like a credenza or a buffet.

SALESMAN: Oh, yes. Let's see now—credenza or buffet. Here's something that looks like a buffet.

CUSTOMER: Yes, but that's mahogany. Don't you have anything in red maple?

SALESMAN: We have an entire section in maple. I think it's over here. (*Leads the customer to another section.*) Here are some maple pieces.

CUSTOMER: Yes, these are lovely. But I need red maple. I think they call this shade Colonial American.

SALESMAN: I don't believe I know what you mean by red maple. Do you mean redder than this? (*Points to the Colonial American.*)

CUSTOMER: Yes, and this isn't it at all. I suppose I will have to try elsewhere.

This salesman did not take the time to learn about the merchandise he was selling. Even though he had been given a manual entitled *Facts About Furniture* by his supervisor and asked to study it, he had not read it carefully.

It is easy to see that if he had known his merchandise he could have been of assistance to the customer and perhaps made a sale. He did not know the name for the furniture he was selling, nor did he know very much about wood. No matter how sympathetic we may be for the salesman because he was new on the job, the fact is that the customer expected assistance, and when she did not receive it, she took her business elsewhere.

Product Knowledge Pays Big Dividends

Knowledge of product helps the salesman in five important ways:

1. It gives him confidence.
2. It helps him through difficult selling situations.
3. It prevents a sales talk from sounding mechanical.
4. It helps the salesman to enjoy his work.
5. It increases the salesman's chances for promotion.

Product Knowledge Gives the Salesman Confidence. The more knowledge the salesman has, the more confident he is that he can satisfy the customer and the more interest and enthusiasm he can inject into his selling. Expert salesmen who know their product "inside and out" show their pride in selling it; and their pride is reflected in their voice, their expression, and their enthusiasm. When a customer observes this confidence, he is more confident, too; he believes that the product he is considering is really worth buying.

Courtesy Eastman Kodak Company

■ **Knowing his product gives the salesman confidence.**

Product Knowledge Helps the Salesman Through Difficult Selling Situations. One of the most common statements made by customers is, "I can buy this same product at a lower price in another store." Unless the salesman knows his merchandise, this resistance on the part of the customer is difficult to overcome. By knowing construction, workmanship, and the raw materials that go into a product, the salesman can more easily prove that his product is worth the price and that what may seem to be a better buy elsewhere is usually not comparable in quality. Customer objections, such as "It seems too light in weight," "This color will get dirty very quickly," or "That price seems awfully high," can be met much more easily if the salesman knows his product thoroughly.

Product Knowledge Prevents a Sales Talk from Sounding Mechanical. The salesman who is prepared to answer any question about his product is not likely to get into a rut in presenting his sales talk. The knowledgeable salesman introduces interesting facts about the history of the product, how it was manufactured, how it was tested, and the experience that buyers have had with it. The salesman who "parrots" merely what is on the label of the product or gives an obviously canned sales talk cannot sound very convincing and thus does not win the customer's confidence easily.

Product Knowledge Helps the Salesman to Enjoy His Work. If you are unusually well prepared for a history lesson in school by having done considerable outside reading on the subject assigned, you are eager to share your knowledge with others; you enjoy the class. The same is true of the salesman who knows his product. Because he is more assured, he really enjoys making a sales presentation. He enjoys sharing his fund of information with a customer who needs this specific information in order to reach a buying decision. On the other hand, the sales presentation can be somewhat painful if the salesman is unsure of himself and is afraid the customer will ask him questions to which he cannot supply the answers. His uneasiness shows through.

The salesman today must possess a constellation of skills and a wealth of knowledge. At his finger tips must be a mass of details about the product he sells, the customer to whom he sells it, and the industry he services.

—Leon Morse, "The Sound of a Different Drummer," *Dun's Review & Modern Industry*

Product Knowledge Increases the Salesman's Chances for Promotion. Top management is constantly sizing up the sales force, looking for those who show signs of leadership. One of the first signs of leadership is a genuine interest in finding out all one can about the merchandise he is selling. The salesman who has extensive product knowledge stands out at meetings, at sales conferences, and on the sales floor. Also, the customers on whom the salesman calls quickly notice his fund of information about the merchandise, and they often let the salesman's boss know how much they appreciate the salesman's competence. When the word gets around that you know your product, you can be sure that you are being looked upon favorably by management as one who has "promotion potential."

A Good Salesman Knows the Industry, Too

A good salesman not only knows his own product, but he also has a good grasp of the industry within which his company operates. If he is selling for a company that makes refrigerators and home freezers, he makes it a point to learn all he can about the refrigeration industry by reading magazines, trade journals, and newspaper articles on the subject and by attending local conventions and conferences sponsored by the industry. If he is selling plastic novelties, he takes it upon himself to study the plastics industry—how plastics are made, sources of supply of raw materials, manufacturing methods, and new developments in the field. Every salesman has an obligation to keep up to date on trends in the industry of which he is a part.

What the Salesman Should Know About His Product

The effective salesman's product knowledge should include the following:

1. Background information about the product
2. Appearance of the product
3. Composition of the product
4. Processes used in manufacturing the product

5. Uses of the product
6. Serviceability and durability of the product
7. Care of the product
8. How the product is priced and the terms of sale
9. Company history and company policies
10. How the product compares with the competitors' products

Background Information About the Product. As a salesman, you will have many occasions to use background information about the product you are selling. If you can make a customer appreciate the effort and patience required to make a lace tablecloth by hand, its value will be greatly enhanced. The history and romance embodied in oriental vases and Persian rugs provides the customer with additional pride and satisfaction in purchasing such valuable articles. A knowledge of the history of furniture helps the furniture salesman to appreciate fine designs and workmanship, both antique and modern, and to pass his enthusiasm on to a customer. A vast fund of information about fishing helps the sporting-goods salesman sell more fishing rods, reels, and flies. A knowledge of the history of cooking utensils has value to a salesman in discussing the advantages of modern kitchenware.

Appearance of the Product. Customers today are very conscious of color, line, and design in many things they buy—furniture, automobiles, luggage, clothing, and so on. Beauty and style sometimes have more influence on the final buying decision than any other qualities of the product. The present-day buyer thinks in terms of ensembles. Will this chair harmonize with my rugs and drapes? Will these shoes match my new Easter outfit? Does this hatbox go with my other luggage? Is this picture "right" for the living room?

Knowledge of color, line, and design will help the salesman to satisfy the customer's desire for beauty and good taste in personal appearance and in the home. When a salesperson expresses a knowledge of artistic principles, the customer's confidence in his advice is greatly increased.

Composition of the Product. The salesman who knows the materials used in his product is better prepared to talk about their selling features, such as wearing qualities and superiority over those in other products. For example, notice the selling confidence displayed by a salesman of housewares:

CUSTOMER: But why will this kettle give better service?
SALESMAN: **This kettle is made of aluminum, Mrs. Cassidy. Unlike an enamel kettle, it will not crack or chip if it is accidentally knocked against the sink**

or stove. Also, aluminum conducts heat quickly and evenly and doesn't scorch food as readily as other cookware.

CUSTOMER (*picking up utensil*): It's so light!

SALESMAN: Aluminum weighs only about one-third as much as iron or copper. But notice how thick this kettle is. It's just as thick as enamelware, yet only one-third as heavy. That means less weight for you to lift every day.

Processes Used in Manufacturing the Product. The quality of the product is determined largely during the manufacturing process—upon the grade of raw materials used, the care given to the production, the quality controls used for the various parts that make up the product, the care given to final inspection, and so on. The salesman should know as much about the manufacturing process as it is possible for him to know. Many companies send their salesmen to the factory frequently so that they can observe firsthand all the steps in the making of the product.

When the salesman knows the problems of manufacturing, he is in a better position to explain to customers why the price is high (or low), why there are delays in shipment, why there are shortages, and the like.

The salesman who knows how his products are made can find use for this knowledge in many ways. For example, note how a salesman of floor tile uses his firsthand knowledge of manufacturing methods to emphasize important selling points:

SALESMAN: Here is our new inlaid linoleum in the new mosaic chip style.

CUSTOMER: Will it wear well?

A knowledge of color, line, and design is extremely helpful to the salesman in the furniture department.

SALESMAN: Extremely well. It is fortified with plastic for longer wear and easier care. See how the mosaic shapes are slightly raised for a unique textured surface.

CUSTOMER: But won't these push through?

SALESMAN: No, they are literally "cooked" in and locked securely by a special manufacturing process. I have seen this particular linoleum being made at the factory. Getting these shapes into such an interesting pattern was quite an engineering feat.

CUSTOMER: It is lovely. Is it easy to install?

SALESMAN: It is very simple. The back pastes directly to the floor—no lining felt is needed. Incidentally, the linoleum is factory-waxed. How large is the room in which you expect to use this linoleum?

Uses of the Product. It is extremely important that the salesman know the specific uses of the product he sells. If he is selling an all-purpose power saw for the home workshop, he should be able to tell the customer the kinds of things he can make with the saw, the kinds of attachments that may be purchased for use on the saw, how to change blades, and so on. If the product has more than one use, the customer should be told about it. For example:

SALESMAN: By substituting this buffing wheel, Mr. Loftin, this saw can be used as a sander and a polisher.

■ Through a tour of the factory, the salesman will gain firsthand information about how his product is manufactured.

Many customers hesitate to buy new products because they don't know how to use them. Note how a door-to-door salesman of stainless-steel cooking utensils shows a customer how to use his product:

CUSTOMER: It sounds wonderful, but I don't know how to cook meat the waterless way.

SALESMAN: It's very easy. Just sear your roast for a few minutes on each side until it is brown. This seals in the natural meat juices and flavor. Then put on this "snug-fit" lid (*showing how tightly it fits*) and finish the roast over a low flame. It's as easy as that.

Know your product. This sounds familiar doesn't it? Yet it continues to be the most common cause for losing a sale. So learn as much as you can about your product or the service you are selling.

You'll probably *never* learn all there is to know about it. Pick up details of successful uses. Learn what it will do; what it will not do. How was it developed? How is it made?

Study it from *every* angle.

Know more about your product than your competitor's salesman knows about his.

—Charles F. Hatmaker, *Notes from a Sales Manager's Handbook*

Serviceability and Durability of the Product. Every customer is anxious to get the most for his money. He is interested in knowing whether the product will give dependable service, how well it will wear, whether it is economical to use, and so on. The salesman should be able to supply this information without hesitation. If he is selling house paint, he can quickly answer such questions as, "How many years can I expect this paint to last?" and "Will it chip or peel?" If he is selling a dehumidifier, he can answer such questions as, "How much does it cost for electricity to run this dehumidifier day and night for a month?" or "Is it noisy?" or "How long will it last?"

Notice how the salesman in the following example assures the customer about the wearing quality of shirts:

SALESMAN: This shirt will last twice as long as the less-expensive brand you were looking at, Mr. Bradley. It is made of two-ply yarn running the width and length of the fabric. That means stronger and longer wear than a shirt that is made of a fabric that has only a single yarn running both ways.

Care of the Product. The salesman often makes a sale by telling the customer how to care for the product properly, thereby increasing its serviceability and durability. See how a salesperson who sells fabrics or ready-to-wear dresses instructs the customer on the care of the article:

CUSTOMER: I've heard these rayon shantungs are practically impossible to launder.

SALESPERSON: Not at all, Mrs. Gordon. Just be sure to wash this fabric with a mild soap, using lukewarm water. Squeeze the suds gently through the material. Don't rub or soak the material. Then rinse thoroughly, and roll it in a turkish towel to remove the excess moisture. When you press this fabric, be sure to press it on the wrong side with a warm iron, never a hot iron.

CUSTOMER: That doesn't sound too hard.

SALESPERSON: No, it's really easy. And with that kind of care it should keep its new look for a long time.

Other examples of instructing customers in the use of a product follow:

Linoleum—how to clean the floor, waxes to use

Power lawn mower—how often it should be oiled, the best type of fuel to use, preparation for winter storage

Paint—how to mix, how to apply for best results, cleaning

Shoes—use of shoe trees, type of polish recommended, how to clean

Roses—when to plant, type of plant food recommended, insect control

Typewriter—how to clean the keys, keeping the machine covered, oiling the machine

Luggage—how to clean, keeping the leather rich-looking, how to pack clothing, recommended uses of various compartments

Information about the care of the product is also important to the industrial salesman: chemicals (How should they be stored?), machinery (How often should it be lubricated? What type of lubricant is best?), raw materials (What temperature is best for storage? Is special ventilation required? Should they be kept off the floor?). Even though many manufacturers supply handbooks to buyers on care of both industrial and consumer products, the salesman should know thoroughly the information that is contained in them. The ability of the salesman to supply answers about product care on the spur of the moment builds confidence on the part of the customer.

How the Product Is Priced and the Terms of Sale. Customers are often confused by the variations in price of the many different types of products available. The salesman, therefore, must be able to explain to them satisfactorily the reasons for such variations. Study the following example:

CUSTOMER: What is the price of this plow?

SALESMAN (*looking at the price tage of the model*): Let's see, it's $159.95.

CUSTOMER (*pointing to another model*): And how much is this one?

SALESMAN (*again looking at the price tag*): Hm-m, just a moment. That's $219.95.

CUSTOMER: What makes this plow higher-priced? The blades seem to be the same length.

SALESMAN: Well—it is made in Philadelphia—er—hm-m.

■ Showing the customer how to care for the product will often help the salesman make a sale.

Contrast this with the following example:

A customer enters a hardware store and tells the salesman he is interested in a barbecue grill with an electric rotisserie. There are eight different models to choose from.

CUSTOMER: I see this grill is $27.50. The one over here (*pointing to a similar grill*) is priced at $21.50. What's the difference?

SALESMAN: **This deluxe model at $27.50 has an aluminum hood; the $21.50 model has a steel hood. The aluminum hood won't rust. Also, note the warming oven and the convenient tray on the deluxe model. These features aren't on the other model.**

CUSTOMER: Oh, yes, I see. Everything else is the same?

SALESMAN: **Yes, they are both made by the same manufacturer. The motor, you will see, is guaranteed for one year. I think you will be glad you bought the deluxe model. You won't have to worry about rusting, and this excellent oven keeps the food warm until you are ready to serve it. This bottom tray, too, is very handy for keeping seasoning, plates, and utensils.**

CUSTOMER: I think you're right. As long as I'm spending this much, I might as well get the best. I'll take the deluxe model.

The salesman should also be familiar with the terms of sale. This is especially important on expensive items, such as refrigerators, pianos, automobiles, and furniture. If the product is not satisfactory, can I return it? For how long is the guarantee? What is the service guarantee? Can this be financed on installment? Who finances it—the store or the bank? What is the carrying charge? What is the maximum length of time one has in which to complete the payments? If I pay for it before the financing period is up, do I get a reduction on the financing charges? These are some of the questions the salesman should be prepared to answer concerning terms of sale.

Company History and Company Policies. The salesman should know his company—its history, its reputation in the community and in the industry, and its policies. Reputable firms are proud of their history of growth, their integrity, their "image." When a salesman is aware of the company's beginnings and growth, his pride is apt to be reflected in his dealings with customers.

Of course, there is no substitute for knowledge of company policies—this knowledge is an absolute "must." What is the policy concerning the return of unsatisfactory merchandise? What is the policy on refunds? What are the credit policies? What about guarantees—does the company stand behind its products? Will the company make adjustments willingly? Will the store or firm make alterations? Will it make installations? These are some of the questions concerning company policy that the salesman must be able to answer.

How the Product Compares with the Competitors' Products. It is not unusual to hear a prospect say, "I can buy this same article from another store (or company) for $10 less" or "I prefer the competitor's product—it is much superior to yours." If the salesman knows competing brands—their quality, selling features, construction, and weaknesses—he can make a more convincing presentation of his own product, pointing out the advantages his product has in these respects. While he does not refer to the specific weaknesses in the competitors' products by brand name, he emphasizes the strong points he knows his product has where others are weak.

Information about competitors' products can be obtained by the following means:

1. Purchasing the competitors' products and testing them. This is a method commonly used by retail stores.
2. Studying competitors' advertisements in newspapers, magazines, and trade journals. By paying careful attention to what competitors feature as strong selling points in their advertisements, the salesman can be prepared to show how his product is superior in these respects.
3. Obtaining sales literature, such as advertising brochures and sales manuals, of competing firms.
4. Soliciting experiences from customers who have bought competing products.

How Product Knowledge Is Used

The questions asked of salesmen by customers vary greatly, of course, according to the type of product. Following are examples of questions that might be asked about three different types of products:

Sterling Silverware

What is the difference between sterling silver and silver plate?
Does sterling silver wear better?
Is there any difference between silver and silver plate in the problem of tarnishing?
What is a good pattern for one who has very modern china?
What does Louis XIV mean?

To answer questions like these, the major silverware companies of America, through the Sterling Silversmiths Guild of America, advocate that sterling silverware salesmen have a good knowledge of composition and manufacturing of sterling silverware, table settings, design (including history of design), the various pieces that make up a table setting, and special pieces used for serving.

Motor Oil

What is meant by different "weights" of oil? Why is a different weight used for summer and winter driving?
Should a heavier-weight oil be used in older cars? Why?
What does the oil pressure gauge indicate?
How can you tell when oil needs to be changed?
What causes oil to thin out?
What is meant by Pennsylvania oil?
What is meant by viscosity?
Does the color of the oil indicate its quality?
What is meant by germ process?

To answer such questions as these, salesmen must know how the product is made, of what the product is made, points of superiority in terms of competing products, the benefits the oil brings to users, and so on.[1]

Life Insurance

Life insurance salesmen must be able to answer questions that arise about the following:

---

[1] *The Salesman and His Job*, instructional material for training salesmen at the Continental Oil Company.

Different types of policies and their specific purposes

Provisions of a standard life insurance contract, settlement options, riders, and
    endorsements

Investment features of life insurance

Computation of premiums

Life insurance trusts

Turning Product Facts into Selling Points

It is one thing to know the important facts about the product you are selling
and quite another thing to convert those facts into customer benefits. To
be meaningful to a customer, facts must be translated into specific benefits to
him. A customer buys benefits and satisfactions, not facts; and these benefits
must be based on the buying motives of the customer. Every fact or feature may
have one or more advantages or benefits that can be turned into reasons for buying the merchandise. Elmer Wheeler, in his book *Tested Sentences That Sell,*
calls these "sizzles"—the points that show the customer the benefits of the
merchandise. For example, if a luggage salesman says that his product has a
"velox surface," he is merely reciting a fact that is meaningless to a customer.
He should follow up this statement by explaining that the velox surface will not
show scratches, will not stain, and will always look like new. To prove his point,
he may pour some ink on the surface and wipe it off. He may run a coin across
the surface to show that velox does not mar. This is selling with "sizzles."

Courtesy Ford Motor Company

The salesman must be able
to turn product facts into selling points. Here he is pointing
out special features about the
motor that will appeal to the
customer.

You can see that there is more than one selling point in that one fact about a velox surface. When the salesman translates the meaning of this term into customer benefits—will not scratch, will not stain, keeps looking like new—he is stressing the points that are important to the customer in making a satisfactory purchase.

Could You Sell a Screwdriver? You are probably thinking, "A screwdriver is such an ordinary item. There isn't much one can say about it. All screwdrivers are pretty much alike." But are they?

To help you to turn product facts into selling benefits, study below the product analysis sheet used by a well-known mail-order firm. It illustrates features of a common hardware item—a screwdriver—and the product benefits that are derived from those features.

Read feature 1 on the product analysis sheet. Now read the two benefits derived from that feature—that is, what it means to the customer. Continue to read each feature thoughtfully; then read the benefit that complements it. Note how each feature has been turned into a benefit for the customer. Compare these selling points with such a statement as this is a "good buy" or a "mighty fine tool." Which gives real product knowledge to the customer?

PRODUCT ANALYSIS SHEET
Product: Screwdriver

Product Features	Product Benefits
1. Hammer-forged.	The bit will not slip easily from the screw slot. The bit is the right size to fit most screws.
2. Made of selected tool steel.	The blade is remarkably tough. Will withstand all kinds of rough usage.
3. Blade is hardened and tempered its entire length.	This means that the bit will not twist or chip on heavy work.
4. Blade runs through length of handle.	The handle is everlastingly locked. The blade is locked securely in the handle so that it is practically impossible to turn or loosen in the handle even under severe strain.
5. Handle is shockproof.	Will withstand up to 10,000 volts of electricity. It is safe.
6. Has plastic "snug-fit" handle.	Handle is long-wearing. It is also comfortable—feels right in your hand.

The Wrong Way and the Right Way. To illustrate the effectiveness of product features when they are turned into product benefits, compare the following sales presentations of two vacuum-cleaner salesmen. In the first example the salesman illustrates the wrong way of selling by presenting facts that are not translated into selling benefits. He fails to arouse customer interest. In the second example the salesman illustrates the correct way of turning facts into selling benefits.

A salesman is showing a new type of vacuum cleaner in an appliance department. He sets up the machine for the demonstration.

SALESMAN: **This little machine is certainly a "jim-dandy," madam.**

CUSTOMER: What do you mean?

(The salesman turns the machine upside down and shows the customer a part of the mechanism.)

SALESMAN: **Well, in the first place, it has an agitator, which ensures balanced agitation.**

CUSTOMER: Oh!

SALESMAN: **In the second place, it has ball-bearing wheels.**

CUSTOMER: Oh!

SALESMAN: **Notice, too, that it has an adjustable rug-thickness control lever.**

CUSTOMER: My, you don't say so! Is that a good idea?

SALESMAN: **Also, notice the positive slide-type bag clamp and furniture bumpers. These are the earmarks of a good cleaner.**

CUSTOMER: It certainly does have a lot of gadgets on it, doesn't it? However, my old cleaner is still quite usable. Thank you for your time. I'll let you know when I'm in the market for a vacuum cleaner.

This case shows what may happen when you don't tie your facts in with the customer's needs. This salesman forgot that customers are primarily interested in what the product will do for them. Facts or technical information should be kept in the background to be used only as supporting evidence.

Now let's see how facts should be presented.

The salesman points to the furniture guard on the vacuum cleaner as he sets up the machine for a demonstration.

SALESMAN: **No danger of damaging that lovely furniture with this reinforced bumper strip, Mrs. Adams.**

(After he has the machine set up, he points to the cord.)

SALESMAN: **Notice the 25 feet of high grade cord on this machine. No skimping here. You can clean all around two rooms without having to change to another outlet.**

CUSTOMER: Will that cord last?

SALESMAN: This cord is made according to fire insurance specifications and stands more right-angle bending than any other cord tested. That means lots of long wear.

(*He spreads some sand on the rug.*)

SALESMAN: This is the worst type of dirt you can get in your house. It's hardest on your rug, and it's mighty hard to get out.

CUSTOMER: How do you figure that?

SALESMAN: Well, these little grains of sand are as sharp as a razor, and they get down into the nap like this. (*Separates nap to demonstrate.*) When people step on these fine razor-sharp particles, the threads of your rug are pressed across these tiny knives, and off goes a thread. That's the reason why a rug wears first near the door. Now as I start this machine, notice how all the sand particles jump around. That shows how powerfully this cleaner is beating the rug.

(*He runs the machine over the edge of the carpet strip and raises the nozzle high enough for the customer to pass her hand under the rug.*)

SALESMAN: Feel the beating action? That's the action that draws up the particles of sand that are deep down in the nap. Also, notice how the nozzle sucks up the rug from the floor and spreads the nap apart. That action loosens the sand and sucks it right out of the rug. All this means perfectly cleaned carpets and rugs for you, Mrs. Adams, no matter what kind of dirt is tracked into the house. By the way, you have small children, haven't you?

CUSTOMER: Yes, a baby boy nineteen months old and a girl of three.

SALESMAN: Well, with a cleaner like this you're ensuring the health of those children. I'm not telling you anything new when I say that dust carries disease germs. Getting rid of such dirt is helping to maintain the health of your children.

(*Mrs. Adams is becoming very interested. The salesman now spreads some kapok on the rug.*)

SALESMAN: Now comes the kapok. This could just as well be dog hair, paper, or lint. Kapok is the worst of all. It sticks to a rug worse than anything else. See how quick and how clean this cleaner picks it up.

CUSTOMER: It certainly does a good job.

SALESMAN: Here, you try it.

(*Mrs. Adams runs the cleaner over the rug.*)

SALESMAN: Notice how easy it goes. A three-year-old child could push it. That's because all four wheels of this cleaner turn on smooth-running ball bearings. No hard, backbreaking work with this machine, is there, Mrs. Adams?

CUSTOMER: It certainly is easy. Could you come this evening so that my husband can see it work?

Notice how the second salesman used his facts in the demonstration. He brought them to life before the customer's eyes. He followed each fact with a statement of what it would mean to the customer. In some cases he stressed the advantage first; then he supported it with facts. This salesman had made a complete study of his product and had his facts and their benefits well organized in his mind.

Product Information Must Be Converted into Selling Features. Product information must be converted into advantages, and they must be presented in a forceful, dramatic way. Every product has a number of sales features, and they should be used to point up the advantages of the product. The Hoover Company in its sales-training program offers an "advantage-proof-action" selling process which works as follows:

1. State and explain advantages.
2. Prove that the advantages exist for the prospect.
3. Ask for buying action.

For example:

> *Advantage:* "Mrs. Prospect, when you empty the Hoover, your fingers never touch the dirt."
>
> *Proof:* "Notice how easily and quickly the Hoover is emptied by using the exclusive Hoover Dirt Ejector."
>
> *Action:* "You certainly want this feature in the cleaner you buy, don't you?"

It isn't recommended that you wind up every statement of advantage with a form of proof and request for action. Sometimes proof is so obvious that it is accepted without any influence on your part, and the prospect may say, either by word or action, "Fine! That's something I want."

This gives you the action you want without asking for it. The important thing is for you to make sure the prospect understands and appreciates what the Hoover will do for her. Then you are getting toward your final goal—the sale.[1]

Sears, Roebuck emphasizes the importance of turning product features into advantages in the following excerpt taken from one of its hardware salesmanship-training manuals.

> Let's consider the words "use value." Here are two salesmen. Each one is selling a Craftsman hammer.
>
> The first salesman urges you to buy a Craftsman on the grounds that it "has a balanced head of chrome vanadium steel, with hardened poll and claws, a turned handle of selected second-growth white hickory with two patented interlocking corrugated wedges."

[1] *The Hoover Sale,* Sales Educational Department, The Hoover Company, North Canton, Ohio, p. 85.

Giving a demonstration of the product is one of the ways the salesman can put product facts to use.

Courtesy John Hancock Mutual Life Insurance Company

The second salesman explains that a Craftsman hammer "is practically unbreakable, will pull out tiny brads or large spikes, has a tough, hard-to-break hickory handle that is comfortable to grip and a head that will not fly off."

Salesman Number Two made use of the *use value* method—Salesman Number One did not.

If you wanted to define use value, you might say that it is "the worth of an article expressed in terms of what it will do for the customer."

Put in another way, use value is the answer to the question, "What of it?" when mechanical or constructional features are mentioned.

Start with what the feature will do for your customer. Then use your technical information to explain why.[1]

There is a right way and a wrong way to use product facts. Follow these five principles in putting facts to use:

1. Facts *must* be put into language the customer can understand.
2. Each selling point should be emphasized in a positive and forceful manner.
3. Selling points should be backed up by a demonstration of the product.
4. Facts should not be stated merely to show off the superior knowledge of the salesman concerning the product. Facts should be used to persuade.
5. Facts must be related to the customer's benefit. Whenever you present a feature, the question in your customer's mind is, "What will it do for me?"

Sources of Product Knowledge. If you were a salesman in a hardware store and the manufacturers had supplied sales facts about the various products carried by the dealer, would you know what they mean? Would a customer know if you

[1] *Hardware and How to Sell It*, Retail Salesmanship Training, Division 9, Salesmanship Manual, Sears, Roebuck and Company, pp. 11–13.

merely repeated those facts? It would be your job to find out what the facts mean so that you could turn them into selling features.

Where would you get the facts about a product that you are selling?

Sales literature of the company might provide the explanation as well as the facts. If not, you could ask the owner of the shop, older salesmen in the shop, or the manufacturer's salesman when he calls. You could consult the dictionary and read all possible information about good tools. You would then be able to explain to a customer what benefits he gets from the product that you are selling.

Retail salespeople can get facts from labels and tags on the merchandise, from the buyer and other salespeople, from well-informed customers, and from the store library, department manuals, advertisements, and reports from the testing bureau. Sources outside the store are the public library, manufacturers' sales literature, competitors' advertisements, United States Government publications and pamphlets, training and educational programs in public and private schools of business, and personal use of the product.

Industrial and specialty salesmen have such sources as company training programs, conferences with company executives, sales manuals, catalogs, company advertising, competitors' advertising, trade and technical magazines, personal use of the product, service calls with firm engineers, and knowledge of the manufacturing process by actual work in the factory. Suppliers who make the raw materials or manufacturing parts of the product are another source of valuable information for the salesman.

SUMMING UP

To do an effective job of selling, you must know the essential facts about the product. The essential facts are those that answer the questions that customers commonly ask about merchandise. In addition, knowledge of your product will:

1. Give selling confidence
2. Help in handling difficult selling situations
3. Prevent a sales talk from becoming mechanical and sounding indifferent
4. Create enthusiasm and enjoyment in your work
5. Advance your chances for promotion

Just stating a fact is not enough. Facts must be converted into forceful selling points (sizzles) that will appeal to the customer. There are many sources of product knowledge that you can utilize in adding facts to your current store of product knowledge.

1. In what five ways does product knowledge pay big dividends to the salesman? Explain each.
2. Give examples of how product knowledge can help the salesman through difficult selling situations.
3. Why should a salesman know the industry of which his company is a part?
4. What ten things should a salesman know about the product he sells?
5. Explain how familiarity with manufacturing processes can help a salesman sell his product.
6. Name several products and list specific suggestions that might be given to customers on the care of each product.
7. "Knowing manufacturing processes helps a salesman to explain pricing policies." What does this statement mean to you?
8. Why is it desirable for a salesman to know something about the history of his company?
9. Why should a salesman be thoroughly familiar with the product of his chief competitors? In what ways can he get such information?
10. What five principles govern the use of facts about products?

For Discussion

1. Describe any sales experiences that you have had in which a knowledge of the merchandise played an important part.
2. "Facts alone are not enough." What does this mean?
3. If you were selling in a hardware store and a customer asked you why a certain wrench had a polished head, and you did not know, what would you say?
4. How can a complete knowledge of his product increase a salesman's income?
5. Can a salesman know too much about his product?
6. Give an example of how knowledge of the history of a product can help in making sales.
7. How can a customer give product information to a salesman?
8. What information would you want to know about women's shoes before you sold to the public? About men's shoes?
9. Should a salesman know all possible facts about all the products of his firm, or only a few of the more important selling features of each one?
10. Is it unwise for a young salesman to listen to people who find fault with his product? Explain.
11. Bring an item to class that you have purchased recently. Analyze its qualities and selling features.

Mabel Larson, a recent graduate, was hired by the Seventh Avenue Department Store and told to report to Mr. Sewell, the buyer in the budget dress department on the fourth floor, at 8:45 A.M. on the following Monday.

Mabel, who was anxious to make a good impression since this was her first job, was there at 8:30. Mr. Sewell told Mabel to start by putting the stock in order and to learn as much about the stock as possible as she arranged it. He told her that if the other salespeople in the department became busy, she was to wait on customers, asking questions of the salespeople nearby.

Mabel racked up the dresses, arranging them so that the manufacturer's label and the store's price tag were easily seen. She soon finished this task and looked for the buyer to get further instructions. Mr. Sewell could not be located.

At that time there were no customers in the department, so Mabel walked around the department just looking at the merchandise. A senior saleswoman asked her to put away some blouses that were piled on a counter. Mabel explained that she was new to the department and would be glad to do it, but she would have to be shown where to put them.

"Arrange them by sizes on this rack," replied the senior saleswoman. She then proceeded to show Mabel how it was done.

Later that morning a customer asked to see the new black rayon suits that were featured in the morning paper. Mabel could not find them immediately, so she interrupted a saleswoman who was showing a customer a blouse to ask about the advertised rayon suits.

"Don't bother me now, dear. Can't you see that I'm busy?" was the answer.

"I didn't think you'd mind," retorted Mabel. "Don't worry, I'll find them."

After further delay, the suits were located. The customer took one from the rack, held it up in front of her, and asked, "Is this acetate rayon?"

"Oh, yes, it is," replied Mabel. (Actually it was viscose rayon.)

"It looks as if it would be hard to wash," said the customer.

"I don't think so," replied Mabel.

The customer looked at the suit for a while; then she put it back on the rack and left the department.

After lunch Mabel became acquainted with several of the other saleswomen. Upon learning that they were graduates of the same school that she had attended, she spent a considerable part of the afternoon discussing old friends.

QUESTIONS

1. How well did Mabel follow the buyer's instructions?
2. What should Mabel have done when she completed her first task?

3. How did Mabel show that she lacked initiative?
4. How did Mabel display a lack of tact and consideration?
5. What should Mabel have done after interrupting the saleswoman and her customer?
6. Criticize Mabel's handling of her first customer.
7. Could Mabel have excused her inability to answer the customer's questions correctly on the basis of its being her first day on the job?
8. Where could Mabel have obtained more knowledge of the merchandise that she was to sell?

Salesmanship in Action

1. From a national magazine select an advertisement that gives a number of facts and selling features about the product. Make a product analysis sheet similar to the one studied in this chapter. List the facts and selling features (benefits) of the product that you selected. Attach the advertisement to the analysis sheet when you hand in the assignment.
2. Assume that you are selling luggage. Prepare a product analysis sheet from the following catalog information about the luggage:
   a. Easy-care vinyl covers featuring special embossed textured finish
   b. Three-ply wood box with molded one-piece frame
   c. Triple-stitched vinyl bindings electronically welded
   d. Tongue-and-groove closings
   e. Hinges with built-in studs
   f. Single snap-open lock with key
   g. Gleaming brass-plated hardware and molded plastic handles with color-matched name tags
   h. Exclusive push-pull action
   i. Celanese acetate lining, three side pockets
   j. Full lid mirror
   k. Cosmetic tray
   l. Price $9.97
3. Prepare a product analysis sheet from the following facts about a dishwasher:
   a. Automatic retractable cord
   b. Sparkling-stripe Texolite top
   c. Quick-loading racks
   d. Exclusive cup racks
   e. Waist-high indicator dial
   f. Exclusive three-cycle push buttons
   g. Water and drain connections
   h. Chrome-cover push plate
   i. Exclusive power shower
   j. Full-length guide arm
   k. Automatic reset detergent dispenser
   l. Handles-up silverware basket
   m. Designed for sanitation
   n. 600-watt calrod heater
   o. Vinyl-cushioned interior
   p. Flushaway drain impeller
   q. $\frac{1}{3}$-horsepower motor

4. A tie department carries three grades of ties in stock: a rayon line selling for $1.50 to $2.50, a wool line selling for $2.50 to $3.50, and a silk line selling for $2.50 to $3.50. What line would you recommend for a customer who is fashion-conscious and quality-conscious, and yet wants a year-round tie? Support your reason.

5. Of the topics that cover the knowledge that every salesman should have about his product (see pages 147 and 148), which do you consider the most important in selling each of the following items?

   a. Fine cotton organdy dress   *d.* Mattress

   b. Electric refrigerator   *e.* Blanket

   c. Motion-picture projector

6. Divide a sheet of paper into two columns. Head the left column "The Retail Salesman" and the right column "The Specialty Salesman." List the kinds of product knowledge that you believe each would need to know to do a good selling job.

7. Divide a second sheet of paper into two columns, using the same headings as in question 6. List all possible sources of product information for each type of salesman.

8. Divide a third sheet of paper into two columns. Head the left column "The Vacuum-Cleaner Salesman" and the right column "The Life Insurance Salesman." Under each heading list the kinds of facts or information needed by that class of salesman.

9. List five products that require a great deal of product knowledge on the part of the salesman. List five products that require little or no knowledge.

Finding Prospects

"HOW DO I locate people who want or need what I have to sell?" The success of many salesmen depends on their finding an effective answer to this question. Of course, the retail-store salesperson usually has no responsibility for going out and hunting for customers, or prospecting. They come to him. They have been attracted to the store by means of newspaper advertisements, letters, circulars, and window displays.

The salesman who calls on customers in their place of business or in the home, however, must find his own prospects. Insurance salesmen; door-to-door salesmen of appliances, encyclopedias, cosmetics, and various home furnishings; the salesmen of products like office machines, stationery and supplies, machinery and tools, and raw materials—all must have many leads to prospective customers if they are to be successful.

Every business has developed its own methods of finding prospects. If a person is selling advertising space in a magazine, his methods of finding prospective space buyers will be somewhat different from those used by a person selling playground equipment to schools and other institutions. An appliance store uses different techniques in locating prospective buyers from those of a paper manu-

Ways of finding prospects
are numerous. This salesman
is scanning the building directory for leads.

Courtesy F. S. Webster Company

facturer. In any event, the ways in which prospects may be found are almost
unlimited. For example, a manufacturer of washing machines suggests to its
dealers that prospects may be found in some of the following ways:[1]

1. Prospects who come into the store
2. Personal visits by the salesman to homes of former customers and new
   prospects
3. Letters to former customers and new prospects
4. Telephone calls to former customers and new prospects
5. House-to-house canvassing
6. Newspaper advertising
7. Exhibits at home shows, fairs, carnivals, and other public gatherings
8. Installations in model homes
9. Installations in cooking schools
10. Contests

[1] Adapted from "How to Get Prospects," *Maytag News*.

11. In-use demonstrations at church, social, and civic affairs
12. Bonuses offered to owners who suggest a prospect that results in a sale
13. Demonstrations at home economics classes in schools
14. Advertisements of used washers in the classified-advertisement section of the newspaper
15. Store and window displays and demonstrations
16. Inquiries of prospects for names of other prospects
17. Marriage announcements in the newspaper
18. Birth announcements in the newspaper
19. "Domestic Help Wanted" ads in the newspaper
20. Listings of new homes under construction
21. Solicitation of names from salesmen of other products
22. Solicitation of names from repairmen, linemen, deliverymen, meter readers, and so on
23. Invitations to selected individuals to come to the store for special open house or similar event

You will see that several of these methods of finding customers are applicable to other products; some apply only to an appliance dealer. In any event, the list is by no means exhaustive.

Building Your Own List of Prospects

You must have gathered from your study of the list above that customers don't "just happen." They must be found. The salesman who thinks his product is so good that people will seek him out to buy from him is sadly mistaken. He must search constantly for the people who have a need for his product or service and who are able to buy it. And he cannot afford to ignore a single lead, because he cannot possibly know in advance who will and will not buy. The good salesman always has more prospects on his list than he can contact; he is constantly jotting down new names and organizations—one name leads to another.

Successful salesmen try to have a definite number of prospects on their list at all times in order to maintain their sales volume. For example, a salesman's goal might be a sales volume of $200,000 a year. He knows from experience that in order to reach that goal he must add fifty new names each month to his prospect list. You can see that he can't let grass grow under his feet—he must be constantly at work to keep the list growing. If the list drops below fifty during a given month, the salesman knows that he must double his efforts to build it up.

Some of the more common sources used by new salesmen in building a prospect list are the following:

1. Family and friends
2. Community organizations
3. Present customers
4. Tradesmen and merchants
5. Telephone and city directories
6. Trade and professional directories and lists
7. Service clubs and social organizations
8. Building permits
9. Miscellaneous lists
10. Newspapers
11. Advertising
12. Store, exhibit, and office contacts
13. Commercial lists

Family and Friends. Both family and friends are important contacts, especially for the new salesman. Because these people are anxious to see the salesman succeed, they will gladly give him information about their friends that may lead to sales. It is much easier to establish friendly relations with people who know someone you know than to go in "cold." The first step, then, for the new salesman is to make a list of prospects from suggestions offered by those closest to him.

Community Organizations. The effective salesman is usually an outgoing person. He makes friends easily and he is constantly widening his circle of friends. One of the most effective ways for the salesman to widen his circle of friends is by working in local groups such as the Junior Chamber of Commerce, trade associations, and service clubs. Another way of meeting people and at the same time of making a valuable contribution to the community is the participation in such causes as Community Chest and Red Cross drives, civic-improvement group activities, Parent-Teachers Association meetings, and various youth activities. Not only does the active person have the satisfaction of contributing his talents where they are needed and appreciated, but he also automatically gains a better knowledge of his community and thereby of his market.

Present Customers. The salesman's satisfied customers are often excellent sources for obtaining new prospects. People like to talk to their friends about their purchases and to show them off. In their conversation they are likely to mention their satisfaction with their purchase and the name of the person or company from whom they purchased. Thus satisfied customers become missionaries for the salesman. (This is one of the most important reasons why the salesman should be honest and reliable, because just the opposite is true: If customers are unhappy, this fact will be made known to their friends, too!) For

The satisfied customer is an excellent source for obtaining new prospects. In this case the customer, encountering the salesman on the street, introduces him to one of her friends.

example, a salesman of air conditioners may make several sales within one block as a result of selling a unit to a popular resident in that block. Some firms estimate that they receive 75 percent of their leads from present customers.

Tradesmen and Merchants. The merchants from whom the salesman buys his own food, clothing, and household necessities, and the tradesmen who service his home usually are willing to furnish information about prospects because of a friendly community interest as well as their desire to hold the salesman's goodwill and his business. These merchants and tradesmen meet and talk with dozens of people every day and their leads can be extremely helpful to the salesman.

Telephone and City Directories. Two directories, available to the salesman in most communities, should not be overlooked as sources of names: the classified telephone directory and the city directory. As you know, the classified telephone directory (Yellow Pages) lists businesses and professional people and organizations, classifying them as to type of product or service offered. For example, an insurance salesman looks under "Trucking Firms" in the classified pages for a list of those who are likely to be interested in liability insurance. The

Painters

ABLE PAINTING CO

SPECIALISTS IN
**FINER RESIDENTIAL
DECORATING**
SERVING METROPOLITAN AREA
Finest Workmanship & Materials
Neat Reliable Service
Reasonable Prices
FULLY INSURED
350-7291

111 Central Ave 350-7291

Adams Malcolm 41 Union.................... 280-9113
Blot August 111 Broad 280-1294
Bryant Peter 8319 Peters Place........... 280-4172
Case Chester 130-44 18 Dr.............. 470-8291
Choice Decorating Co 18 E Grace 280-9112

CITYWIDE PAINTING & DECORATING CO

PAINTING & DECORATING
• INTERIOR
• EXTERIOR

BRUSH — SPRAY
SHAFTEX REMOVED FROM WALLS
Member of P.D.C.A.
99 Willard Way 470-1230
If No Answer 280-1491

Courtesy New York Telephone Company

■ The columns of the classified telephone directory list businesses and professional people according to type of product or service offered.

paper salesman finds lists of printers, publishers, and stationers. The salesman of medical supplies finds lists of doctors, dentists, hospitals, and clinics. And so on.

The city directory contains the names, addresses, and occupations of residents of the community. In addition to an alphabetic listing, the city directory provides another listing by streets. Some city directories contain classified lists of businesses, professions, and certain occupations.

Trade and Professional Directories and Lists. There are several national directories that are helpful to the salesman of particular products and services. Typical of such directories are *Thomas' Register of American Manufacturers, American Medical Directory, Poor's Register of Directors and Executives of the United States and Canada,* and *Lawyer's Directory.*

In addition, there are often local directories (or membership lists) of various groups, such as cost accountants, office managers, insurance underwriters, attorneys, sales executives, teachers, purchasing agents, advertising directors, contractors, and so on. Often the salesman is a member of one or more of these groups; for example, an experienced salesman of office equipment may qualify for membership in the local cost accountants association or office executives association.

Service Clubs and Social Organizations. Members of service clubs, such as Rotary, Lions, Kiwanis, and Optimists, are often valuable contacts for the salesman. The same is true for social groups, such as women's clubs, alumni associations, automobile clubs, fraternal orders (Masons, Elks, Knights of Columbus, and so on), country clubs, and various sports and hobby clubs.

Membership lists of such organizations are not always easy to obtain. However, an alert salesman can sometimes obtain a membership list by performing some special service for the group, such as giving a demonstration, providing door prizes and bridge prizes, lending equipment, and so on.

Building Permits. Building permits (permission from the local government to construct a home or building) are published in local newspapers. These are valuable prospects for the salesman of lumber, building materials, appliances, shrubs, and other home needs.

Miscellaneous Lists. Records in city, county, and state government offices are often used by the salesman as a source of prospect. In the county assessor's office, for example, the salesman can find the name, address, and assessed valuation of each property owner in the county. City tax lists, registrations of voters, names of people who own car licenses, and so on, are examples of lists to which the salesman usually has access.

Newspapers. The local newspaper can be a "gold mine" of leads for many salesmen. News stories about newcomers to the community, new businesses or expansion of existing businesses, appointments of individuals to new jobs, election of officers in civic and social organizations, birth announcements, actions taken by city government—all are typical of events that may lead to new prospects. An individual's promotion to a higher position, for example, may indicate his readiness for more insurance, another car, a new home, and so on. The want ads provide clues, too, especially to those who sell automobiles, building materials, and household appliances.

A note of warning: Never use newspaper stories of personal misfortunes to build a prospect list. Accidents, serious illnesses, deaths, separations, divorces, and various other personal tragedies are never used by the ethical salesman as a means of selling his product or service. The good salesman respects the individual's rights to privacy during times of distress.

Advertising. Leads are often provided the salesman by the firm that employs him or by the manufacturer of the product. One of the most effective ways in which these leads are obtained is through advertisements in newspapers and magazines and on radio and television. Newspaper and magazine advertisements frequently contain coupons which invite the reader to send for a free booklet or sample, and from those who respond a prospect list can be developed. If you thumb through a local newspaper and such magazines as *Better Homes and Gardens,* the *Saturday Evening Post,* and *Life,* you will find many examples of this type of advertising. Insurance companies, publishers of encyclopedias, and manufacturers of various products for the home find coupon advertising especially effective for building prospect lists. The people who respond to advertising of any type are considered to be good prospects, and their names are passed along by the advertiser to individual dealers and salesmen in the appropriate geographical areas.

Store, Exhibit, and Office Contacts. When visitors come to the store to see a special demonstration or an advance showing, they are often asked to fill out a card which asks for their name and address. These cards are then turned over to the salesman for later follow-up. Automobile dealers and TV appliance stores often use this technique. Similar opportunities for obtaining prospect lists are found at exhibits, fairs, and conventions. For example, manufacturers of office supplies and equipment receive some of their most effective leads at business shows that are held in various major cities each year. Encyclopedia salesmen obtain valuable leads at county and state fairs.

When the company has no store or showroom in the community, prospects often come to the office of a dealer for information about his products. Those who take the trouble to do this are considered very good prospects for the salesman.

Commercial Lists. Lists of prospects may be purchased from local commercial mailing-list organizations in most large communities. In addition, such organizations as R. L. Polk and Company and the Reuben H. Donnelly Corporation sell mailing lists on a nationwide basis. These lists may be purchased by geographic area and according to the type of product or service in which those listed are considered prospects. Commercial lists such as these provide not only the names and addresses of individuals but also information about their buying power and probable buying readiness.

Prospecting Methods Vary

Prospecting for customers is more important for some types of selling than for others. While it was mentioned earlier that retail salespeople do not generally prospect for customers, it should be pointed out, however, that prospecting is

Courtesy Andersen Corporation

■ Those who respond to advertisements in magazines and newspapers are often good prospects.

done by the store to bring customers in. In a sense, advertising is a form of prospecting, since the advertising message is usually prepared with the wants of a definite group of people in mind and is placed in media that will reach this group. Window displays, impressive storefronts, personal letters, sales letters, circulars, and telephone calls are other methods of prospecting used by the retail store.

In some cases retail stores—appliance, radio-TV, and furniture stores, for example—employ outside salesmen who call on prospects in the home or office. These salesmen use the prospecting methods common to all outside specialty salesmen.

Route salesmen of dairy and bakery products and cleaning-pressing service are encouraged to be on the lookout constantly for new prospects. They are especially alert to "For Sale" signs on homes, new homes under construction, and changes in family status. Route salesmen have learned through experience that the one who gets there first usually has a much better chance of getting the business. Sales meetings in a typical dairy company are devoted in large measure to ways of prospecting.

Automobile agencies encourage salesmen to develop prospects on their own initiative. These salesmen are told that "for every sale you make to a prospect who comes into the showroom, you should make ten sales to prospects you originate yourself." Such prospect lists are built by watching the want ads, by obtaining information from prospects who come into the showroom, by asking satisfied customers to supply names of friends and relatives who need a new automobile, and by actively participating in various community events.

Prospecting methods of salesmen for manufacturers and wholesalers are likely to be quite different from those used by specialty salesmen. Because the manufacturer's and wholesaler's salesmen are limited in the type of customer they serve, they may do only a minimum of prospecting, if indeed any. For example, a wholesale hardware salesman will call only on retail hardware stores and manufacturing firms that buy hardware in large quantities. The number of such businesses in his territory is, of course, limited; even when new ones are opened, advance information is given him by the firm that employs him. The wholesale salesman of drugs may call only on retail drugstores, and his situation is similar to that of the wholesale hardware salesman. The trend in sales organization is toward specialization. A large drug manufacturer may have one group of salesmen who call only on wholesale druggists, another group who call only on hospitals, and still another who call on doctors. Many salesmen for wholesalers and manufacturers are really service specialists. Their chief job is keeping their customers informed of new products, assisting their customers with display and sales promotion, and handling service problems such as shipping and billing. These salesmen are usually not responsible for developing prospects; that job is left to the advertising department of the firm.

Common Methods of Prospecting

When the salesman reaches the point where he has no prospects to see, he is of little value to his employer, and his earnings may be reduced to zero. Because new prospects are so vital, the salesman usually gets considerable assistance from his supervisors in keeping a fresh list of prospects always on hand. The following methods of prospecting have been developed by large firms and sales experts:

1. The endless-chain method
2. The center-of-influence method
3. Home demonstrations
4. Personal observation
5. Sales-associate plan
6. Cold canvassing

Endless-Chain Method. The basis of the endless-chain method of prospecting is to obtain names of other prospects from everyone on whom the salesman calls. For example, you sell Mr. Williams a tape recorder. Upon closing the sale, you ask him if he knows someone who might also be interested in this recorder. He mentions that a fellow member of Rotary, Charles Watson, has discussed such a purchase with him. You see Mr. Watson, and he buys. At that point you ask Mr. Watson for the name of persons he knows who might be interested, and he refers you to Frank Kingsley. You see Mr. Kingsley, and the chain continues.

The endless-chain method often results in an amazing number of prospects. For example, suppose you try to get the names of two prospects or "suspects" from every person you interview. ("Suspects" are those that are only *suspected* of being in need of your product.) If you are successful, the first visit would yield two new names; these two prospects should yield four additional names; these four should yield an additional eight; and these eight should provide you with sixteen new names—or a total of thirty new prospects.

When a customer gives you the name of another person who is either a "suspect" or a prospect, it is called a *referred lead.* Many salesmen consider referred leads to be the best type of prospect. Of course, you won't sell your product to all referred leads, but when you have their names you should make every effort to do so.

In obtaining referred leads, it is best to have permission from the customer to use his name in seeing those prospects. For example, the customer may say, "Go and see Charlie Watson, but don't tell him I sent you." This is not an effective lead; you will really be calling on Mr. Watson "cold." It is much better to have the customer say, "Go and see Charlie Watson, and tell him I sent you." The use of a name immediately establishes a friendly connection between you and the new prospect. If the customer does not volunteer the use of his name, you might ask, "Do you mind if I use your name in talking to Mr. Watson?" In calling Mr. Watson for an appointment, you could say, "Mr. Watson, last week Frank Williams bought an Empire tape recorder from me, and he told me he thought you would be interested in one, too. When could I see you to give you a demonstration?"

In obtaining referred leads, the Connecticut General Life Insurance Company strongly recommends that the salesman seek a personal introduction from the individual who gave him the lead. This company lists six types of personal introduction and they are discussed here.

In-Person Introduction. The in-person introduction is the best referred lead you can have. Here the customer takes you to the referred lead and introduces you personally. Ask the customer beforehand not to try to explain your work to the referred lead, to praise you as a clever salesman, or to remain after the

One of the best types of prospect is the referred lead. Having the customer telephone the referred lead to tell him about the salesman makes an effective introduction.

introduction has been made. Make your sales approach after the customer leaves you and the prospect alone.

Letter of Commendation. Another type of personal introduction is a letter of commendation from a customer in your behalf. If the customer is willing to send such a letter, the salesman may show him samples of letters that others have written and ask him to select the one he likes. Then the salesman volunteers to type it up on the customer's stationery if the customer prefers not to bother with this chore.

Letter of Introduction. Sometimes a customer is willing to write a letter of introduction for you to his friends. Such a letter is addressed to the referred lead and merely introduces you as representing a certain company. It implies, of course, that you have the customer's recommendation. The letter may be mailed or given to the salesman to deliver.

Telephone Introduction. A telephone introduction is also effective. In this case the customer merely picks up the telephone and tells a friend that he is sending the salesman to see him.

Card of Introduction. Some salesmen carry a card of introduction with them. When this is filled out by the customer (name of the referred lead and signature of the customer), it becomes an effective introduction to a new prospect.

Telephone Commendation. In obtaining referred leads from a customer, it is well to ask him if it is all right for others to telephone him for reactions to yourself and your product. Whether the new prospect telephones the customer or not, it is valuable sales ammunition to be able to say, "Mr. Jackson said that he would be glad to give you the results of his experience with our company if you would telephone him."

Center-of-Influence Method. In the center-of-influence method of prospecting, the salesman concentrates on cultivating the friendship of influential persons in his territory. These persons are called centers of influence; and they help the salesman to obtain prospects by referring him to others, making appointments for him, providing him with information on what is going on in the territory that is of consequence to him, and urging acquaintances to buy from him.

The salesman must choose his centers of influence carefully, for not all well-known people—regardless of their position—can provide the help he needs. Centers of influence are selected with two main factors in mind:

1. The age group with which they have the greatest influence
2. The income group that the salesman wants to reach

A person may be influential with a number of people in the community and still have no influence with the particular group the salesman wants to reach. A local golf pro may be a center of influence for a salesman in a sporting-goods store, but he would ordinarily be of little help to a salesman of building materials.

Some of the persons who make good centers of influence for most salesmen are prominent club men and women, ministers, leading business executives, bankers, attorneys, doctors, and officers in civic and professional organizations. The best way to cultivate centers of influence is to be one yourself—mixing in with these people in various civic efforts, as mentioned previously. A purely "commercial" approach to establishing centers of influence will not work. You must be able to demonstrate that you are worthy of assistance, and this means giving your best to the community in which you live and work.

Home Demonstrations. Some companies market their products directly to the consumer by getting a group of people together for a salesman's demonstration. One of the best-known companies that market in this way is Stanley Home Products, Inc. This organization relies mainly on dealer-salesmen who sell in the evening or at any other time when they can get a group of prospective customers together. The plan works this way: A Stanley salesman asks a prospect if he may use her home as a gathering place for women in the neighborhood so that he may demonstrate his product. For this service the hostess receives a gift, the value of which is based on the amount of sales that the salesman makes during the evening. Often a party is held at which games are played and guests compete for prizes. From such meetings the salesman frequently obtains firm orders as well as prospects for later sales.

A similar plan is used by cooking-utensil distributors. A prospect is asked to

■ The salesman can often obtain leads by participating in the activities of his community.

invite several friends and neighbors to her home for dinner—the dinner to be supplied by the salesman. The salesman or a special assistant arrives early and prepares the entire dinner, using the company's utensils, of course. A number of prospects are obtained for later follow-up.

Personal Observation. The alert salesman can accumulate many leads simply by observing newcomers in the area or by spotting worn-out or outmoded products (an excellent method for a tire and equipment salesman). He can also obtain leads through conversations at club meetings, social gatherings, and professional meetings. In fact, many of the methods of prospecting already discussed depend in large measure on the salesman's power of observation.

Sales-Associate Plan. Under the sales-associate plan, people in various occupations are engaged as "spotters" to obtain prospects on whom the salesman can call. Generally these people are given a commission on the sales made to these prospects, although sometimes they may be paid a flat fee.

Sales associates are paid for supplying information about prospects only when sales result. If the information about a lead is already in the salesman's hands or if the prospect already has been canvassed by the salesman, the associate is not paid. Sales associates are not permitted to do any selling. They merely pave the way for the salesman to call. For example, the associate may call on homemakers in a given neighborhood and inquire as to the types of appliances owned and the condition of the appliances. In the process of gathering this information, the associate endeavors to make an appointment for a regular salesman to call to show the newest equipment.

Some salesmen pay other workers in their territory to obtain qualified leads—for example, meter readers, postmen, movers, repairmen, and deliverymen—who can furnish information about new developments and new prospects in the community. The term "bird dog" is used for this type of associate.

Cold Canvassing. An example of cold canvassing is the door-to-door salesman who goes from house to house trying to interest people in his product. He has no particular leads; he takes his chances that among all the people he sees he will find customers. Sometimes he merely introduces himself and gives general information about his product, hoping to return later to conduct a demonstration. For example, here is how a salesman of cooking ware canvasses for prospects from door to door:

SALESMAN: **Good morning, Mrs. Carroll. I'm Fred Elliott with Kitchen Specialties. We have just opened a new branch office in Fairview County, and we are anxious to acquaint everyone with our location. May I give you this booklet describing our new health method of cooking.**
PROSPECT: Thank you.
SALESMAN: **Do you have a complete set of stainless-steel cooking ware, Mrs. Carroll?**

This conversation leads into a discussion of the cooking equipment of the "suspect" and provides the salesman with a chance to make a future appointment to demonstrate his product.

Methods of canvassing for prospects vary according to the product. Canvassing for prospects for cooking utensils or bakery goods will be different from canvassing for prospects for roofing materials. Every family is a likely prospect for cooking utensils and bakery products whether they live in an apartment or a house. Only homeowners who obviously need new roofs are prospects for roofing materials.

In all canvassing it is necessary that the salesman screen his prospects to find out whether they need or desire his product and whether they have the money to pay for it. In the case of cooking ware, this screening would be done on the first call. Screening prospects for roofing materials would be done before the call. In canvassing for products that appeal to housewives, the salesman generally finds it best to call in the morning between 9 and 12, because more women are at home during those hours. If he calls in the afternoon, he may interrupt a social gathering. The salesman's afternoon and evening hours are then kept free for calls by appointment or for call-backs to complete previous demonstrations. Industrial and specialty salesmen, on the other hand, cannot easily predict when it is best to call on prospects. They must find a time when the prospect is not likely to be too busy, which may be in the morning or afternoon, according to the business.

Even cold canvassing should not be done haphazardly. Of course, some sales are bound to come just by pushing doorbells anywhere; the law of averages will take care of that. However, the salesman's time and effort are more productive if he has a systematic plan worked out before starting his canvassing.

Evaluating Your Prospects

Some salesmen assume that everyone is a prospect for their goods or services. They are wrong. One of the main differences between an effective salesman and a weak one is that the successful salesman makes sure he calls only on real prospects; the weak one wastes his time and that of his company by calling on just anyone.

The salesman should evaluate every prospect to determine whether or not he is worthy of concentrated attention. He should ask himself the following questions about every prospect or "suspect":

1. Does he have a need or desire for the product?
2. Does he have the ability to pay for the product?
3. Does he have the authority to buy?
4. Is he accessible—that is, is it possible to get an appointment or communicate with him?
5. Does he meet the special qualifications necessary to buy this particular product?

Need for the Product. The first qualification of a good prospect is that he need or want what you have to sell. His needs may be physical—the need for food, clothing, housing, transportation, or money. Or the prospect's needs may be emotional—the desire for comfort, recognition, beauty, love, pleasure, or adventure.

As you know, the prospect is not always aware of his needs. It is the salesman's job to help the prospect recognize them. One reason that people do not recognize needs is that they tend to think in terms of one specific need rather than a number of needs the product will satisfy. For example, a car owner may think like this: "The old buggy doesn't look too good and it's got lots of mileage on it, but it gets me to and from work. I'll keep it awhile longer." This person recognizes only one need that the car serves—getting him to and from work. Yet the alert salesman can quickly call to the car owner's attention other needs that had not occurred to him. What about the Mrs. when she takes the children to school—is the car safe? Would the present car give satisfactory service on a long vacation trip? Is there a boy or girl in the family who is about to reach driving age? What about the family shopping—wouldn't it be easier for the Mrs. if she had a better car? Are there additional uses—both business and pleasure—that would be made of a new car that are not now being made of the present car? These are some of the other needs that a prospect might not even have thought of; he was concerned only with the basic need for transportation.

The good salesman can find additional needs for a product by learning everything possible about the prospect before talking with him or during the interview. If he is selling vacuum cleaners and the homeowner already has a fairly new one, he can point out the value of having two cleaners—one for each floor of the house, or a hand cleaner for small jobs. If he is selling power mowers, he may point out the prospect's need for a larger, riding-type mower that will permit him to do the job much faster and in greater comfort, thereby saving time and energy for family recreation.

Ability to Pay. Many "suspects" who have need for a product are disqualified as prospects because they cannot afford it. However, as you know, some people who are financially able to pay often use the excuse "I can't afford it" when they really mean they are not convinced they want or need the product. Those who use this merely as an excuse are really excellent prospects, and they should not be confused with those who really cannot afford to buy. The young father who is struggling to meet the payments on the new car is obviously not in a position to buy an additional car, no matter how much he believes he needs it. The salesman must gather all the evidence he can that the prospect is really able to purchase his product. The salesman who unloads his merchandise on an already overburdened and gullible prospect is unethical. Some people simply do not know when they are overextending themselves in their buying.

If the product the salesman is selling is expensive—such as a car, a refrigerator, a stereo-television combination, or a set of encyclopedias—he should try to break down his prospects into groups according to their probable ability to pay. He will then work hardest to sell to those who are in the higher-income groups. Salesmen often carry several quality and price lines, and by breaking down their prospects into income groups, they can determine which line to present to a particular prospect. Incidentally, don't make the mistake of sizing up a prospect's ability to pay by your own—that is, determine the prospect's ability to pay on the basis of his own income level, not yours.

Authority to Buy. Make sure that the prospect who needs your product not only has the ability to buy but also has the authority to buy. For example, if you call on the chief pressman of a printing plant and sell him on the need for a new printing press, you must remember that he probably does not have the authority to make the final decision. Usually he will have to consult with the general manager and perhaps the purchasing agent for the firm, so you may have to make your presentation to these people, too. The housewife who wants to purchase an electric range from your store will usually have to consult with her husband before a decision is made. And the man who wants a new suit often feels compelled to have his wife's approval before he acts.

The salesman must learn as early as possible whether the prospect has the authority to buy; if the prospect cannot make the decision, the salesman must focus his attention on the person who can. No matter how successful the salesman is in convincing others of the need for a product, if he cannot convince the person who has the authority to buy, he cannot make a sale.

Concentrating on the person who has the authority to buy does not mean that the salesman neglects others, especially those who may actually use the product. The salesman of the printing press mentioned earlier won't get very far with the general manager if he has not convinced the chief pressman, too. Sometimes those who have no authority to buy can be of tremendous influence. For example, consider the case of a typewriter salesman. One of his customers, a large firm, needed several new typewriters and was seriously considering a competing brand. The salesman called the office manager of the company, but he was not in; however, on his way out the salesman stopped to chat with the office manager's secretary. He talked to her about her work—the kinds of typing problems she encountered, the features she would like most in a new typewriter, and the like. Then he mentioned the machine he was selling and described its various features.

■ The person who makes the selection may not always have the authority to buy. In this case the salesman may find that a follow-up call will be necessary later.

Before he left, he had obtained her permission to send a machine to her for a one-week trial period (with the approval of her boss, of course). When the salesman called back a week later, he found that the secretary was sold on the typewriter and hoped that the company would purchase that model. She made it easy for the salesman to get an appointment with the office manager. Needless to say, the secretary had already done the selling for the salesman, even though she herself did not have the authority to buy.

Accessibility of the Prospect. Some prospects are so difficult to approach that they cannot be placed very high on the list of potential customers. Accessibility, therefore, is an important consideration in evaluating prospects. A person may meet all the other qualifications beautifully, but if he is not available or is unapproachable, you may as well cross him off your list. One example of inaccessibility is the high-ranking business executive who is too busy to see a salesman and surrounds himself with barriers to prevent such interruptions. Another is the prospect who works irregular hours and who can never be counted on to be "in" to the salesman. Some prospects may be accessible physically but are so disagreeable that the salesman cannot "get through" to them with his sales message. Don't give up too easily on these people—their disagreeableness may be a defense mechanism. After all, they have needs, and a good salesman exhausts every possible way to prove that he can satisfy those needs before he tosses in the towel.

Special Qualifications. Sometimes a "suspect" must have certain qualifications before he can be considered a real prospect. For example, an individual considering life insurance must be able to pass a physical examination, and even though he meets all the other requirements of a good prospect, he cannot become a policyholder if he is in poor health. Some products, such as certain drugs and chemicals, may be sold only to certain individuals and organizations. Most wholesalers make it a strict policy to sell only to authorized retailers and dealers—never to individual consumers, even though many consumers may qualify as excellent prospects and jump at the chance to buy directly from the wholesaler. Sometimes the type of product and the area in which the prospect lives have a bearing on the evaluation of the prospect. For example, an individual who lives in an area where there is soft water is automatically eliminated as a prospect for water-softening equipment, and so on.

Obviously these are only some of the factors that must be considered in evaluating prospects. There are many others, depending on the product or service. The important thing to remember is that you must evaluate all your prospects according to the five factors just discussed.

SUMMING UP

The salesman knows he must have a good prospect list if he is to be effective, and this list must be replenished and enlarged constantly. It cannot be assumed, however, that everyone is a prospect. Every prospect must be evaluated in terms of his need, his ability to pay, his authority to buy, his accessibility, and his qualifications to buy. Some of the more common methods of prospecting used by the salesman are the endless-chain method, center-of-influence method, home demonstrations, personal observation, sales-associate plan, and cold canvassing.

Reviewing Your Reading

1. What are some common sources used by salesmen in building prospect lists? List at least eight.
2. Why are the salesman's satisfied customers an important source of prospects?
3. How does the classified telephone directory help the salesman in locating prospects? The city directory?
4. What field of selling seems to require the most prospecting? Why?
5. Describe the endless-chain method of prospecting.
6. Give examples of how prospecting methods vary according to the business.
7. How can a salesman make the use of referred leads more effective?
8. What is the center-of-influence method of prospecting? Illustrate how it might be used.
9. What two factors must be kept in mind in selecting a center of influence?
10. What is the difference between a prospect and a "suspect"?
11. Describe the sales-associate method of prospecting.
12. What is a "bird dog," as used in sales language?
13. How can a salesman use cold canvassing to obtain prospects?
14. What is meant by "evaluating your prospects"?
15. What five questions should the salesman use to evaluate prospects? Discuss each briefly.

For Discussion

1. Discuss the advantages and disadvantages of cold canvassing.
2. Why do you think every business must develop its own methods of locating prospects?

3. When canvassing homes, how should the salesman conduct himself on the homeowner's doorstep?
4. What products might appeal to a list of homeowners obtained from tax assessment rolls?
5. How would you use the personal-observation method of prospecting if you were a tire salesman?
6. How might the salesman use gifts to obtain prospects?
7. What advantages and disadvantages do you think there would be in canvassing in pairs?
8. Name organizations in your own community that might be important sources for prospects.
9. In what community activities should a life insurance salesman take an active part from the standpoint of building a prospect list?
10. Some door-to-door salesmen jot down in a notebook the number of every house called at. What do you think is the purpose of this information?
11. How does prospecting for customers for printing inks differ from prospecting for customers for household brushes?

Salesmanship in Action

1. Assume that you are a salesman for a retail floor-covering firm and that your specific responsibility is to obtain customers other than those who come into the store. Where would you get your prospects? List the sources in the order of their probable effectiveness.
2. Using the classified pages of the telephone directory or a city directory, select several classifications of businesses or professions and list products or services you might sell to them.
3. From your local newspapers, clip several items that might be of significance to you in building a prospect list. Assume that you are selling life insurance.
4. Turn to the list on pages 168 and 169. Choose one of the sources and write a report on it—advantages, how it works, and points to be emphasized.
5. On page 182 it is mentioned that cold canvassing should not be done haphazardly, that the salesman should have a systematic plan. Write a paragraph describing what you believe to be a systematic plan for a kitchenware specialties salesman.

Salesmanship in Action

Part Three

You wouldn't think of taking an automobile trip into strange country without a road map. The smart salesman uses a "map," too, when he makes a sales presentation. His "map" is a carefully made plan that he has prepared in advance—how he is going to approach the customer, what he will emphasize in his talk, how he will demonstrate his product, how he will anticipate and meet objections, how he will close the sale. Effective selling requires planning; no good salesman goes into an important sales situation "cold." Semper paratus!

Organizing Your Sales Presentation

IF YOU have ever taken part in a formal debate, you know how important it is to prepare for it in advance. Because each speaker in a debate is allowed only a limited amount of time to state his case, he has to figure out well in advance not only what his arguments are but also the most convincing way to present them. No oratorical power or last-minute inspiration can compete with this thorough advance preparation.

The salesman is in the same position as the debater. His job is to try to persuade a prospect to accept the idea of buying his product—and he has a limited amount of time in which to do it. Before the prospect loses interest, the salesman must present to him in the most concise but forceful way possible all the reasons why he needs the salesman's product. This obviously cannot be done on the spur of the moment. The only way for the salesman to be confident that he can present a sound, logical, accurate story that includes *all* the important selling points in their most effective order is by using a presentation that has been carefully prepared in advance.

Types of Sales Presentations

There are three types of prepared sales presentations that the salesman may use: (1) canned, (2) planned, and (3) programmed.

The Canned Sales Presentation. The canned sales presentation (sometimes called a standardized presentation) is usually prepared for the salesman by the company. It sets forth in every detail the things that are to be said and done in the presence of the prospect. The salesman is expected to memorize the presentation and deliver it pretty much as is. Here is the story of how it started:

> In the early days of its founding, the top salesman for the National Cash Register Company was Joseph H. Crane. One day at the factory, in 1886, John H. Patterson, the founder, asked him, "How do you sell so many cash registers?"
>
> Crane replied, "I have built up a selling talk."
>
> "How did you happen to do this?" Patterson asked.
>
> Crane replied, "One day I had my cash register in a hotel room. I talked with three different prospects, but I failed to make a sale. Then I began to think. I went back over my sales talk with the first prospect and realized that I had overlooked some important points. I put them down on a pad. I did the same thing with the talks to the second and third prospects. I now had a complete selling talk. Later I invited one of the prospects back to the hotel and, using the prepared talk, sold him a register."
>
> "Suppose you try the talk on me," said Patterson. When Crane had finished, Patterson remarked, "That talk would induce me to buy a cash register." And he converted Crane's sales talk into "The NCR Primer," considered to be the first standardized sales procedure ever used.[1]

The canned presentation is usually prepared by a team of experts who know the product "inside and out," understand sales psychology, and bring a creative ability and a capacity for organizing that the individual salesman, especially the beginner, could hardly be expected to match. Such a presentation offers a big advantage in that it makes sure that all the merits of the product are presented accurately and completely.

However, there are several serious disadvantages to a canned presentation. Many good salesmen feel that it takes the *man* out of sales*man*ship. They argue that the company might as well send the prospect a phonograph record, since the salesman's initiative and sales ability seem to count for so little.

You have probably heard canned presentations delivered by door-to-door salesmen and may have seen how difficult it can be for them to give someone else's words a ring of sincerity. In such instances the salesman may sound like

[1] Adapted from *Our Story of Sales Training*, The National Cash Register Company, Dayton, Ohio.

■ Planning his sales presentation. Before the salesman calls on a prospect, he must know what he is going to say during the interview.

Courtesy Hilton Hotels

a parrot, for he is simply mouthing what someone else has told him to say. This doesn't do much for his self-confidence. It may even make him seem ineffective and perhaps ridiculous to the prospect.

In the canned presentation the salesman may not be prepared to ad-lib; and if the prospect interrupts the salesman with questions, the salesman may get flustered or embarrassed. Once the flow of his memorized spiel has been halted, he finds it so hard to continue again that he is apt to insist on rushing forward in spite of anything the prospect can say. The following statement that a customer made about a salesman who was giving a canned presentation is an example:

> Evidently he [the salesman] had been told that he absolutely had to stick to his script and make his demonstration before asking for the order. I knew I wanted to buy and was only interested in finding out about delivery and trade-ins. But I just couldn't seem to get through to him. He was so busy looking for a place to plug in his demonstration model he didn't even hear me. Took me ten minutes to get him to allow me to order.[1]

Those who favor the canned presentation feel that the difficulties just mentioned can be overcome. They say that the salesman should compare himself to an actor in a play. Like the actor, he has to make the words that have been written for him come alive through his tone of voice, facial expressions, and gestures. He will be able to do this more easily if, instead of simply memorizing the

[1] Robert N. McMurray, "The Salesmen Who Turned into Parrots," *Sales Management*, Aug. 16, 1963, p. 53.

canned talk, he makes every effort to understand it. He should ask himself what each part of the presentation is trying to accomplish, which buying motives are being aroused, and what is significant about the order of the points. Those who favor the canned presentation argue that a genuine analysis of the canned presentation will make the salesman believe in it when he delivers it and will make him feel more like the master than the slave of the material. Because he understands what he is doing, he will be more confident that he can get back to his "script" after the prospect has interrupted it with questions or comments, and he will therefore not be as insensible as the salesman in the example cited. Some companies encourage their salesmen to rewrite the canned talk in their own words, which results in a more natural and conversational delivery.

In spite of the arguments in favor of the canned presentation, it cannot be denied that the canned presentation is a form of group selling. It is true that the team of experts must think in terms of how various individuals of different temperaments will react when they are working out the canned presentation. But these individual reactions have to be *averaged* in order to arrive at the final tight form of the finished talk so that the talk can be used for every prospect rather than any one particular prospect. This means that the canned presentation not only takes the salesman's personality out of the sale but also makes the prospect a generalization instead of an individual. Thus the canned presentation may be seen as a form of group selling rather than personal selling.

For this reason, the canned sales talk can be used best for products to which people will react in the same way. For instance, vacuum-cleaner salesmen can use a canned sales talk successfully because all housewives share about the same desire to clean their homes thoroughly and quickly with a well-built instrument that will last. It makes no difference whether the housewives are young or old, modern or old-fashioned, clubwomen or homebodies; they all want the vacuum cleaner for the same basic purpose. But when the appeal of the product is very individualized, for example, as it is with furniture, where education, tastes, habits, and income are the bases of selection, the use of a canned presentation is usually not effective.

The Planned Sales Presentation. It may be true that when the salesman plans his own sales presentation he does not come up with the polished masterpiece that a team of experts can produce. But many companies feel that when the salesman prepares the presentation himself he paves the way for genuine harmony with the prospect—something the technical perfection of the experts cannot rival. He can "zero right in" on John Doe and use his understanding of Doe's background, attitudes, and habits to make a presentation directly aimed at *him.* This is personal selling.

Although in preparing a planned sales presentation the salesman is ultimately responsible for how the material is put together, his company does not throw him out on his own. Usually the company gives him a training course that stresses product knowledge, prospecting methods, the psychology of selling, and sales techniques. The company will also keep the salesman supplied with pamphlets and brochures issued about the product and the competitors' products, and sales meetings will give the salesman a chance to get advice from the company's seasoned salesmen. The company may supply sales aids in the form of audio-visual materials. Some companies provide the salesman with a canned presentation but suggest that it be used only as a guide, helping the salesman see the possible form and flow of a sales talk. All this assistance goes a long way in helping even the average salesman to do a really good job in working out a presentation.

If the salesman writes out his presentation exactly, memorizes it, and then delivers it word for word, he has merely created a canned sales talk of his own to which all the objections about rigidity will still apply. What the salesman should do instead is to work out all the points that should go into the presentation (exactly how the salesman should arrive at these points will be discussed later in the chapter) and then think of these points as building blocks. He should have a definite, predecided plan for placing the blocks in their most logical and effective order to make an appealing, convincing, and complete sales talk that flows

■ The salesman should be more than a walking phonograph record. He must never sound as though he is giving a memorized sales talk—whether his presentation is canned, planned, or programmed.

continuously from the opening sentence to the point where the order is signed. This blueprint will keep the salesman from rambling all over the subject and will give the sales presentation the concise, immediate quality that spells success in selling.

But—and here comes the single most important advantage of the salesman's preparing his own presentation—the blocks do not always have to be placed in the same order. In the planning stage itself the salesman can decide on changes in the order that will make the presentation more directly appealing to a particular prospect. The salesman can even decide to leave some blocks out of the blueprint and take them along as "spares." But even more important is the fact that when the salesman gets into the actual sale he can shift the order of the blocks if he has to and still finish his building. This gives the salesman one of the most vital tools in selling—*flexibility*. It puts the prospect right in the middle of the picture where he belongs, for it makes room for his reactions, questions, comments, and objections. The salesman, instead of becoming confused and unhappy when he discovers that he is faced with a real live man who responds in a very personal way, is able not only to stay in full control of the interview, but actually to take advantage of the prospect's individuality to carry his sale to a conclusion.

Thinking of the materials as building blocks is also a timesaving device. After the salesman has fashioned the blocks the first time, his planning for each sale comes down to which of these prefabricated parts he needs for a particular prospect and how he should put the parts together. This is obviously easier than starting from scratch every time.

The Programmed Sales Presentation. Many products can be sold by submitting a written plan to the prospect that contains all the essential information. This is the basis of the programmed sales presentation. However, a written sales plan can be used successfully only for products with a highly individualized application, such as life insurance, especially-designed machinery for factories, plans for air conditioning or heating units for a large building, interior-decorating designs, and so on.

Usually a written sales plan can't be made up until the prospect has been approached and has given the salesman certain information. To make up an insurance plan, for instance, the salesman has to know such intimate details as the prospect's age, marital status, number of children, financial income and commitments, debts, savings, job security, and expected age of retirement. So the salesman must sell both himself and the *idea* of insurance to the prospect before he can get these details. After that, he makes up a brochure with an attractive cover and a personal title, such as "Life Insurance and Retirement

Fund Program for Charles W. Bowman." The brochure will then set forth down to the last detail the way this program will work for Charles W. Bowman.

In the programmed presentation the salesman is appealing to the prospect's intelligence. The salesman may actually have to do a great deal of persuasive talking to interpret the brochure to the prospect and to make the program sound attractive. But all the time the brochure seems to be saying, "You see, here are all the facts. There's no high-pressured ace up my sleeve. Everything's right here and you can figure it out for yourself." This provides real psychological comfort for the prospect who is about to part with a great deal of money.

Because of its time-consuming nature, the programmed presentation can sensibly be used only for expensive products that bring the salesman a large commission. The insurance salesman can afford to gamble the time needed for preparation of the brochure, since the large "take" on one success will make up for several losses.

The Five Essential Steps in Every Presentation

Every sales presentation, whether it is canned, planned, or programmed, must be built around the five basic steps to a sale, which were introduced in Chapter 1. As you will recall, these steps are (1) gaining attention, (2) arousing interest, (3) building desire, (4) winning conviction, and (5) getting action. The fact that the prospect must be led through all five of these steps if a sale is to take place gives the salesman a definite directive for planning the order in which he will place the building blocks that he is prefabricating for his sales presentation.

Richard C. Borden, one of the country's foremost sales experts, has drawn a comparison between the function of a sales presentation and that of a match. Study a match and what do you see? The tip is made of phosphorus so that it will light at the first scratch. Right below the tip is the sulfur. The sulfur converts the flash from the phosphorus into a flame that ignites the main fuel, or wooden shaft, of the match. The wooden shaft is coated with paraffin so that the match can burn long enough to do its job, which is to light a fire.

Let's see how Mr. Borden's comparison fits in with a salesman's attempt to make his sales talk follow the five selling steps:

1. *Gaining attention* (the phosphorus). The purpose of this first step in the selling process is to win the favorable and immediate attention of the prospect so that he is willing to hear more about the product. Just as people want a match to light at the first strike, so too people expect a salesman to make his opening remarks arresting and worthwhile. Here is a sure-fire attention getter that an appliance salesman who is calling on a housewife can use as the phosphorus at the tip of his sales talk:

Courtesy Whirlpool Corporation

■ This salesman can create a desire for his product by explaining its merits from the prospect's viewpoint.

SALESMAN: Mrs. Adams, how would you like a present of more than an hour of free time every day of your life?

PROSPECT: What a question! What woman on earth wouldn't like that?

2. *Arousing interest* (the sulfur). Having gained the prospect's attention, the salesman must now translate this into interest in the product. There must be some sulfur right below the tip of the sales talk to make the interest take fire. The salesman will be most successful in arousing interest if he can make one of his product facts tie in with a special problem or interest of the prospect.

SALESMAN: I'm talking about Royal Electric's new Portomatic dishwasher, Mrs. Adams. I know you wouldn't want to spend the money to install a regular dishwasher here in your apartment, but now you can be freed from the drudgery of dirty dishes without that extra expense. And, of course, you'll be able to take the dishwasher with you when you move.

3. *Building desire* (the main fuel). This is the main body of the presentation and is the part of the sale where the salesman explains all the merits of the product *from the prospect's viewpoint*. The question is not just what advantages the product has but how these advantages will benefit the prospect. The salesman must make his points in a concise, clear, and interesting manner, forestalling the most obvious objections as he goes, so that the prospect can see that the benefits of this product are so great that he should no longer be without it.

SALESMAN: You can see from this picture, Mrs. Adams, that the Portomatic is a very convenient size for an apartment kitchen. It's only 19 inches wide, so it will fit right there in that corner next to your table. You can roll it with a fingertip right up to the sink when you need it. The hoses are very simple to connect, and one of the best features of this particular model is that it has a new faucet attachment that allows you to draw both hot and cold water from the tap while the dishes are washing. This used to be one of the great objections to portable dishwashers, because you couldn't get any other sink chores done in the kitchen while they were connected; but that's all taken care of in this new model.

And talking about improvements, have you ever watched your friends practically wash their dishes before loading them in their old-style dishwashers? The Portomatic has a special prerinsing cycle that washes food particles down an extra-wide drain. All you have to do is remove the large scraps of food and the machine will do the rest.

This example is meant only to give you an idea of the general way in which the salesman can handle step 3. There are, of course, many other selling points about the dishwasher that the salesman will be ready to discuss—its baked-on enamel finish which will keep it new looking for years, the ease with which it can be loaded, its quiet operation which won't disturb the neighbors, the two-year factory guarantee which ensures good performance, and so on. The salesman is trying to make the flame of interest ignite the shaft of the match, which is desire for the product.

4. *Winning conviction* (the main fuel is still burning). If a match is not used quickly enough, it goes out or burns the fingers and must be dropped. Likewise, the salesman must be prepared to time his presentation so that the prospect is convinced of his need to buy before the flame of his interest goes out.

The salesman must be able to recognize when the prospect's conviction is final enough for the salesman to ask for an order. This point can come very early in the presentation. Just as the match is ready to use as soon as it is lit, so the prospect may be convinced that he should buy long before the salesman has used more than the first few building blocks in his blueprint.

This is especially true when large-scale advertising has already whetted the prospect's interest in the product. One can imagine that Mrs. Adams, the prospect for the dishwasher, might be ready to close very soon after she discovers that the dishwasher does not need permanent installation. This single selling point could conceivably carry her through steps 2, 3, and 4 all at once, for she is an avid reader of the slick women's magazines and she already is convinced that she is woefully deprived because she doesn't own a dishwasher.

Plan every call. If you have no better reason for a call than "I just dropped in," don't drop in. Every call must be based upon a specific sales plan and specific sales strategy. Know what you are going to say before you go in.

—E. B. Weiss, "The New Rules for Personal Selling," *Dun's Review & Modern Industry*

On the other hand, Mrs. Adams may be the type who always seems to need just one more reason before she can make up her mind. In this case the salesman will probably have to go through his entire sales talk, patiently answer all the objections that Mrs. Adams raises, and then even add a strong summary of the points which seemed to appeal to her most.

Even if the salesman knows a great deal about his prospect before he goes into the sale, step 4 is still going to hold some surprises for him. This is why the plan for the presentation *must* be flexible.

5. *Getting action* (using the match). Once the prospect is convinced, the salesman must get him to take action *now*. The salesman wants to light his fire with this one match. To do this, he must make immediate action seem desirable to the prospect with such remarks as, "Fortunately we received several of these dishwashers in our last shipment from the Royal Electric Company, so tonight could be the last night that you ever have to do dishes by hand again."

He should also make action easy for the prospect. "If you'll just sign this order form, Mrs. Adams, I'll see that your new dishwasher is delivered in the morning."

Of course, there will be times when one match can't do the job. In that case the salesman should try to obtain an appointment for a return call. The salesman's objective is to keep the prospect from shutting a final door on the sale.

Principles of Building a Sales Presentation

Building a sales presentation is a logical, orderly process. It is also a time-consuming process; but as has already been said, much of it has to be done only once. Because the salesman is going to have to refer to his presentation facts again and again, he should write everything out clearly, following the suggestions given here:

1. *List the five basic steps in the selling process.* These steps are the heart of the presentation. As a reminder of their importance, you should write them down. Also, by writing them down, you can refer back to them readily.

2. *List all the buying motives that could induce prospects to buy the product.* Think of all the people whom you know well, and try to figure out what motives would prompt each of them to buy the product. This will give you a list of motives that goes beyond the obvious. Then rewrite the buying motives in the order of their strength.

3. *List all possible facts about the product.* Start by writing down all the facts that come to your mind as you think about the product. Then add to your list

the facts contained in the company's advertisements, pamphlets, and bulletins. If you sell tangibles, you will come to a better understanding of any technical facts by making a careful study of the product, seeing exactly how it works— even taking it apart if that's possible. Clear up your doubts by talking to the men in the production department, the advertising and public relations departments, and the senior salesmen. Include in your list any facts about the company which are pertinent to the sale of the product.

4. *Translate these facts into selling points that tie in with the buying motives that you selected.* Take every fact and ask yourself what it would mean to the prospect. Here are two examples from a Sears, Roebuck sales-training manual that show how to turn product facts into benefits, which salesmen refer to as "sizzles":

> The Craftsman plane is perfectly machined, with the cutter and frog fitting firmly to the bottom. What of it? It prevents vibration or "chatter" and so leaves a smooth, even surface.

> Our Craftsman wood chisel is made of special-analysis, properly tempered steel. What of it? The chisel will last a long time. The cutting edge will stay sharp.

Notice how the salesman in each case has turned technical information into a direct appeal to the prospect's desire for efficiency, quality, and ease of use.

To answer the question "What of it?" in connection with each of the facts about your product, you should prepare a product analysis sheet, as was suggested in Chapter 9. While you are doing this, be aware of the fact that different buying motives can sometimes tie in with a given fact about a product. An example of this is seen by the salesman of a small foreign car. Some people see the economy features of the car as a way to save money; other people see these same economy features as a way to indicate to their neighbors that they already have more status than they can use and don't need to seek more by driving a big, expensive car.

5. *List the demonstrations that you will use to emphasize the selling points.* Try to think of ways to demonstrate as many selling points as possible. Remember that the prospect absorbs information through all five of his senses: he sees, hears, touches, smells, and tastes. Try to get to the prospect through several of his senses. The prospect hears from the salesman about a wonderful new perfume, which is described in glowing words, but that perfume won't be sold until the prospect smells it. Most automobile salesmen try to get the prospect behind the wheel of the car as soon as possible so that the prospect can feel the car's comfort and action. Try to appeal to the prospect's sense of sight most of all, with pictures, graphs, models, cutaway parts of the product, and everyday

gadgets that will illustrate a point. But keep the demonstration simple; if it is too technical, it will confuse, not clarify.

6. *List all possible objections to the product or the sales proposition.* The best way to overcome possible objections is to anticipate them. Here again try to think of the differences in people. One family loves the style of an old Victorian house but objects because it is too big. A second family thinks that bigness is the greatest advantage of the house but can be talked into buying only if the real estate agent can overcome their aversion to the style.

The salesman should prepare an objection analysis sheet. He should plan to incorporate into the sales talk the more obvious objections. Most salesmen feel, however, that it is better to accent the positive and to leave most of the objections until the prospect brings them up. The important point here is that the salesman should not be caught off guard by the prospect's objections. He should have his answers ready.

7. *Plan selling-point stories.* Build a story around each selling point. Put human interest in your stories, using examples that are close to the prospect's experience, humorous incidents, and timely news accounts. Weave questions into your stories that call for a "yes" answer, so that the prospect gets the "yes" habit.

Use analogies whenever you can. An analogy is a similarity between two things that are different in all other respects. Here is an example of an analogy between an apartment building and the prospect's health:

SALESMAN: **Mr. Baxter, I'm sure you realize that your way of life is directly related to your income. If your whole income came from the rents in a big apartment building, you certainly would not be so careless as to leave that building uninsured. But even though your income would stop if you weren't physically able to work, you don't have any disability insurance.**

Put the prospect into your selling stories whenever you can. Instead of saying, "The advantage of this range is that it has two ovens," say "*You* will enjoy preparing a meal on this range, *Mrs. Jones.* When *you* cook *your* Sunday dinner, *you* can bake *your* pie in this oven at the same time *your* roast is cooking in the other oven."

Make your sales stories sound as though they are a natural part of the conversation by using the words *for instance* and *for example:*

"For example, Mr. Barnes, let me tell you how a company about the size of yours over in Valley Town uses our photocopier."
"For instance, Mrs. Harwood, let me tell you why our company calls this model our 100 percenter."

"For instance, do you remember the house that burned down over in Park View last year? The insurance company found that the cause was defective wiring, which could have been remedied."

8. *Pick out the material that you want to use in your sales presentation and arrange it according to the five steps of the sale.* Ask yourself which point would make a good opener, and then try to see how the other steps to the sale can be handled. For the demonstration step, arrange your material so that it packs the most wallop.

After you have planned how you will arrange your material, take another look at it to see how the order can be changed to meet the reactions of the prospect. Ask yourself what you will do if the prospect brings up price before you are ready to discuss it or objects to the design when you would like to be discussing how much better your product works than all the machines like it. In other words, practice flexibility.

■ Using such words as *for example* or *for instance* will make your sales story sound as though it is a natural part of the conversation.

And remember that the prospect should never know that there are definite parts to your sales talk. The parts must flow into each other both easily and smoothly.

9. *Write a summary paragraph of the principal reasons for buying the product.* You must realize that there are prospects who will agree with every point you make as you go along; yet they will still be hesitant about buying. This type of prospect needs you to pull everything together for him so that he can see that "all the trees make a forest." You should plan an overall summary, but in the actual sale you will want to stay alert to the points that seem to have the most appeal to the prospect so that you can emphasize those points in presenting your summary to him.

Building a Sales Presentation for an Electric Percolator

For the sake of illustration, let's see how a sales presentation for an electric percolator might be developed. Assume that the salesman works for a housewares store that is trying to promote a new electric coffee maker and is sending the salesman to call on housewives in their homes. This same presentation, with a few minor changes that will be apparent to you, could be used by the salesman when he is selling the percolator in the store.

To keep the example brief and to emphasize certain points, only the major points of the presentation are included here.

First, the salesman writes down the five basic steps in the sale. This is the general outline of the sales presentation:

1. Attention ⎫
2. Interest   ⎬ —Approach
3. Desire   —Presentation of product
4. Conviction—Handling objections
5. Action   —Close

Second, he makes a list of the buying motives that would make a prospect want to own this appliance:

1. Convenience
2. Efficiency
3. Savings in time and labor
4. Pride of ownership
5. Imitation
6. Ease of operation

Now come the third and fourth steps, which can be combined. The salesman selects all the facts and selling features of his product that he can use in his presentation. He decides to use a product analysis sheet as shown. Notice how the salesman uses his facts to point out the benefits that the customer will receive. These benefits (sizzles) are based on the buying motives of the customer.

PRODUCT ANALYSIS SHEET
Product: *Minute Maid Electric Percolator*

Sales Facts and Features	Sales Appeals (Sizzles)
1. Stainless steel body	Attractive addition to your table; does not tarnish or get dull; is durable.
2. Electric current—A.C.	Can be used in any type dwelling—city apartment or rural home.
3. Completely automatic	Does not have to be watched; hostess can spend more time with guests; no danger of coffee spilling over and soiling stove and kitchen floor.
4. Heat control	Keeps coffee warm for a long time without spoiling flavor; no necessity to make a "fresh" pot.
5. Clean, modern design	Easy to wash and clean; no danger of losing or breaking parts.
6. Speed of operation	Can boil 12 cups of coffee in 10 minutes.

Fifth, the salesman thinks about the demonstration he will employ to put across his selling points, so he jots down the following:

Demonstration No. 1. To show Minute Maid electric percolator. Have sample model in complete working condition. Have cloth handy to keep it shiny and clean at all times.

Demonstration No. 2. To show features of Minute Maid percolator. Have cord wrapped around base of machine in neat manner. Keep supply of coffee, sugar, and powdered milk along with order pad.

Demonstration No. 3. To show material of which percolator is made. Have strips of stainless steel available for this purpose. Also, have samples of other materials for making comparisons.

Demonstration No. 4. To show portfolio of pictures in which Minute Maid percolators are used in prominent homes, leading hotels, and clubs.

Sixth, the salesman makes a list of all possible objections to the product. Four chief objections to the percolator seem to arise, and they can be listed as follows:

1. I can't afford it.
2. I can get other models cheaper.
3. I don't like stainless steel.
4. It will use too much electricity.

OBJECTION ANALYSIS SHEET

Product: Minute Maid Electric Percolator

Principal Objections	How to Answer Them
1. I can't afford a Minute Maid.	"I can appreciate how you feel, Mrs. Nelson. Naturally, you want the most for your money, but if you could be sure in buying the Minute Maid that you were getting the most value for your money, you wouldn't hesitate, would you?" 1. Review what the Minute Maid will do. 2. Call attention to the *exclusive* features of the Minute Maid. 3. Explain low down-payment and easy-payment plan.
2. I can get other models for less.	Use same approach as for No. 1.
3. I don't like stainless steel. I'd rather have a percolator that is made of another material.	"I can understand why you might feel that way, Mrs. Nelson. But stainless steel really has many advantages. It is tough and durable (demonstrate), will not corrode (demonstrate), is easy to clean, and will always keep its high luster."
4. It will use too much electricity.	"The amount of current required to heat a full percolator of coffee is very small. You will probably find that you are actually saving money. *Then bring out evidence that Minute Maids are used in prominent homes and in leading hotels and clubs.*

Now the salesman is ready to connect these points. He is ready to build his sales stories on each selling point. Then he will bring the stories together, using "for instance" and "for example" and putting the prospect into the picture as much as possible. Notice how smoothly the following sales presentation flows along:

SALES PRESENTATION
Minute Maid Electric Percolator

SALESMAN: Mrs. Nelson, my name is Paul Johnson. I have something here to show you that will save you money and help to ease your cooking chores. It will only take a moment. May I step in?

(*Use following statement if customer says she has a percolator.*)

SALESMAN: I can understand that, Mrs. Nelson. However, I know you are interested in the latest improvements in electrical utensils. It will only take a moment, and what I will show you may prove of great value. May I take that moment?

(*Bring percolator into house and start demonstration immediately.*)

SALESMAN: Notice, Mrs. Nelson, how easy the Minute Maid is to carry and handle. It is so compact that you can easily store it on a shelf or in the cupboard. It's attractive, too, and you can use it to decorate your table or dining room.

(*Explain each part of the percolator as you prepare to make coffee.*)

SALESMAN: Now, Mrs. Nelson, I'd like to make four cups of coffee with this ordinary store brand of coffee which I have with me and show you how easy it is to operate the Minute Maid. Would you like to plug it in and set the controls?

PROSPECT: It does seem quite simple.

SALESMAN: Yes, indeed. Mrs. Nelson, do you sometimes find it difficult to make your coffee the strength and flavor that you would like?

PROSPECT: Well, it is difficult to get a perfect cup always—just as you would like it to be.

SALESMAN: Yes, I understand. But with the Minute Maid this problem will be solved. You'll know, positively and definitely, that you can make cup after cup of perfectly blended coffee, because the guesswork will be gone. The Minute Maid will give you the guaranteed results with every cup of coffee.

(*Objection may arise at this point.*)

PROSPECT: That may be true, but won't it increase our electric bill?

SALESMAN: Actually, Mrs. Nelson, it probably will cost you less than what you are paying right now for making coffee on your stove. The small amount of electric current used by the Minute Maid makes it very inexpensive to operate. That's why the Minute Maid is used not only by other housekeepers but by our finest hotels and clubs, too.

(*Display pictures to prospect.*)

SALESMAN: And now, Mrs. Nelson, I see that the Minute Maid is ready. Won't you join me in sampling the flavor of this coffee?

PROSPECT: It certainly is delicious.

SALESMAN: Just remember, Mrs. Nelson, you will get coffee like this every time you use the Minute Maid; and there will never be any embarrassment or waste, because the Minute Maid will automatically shut itself off when the coffee is ready to be served. Now that you have seen and tasted the benefits of the Minute Maid, I'm sure you will agree that it will do a real job of saving you money, time, and energy.

PROSPECT: How much is it?

SALESMAN: Owning a Minute Maid is a matter of only a few cents a day. It costs less daily than a good magazine, a bottle of milk, or any other item you may buy daily. Let me show you how easy it is to own a Minute Maid. (*Explain E-Z Installment Plan.*)

SALESMAN: Considering all that the Minute Maid will do for you, Mrs. Nelson, I'm sure you won't want to be without it a single day longer. If I can get your OK now, I can deliver your beautiful new Minute Maid by the end of this week. Would Friday or Saturday suit you best? Thank you, Mrs. Nelson. If you will just place your name here, we will have it for you on that date. You will get a lot of satisfaction and enjoyment out of your coffee making from now on. (*Write up the order.*)

The Multicall Presentation

Earlier in the chapter it was stated that sometimes the first presentation is not enough to convince the prospect to buy. The salesman who sells technical or high-priced goods frequently has to call on the prospect several times before a buying decision is made.

It is very important that these follow-up calls be planned carefully. If the salesman's preparation for the first call has been as thorough and careful as has been recommended in this chapter, his preparation for subsequent calls will be greatly simplified.

But obviously the salesman can plan only one interview at a time. And furthermore, he should go into each one *planning to make a sale.* He should give the first interview everything he has, assuming that because his material is well prepared he will be able to conclude the sale successfully. If he does not get an order, he should make a request similar to this one for another appointment:

SALESMAN: Mr. Chase, I realize that it's sometimes hard for a busy man like yourself to come to a decision right away. Why don't you think over my proposition at your leisure and then let me talk to you again about it? How about next Tuesday at this same time?

■ In planning for his follow-up call, the salesman should go back over his previous sales presentation to try to discover what went wrong.

Then the salesman should go back to his written plans for his presentation and study them carefully, analyzing why they were not successful. He should give a great deal of thought to the unsuccessful interview and try to remember every-thing the prospect said to help him to get a lead on what the block is. As an example, suppose the salesman decides that the prospect's main objection is that he is afraid to place such a large order with the salesman's company because the company is relatively new and small. Actually the salesman had anticipated this objection and did have an answer prepared. But on going back over the interview, he can see that his answer wasn't strong enough. So before the next interview the salesman will arm himself with very detailed statistics about his company's security and he will also obtain some testimonials from satisfied customers. He will plan to dwell on the advantages of dealing with a small com-pany rather than a large one in his second presentation, stressing more personal service and more direct interest in the customer's welfare.

The salesman must guard against saying the same thing in the same way dur-ing the second interview. This will only annoy the prospect, who will feel that he has heard it all before and so why listen? In planning the second interview, the salesman has the advantage of knowing more about the prospect, so that he can tailor his presentation more exactly to the prospect's measurements. He should look at his product analysis sheet again, trying to see it through the eyes of the prospect. He should then be able to come up with a more direct appeal.

SUMMING UP

The salesman cannot go into an interview and give an effective story containing all the important selling points on the spur of the moment. He must be fully prepared with a canned, planned, or programmed sales presentation.

The canned presentation, which is prepared for the salesman by his company, is memorized and delivered word for word. Even though the product is presented accurately and completely, this method has several disadvantages: it lacks flexibility; the salesman may sound like a parrot; and since it takes both the salesman and prospect, as distinct individuals, out of the sale completely, it cannot be said to be a good example of personal selling.

The planned presentation, on the other hand, is personal selling at its best, for it takes full advantage of the salesman and the prospect as people. In this method the salesman analyzes his material and plans his own sales presentation, not memorizing a word-for-word talk but blueprinting the plans so that he knows exactly what he is going to say and yet can shift his plans in accordance with the prospect's reactions.

In the programmed presentation the salesman submits to the prospect a written plan that is very detailed. This method is especially time-consuming and should only be used for expensive products of very personal appeal.

The five basic steps to a sale,—(1) gaining attention, (2) arousing interest, (3) building desire, (4) winning conviction, and (5) getting action—are the heart of every sales presentation. To build a logical, orderly sales presentation, the salesman should begin by listing these five steps. Next he should list all the buying motives that could induce prospects to buy the product and all possible facts about the product. He should prepare a product analysis sheet to tie in the buying motives with the product facts by asking himself why and how each fact is important from the prospect's point of view. Then he should think of all the demonstrations that he could possibly use to emphasize his selling points. The salesman should anticipate all possible objections to the product in an objection analysis sheet. He should plan stories around each of his selling points. Then he should pick out the material that he wants to use in his sales presentation and arrange it according to the five steps of the sale. As the last step in his preparation for the sale, he should write a summary paragraph of the principal reasons for buying the product.

If the salesman is unable to get an order in the first interview, he should try to obtain another appointment. The second interview should be planned very carefully on the basis of what went wrong in the first one.

1. Why is it important that the salesman's sales talk be prepared in advance?
2. What is the main advantage of the canned sales presentation?
3. List three disadvantages of the canned presentation.
4. When can the canned sales talk be used most satisfactorily?
5. What is the planned sales presentation?
6. When the salesman is planning his own presentation, does his company give him any assistance? Explain your answer.
7. Describe the programmed sales presentation.
8. Why is the programmed presentation recommended only for expensive products that bring the salesman a large commission?
9. List the five steps to a sale and tell how each is important to the salesman when he is planning a sales talk.
10. Does the opportunity to close always come at the same point in the sale? Explain your answer.
11. List the nine things that the salesman must do to build a sales presentation.
12. Why is it important that the salesman plan very carefully any follow-up calls that he has to make when the sale is not concluded successfully in the first interview?
13. What advantage does the salesman have in planning his second interview with a prospect?

For Discussion

1. What does the statement "The canned presentation takes the *man* out of sales*man*ship" mean?
2. Why should the salesman who is required to give a canned sales presentation try to understand it?
3. Why does the presentation that the salesman plans himself represent real personal selling?
4. How can you personalize a sales talk?
5. What is your own opinion about using a canned sales talk? Do you think such a talk is effective with most people?
6. Is there any difference between planning a speech and planning a sales talk?
7. If you were working for a company that insisted on your memorizing and using a canned sales talk, is there anything you could do to make it sound natural and pleasing?

8. What does the fact that the prospect has five senses have to do with planning a sales presentation?

9. How could a retail salesperson use the nine-step method for planning a sales presentation as outlined in this chapter?

Tom Mason is a salesman in the lighting-fixtures department of a large department store. One of his chief problems is to help people select the proper lighting fixtures for their new homes (usually at the time the homes are being built). His problem is complicated by the fact that often the prospect is trying to stay within the fixtures budget allowed by the building contractor. The following is a typical sales situation in Tom's selling day. A customer has entered the department and is examining a new three-way lamp.

SALESMAN: **Good morning. May I help you?**

CUSTOMER: Well yes. I need fixtures for the Colonial home I am building.

SALESMAN: **Won't you please be seated first, Mrs. __ , Mrs. __ .**

CUSTOMER: Jennings. Mrs. Ralph Jennings. I'm building out in the Rushwood Tract. (An exclusive area limited to homes costing over $40,000.)
(Salesman places an order blank in position on his desk.)

SALESMAN: **Mrs. Jennings, here is an authentic coach-lantern style that will set off your Colonial doorway to advantage. Keep in mind that the outdoor lantern becomes an architectural feature of the house. It must be suitable in scale and proportion as well as in style. This is the right size for a doorway like yours.**

CUSTOMER: But two of these would cost $50, and the entire allowance for fourteen fixtures is only $175.

SALESMAN: **Mrs. Jennings, it is possible to supply lights for the fourteen outlets for the $175 allowance. If you feel later that this is what you want to do, I'll be glad to show them to you. But when you consider that your house is costing more than $40,000 and you have put so much care and thought into its design and furnishing, wouldn't it be false economy to ruin the effect of your investment with inappropriate fixtures? If you stop to think, you'll realize that the rug on the floor in just one room will cost more than the sum allowed for all the lighting fixtures in the entire house—the lighting fixtures that are to show off all the other fine furnishings to advantage. If you will let me help you to economize where it is possible, you will see that the fixtures you really want and should have for your home are not too far from the allowance figure.**

CUSTOMER: Perhaps you're right.

SALESMAN: Actually, Mrs. Jennings, it's your own money that you're spending. The builder was interested only in keeping the contract price of the house at a minimum. He included a figure for fixtures that would permit him to cover the outlets if he had to. If he included more expensive fixtures, which you might prefer, he would have to allow a lot of leeway and charge overhead and expense in addition. That would have increased his overall price for the house.

CUSTOMER (*hesitating*): Well, er—I'm not sure I will want to order anything today. I want to look at the fixtures first.

SALESMAN: Of course. I understand, Mrs. Jennings. But to help you with your fixtures selection, I'll need some information about the rooms in which they are to be used. This will save you time. (*Lists the rooms and the electrical outlets of each room.*) Mrs. Jennings, you've mentioned the main hall. Is there a rear hall? If so, you will need a fixture for that also.

CUSTOMER: Yes, there is.

SALESMAN: That means a total of fifteen fixtures.

CUSTOMER: That's correct.

SALESMAN: Now when will your new home be ready to move into?

CUSTOMER: I expect to move in about two weeks from now.

SALESMAN: That's fine. Now let's start with your front porch, Mrs. Jennings. (*Escorts prospect to display of porch lanterns first and then proceeds to go through entire selection.*)

SALESMAN: Now here are your dining room fixtures, Mrs. Jennings. I would like to see you get something in crystal. How do you like this? (*Points to a particular chandelier.*)

CUSTOMER: That's a nice crystal fixture, but it's too large for my dining room.

SALESMAN: I'm glad you mentioned size, Mrs. Jennings. I have taken into account the size of your dining room, 12 by 14 feet, as well as an 8½-foot ceiling. If this were a bronze or other heavy metal chandelier, it would be a bit large. But in crystal it is correct to use a somewhat larger fixture because the material itself is lighter and airier—not so heavy-looking. In fact, that is one of the attractions of crystal. It is light and gay, and notice how it lends a sparkling air of festivity to your table settings. (*He swings the fixture slightly so that it throws off a sparkling beam of light.*)

Besides, Mrs. Jennings, it is hung high in the showroom to permit walking under it. But at the correct height, 5½ feet above the floor and over your table, you'll be seeing it at the angle that the designer intended.

CUSTOMER: I see. Yes, I believe you are right at that.

SALESMAN: You will always be glad you chose a crystal chandelier for your Early American dining room.

Now here are the hall fixtures. Don't you agree, Mrs. Jennings, that the gleaming brass of this Colonial hall lamp will add warmth to your entrance and harmonize with the hardware?

CUSTOMER: Yes, I would love that fixture for my hallway. You certainly have shown me some beautiful things.

SALESMAN: They are beautiful, aren't they? Now, Mrs. Jennings, why don't we go back over the items you liked, which I have listed. You may ask me any questions you wish about price, and then we can try to effect economies whenever you feel it is necessary. After that, we can add up our list and get the overall cost.

CUSTOMER: Well, I'm still doubtful about that crystal fixture in the dining room. I think I would like a tollhouse fixture in brass better.

SALESMAN: Certainly, Mrs. Jennings, we can arrange that. How about that model with the black and white cap? Do you like that one?

CUSTOMER: Yes, I believe that would be all right. That is $24.75 isn't it?

SALESMAN: It is $24.50. Your builder's discount would amount to $9.80, which would make it only $14.70. That's a beautiful fixture, isn't it? Notice, too, that it has four bulbs rather than the conventional three. That means extra light where you want it.

CUSTOMER: Do you have all the items listed?

SALESMAN: I believe so. (*Checks list with the prospect.*) I've added the list now, and with your discount the entire amount is $214.80. That includes the three extra fixtures you wanted for your service porch, extra bath, and patio. (*Customer appears to be thinking it over.*)

QUESTIONS

1. Write a close for this salesman that in your opinion will get buying action from the customer. Keep your close brief, perhaps one or two paragraphs at the most.

2. Did the customer raise any objections in this case? How did the salesman handle them?

3. Indicate where the five basic steps to the sale were first noticeable.

Basic Step	Sales Presentation
Attention	
Interest	
Desire	
Conviction	
Action	

4. Make a list of the buying motives used in this sales presentation.
5. What demonstration did the salesman use?

Salesmanship in Action

1. Select a product that may be sold to people in their homes, such as an automatic washer, refrigerator, vacuum cleaner, life insurance, water softener, insulation, roofing; or any other product you care to select. Obtain sales information on this product from company or dealer sales literature and from magazine and newspaper advertisements. Prepare a planned sales presentation as described in this chapter. Be prepared to make this presentation before the class with or without demonstration aids, as the instructor may direct.
2. Make a list of attention-getting questions that you could ask at the beginning of a sales presentation on an automobile, an electric refrigerator, a six-room house, and life insurance.
3. In a newspaper or a magazine, select an advertisement that provides an abundance of information on a product. Prepare a product analysis and an objection analysis. Clip the advertisement to your analyses sheets and hand them in together.

Making the Approach

THE FIRST few moments the salesman spends with the prospect are undoubtedly the most important of the entire interview. The impression he makes in those early minutes is going to determine the buyer's attitude toward the entire sales presentation. Thus success or failure are directly dependent upon what is called, in the language of the salesman, the approach.

In the approach the salesman is trying to accomplish the first two steps in the selling process. He wants (1) to gain the favorable attention of the prospect and (2) to arouse interest in the product or service that he is selling. If the salesman is not able to accomplish these goals in the first two minutes in which he faces the prospect, then his chance to demonstrate his product will be lost along with the sale.

The setting in which the meeting with the prospect occurs will vary, of course. It may be in the prospect's office, in his factory, or in his home. It may also be in a retail store, such as a specialty shop. While the approach used will vary according to the setting, the basic principles of making the approach are the same. The major emphasis in the first part of the chapter will be on those situations in which the salesman seeks out the prospect. Later in the chapter special additional hints for retail-store selling will be given.

214

The Preapproach

Making a successful approach is not a matter of luck. It is a matter of intelligent and thorough advance preparation. In fact, the salesman can measure his chances of success against the completeness of his preparation almost like a mathematical formula. This advance work for the actual meeting with the prospect is called the preapproach, and it requires the salesman to consider (1) his appearance, (2) his attitude, (3) his knowledge of his product, (4) his knowledge of the prospect, (5) the organization of his sales presentation, and (6) his timing.

The Salesman's Appearance. No matter what kind of salesman you are or where you are going to meet your prospect, you cannot begin the sale of your product or service until you have sold yourself by your appearance. The prospect is going to make a lot of deductions about you from what he sees. A loud tie, dirty shirt cuffs, too much makeup on a woman, shoes that haven't been shined, all tell a story to the prospect. Thus a basic part of your advance preparation is checking every detail of your appearance before you face your prospect to be sure that you are presenting yourself in the best possible light.

■ Check yourself in a full-length mirror before you leave for a sales interview. You must sell yourself before you can hope to sell your product.

The Salesman's Attitude. The salesman has to toe a very fine line between natural friendliness and overfamiliarity and between self-confidence and an air of superiority. The prospect is obviously not going to take the time to listen to a man who looks as though he couldn't be unhappier about the whole thing and would rather be a hundred miles away, but neither does he want to hear out a man who is cocky, brash, or ill-mannered.

With this in mind, you as the salesman should take the time in your preapproach planning to review your attitude. One important clue for achieving the proper degree of friendliness and good manners is to picture yourself as the prospect's guest if you are calling upon him, or as his host if you are a salesperson in a retail store.

The second main clue for success is a positive attitude. If you believe in yourself, in your product, and in your firm, you will not need to take the negative approach of apologizing for taking up the prospect's time. You should feel that you are in a position to offer the prospect something that will benefit him, and your attitude should reflect your confidence in doing just that.

In other words, when you are getting ready to approach a prospect, you should plan to do so with the idea in mind that you are going to get an order. At the same time, you might as well ask for the largest sale possible. Think in terms of diamonds, not pebbles! Here is an example:

> A salesman walked into the office of a buyer who was famous for giving salesmen a hard time. Because of the buyer's reputation, the salesman didn't really expect to make a sale. But he had worked hard on his presentation; and after he had delivered it, he was astonished to hear the buyer say, "That sounds very good. I'll place an order."
>
> Still unbelieving, the salesman replied, "Thank you, Mr. Bronson. Shall I put you down for 10 gross? We can make delivery next week."
>
> The buyer nodded his head, and the salesman filled out the order blank. Then as the salesman was about to leave, Bronson made this parting remark: "It may interest you to know that I really need 100 gross, and I was prepared to order them all from you. But since you seemed satisfied with 10 gross, I'm sure you won't feel hurt if I spread the rest of the order among your competitors."

The Salesman's Knowledge of His Product. The day of the fast-talking, high-pressure salesman is gone. With so many goods and services on the market and with so many companies making slightly different versions of the same goods, the salesman must know what he is talking about. He must be prepared to discuss his own product as completely and accurately as possible. He must not get caught short on technical details. This is just as true for a man who is selling a new refrigerator to a housewife as it is for a man who is trying to sell an air-conditioning system to the contractor for a large office building.

The salesman must also be prepared to discuss the competition. For instance, in 1963, twenty-three types of electric and gas automatic clothes dryers were placed on the market in the medium-priced field alone. This kind of statistic means that the salesman who doesn't know the differences between his product and all the others like it is going to get caught short when faced with the sophisticated buyer. The principle also applies to retail selling, where the salesperson must be prepared to explain, for instance, the relative merits of blankets made by different manufacturers and selling for greatly varying prices.

It is highly unlikely that the salesman will need to call forth every fact in his possession every time he makes a sale. But knowing that he has the facts at his fingertips if they are needed will allow him to face the prospect with assurance.

The Salesman's Knowledge of the Prospect. In his preapproach planning, the enterprising salesman can find out a great many facts about his prospect which will enable him to tailor his approach to the prospect's individual needs with a considerable degree of accuracy. Facing a man about whom you know nothing can be a very unnerving experience even if you are a fast-thinking individual. It is not worth the gamble to the salesman who wants to be sure of success.

The alert salesman will find many ways of collecting this advance information about his prospects. The most obvious way is by a thorough reading of the local newspaper. It will provide a wealth of information about such events as mar-

From General Business Filmstrip Series, McGraw-Hill Text-Films

■ The alert salesman can often find worthwhile information in the local newspaper about the prospects he intends to call on.

riages, births, building permits issued, business promotions and expansions, and the fact that Mr. and Mrs. Harry Brown just returned from a trip to New York. All these stray bits of information add up to who's who and what's what in the town, politically, socially, and economically, and provide the salesman with a base of knowledge that will be invaluable to him.

The other major source of information for the salesman is people. Fellow salesmen, satisfied customers, the salesman's friends and family, the hotel clerk, the barber, the gas station attendant, and the waiter, all will talk to the salesman who is friendly and pleasant and will pass on stray bits of information that the salesman can piece together.

The five main areas of interest about any prospective customer that the salesman should investigate are (1) the prospect's name, (2) his ability to buy, (3) his authority to buy, (4) his need for the product, and (5) personal data about the prospect.

The Prospect's Name. The most basic thing that the salesman must know is the prospect's name and its correct spelling and pronunciation. This applies to every area of selling. The salesman who asks to speak to "the buyer" makes the receptionist think he is too inexperienced to deserve any consideration. Even the door-to-door salesman can ask as he leaves each house the name of the family next door. "Good morning, Mrs. Johnson," obviously has more impact than "Good morning, madam."

In the grocery store, the dry-cleaning store, and the dress shop, the salesman almost certainly won't be able to learn the customer's name ahead of time; but the sooner he can find out what it is, the better off he will be. And by all means, he should remember it when the customer comes back. When the salesperson knows the customer's name, the customer feels that his business is appreciated.

The Prospect's Ability to Buy. The salesman should find out what the prospect does for a living and get some indication of his credit rating. Can he afford the salesman's product and will he pay for it? The industrial salesman should find out about the buyer's firm. How long has it been in business? What does it make and to whom does it sell? Is it reputable in every way?

The Prospect's Authority to Buy. The salesman should know whether he can really settle the sale with the person that he is contacting. Perhaps the man always consults his wife before he buys. If so, the salesman must be prepared to sell her, too. If the prospect is a buyer, the salesman should know the buyer's position in the company. What is his title and the degree of his authority?

The Prospect's Need for the Product. The most successful salesmen sell their customers not just a product, but satisfaction. You as the salesman should discover whether the prospect needs what you are selling. Perhaps he already wants it or perhaps you will have to sell him the idea that he wants it, but your product must be something that he can use. Even if you should succeed in selling him something that he doesn't need, you may be sure that you won't ever sell him anything again.

Personal Data About the Prospect. The prospect's age, his marital status, the number of children in his family, his educational background, his neighborhood, his religion, his political affiliation, the organizations to which he belongs, his personality, and how he spends his free time, all give the alert salesman information that he can use. Personal data of this type will help the salesman to decide ahead of time which angles to use in his sales presentation. As an example, think how much it would help a car salesman to know before he makes his approach whether his prospect is (1) a single girl with a top job as a secretary who likes to go skiing every chance she gets, (2) a middle-aged drugstore clerk with five children and an interest in camping, (3) a young business executive on his way up who has just been admitted to the Country Club, or (4) a retired widower who is president of the Historical Society and writes letters to the editor against everything new.

The Salesman's Organization of His Sales Presentation. The smart salesman knows that he cannot count on some magical inspiration coming from out of the blue to give him just the right words he needs to persuade the prospect to buy. He knows that he must use the preapproach stage to combine his knowledge of his product and the information that he has been able to gather about the prospect into an orderly sales presentation.

He knows that this sales presentation must carry the prospect through the five steps of the sales process: (1) gaining attention, (2) arousing interest, (3) building desire, (4) winning conviction, and (5) getting action. He also knows that he must use every means he can think of to make the presentation vivid and interesting. The presentation must be carefully planned, and even rehearsed, so that every feature of the product that will appeal to the particular prospect is brought out in the order most likely to lead the prospect through the five steps of the sale.

But, at the same time, the plan must be flexible, because the prospect is not going to do or say exactly what the salesman expects. The salesman must be prepared to adjust his plan to allow for the prospect's questions and for new information that comes out during the interview about the prospect's needs and personality.

The Salesman's Timing. The best-planned sales presentation will be useless unless the salesman gives some thought to when he can best approach the prospect. If the salesman is selling attic fans, he may be welcomed enthusiastically by a householder in the middle of a heat wave. In the middle of the winter, however, the same householder would probably refuse to talk about attic fans or air conditioners, whereas he might be very much inclined to listen to a man who wanted to sell him a piece of automatic snow-removal equipment.

It is true that sometimes what seems to be impossible timing can be turned to the seller's advantage. Stores can and do sell furs in August. But such situations must be handled carefully. In this case careful advertising, backed up by smart salesmen, convinces women that they are being given an absolutely unprecedented chance to get a bargain by buying off-season.

At any rate, it is obvious that timing is a subject that the salesman cannot ignore. The time of the day or the day of the week can be as important as the season of the year. The specialty salesman who calls on a small retail merchandiser of men's wear late Saturday afternoon is asking for a quick "no." Likewise, it would hardly be smart to try to sell this same merchandiser a brand new and rather revolutionary item that needs a lot of explaining when he is in the middle of taking inventory. And the door-to-door salesman whose sharp jab of the doorbell comes just as the baby is getting to sleep will never have a chance.

The Approach

In the successful approach the salesman is able to win immediately the favorable and undivided attention of the prospect and then to hold it long enough to be able to go on to the presentation (the next step in the sale, which will be discussed in Chapter 13). The salesman has only a very few minutes in which to gain this interest. If he fails to gain it, he cannot hope to make a sale. But he will not fail if he pays sufficient attention to the essential ingredients of the approach: (1) the right setting, (2) the strong opener, and (3) the relationship of the approach to the sales presentation.

The Right Setting. The salesman has now moved from the hypothetical planning of his meeting with the prospect to the actual meeting itself. He is ready to stand face to face with the prospect at last. If all the plans that he has made so carefully are going to work out, he will have to be prepared to take the initiative in creating the right setting for the sale. There are three main aspects to creating the right setting: (1) establishing a friendly atmosphere, (2) getting past the secretary or receptionist, and (3) handling the unwilling prospect.

Establishing a Friendly Atmosphere. The salesman's first job is to get the interview started on a friendly basis. It is not unusual for people to react initially to a salesman with resistance and suspicion. No one likes to put himself in the position of being dominated by someone else. The prospect, especially if he is none too sure of himself in the first place, is afraid that if he listens to the sales talk, he is going to be persuaded to buy something against his will. The disad-

H. Armstrong Roberts

■ It is important to establish a friendly atmosphere at once. The first impression and opening statement will influence the entire interview.

vantages of this principle are felt most keenly by door-to-door salesmen, who routinely receive such stock answers as, "Sorry, I'm too busy," "I'm not interested," or "I don't want any."

But the salesman can prevent the prospect from throwing up this wall of resistance. Knowing that it is easier to talk to a friend than it is to a stranger, he should try to make the prospect his friend. The sales interview can then proceed along the lines of an informal, amiable conversation instead of being a stiff, awkward, formal meeting between two strangers.

The salesman's appearance, general bearing, and tone of voice obviously have a great deal to do with establishing a friendly atmosphere, as does the principle, mentioned earlier in the chapter, that the salesman should consider himself the prospect's guest if he is calling upon the prospect or the prospect's host if he is a salesman in a retail store. If the salesman follows these principles, the proper degree of courtesy should be easy for both the salesman and the prospect.

The proper social preliminaries also have a lot to do with making the atmosphere of the approach a friendly one. The salesman should introduce himself to the prospect, giving his own name and the name of the company that he represents. He should use the prospect's name, pronouncing it correctly. The introduction is as simple as this: "Mr. Fowler, I'm George Davis of the Ever Ready Tire Company."

The problem of whether the salesman should shake hands with the prospect is one that depends on the situation. If the prospect extends his hand, obviously the salesman should shake hands with him, clasping his hand firmly but not pumping it. However, the salesman should not force a handshake if the prospect seems reluctant. The salesman will have to play this by ear, remembering that a handshake works very much to his advantage since it lends cordiality and friendliness to the interview.

The salesman should always try to sit down once the introduction is over. This places the salesman in a more natural and comfortable position for engaging the prospect's interest and allows the salesman to control his sales material more effectively. If the salesman remains standing throughout the sales presentation, he gives the impression that he is about to leave at any moment or expects to be dismissed. If you as the salesman have managed to make the prospect think of you as a guest, he will almost always ask you to be seated. If he does not, you may make a motion toward a chair or ask permission to sit. If your sales presentation requires you to remain standing, you should be sure that the prospect is comfortably seated, thus indicating his willingness to listen to your presentation.

Your overcoat and hat should be placed inconspicuously on a vacant chair or on the floor near where you sit, or better yet, they should be left in a reception room or outer office. *Never use the prospect's desk as a place to deposit your personal belongings.* If you must place your sales material on the prospect's desk to make an effective presentation, ask the prospect's permission first.

Getting Past the Secretary or Receptionist. It is not always possible for the salesman to get in to see the prospect directly. There may be a very major

■ The salesman may have to sell himself to the secretary or receptionist first. He should treat her with respect.

obstacle in the salesman's way in the form of a secretary or receptionist. Many busy men delegate a great deal of authority to their aides and give them the power to decide who should be admitted to the inner sanctum. In such a situation the salesman is going to have to sell himself to the secretary first.

Most women who have been given such a degree of authority are serious about their work. They also have a sense of pride that their employers put so much trust in them. They will, therefore, appreciate being treated like responsible people. They will *not* appreciate a "palsy-walsy" approach or one that implies that the salesman thinks he is this year's gift to women.

If the salesman has to wait before he is admitted to the inner office, he should use his time to good advantage. He should not waste the secretary's time by talking to her unless she takes the initiative. Instead, he should review his plans for the interview, reread some of the material about his product, or plan new ideas for sales presentations. If he looks as though he values his time, the secretary will be more inclined to value it, too.

Handling the Unwilling Prospect. Sometimes after the salesman has been announced, it becomes clear to him that the prospect is not really willing to talk to him. The prospect may meet the salesman at the door to his office or somewhere in the outer office and say, "Yes, sir, what can I do for you?" If the salesman is inexperienced, he may try to start his sales talk then and there. But all the time he is talking, the prospect will only be trying to think of a way to get rid of him. The experienced salesman knows better than to try to make a sale under such circumstances. He smiles and says, "Mr. Prospect, I know that you're too good a businessman to buy something on the spur of the minute. Could we talk about this in your office?" If this tactic doesn't work, the salesman should excuse himself and ask for an appointment when the prospect is less busy.

Sometimes the salesman is ushered into the prospect's office, and the prospect barely looks up while he continues with what he is doing. "Go ahead with your story," he may say. "I can listen to you while I get these papers signed." This situation must be handled tactfully, but firmly. The salesman may say, "I don't want to distract you, Mr. Prospect. I'll be glad to wait until you are finished." Or the salesman may say, "Mr. Prospect, I would rather wait until you are through. This proposition will not benefit either of us if your attention is divided while I am presenting it to you." In any event, the salesman should not begin his interview while the prospect's attention is focused elsewhere.

The Strong Opener. The first twenty-five words you say to the prospect after you have introduced yourself are the most important words in the entire interview. They set the stage for the presentation that is to follow and make the prospect decide whether or not he wants to listen to what else you have to say.

These first few words are known as the opener, and they must be positive, definite, and to the point. As an example of how a salesman can muff each of these requirements in just sixty seconds, consider this dialogue:

SALESMAN: Mr. Conklin, my name is Peter Harris. I'm with the Flash Engineering Company, and in view of the fact that—er—since you have such a large plant—I mean, you wouldn't be interested in seeing our line, would you?

PROSPECT: It depends on what you are selling.

SALESMAN: Well, we have several products, Mr. Conklin, and they're all unbeatable. Our main line is soundproofing, but we also handle insulation jobs.

PROSPECT: That's just great, but would you mind telling me what you think you can do for me?

The salesman in this example is guilty of three major mistakes. When he says, "You wouldn't be interested in seeing our line, would you?" he is giving the prospect too easy a chance to answer "no." His statement that his company makes *several* products that are *unbeatable* is vague, indefinite, and exaggerated. And finally, he has not been able to get to the point, so that the prospect has become annoyed with the effort of having to fish for the purpose of the salesman's visit.

The salesman can eliminate the chance that he will make such mistakes with careful planning. In addition, he should make use of everything he knows about buying motives and human nature to frame his opening remarks so that they are strong, vivid, and appealing to the particular prospect. Experienced salesmen base their openers on one of the following ten types or on a combination of them:

1. The question	6. The service
2. The curiosity arouser	7. The referral
3. The appeal to special interest	8. The anecdote
4. The gift	9. The exhibit
5. The survey	10. The product

The Question. Asking the prospect an interesting question is an excellent device for gaining attention, because most people will automatically answer a question that is put to them. However, the question should be worded in such a way that the prospect can only answer "yes." For example, the question "I know you're pretty busy, Mr. Prospect, but could I show you our new carbon paper?" should be contrasted with "Mr. Prospect, could your office benefit from a new carbon paper that will give you eight perfectly clear copies of everything your secretary types?" The first question is negative, weak, and apologetic. The second one is positive and interesting, because it promises the prospect greater efficiency and economy.

Another form of negativism to be avoided is the question that creates an unpleasant impression in the prospect's mind, such as "Supposing one of those trucks of yours blew a tire and killed a driver, how would you feel then?" or "What would your family have for support if you died tomorrow?"

The successful question opener should bring the buyer and the product together. For instance, a freezer-plan salesman might say to a prospect, "If you could find a way of feeding your family better for a third less than you are spending now, you would be interested, wouldn't you?" This question sets forth the main merits of the freezer plan in such a way as to appeal to the prospect's interest in economy and in his family's welfare.

Another effective type of opening question is the one that has a challenge concealed in it. For example, "Mr. Prospect, do you have a sales force that could sell a top grade line of marine paint?" This question challenges the prospect's efficiency. He wouldn't want to admit that he was the boss of an inferior sales force, so he will answer the question affirmatively.

The successful question opener should be (1) positive, (2) to the point, (3) vivid, (4) appealing, and (5) challenging.

The Curiosity Arouser. This type of opener is based on arousing the prospect's curiosity and making him want to hear more. Curiosity is one of your prospect's traits that you can count on; it's a quality that everyone shares. For example, a glass-container salesman might use the following question to open an interview with a prospective customer: "Have you ever heard of a glass bottle that won't break if it's dropped on a cement floor?" The customer thinks to himself that dropping a glass bottle on a hard floor without breaking it would be a pretty neat trick. He is curious enough to let the salesman tell him how this could be possible.

Another example is that of the toy salesman who sells to department stores. He walks into a buyer's office carrying a package that is an odd shape. Without mentioning the package, he begins to talk about the wonderful toy he is going to show and some of its unusual features. As he talks, the buyer becomes more and more curious to know what is in the package and when the salesman is going to get around to opening it.

The Appeal to Special Interest. This type of opener is especially effective because it is aimed directly at the personal interests of the particular prospect, whether it be the prospect's family, home, health, job, or hobbies. This opener will work best if the salesman is not approaching the prospect cold but has learned about his particular interests in his preapproach preparations.

As an example, a man selling power lawn mowers has Mr. Harry Morse on his prospect list, because Mr. Morse has a large lawn and can't afford a gardener.

The salesman also discovers that Mr. Morse has spent all winter building a sail-boat in his garage. The salesman makes this opening statement: "Mr. Morse, I know how you can free yourself to spend many more hours in your sailboat this summer." The salesman has, as the old saying goes, "hit the nail right on the head." Mr. Morse couldn't put up any resistance if he tried.

In the example just given, the salesman was able to relate the product directly to the prospect's special interest. But the special-interest opening can also be effective when there is no possible connection between the product and the prospect's personal concerns. For example, a salesman for a tie manufacturer learns that one of the difficult department store buyers on his list is an avid bird watcher. The salesman is smart enough to do a little boning up on birds at the local chapter of the Audubon Society. He is then prepared to indicate to the buyer in his opening remarks that he shares and understands the buyer's interest in birds. This has nothing to do with the ties that he is trying to sell, but it will make the buyer look on him, and hence his product, with favor.

A word of caution must be said about the special-interest opening. The sales-man must avoid the obvious. He should remember that the picture on the prospect's desk of his family or the moose head on the wall of his office are there for all the other salesmen to see, too, and that the prospect will be grateful for not having to tell for the two hundredth time where his children are in school or how he shot the moose.

The Gift. Giving a gift to the prospect can be a very effective beginning for your sales presentation. The prospect usually feels grateful enough or obligated enough to give you his attention in return. The gift may be a novelty, such as a calendar or memorandum book, or a sample of your product or the prod-uct itself. But the closer the relationship is between the gift and the product, the more effective this approach will be. A large brush company instructs its door-to-door salesmen to start out by presenting a small brush to the housewife and to say, "Good morning, Mrs. Prospect. I have an all-purpose brush here as a pres-ent for you. You will find many different uses for it. Don't you think it's well made? All our brushes are as sturdy as this one."

An office-furniture salesman may present his prospect with a brass ash tray framed in a sample of the wood used in his line of furniture. Salesmen for drug companies routinely visit doctors' offices loaded with free samples of the drugs they are selling. Some of the drug salesmen are even able to present the doctors with elaborate pharmaceutical directories that their companies bear the expense of printing, because these directories make such an effective way of gaining the doctors' attention.

The idea of the gift may also be used to keep a continuous opening with a customer. A car salesman picks up from the registration application the birth-

■ Presenting the prospect with a gift often makes an effective sales opener.

Courtesy The Fuller Brush Company

day of Mr. David Richards, to whom he has just sold a car. Every year on Mr. Richards' birthday the salesman sends him a birthday card and a small present, such as an ice scraper or a specially treated cloth for wiping the windshield. When Mr. Richards is ready for a new car, the salesman will already have his opening.

The Survey. In some situations the salesman is not able to find out in his pre-approach work enough about the prospect's exact operation to know whether or not the salesman's product will benefit the prospect. In this case the salesman asks the prospect for permission to make a survey. A good example of this would be the IBM salesman who suspects that the D. W. Smith Department Store could save time and money and gain efficiency by putting its payroll, billing, and inventory on IBM machines. However, the salesman knows that the rental of the machines sounds at first like an expensive proposition. To prove the value of the machines, the salesman needs to collect data about the store's present operations. He approaches the store's president and obtains permission to make the survey. He studies the situation carefully and draws up statistics comparing the present operations and their costs with the machines and their cost. He then goes back to the president and says, "Mr. Smith, I have completed my survey of your payroll, billing, and inventory operations, and I can prove with actual figures that the IBM machines can do the work much more quickly and accurately and actually cost less in the end."

The idea of the survey opening can be adapted by the door-to-door salesman who says to the housewife, "Good morning, Mrs. Brown. I'm George Davis and I represent the Heato Company. We're making a survey in this neighborhood to find out how many families use stainless-steel cooking utensils. Do you have a set of stainless steel?"

A negative answer qualifies the housewife as a good prospect, and the salesman then tries to make an appointment to demonstrate the product. If the woman says that she has a set, the salesman asks her how long she has had it, whether it is lightweight or heavy stainless steel, and whether she likes it. This questioning may bring to light the fact that the old set is not giving satisfactory service or that some of the pieces are missing. Also, the comparison of the new utensils with the older ones may serve to make the housewife feel dissatisfied with the old set and curious about the new one.

The Service. This opening is similar to both the gift and survey openings. As in the gift opening, the idea is to give the prospect something for nothing so that he will feel grateful enough or obligated enough to let the salesman demonstrate his product. But in this case, what is being offered is a service rather than a material gift. The similarity with the survey opening is that the salesman is using the same approach to try to find a need for his product.

A good example of the service approach is the appliance salesman who calls on the housewife and says, "Good morning, Mrs. Jones. I'm John Conroy with the Rockwell Electric Company. We're calling on homemakers this week to offer a free inspection of electrical appliances. May I see your appliances and check them for safety?" The salesman must then make a legitimate inspection of the housewife's appliances, checking the cords for fraying, seeing whether large appliances are grounded and whether the fuse load is sufficiently distributed, and so on. After the salesman has made his inspection, he can discuss the appliances with the housewife, pointing out any problems. If done in the proper manner, this could very well lead to a sale. If the sale is not made right then, the salesman need not feel that his time has been lost. When the housewife is considering appliances in the future, she will remember the helpful salesman.

The Referral. Experienced salesmen consider that they are indeed fortunate when they can use this type of opening. In this case a satisfied customer gives you the name of one of his friends that he thinks would benefit from your product and says that you may use his name. There could not be a more ideal set-up than to be able to call on a prospect who has been recommended to you by a satisfied customer.

But this situation must be handled with great tact. For instance, assume that you are selling electric typewriters. Your last customer, George Brown, has given you the name of his friend, Philip Owen of the Bishop Manufacturing Company, as a good prospect. The inexperienced salesman might ruin his chances for a sale by saying, "Mr. Owen, my name is John Roberts. Mr. Brown of the Loughlin Company said you needed an electric typewriter, and I want to show you ours." This opener is worded in such a way that it may make Mr. Owen suspect Mr. Brown's motives, or it may cause Mr. Owen to resent the idea that Mr. Brown is making decisions for him. He may react this way: "Brown said that? Well, what makes him so sure he's right?"

The tactful salesman will say instead, "Mr. Owen, my name is John Roberts, and I'm with the ABC Electric Typewriter Company. I wonder whether you have seen our new electric typewriter. Mr. Brown of the Loughlin Company is very much impressed with the way it has stepped up efficiency in his department. As a matter of fact, he told me specifically to mention his name to you. He thought you might be interested to know that he is so pleased."

The Anecdote. Sometimes it is desirable to open a sale in a leisurely fashion. This is especially true when you are well acquainted with the prospect. In such a case you may use a brief, interesting story as an opener. It may be humorous or serious, but you must be able to make it relevant to your sales proposition. Here is an example that a man selling to a buyer for a specialty shop might use:

> Mr. Buyer, recently I saw a wonderful cartoon in a magazine. There was a worried-looking group of businessmen seated in front of a sales chart that pointed downward, and the caption read, "We've tried the hard sell, and we've tried the soft sell. Maybe the product's no good." But you won't have any trouble moving our new sports shirts, Mr. Buyer, hard or soft sell.

The following example is one that almost any kind of salesman might adapt:

> Mr. Prospect, our sales manager has a favorite story that he tells new salesmen. He tells about the couple who were in the middle of their dinner when suddenly the lights went out. They looked all up and down the street and found that everybody else's lights were out, too. So they figured there was trouble somewhere in the power line and they'd just have to wait it out. Several hours later they were getting pretty bitter about the inefficiency of the electric company. After another hour the husband called the company to complain and was told that no one in the service department even knew the lights were out. Everyone in the neighborhood had just assumed that someone else had phoned in the trouble. Now the point of the story, Mr. Prospect, is that in our company we feel we can't afford to make any assumptions or take anything for granted. We've got to stay on our toes to stay ahead of the field in efficiency and quality.

The Exhibit. This opener is based on the old theory that a picture is worth 10,000 words. Pictures, models, and statistical charts make excellent attention getters for the salesman, for they immediately catch the eye of the prospect. But they must be well planned and they must be directly related to the product.

A man who is trying to sell a large corporation a site for a new factory that is in a distant city might take along a slide projector and a small screen to show the appropriate executive detailed pictures of the site and the surrounding area right in the executive's own office. This is a device that will be greatly appreciated by the busy executive, because it will show him quickly whether the site is worth considering.

The office-furniture salesman carries with him a box model of a typical office. In it he has a scale-model set of old-fashioned office furniture, and he shows this to the prospect first. Then he removes the old-fashioned furniture and substitutes scale models of the furniture he is selling. The prospect can see at a glance how much more efficient the same space would be with the new furniture.

The Product. Sometimes the best possible approach is simply to hand the prospect the product. This is especially true when the product is very unusual or exceptionally well made, so that it speaks for itself. Suppose, for example, that a salesman is the representative for the Morris County Society of Craftsmen. One of the craftsmen makes wooden trays of black walnut that are exceptionally beautiful. The salesman goes into the office of the buyer for an exclusive housewares store and simply hands him a tray. The salesman knows the kind of quality merchandise that the store handles and the discriminating clientele to which it sells. He knows that he is not taking any risks when he lets the product do the talking to this particular buyer.

■ A good way to arouse the prospect's interest during the approach is to show her the actual product or an illustrated brochure.

The theory of the product approach is also used in retail selling whenever the salesperson sees a customer actually examining merchandise. Here the salesperson approaches the customer with a well-planned opener about the product. For example, a salesperson in a hardware store, observing a customer examining a saw, may step up and say, "That saw is tempered, ground, and honed. That means that it's sharp and will stay sharp." Or if a customer is looking at ruffled nylon curtains in a decorating department, a salesperson may approach and say, "Those curtains will look exactly like that after many washings, and with the barest minimum of ironing, too."

As can be seen from the examples given, the product approach in retail selling is based on the psychology of keeping the customer's mind on the merchandise, rather than diverting his attention by a greeting. Of course, this approach requires product knowledge. If the salesperson doesn't know the facts about the merchandise, he cannot expect to use this type of approach successfully.

The Relationship of the Approach to the Sales Presentation. In studying salesmanship, it is necessary to break down the component parts of the sale in order to analyze them. But the student must realize that there are not any apparent parts to the interview in the sale situation itself. All the parts must flow together in a completely natural way.

This realization of the necessity for smoothness in the interview is the key to the salesman's timing for ending the approach and beginning the presentation. The salesman should begin his presentation *the minute he senses that his prospect's interest has been aroused.*

In order for the salesman to sense this exact minute, he must be alert to the prospect's reactions. For the experienced salesman, the approach is a "two-way street." All the time that he is trying to make a favorable impression on the prospect, he is also taking mental note of his own impressions of the prospect. Even if he has learned a great deal about the man in his preapproach work, he still has to keep adding to his information while he is making the approach. If he is alert enough to do this, he will be able to make the transition to the presentation easily, and he will also be able to fit the presentation more exactly to the prospect's needs and personality.

Applying the Principles of the Approach to Retail Selling

Although the general principles of the approach that have been discussed in this chapter apply also to retail selling, there are some additional pointers that will prove helpful to the retail salesman. These pointers will be discussed as follows: (1) the salesman's appearance, (2) the friendly atmosphere, (3) the salesman's opening remarks, and (4) the salesman's analysis of the customer's needs.

The Salesman's Appearance. Because the salesman's appearance in retail selling is so important, many stores have quite definite rules about what their salesclerks should wear. An exclusive New York department store insists that all its salesgirls wear black, simply tailored dresses with white collars or with a single strand of pearls. Shoes have to be medium-heeled black pumps, and makeup and hair styles must be simple but stylish. The collective effect of all these carefully groomed salesgirls makes the customer feel that in this store everything is exceptionally well run and that shopping here will be a pleasure.

This store's rules are far more rigid than most, but the basic principles of dress are the same in every store, including the butcher shop and the ice-cream parlor. Clean, neat, well-groomed salespeople reassure the customer that he has come to the right place to get his needs satisfied.

The Friendly Atmosphere. The necessity for establishing a friendly atmosphere for the sale is just as important to the retail salesperson as it is to the specialty salesman. The person shopping in a retail store is very often tired, harassed, or hurried. For instance, a woman has had to bring her two small and lively children with her to shop. A man has run out on his lunch hour to buy his wife a present. A school teacher is trying to fit in a little shopping at the end of the school day. These three people are all easily annoyed. It is up to the salesperson to try to relax them by being as friendly, courteous, and helpful as he can.

The first ingredient for establishing a friendly atmosphere is promptness. The customer considers that his own time is very valuable. He does not want to stand around waiting for the salesperson to finish arranging stock. Any such duties must be postponed immediately upon the customer's arrival. Nor does the customer want to wait while the salesclerks finish their conversation with each other about last night's date or next week's party.

If a salesperson finds that he cannot wait on the customer immediately because he is busy with another customer, and no other salesperson is available, he should *acknowledge the customer's arrival* by a pleasant greeting. It helps to say, "Good morning. I'll be with you in just a minute." If his present customer is occupied in examining an item, he may excuse himself for a moment and wait on the second customer or display some items for the newcomer to examine while that person is waiting. But this should only be done with the permission of the customer on whom he was waiting first.

Sometimes when the customer arrives, the salesperson is busy writing up a telephone order or finishing up an order that is a charge and send. In this case, too, he should acknowledge the customer's arrival and explain that he must finish the order but will be with the customer in just a few minutes.

Besides being prompt, the salesperson should indicate his desire to be helpful. His whole attitude should say, "I want to find out what your buying problem is, and I want to help you solve it to your complete satisfaction." If the salesperson will take the attitude that the customer is his guest, it will be easy for him to serve the customer's best interests.

The Salesman's Opening Remarks. The customer should be approached with a smile and a pleasant greeting, such as "Good morning, sir." Such service approaches as "May I help you?" or "Are you being helped?" are also pleasing to the customer as long as they are said sincerely and not just parroted. However, the salesperson should avoid any remarks that put the customer on the defensive, such as "What can I sell you?" or "Do you want to buy something?" Such remarks only irritate the customer and make him suspicious of the salesperson's motives throughout the sale.

The Salesperson's Analysis of the Customer's Needs. The fact that the approach is a "two-way street" is especially important to the retail salesman, who does not usually know anything about the customer beforehand. It is vital that the salesperson study the customer carefully during the approach so that he can judge what direction the sale should take. The salesperson should listen carefully to the customer's opening remarks to determine the customer's exact need and decide what merchandise will fill it. This close attention will also serve to flatter the customer and make him believe in the sincerity of the salesman's desire to help him.

If the customer does not readily indicate what he wants, then a few well-chosen questions concerning the intended use of the merchandise must be asked so that the salesperson has a more definite idea of what articles to show. The salesperson can also use his observations of the customer's clothes, actions, and general remarks as a guide to the kind of merchandise to show. But he must be careful not to become so sure of his judgment of the customer that he stops listening to what the customer has to say.

Asking the customer point-blank how much he wants to spend is not a good idea. Instead, the salesperson should start showing him items in the medium-priced range and then work up or down, according to the customer's reactions. It is also important not to display so many items to start with that the customer gets confused. Instead, the salesperson should show the customer just enough merchandise to enable him or her to make comparisons. Two or three neckties, three or four shirts, two or three blouses, one or two dresses, or seven or eight pieces of costume jewelry are usually all that should be displayed at one time. These are good rules for specific merchandise. But all the time that the salesperson is waiting on the customer, he should stay alert to the customer's responses so that he will be able to find the exact item to suit the customer's needs.

SUMMING UP

In the approach the salesman is trying to accomplish the first two steps in the selling process. He wants (1) to gain the favorable attention of the prospect and (2) to arouse interest in the product or service he is selling. He has only a few minutes in which to accomplish this.

Because the first few minutes with the prospect are so important, the salesman prepares himself for the meeting as intelligently and thoroughly as he can. This advance preparation is called the preapproach; and it requires the salesman to consider his appearance, his attitude, his knowledge of his product, his prospect, the organization of his sales presentation, and his timing.

To succeed in the approach, the salesman must give proper attention to the three essential ingredients of the approach: the right setting, the strong opener, and the relationship of the approach to the sales presentation. In trying to create the right setting for the sale, the salesman must take the initiative in establishing a friendly atmosphere, and he must be able to get past the secretary or receptionist and to handle the unwilling prospect. His opening remarks, which are the most important words of the entire interview, must be positive, definite, to the point, vivid, and appealing to the particular prospect. Finally, the salesman must stay alert to the prospect's reactions so that he can gauge the exact moment when he can start his presentation. He should do this the minute he senses that the prospect's interest has been aroused.

All the principles of the approach can be applied to retail selling, with special emphasis on the salesman's appearance, his efforts to create a friendly atmosphere, his opening remarks, and his analysis of the customer's needs.

Reviewing Your Reading

1. What is the salesman trying to accomplish in the approach?
2. How much time is involved in the approach?
3. What does the salesman call the advance work that he does before he makes the approach?
4. What are the six categories that the salesman should consider in the preapproach?
5. Why is the salesman's appearance so important to the success of the approach? Is the salesman's appearance also important in retail selling?

6. What is the most basic thing that the salesman should know about the prospect? Why is this so important?
7. How does it help the salesman to know details about the prospect's personal life? Give three specific examples of how this works.
8. Why is it necessary that the salesman's plans for his presentation be flexible?
9. Why should the salesman consider what would be the best time to approach the prospect?
10. Why do some people react initially to a salesman with resistance and suspicion?
11. Should the salesman make it a rule always to shake hands with the prospect?
12. Why is it important for the salesman to make a favorable impression on the secretary or receptionist? How can the salesman accomplish this?
13. If the salesman does not have the prospect's full attention, should he begin the sale? Explain your answer.
14. What are the ten types of opening statements? Describe each one briefly.
15. How does the salesman know when he should end the approach and begin the presentation?
16. Why is promptness essential in retail selling?
17. What opening remarks can a salesman in a retail store make that will be pleasing to the customer? What remarks will be displeasing to the customer?
18. How does a good retail salesman handle the problem of finding out how much the customer wants to spend?

For Discussion

1. Think back to a recent sales situation in which you were the customer. Describe the efforts the salesperson used to interest you. Was he successful or unsuccessful? What would you have done under the same circumstances?
2. Assume that you are a salesman for movie cameras. Prepare a question opener for each of the following prospects:
   a. Young couple with a new baby
   b. Elderly widow who is going to Europe for the first time
   c. Man whose young son is the star pitcher for the Little League
3. Assume that you are a salesperson helping a customer to decide on a blouse. Another customer is waiting to be served and seems impatient. How would you handle this situation?
4. The product approach is used in retail selling to keep the customer's mind on the merchandise that he is examining. What remarks could you make about the following items?

a. Vacuum cleaner   e. Copper teakettle
b. New style of necktie   f. Electric coffee maker
c. Woman's suit   g. Bathroom scales
d. Oriental rug   h. Tricycle

5. A customer had been waiting a long time for service and was finally approached by a salesperson who greeted her by saying, "May I help you?" The customer replied, "Well, I should think so! What do you think I've been standing here for? A bus?" If you were this salesperson, what would you do next?

6. Discuss how you would approach a customer in a retail store who wants to be approached and another who does not want to be approached.

Sales Problem I

Read and criticize the following sales situation which occurred in a retail dress department:

CUSTOMER: I'd like to see some of those rayon print dresses you have on sale.

SALESPERSON: **What color would you like to see?**

CUSTOMER: I want a navy blue or black—something dark.

SALESPERSON (*looking on rack holding all large sizes*): **I'm afraid I can't fit you in either a dark blue or a black in the sale dresses. May I show you what we have in the regular stock?**

CUSTOMER: They cost more, don't they?

SALESPERSON: **Yes, but they are usually newer styles and better dresses.**

CUSTOMER: No, I'll just look at the dresses on this rack.

SALESPERSON (*showing a gray dress*): **I suppose you wouldn't want a gray one?**

CUSTOMER: No, I believe not.

SALESPERSON: **Nor a light blue?**

CUSTOMER: No, I don't think so.

SALESPERSON: **Here are a beige and a tan in your size. These are nicer dresses.**

CUSTOMER: No, I don't wear light shades.

SALESPERSON: **Then you wouldn't want a white one. This is an organdy.**

CUSTOMER (*still looking about and hesitating*): No, I look too large in white.

SALESPERSON: **Sorry we couldn't fit you. Come in again sometime.**

CUSTOMER: Well, perhaps I'd better, although I did want to get a dress today.

QUESTIONS

1. What mistakes did the salesperson make?

2. Rewrite the sale, correcting the mistakes that were made and adding any selling techniques that you would have used.

A door-to-door salesman tells the housewife that he is representing a public-opinion poll and that he would like to ask her a few questions. He shows her some credentials that seem to prove what he says. Once inside the house, however, he immediately launches into a "hard-sell" talk on why she should subscribe to his magazines.

QUESTIONS

1. Do you think the salesman's approach is a good one?
2. What do you think the housewife's reaction will be when she discovers the salesman is really selling magazines?
3. Prepare what you think would be an effective approach for a door-to-door magazine salesman.

George Ashcraft is the owner of a new music store in a fast-growing suburban district, located about 20 miles from a big city shopping center. The store has a complete line of musical instruments, radios, high-fidelity and stereo equipment, television sets, sheet music, and records.

When he first opened his store, Ashcraft took quarter-page advertisements in a local newspaper, which is delivered to all residents free of charge. Then to promote sales, he decided to call at every home in the immediate area of his store to tell the residents about the store. Since there are more than 2,000 homes in the area, he decided to make his calls short and snappy, allowing no more than one minute for each call. He introduced himself to the householder, presented his business card, and briefly stated that he had recently opened a new music store in the neighborhood.

After one week, during which he called at approximately 400 houses, Ashcraft became discouraged. Not one call had resulted in any business for the store. Moreover, since he had spent all his time soliciting, Mrs. Ashcraft had had to take care of the store, and sales were slower than they might have been had Ashcraft been there himself.

QUESTIONS

1. What do you think was wrong with Ashcraft's solicitation method?
2. Write out a door-to-door approach that you believe would have achieved better results for Ashcraft. (Review the types of approaches discussed in this chapter.

1. Prepare a list of ten things to avoid in the retail sales approach. For instance, you could start with the following:

    a. Avoid lengthy conversations with other salespeople.

    b. Avoid chewing gum.

    c. Avoid asking, "How much do you want to spend?"

2. Prepare a list of five things to avoid in the specialty sales approach.

3. Assume that you are selling a new type of lawn sprinkler from door to door. The sprinkler is timed to move along the lawn automatically, so that the householder has only to turn it on and then reset it occasionally to get his whole lawn watered. It delivers about 6 gallons of water a minute and has a four-position spray-control dial. It sells for $9.95. Decide on four out of the ten approaches discussed in this chapter that you could use to sell this sprinkler, and write out in dialogue form exactly what you would say and do.

4. Prepare three different product approaches that you could use if you were selling the same sprinkler in problem 3 in a hardware or garden supply store.

5. Assume that you are an industrial salesman calling on purchasing agents in their offices. You are selling a liquid plastic floor compound that works perfectly on wood or linoleum. It seals floors with a skidproof satin gloss and makes waxing them unnecessary. It is easily applied. All you have to do is wipe the compound on with a cloth and let it dry for one hour. A gallon costs $6. From the ten openers discussed in this chapter, choose five that you could use to sell this product. Write them in dialogue form, making them brief and to the point.

6. Write out for each of the following a question opener that you think will gain the attention of the prospect:

    a. Portable typewriter to be sold to a college student

    b. Fur coat to be sold to a woman whose husband has just received a promotion

    c. Electric train to be sold to the father of three small boys

    d. Set of encyclopedias to be sold to the same man

    e. Automobile seat belts to be sold to a man who commutes to work on a superhighway

13

Conducting the Presentation

YOU HAVE MADE a successful approach: you have gained the favorable attention of the prospect and you have aroused his interest in the product. Your next step is to translate this interest into desire, for there is a big difference between the two. A visitor to Paris is interested in the Eiffel Tower, but he doesn't want to own it. Similarly your prospect may find your product fascinating. He may smile appreciatively and say, "What won't they think up next?" He may even go home and entertain his family at dinner by telling them about the amazing new product that he has just seen. But he won't buy it unless you make him *want* it. You have to show him clearly and conclusively why he needs this product, what it will do for him, and why he would be making a mistake to try to get along without it any longer.

The part of the sale where the salesman attempts to turn the interest that he has gained for his product into the desire to own it is known as the *presentation*. It is the heart of the selling process.

239

■ The presentation—turning interest into desire—is the heart of the selling process.

Courtesy The Singer Company

Nine Rules for a Successful Presentation

There are nine basic rules for a successful presentation:

1. Prepare your presentation carefully in advance.
2. Concentrate on the particular prospect.
3. Tell your story well.
4. Appeal to the prospect's five senses.
5. Dramatize your presentation.
6. Put the prospect into the act.
7. Get the prospect to commit himself.
8. Know how to handle interruptions.
9. Know where to start and when to stop.

Prepare Your Presentation Carefully in Advance. It is a cardinal rule in selling that the salesman cannot rely on his ability always to say exactly what he wants to say on the spur of the moment. This ability is very rare, and then even at its very best it is no substitute for careful advance preparation. The salesman who thinks out ahead of time what he is going to say about the product and how he is going to say it to the particular prospect will consistently outsell the salesman who works on a hit-or-miss basis. The prepared salesman can tell his story in a fraction of the time it takes the unprepared salesman—and with much more wallop. The knowledge that he can do this gives the salesman a special feeling of self-confidence that is both attractive and reassuring to the prospect.

When the salesman plans his presentation, he first decides the best way to tell his sales story in general—that is, to any prospect. From that general plan he decides how he will tell the story to that *particular* prospect. The more he has learned about that particular prospect in his preapproach work, the more specifically he is able to plan his presentation to suit that prospect. But at the same time, the salesman must keep his presentation flexible, since he has no way of knowing exactly how the prospect will react during the interview. The salesman will then be able to adapt his presentation to the exact needs of the particular prospect when he meets the prospect face to face.

Concentrate on the Particular Prospect. The salesman goes into the sale knowing that he is about to face a person who is quite different from everyone else and who is therefore likely to react to the salesman and the salesman's story in an unpredictable way. The salesman has to tell his story in terms that this particular prospect can comprehend. The prospect must be made to understand what benefits and satisfactions he, especially, stands to gain by buying the product. In order to get through to the prospect as personally and directly as possible, the salesman should consider the following four points: (1) the you attitude, (2) the prospect's temperament, (3) the prospect's needs and desires, and (4) the choice of material for each interview.

The You Attitude. The frequent use of the prospect's name and of the words *you* and *your* is, of course, one way to personalize a sales talk. But the really good salesman has developed what has been called *the you attitude*, which simply means that he is able to imagine himself in the prospect's shoes. He tries to think like the prospect and to see his product through the prospect's eyes.

The travel agent is a good example of the kind of salesman who can be more successful if he has the you attitude. In a day's time the agent may see three people who want to go to Bermuda—a young man who is planning a honeymoon, a recently graduated nurse who will be traveling with her roommate, and a wealthy elderly widow who wants accommodations for herself and her companion. Actually the travel agent has his own favorite hotel in Bermuda, and if he didn't have the you attitude, he would simply send all three clients to the hotel that he himself enjoys so much. But the sympathetic travel agent forgets his own preferences and tries instead to imagine what it is that each of these people really wants from a Bermuda vacation. As a result, the honeymooners are sent to the hotel that caters to young couples their own age, the young nurse and her girl friend go where there is very likely to be much excitement and possibly many young men, and the elderly widow gets all the luxurious gentility that she is accustomed to.

The Prospect's Temperament. One of the main reasons why the salesman's plans for his presentation must be flexible is that he must be able to adapt what he says and how he says it to the temperament of the prospect. The salesman is not usually able to get much advance information about temperament, and what he does get may be misleading because people show different facets of their personalities at different times. For instance, a man who knows Mr. George Hall socially suggests to the salesman that Mr. Hall might be a prospect. The salesman is told that Mr. Hall is an extremely friendly and pleasant man, which of course he is—socially. But it turns out that in his office Mr. Hall is not quite so friendly. Once he is behind his desk he is aggressive, opinionated, and extremely hard to reach.

Since accurate advance information about temperament is so hard to get, the salesman tries to gather all the information that he can about the prospect during the approach and throughout the presentation. By listening carefully to what the prospect says and by observing his mannerisms, the salesman can qualify the prospect as to type and then alter the plans during his presentation accordingly.

When the salesman is trying to "type" the prospect, he must remember that the most fascinating thing about working with people is that they do not fit into neat little pigeonholes. Every individual combines the elements of several types in varying proportions. But at the same time, a list of general types and suggestions for dealing with each one can point the way for the beginning salesman. Such a list, taken from one of the sales manuals of the Burroughs Corporation, is given on the opposite page.

The Prospect's Needs and Desires. As you learned in Chapter 8, every person has certain needs and desires that are both personal and individual. In order to make a sale, the salesman must find out what those needs and desires are and then show the prospect in very definite terms how his product can satisfy them. If the salesman is able to pinpoint these buying motives in his preapproach work, so much the better; but he must stay alert during the sale itself for any clues that are to be found in what the prospect says and does.

■ By discovering his customer's needs and wants, the salesman can then proceed to show her how his product will satisfy those needs and wants.

HOW TO HANDLE DIFFERENT TYPES OF CUSTOMERS

The Type	Key to Strategy
1. Deliberate, methodical, fair-minded.	Slow down—explain details.
2. Impulsive, fast, changeable.	Speed up—omit details.
3. Skeptical, suspicious, "show me."	Agree on minor points, and expand. Be conservative in assertions.
4. Nervous, irritable, high-strung.	Use a quiet, tactful, soothing manner.
5. Pessimistic, grouchy, complaining.	Listen patiently, and ask questions to find the real reasons. Hear him out.
6. Egotistical, opinionated, "high-hat."	Flatter his ego. Concentrate on the immediate sale.
7. Argumentative, blustering, insincere.	Courage and sincerity create respect —and will win.
8. Timid, nonassertive, "poor mixer."	Reassure his timid soul by your quiet manner, simple explanation, and sincere compliments.
9. Talkative, friendly, sociable.	Lead him back repeatedly by using his own words to renew your sales talk. Otherwise, "Be bright, be brief, be gone."
10. Silent, secretive, clamlike.	Be more personal than usual to draw him out.
11. Procrastinator, staller, "putter-offer."	Emphasize the losses caused by delay, and flatter his power of decision. Use action to overcome indecision.

"The Prospect and How He Thinks," *Burroughs Salesmanship, A Course in Selling Principles*, Burroughs Corporation, Detroit, p. 11.

As an example, consider the case of a salesman for a company that remodels kitchens. In a newspaper ad his company has offered a brochure of its kitchen designs to anyone who will send in the coupon in the ad. Four women from the same section of town have sent in the coupons, and these are turned over to the salesman after the brochures have been mailed out. By asking around, the salesman finds that all four women are middle-aged, they belong to the local country club, their husbands are all executives, and all four live in well-kept but older houses. The picture that emerges is that the salesman has four legitimate prospects, each of whom can afford a new kitchen and is probably serious in her request for information.

This salesman is an old hand at dealing with housewives, so that he knows, in spite of their similar tastes and environment, each is quite different from the other. During each interview he tries to get at the real reason why each woman wants a new kitchen. He finds that Mrs. Harrison's motive is doing the Joneses one better. Two members of her bridge club have a new kitchen, and she is literally eaten up with envy. Money is no object as long as she can get a kitchen that will top those of her friends. Mrs. White's chief desire is for beauty. The rest of her house is elegantly decorated, so she's very unhappy with the drabness of the old kitchen. Mrs. Laing sees herself as an amateur time-and-motion expert. She wants a kitchen that is organized for the greatest possible efficiency. The fourth prospect, Mrs. Barker, is thinking in terms of economic gain. Her husband is going to be transferred, and they feel that they can get a much greater return on their money if they do over the kitchen before they try to sell the house.

The salesman will be well repaid for the effort that he has made to get at the real motives of these four prospects. First of all, he will say exactly the right things to each of them and thus will be able to close each sale successfully. Secondly, he will have four very satisfied customers, because he will be able to give each woman the new kitchen that exactly answers her particular needs and desires.

The Choice of Material for Each Interview. The product that you are selling has many features to recommend it, and in your advance planning for your presentation you should plan exactly how you can best demonstrate each one of those features. But once you are actually in the sales situation and have made your observations about the prospect's personality and motives as recommended above, you will realize that some of your selling points are not going to be of any interest at all to this particular prospect and that you can hit twice as hard as you had planned on some of the other features. For instance, suppose that you are selling Cadillac cars. The prospect indicates to you early in the sale that he has never driven over 50 miles an hour in his life and never intends to. So you leave out of your sales story any reference to how well the Cadillac holds the road at high speeds and how powerful its engine is. Instead you emphasize and reemphasize the car's comfort and safety features.

When a salesman merely goes down through a list of the features of his product, giving each one equal billing, he is in effect saying to the prospect, "I'll tell you all about my proposition, and you figure out how it will work into your situation." But most people don't have the patience to do this, and indeed many simply can't find the connection on their own. Therefore, the salesman must accept the full responsibility for bringing the prospect and the product together through his choice of material.

Tell Your Story Well. The salesman should remember that his main purpose in telling his sales story is to communicate ideas to the prospect. This is possible only if the salesman can get the prospect to *really listen* to what the salesman is saying. Because listening is actually a quite difficult art, the salesman has to do all that he can *to make it easy for the prospect to listen.*

The salesman will make a good start on getting the prospect to listen if he will give some attention to the mechanics of speaking, as was discussed in Chapter 7. His voice should be pleasant, his pace should be natural and conversational, and he should vary both the tone and the volume as he talks. The salesman should aim for such clarity in what he says that the prospect not only can understand him but also cannot possibly misunderstand him. To do this, the salesman has to talk in terms that are familiar to the prospect. For the average layman, technical terms should be translated into everyday language. Short, simple words should be used in preference to more complicated words that may be over the prospect's head.

Another way to achieve clarity is to arrange the selling points in logical order —there should be no sudden or abrupt transitions from one thought to another. Each point should lead smoothly into the next point, so that the prospect never has to attempt to make the connections himself.

And while words should be short and simple, they should be very specific, with precise meanings that no one could take any way but the way the salesman intends. One familiar example of lack of precision is the word *funny,* which can mean amusing, witty, ridiculous, queer, or eccentric. Nine times out of ten when you say that someone is funny, the person to whom you are talking will say to you, "How do you mean that?" Such ambiguous words should be avoided. Also, if a certain word is too vague in meaning, the salesman should pin it down with words that qualify it correctly. For example, a customer in a dress shop is extremely pleased with the style of a certain dress but doesn't like the color. If the salesgirl says to her, "I can get that dress for you in red," the customer feels too vague about the color to take a chance on ordering the dress. But if the salesgirl says Chinese red or cranberry red or true red, the customer feels more sure about placing an order.

The salesman should also avoid those words and expressions that have become so hackneyed that they no longer mean anything at all. Statements such as "This little number is really a honey" or "You can't go wrong on this one" don't say anything to the prospect. And such clichéd words as *nice, good,* and *fine* have become virtually useless. It is also ineffective to use words that overstate the case for the product, such as *terrific, sensational, unbelievable, stupendous, incomparable,* and so on. While these words used to work for the sideshow barker who was trying to entice the "suckers" inside, they are out of place in modern selling.

At the same time that the salesman is trying to be as clear, specific, and accurate as possible, he must also try to make his story interesting and vivid. To do this, he should use figures of speech that are not only colorful but also appropriate to the prospect's experience. A simile, metaphor, or analogy concerned with deep-sea fishing would almost certainly fail to click with a prospect who has grown corn in Iowa all his life. But if the salesman is trying to sell the farmer a new heating system for the farmhouse, he can count on this kind of statement to put across his point: "Mr. Farmer, with this furnace, even in the coldest weather every room of your house will be as comfortably warm as a cornfield at noon on a June day."

The last point to be made about the salesman's story is that it must make an appeal to the prospect's reasoning. The farmer just mentioned wants to know how difficult the new heating system will be to install and its cost, how much it will cost to operate the heating system, what kind of service he will get, and so on. The salesman will have to present these points so that the farmer feels that he is doing the logical, rational thing by making this purchase. If the prospect is a professional purchasing agent, this emphasis on facts becomes the most important part of the sale. But even the ordinary prospect likes to feel that he is being very levelheaded and businesslike about his purchases. In fact, the more emotional he actually is about the purchase, the more he wants the salesman to rationalize it for him.

Appeal to the Prospect's Five Senses. When he talks, the salesman is trying to make an impression on the prospect's mind through the prospect's sense of hearing. But the prospect has four other senses, too, which carry information to his brain—sight, touch, taste, and smell. Each of these senses is so essential to the individual's perception of the world around him that we say he is handicapped when he has lost the use of any one of them. But at the same time, they are not equal in their importance. Taste, touch, and smell are together at the bottom of the scale; next comes hearing; and then at the top is the sense of sight, which accounts for about four-fifths of your total impressions. Also, what you see is registered faster and retained longer than the impressions gained through the other senses. These facts tend to make the sense of sight the most trusted of all the senses as is evidenced by how often you hear such remarks as "I'll believe that when I see it" or "I never would have believed it if I hadn't seen it with my own eyes."

Courtesy Fairchild Camera and Instrument Corporation

■ The salesman must appeal to his prospect's sense of sight as well as to his sense of hearing.

One significant fact about the senses is that while you can learn through any one of them, you can learn *more* and learn *better* when you collect data about the same subject through more than one sense at a time. It has been estimated that a man remembers 20 percent of what he hears, 40 percent of what he sees, and 80 percent of what he both hears and sees.

The first rule for the salesman that comes out of these facts is *never tell what you can show.* Think how many words you would have to use and how long it would take to describe something as simple as a chair, for instance. And when you finished, even if the prospect had managed not to go to sleep in the middle of your lengthy description, he probably would say doubtfully, "I think I see what you mean." But show him a picture of the chair or the chair itself and he will get the message immediately and accurately. This means that if the salesman cannot use the product itself, he should use pictures, graphs, charts, diagrams, movies, portfolios, brochures, catalogs, material swatches, color cards, scale models, cross sections, parts of the product testimonial, or anything else that the prospect can *see.* If the salesman is selling intangibles, such as an insurance program, and can't think of any visual aids at all, he can at least use a pad and pencil to jot down the important points of his presentation as he goes along. Then at the end, he can *show* the prospect the summary. But the salesman who does not in some way take advantage of the prospect's sense of sight is "flying on one wing."

The second rule for the salesman is *never simply show what you can also tell.* The best example of this point is a corkscrew. You could not possibly describe a corkscrew adequately without showing it. But on the other hand, if you simply handed it to a prospect who had never seen one before, he wouldn't know how to use it. For maximum effect, you have to combine the showing and the telling. When the prospect is looking at a picture, he may not see what you want him to see, so supply the words that will direct his attention where you want it. Also, some of the most important features of the product may be hidden. For instance, on the automatic washer the prospect can see only the enamel outside; you have to supply the information that it is enamel baked over steel. This principle of showing and telling simultaneously provides the repetition that is so essential for getting through to the prospect and yet doesn't bore him.

The salesman should also *explore every possibility for using the other senses.* *Show* the prospect a fabric, *tell* him that it's soft and supple, and then prove your point by letting him *feel* it. Put the product or product part into his hands whenever possible. Let him manipulate it, feel the weight of it, find out how hard or how smooth or how rugged it is. Get him to sit in the chair, lie on the mattress, drive the car, turn the dials on the television set, or swing the tennis racket. Let him smell the flowers, the perfume, the freshly ground coffee, or the newly baked rolls. Get him to taste the difference between two cheeses. Let him hear the lively fizz of a beverage being opened, and then let him taste it. Remember that famous steak houses cook their steaks where the customers can hear the sizzle.

As a final application of the information about the senses, the salesman should *remember that sometimes the absence of a sensation can be a selling point.* The salesman should capitalize on the fact that the cleaning fluid has no unpleasant odor, the water heater doesn't make any noise, and the light source can't be seen.

Dramatize Your Presentation. A certain amount of "stage business," or showmanship, has to go into every presentation. This is the ingredient that saves the presentation from being ordinary and humdrum. It is not a difficult ingredient to understand. You already know that the good storyteller puts drama into his story by using pauses to pique the listener's curiosity and by choosing vivid, colorful words that are full of action. And you realize that the appeal to the senses has an element of the dramatic built into it, too. The important thing is that the salesman should learn how to heighten this. The jeweler is going to show the prospect a pearl necklace. He opens the case slowly, takes out the necklace gently with both hands because it is so precious and must not be dropped, holds it for a few minutes so that it catches the light, and then places it lovingly on a velvet pad. He is appealing to the prospect's sense of sight, of course, but with a very important plus.

A hat salesman dramatizes a wrinkle-resistant hat by crushing it in his hands, stepping on it, and then straightening it out and showing that it is as good as new. A toy salesman demonstrates the sturdiness of a toy truck by standing on it. A salesman for a new plastic surface coating demonstrates the indestructibility of this new material by trying to scratch the surface of a board that has been coated with it. He also tries to burn it with a match, pours ink and acids on it, and then hits it hard with a hammer.

Suspense is built into each one of these examples. Will the hat be ruined? Will the toy truck crumble? Will one of the acids eat through the plastic? This brings up the obvious point that each salesman had better be sure that the answer to such questions will be "no." If he says, "You see how easy it is to close up this sewing machine," then it had better be easy to close! The salesman should practice ahead of time the "stage business" that he is going to use to be sure that everything is in good working order. He should not be satisfied with planning *what* he is going to do; he should also know exactly *how* he is going to do it.

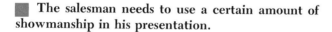 The salesman needs to use a certain amount of showmanship in his presentation.

Put the Prospect into the Act. The best example of the importance of putting the prospect into the act is the story of an expert typist who decided to sell typewriters. He thought he would be a natural at selling them since he could demonstrate his lightning speed and great accuracy. But he turned in only a fraction of the sales of another salesman who typed very poorly and awkwardly. The latter salesman would simply put the machine in front of his prospect and say, "Here, just try this keyboard. Doesn't it work lightly and smoothly?"

The prospect doesn't want to know whether the salesman can operate the product; he wants to know whether he can operate it himself. The vacuum-cleaner salesman can make a brilliant demonstration of all the things the vacuum cleaner can do, but he will be closer to the end of the sale when he places the vacuum cleaner in the housewife's hand and says, "Here, you try it." This makes the woman feel that she is making up her own mind and takes away any latent feeling that she is being persuaded against her will. Also, once the vacuum cleaner is in her hands, she gets the feeling of ownership and begins to think in terms of how awful it would be *not* to own this machine that she can handle so easily.

When a salesman is selling intangibles, it is harder to get the prospect into the act, but the clever salesman can figure out a way of making this principle work for him. If he is selling stocks and bonds, for instance, he can hand the prospect a pencil and pad and say, "Now I'm going to show you how you can get $5,800 or more for $5,000, and you can figure it out for yourself."

It is also effective to put someone close to the prospect into the sale, as for instance, a child. The salesman of a convertible sofa says to the woman, "It's so simple a child can operate it"; and then to prove his point beyond any doubt, he gets the woman's six-year-old daughter to open up the sofa. The salesman of a mobile book cart for a school gets one of the pupils to push the cart to demonstrate its lightness and maneuverability to the principal.

Get the Prospect to Commit Himself. The salesman must keep his finger on the pulse of the interview. It is essential for him to realize that the sale is not a *monologue* on his part, but a *conversation* between two people. Remembering this will make it easy for the salesman to keep track of the prospect's reactions.

The salesman should be sure that the prospect understands each selling point before he moves on to the next one. If the prospect does not make any comment on his own, the salesman should ask a question to see what he is thinking. The question should not be something like the overworked "See?" or "Do you understand what I mean?" These questions insult the prospect's intelligence, for they cast doubt on his ability to get the point. The salesman would be more tactful if he said, "Did I make that point perfectly clear? I'm afraid I

██ Putting the customer into the act helps to give him the feeling of ownership.

didn't put it very well." Such a question invites a frank answer from the prospect and gives the salesman the opportunity to clear up any doubts right then and there, so that they don't block the closing of the sale.

The salesman can also check on whether he is getting his point across by asking such seemingly innocent questions as, "Doesn't your experience check with that, Mr. Prospect?" or "Isn't that large freezer chest across the top a worthwhile feature?" The answers to such questions will indicate to the salesman whether his explanations have been full enough and also which points are and are not especially appealing to the prospect. Suppose, for instance, that the prospect replies that the freezer chest across the top of the refrigerator is nice, but that she doesn't care much one way or the other because there are only three in the family and they use very few frozen foods. The salesman would then know that he shouldn't emphasize this particular point further but should hit harder on the capacity of the main part of the refrigerator and the storage space in the door.

By getting agreement from the prospect on each selling point in the presentation, the salesman gets the prospect into the mood for the final "yes" that closes the sale. Here is an example of how a retail salesman gets agreement from his customer:

SALESPERSON: Mr. Wendell, you say you want a traveling case that will wear, isn't that right?

CUSTOMER: Yes, that's right.

SALESPERSON: This piece of luggage is made of top-grain leather, much thicker than the less-expensive pieces. Also, notice the rounded leather-reinforced edges that resist handling and wear. Then, too, the catches and locks are made of the finest-quality steel and put together with the same care that goes into the making of a fine watch. You would agree that all these things are essential for long wear, wouldn't you?

CUSTOMER: Yes, that seems very logical.

SALESPERSON: You will also want a piece of luggage that is distinctive when you travel, isn't that correct?

CUSTOMER: Yes, that's so.

SALESPERSON: That's why this bag is such a good seller. It combines sound construction with beauty and distinction. You wouldn't be ashamed of carrying this case around, would you?

CUSTOMER: Certainly not. Tell me, does this case have a solid wood frame?

SALESPERSON (*tapping the case*): Absolutely. You can tell by the sound. That's another thing you want to make sure of in luggage of good quality. Isn't that true?

CUSTOMER: Yes, it is.

SALESPERSON: Now let me show you all the little extra things about this piece of luggage that make it such a popular item.

Know How to Handle Interruptions. The salesman's recognition of the fact that the sale is a "two-way street" will make him welcome the interruptions that come from the prospect himself in the form of questions and comments. In order to overcome the prospect's reservations, the salesman has to get them out into the open. But there are other interruptions to the sale that are not so welcome. The businessman may get a telephone call that goes on for ten minutes, or his secretary may come in with an urgent message. The housewife may have to run outside to comfort her little boy who has fallen down. Such interruptions are very unfortunate, because they break the mood that the salesman has worked so hard to create.

When the interruption is over, it is a mistake for the salesman simply to start in where he left off. The prospect usually makes this evident, because he invariably says something like, "Now where were we?" Since he can't think about two things at once, he had to stop thinking about what the salesman was saying while he handled the other problem. Now he can't quite get his attention focused again. The salesman should help him by going back a little in the sale and reviewing some of the points that had been made prior to the interruption. This gives the prospect time to recall the thoughts and feelings that he has had so far about the product. Here is an example:

SALESMAN: **Mr. Retailer, just before your phone call, we were talking about how tough the Wearever overalls are and how long they last. I was telling you about the reinforcement of the seams that really holds at all the points of special stress. Now I'd like to show you a piece of the denim from which our overalls are made. Just feel the strength of the weave in that material.**

Sometimes the interruption is one that not only distracts the prospect, but puts him in a very bad humor. Perhaps a piece of business information has been relayed to him that is going to create real problems for him, and he is distracted and worried about it. In such a case the salesman might as well realize that he is not going to be able to recapture the interest that he had built up. He should take the initiative in suggesting that the rest of the sales talk be postponed until a time more convenient for the prospect. He can say, "Mr. Prospect, I can see that you have something else that needs your attention. Why don't I arrange another appointment with your secretary so that I won't hold you up today?" Usually the prospect will be grateful enough for the salesman's consideration that he will make a special effort to be courteous to the salesman on the return visit.

Know Where to Start and When to Stop. The usual answer to the question of where to start and when to stop is to start at the beginning and stop when you have reached the end. But for the salesman involved in making a sales presentation, the answer is not so simple. The salesman very often has to forget the beginning that he has planned for his presentation and jump in in the middle. And often he will find that his opportunity to close the sale has come long before he has covered all his selling points.

The key to the salesman's course of action is in a simple question that he should keep asking himself: "In what stage is the prospect's mind?" A busy prospect does not want to listen to all the reasons why no home should be without color television when he has already fully made up his mind to buy a set and only wants to find one that is priced right. On the other hand, the prospect may be undecided. For example, a man goes into a store to buy a pipe. Most pipe buyers know exactly what they want; however, this man has never smoked a pipe before and really doesn't know the first thing about them. He has been a heavy cigarette smoker but has decided that a pipe would be better for him. Unless the salesman tells a full sales story, the prospect will not be able to make a decision.

As you can see from these two examples, there can be a wide variation in how far along the prospect has gone toward a buying decision before he even meets the salesman. By listening carefully to what the prospect says in the beginning of the sale, the salesman can judge where to start his sales story. And by continuing to stay alert during the presentation, the salesman can sense the right moment to try for a close. Since this right moment for the closing may come at any time during the sale, the salesman must watch continuously for signals that the prospect is convinced enough to buy. The subject of when and how to close a sale will be discussed fully in Chapter 15, but the point to remember now is that the salesman cannot possibly plan the time of the closing in advance. On this point, as on so many other points in the presentation, the salesman must be prepared to be flexible.

The Presentation in Retail Selling

Many of the examples given so far in this chapter are examples from retail selling, because the principles of making a retail presentation are basically the same as the principles involved in any other presentation. But there are certain additional suggestions that can be made to the student who is interested in retail selling. This information can be divided into four categories: (1) deciding what merchandise to show, (2) handling specific requests, (3) making the merchandise seem desirable, and (4) making product knowledge work.

Deciding What Merchandise to Show. The retail salesperson's main job is to display the right goods to the customer and thus help him come to a buying decision. The salesperson does this by listening very carefully to what the prospect says during the approach and throughout the presentation. Like any other salesman, he has to find out what the prospect really wants.

The retail salesperson should let the goods that he shows ask some of his questions for him—that is, he should begin showing goods before asking questions that would tend to pinpoint the customer's wants. This way he can get the answers to his questions from the customer's reactions to the goods. For example, a woman goes into a linen store and asks to see some place mats. Instead of asking her immediately about color and design, the salesgirl begins to show her some mats. The first set shown is yellow and brings forth the response that the customer would prefer all-white. For the second set the salesgirl chooses white organdy, and the customer says she does want something that is elegant-looking but would prefer linen. The third set is white embroidered linen, and the customer now seems very interested but still hesitant. The fourth set, also white embroidered linen but with a slightly different design, suits the customer perfectly.

■ It is often up to the retail salesperson to decide what merchandise to show. The customer will buy only if the salesperson is able to display the right goods to her.

Courtesy Joseph Magnin, San Francisco

There is a very sound principle behind this recommendation to start showing goods immediately. The more qualifications you let the customer tack onto his initial request for a product, the more you increase the odds that you won't be able to answer the request. A woman says, "I want an evening dress." Fine. You have plenty of evening dresses. You ask, "What size?" She answers, "Size 12." Then you come back with, "What color?" She replies, "It must be royal blue, and I want it with a beaded top." That does it. You simply don't have a dress that meets all those requirements. You have asked too many questions before showing her anything.

The customer who has made such a definite request can sometimes be talked into looking at other items (this will be discussed in more detail below); but very often, by the time the customer has gone all through his list of qualifications, he has talked himself into the idea that that exact item is what he really wants and he won't settle for anything else. By showing merchandise right away, before the customer can become so definite, the salesperson can usually give the customer some new ideas about the kind of product that will answer his needs.

Handling Specific Requests. It is a rule in retail selling that the specific requests of the customer must be honored. Nothing makes a customer more angry than being shown everything but the one thing he has said he wants. This is why the salesperson tries to keep the customer from getting too specific too soon. But suppose the customer is quite determined, and the item that he says he wants is not in stock. Is there anything the salesperson can do?

The salesperson should realize that every store has to be selective about what merchandise it will and will not carry. Sometimes he can handle the determined customer by explaining the store's reasoning. For example, a man goes into a hardware store and says, "I want some Quik-Off paint remover." The salesman can say, "I'm sorry, sir, we don't carry that brand," or he can say, "We don't carry that brand because we have found that while it is very effective in getting off the paint, it is too thin and is hard to control. We carry Lift-Clean remover. It's every bit as effective as Quik-Off, but much easier to work with." The customer will be grateful for this kind of frank answer and probably will accept the substitute. The salesman has shown that he is eager to serve the best interests of the customer.

The salesgirl who has to deal with the woman who wants the size-12 royal blue evening dress with the beaded top can also indicate a real desire to be of service. This might not pay off in an immediate sale, but it will make the customer think well of the salesgirl and the store. The salesgirl can say tactfully, "I'm terribly sorry we don't have a dress like that. I think you may have a hard time finding one, because royal blue is not one of the big colors this spring. While you're here, why don't you just look at what else we have; and then if you don't find the dress you have in mind elsewhere, you can always come back." This kind of answer saves the customer's pride and makes it easy for her to return to the store if she has to.

Making the Merchandise Seem Desirable. The decor of the store, its lighting, and the way the goods are displayed, all play a large part in making the merchandise seem desirable to the customer. Also, the salesperson's attitude is a very important factor in how the customer feels about the merchandise.

The salesperson should handle the goods as though he thinks they are very valuable. Suppose, for instance, that the salesperson sells leather handbags for women. The handbags are all kept in a case behind the counter, and the salesperson has to take them out of the case and hand them to the customer. If he reaches hurriedly into the case, grabs a couple of bags, and flings them down on the counter, the customer will think that these are pretty ordinary bags. But if the salesperson handles the bags reverently from start to finish, the customer will get the impression that the bags must be something special.

This salesperson should also give the customer a brief sales talk about each bag to increase the customer's desire for it. For instance, he could say, "Just feel the leather in this bag. It's the softest and finest calfskin we have in any bag in

■ Product knowledge not only increases sales but is helpful to the customer as well. In explaining the essential facts about his product, the salesman is making effective use of his product knowledge.

the store. And please look at the construction details. When you see that kind of perfection, you know that you have a top-quality bag."

The salesperson should be able to make this type of brief, but interesting and specific, comment about each piece of merchandise that he shows. He should try to hit on the chief selling feature of each item. In making this comment, the salesperson should use a positive vocabulary. For example, he should avoid the word *cheap*, which has a bad psychological connotation. Instead he can say *inexpensive* or *reasonably priced*. And consider the difference between the words *foreign* and *imported*. Foreign brings up a negative image of alien and strange, but imported has an exotic sound that goes with perfume and champagne.

Making Product Knowledge Work. It was just recommended that the retail salesperson have a brief, interesting comment to make about each item that he shows. But he must be prepared to back up this comment with something more substantial—the complete story about the product. He should know what the product is made of, how it is made, what its uses are, how it should be cared for, how long it can be expected to last, what it costs and why, and how it compares with competing items. There are certainly many times when he won't need this information, but he must have it at his fingertips so that he can answer any questions the customer asks. For example, a customer is looking at pants for her little boy and she says, "These are certainly good-looking pants, but I don't dare buy anything that can't be washed." If the salesman doesn't know his stock, the sale will be lost. If he does, he can say, "That's a new wool, cotton, and nylon blend that can be put right into the washing machine; and it doesn't even need ironing. It couldn't be easier to care for; and I do think it's so much better looking than the plain cotton, don't you?"

SUMMING UP

In the approach the salesman gained the favorable attention of the prospect and aroused his interest in the product. His next step is to translate this interest into desire. In the presentation stage of the sale, the prospect must be shown why he needs the salesman's product, what it will do for him, and why he would be making a mistake to try to get along without it any longer.

The salesman must prepare his presentation carefully in advance so that he knows what he is going to say and how he is going to say it. But at the same time the salesman's plans must be flexible, because every prospect is a distinct individual and is not going to do or say exactly what the salesman expects. The presentation is most effective when it is aimed directly at the particular prospect. The salesman, therefore, must stay alert during the presentation to clues about the prospect's temperament and real needs and desires and then choose the selling stories that will be most interesting and most applicable to the particular prospect. In telling these stories, the salesman should try to be clear, specific, accurate, positive, and interesting.

In the presentation the salesman should appeal to as many of the prospect's five senses as he can, because this is the way to repeat the sales points to the prospect without boring him. It is also important that the salesman dramatize his presentation as much as possible to keep the prospect interested and anxious to know what comes next. Letting the prospect participate in the presentation is also an excellent way to hold his interest and to make him feel that he would like to own the product.

The salesman should keep his finger on the pulse of the interview. He should ask questions as he goes along that will show him whether he is making his points clear and how the prospect feels about each point. If the prospect shows a lack of interest in one point, the salesman can stop emphasizing that point and hit harder on the ones that appeal to the prospect more.

The salesman must know how to handle the interruptions that take the prospect's mind off the sales story. He must also be alert enough to judge the stage of the prospect's mind so that he knows where to start and when to stop his presentation.

The principles of the presentation for the retail salesman are basically the same as the principles involved in any sales presentation. But it is helpful to the retail salesman to consider four categories of additional suggestions: (1) deciding what merchandise to sell, (2) handling specific requests, (3) making the merchandise seem desirable, and (4) making product knowledge work.

1. Do the terms *interest* and *desire* mean the same thing in selling?
2. List the nine rules for making a successful presentation.
3. Why does the salesman have to plan his presentation in advance?
4. What are the four points that the salesman should consider in order to get through to the prospect as personally and directly as possible?
5. Why should the salesman have to be concerned about "making it easy for the prospect to listen"?
6. For the salesman, what is the significance of the fact that the sense of sight accounts for about four-fifths of one's total impressions?
7. How can the absence of a sensation be a selling point?
8. Why is it important that the salesman practice the dramatization he will use during the presentation?
9. Why did the salesman who typed poorly sell more typewriters than the salesman who was an excellent typist?
10. What is wrong with the question, "Do you understand what I mean?" What could the salesman say instead?
11. How does the salesman know where to start his presentation and when to stop it?
12. Why is it a good idea to start showing merchandise to the retail customer as soon as possible?
13. Why does the retail salesperson need product knowledge?

1. On page 241 there is an example of a salesman who has "the you attitude." Give another example to illustrate the importance of this point.
2. If you were selling pianos, how would you demonstrate the following features?

    a. Rich, true tone   *c.* Easy keyboard action

    b. Fine construction   *d.* Accessible pedals

3. Here are five products that you could not take into a prospect's office or home. What visual aids might you use?

    a. Diesel engine   *d.* Freezer

    b. Real estate lot   *e.* Insurance protection

    c. Child's jungle gym

4. You are examining a tennis racket. The salesperson takes it from you as he is talking about it and puts it back in the display. Later he asks you to buy it. How would you be affected by this type of presentation?

5. Assume that you are selling women's coats and have a customer who insists that she should have size 12 and cannot wear a larger size. It is obvious that the smaller size will prove uncomfortable, and it is likely that she will return the coat. What should you do?
6. Assume that you are a salesman for a wholesale firm. How could you use a product display to help sell your products to retail dealers?

A large clothing firm with many branches is having its big summer sale, an annual event. Notices have been sent to the store's regular customers, offering them a chance to preview the stocks before the sale is advertised in the papers. The first day of the preview, a young man walks into the Campus Shop at the main store and browses among the suits. After a few minutes, he is approached by a salesman.

SALESMAN: **Yes, sir?**
CUSTOMER: I'd like to see something in a suit—something in brown, I guess.
SALESMAN: **What size do you wear?**
CUSTOMER: A 34 short, I guess. A 33 regular might do, however.

> (*The salesman looks through the racks, selects two suits, a blue gabardine and a gray flannel, and holds them up for the customer to see. The young man studies them for a few minutes but cannot seem to make up his mind. He turns to the rack, finally picks out a brown covert suit, and tries on the coat. Then he walks over to the mirror. Up to this time the salesman has made no comment, but now he speaks.*)

SALESMAN: **That's a smart suit.**
CUSTOMER: How much is it?
SALESMAN: **$59.95.**

> (*Hearing the price, the customer takes off the coat and walks over to the rack to look for another suit.*)

SALESMAN: **That's about all we have in your size, except for the two I showed you before.**

> (*One of the first suits shown is still lying on a table nearby. The customer walks over to examine it.*)

QUESTIONS

1. Give your opinion on how well or poorly the salesman presented his merchandise.
2. What selling features did he introduce?

3. What selling features could have been used?
4. Describe the presentation you would have used to put over your selling points.

1. Write out a presentation procedure for a selected product that you can bring to class, and be prepared to give the presentation before the class. Follow the nine principles for a successful presentation as discussed in this chapter.
2. Make a list of the selling features that you might present for the following products, arranging the points in the order of importance. Prepare a list of specific statements you would use for each item.

   a. Electric range
   b. Electric refrigerator
   c. Quick-drying enamel
   d. House paint

   e. Tractor
   f. Woman's lounging robe
   g. Set of fine china dishes

3. Write out at least three ways in which you would include the customer in making a presentation for each of the following items:

   a. Potted plant
   b. Box of stationery
   c. Tennis racket

   d. Cocker spaniel
   e. Flowered cotton yard goods for drapes

Turning Objections into Sales

AS YOU KNOW by now, the successful sale involves two-way communication: the salesman's presentation and the prospect's reaction to it. Sometimes the salesman concentrates so hard on preparing and presenting his sales story that he doesn't think about the prospect and whether or not the sales story is getting across.

It would be simpler if the salesman could at least count on the prospect's hearing and completely understanding every word the salesman says. But every prospect is different, each having his own listening and thinking patterns. So the salesman's first problem is to stay alert to how much of his sales story is getting through to the prospect. Secondly, the salesman must try to analyze the prospect's reactions to the sales proposition. The salesman's most effective means of accomplishing these goals is *to get the prospect to talk.*

When the subject of objections is viewed against this background, it becomes clear that objections are an essential part of the sale. What could be more helpful to the salesman than getting the prospect to come right out and say what is on his mind? Thus it would be a serious mistake for the salesman to fear objections or try to avoid them. The smart salesman welcomes and encourages objections, because he knows that he can capitalize on them, using them as tools to make his sales presentation all the stronger and thus win conviction. The techniques for turning objections into sales are the subject of this chapter.

Objections Versus Excuses

It is important that the salesman learn to distinguish between real objections and mere excuses, since the techniques for handling them are quite different. The objection is an honest block to the sale that comes about because the prospect either does not fully understand the salesman's proposition or does not fully agree with it. The sale cannot be closed until the salesman has removed the block by answering the objection to the full satisfaction of the prospect. The prospect believes that the objection is valid, and the salesman must take it seriously. Objections may be based on (1) *the need* of the prospect for the product; (2) *the product* itself or some attribute of it; (3) *the source* of the product, which includes both the company offering the product and the salesman himself; (4) *the service* that goes with the product, including delivery, installation, guarantees, maintenance, replacement of parts, display materials, and so on; (5) *the price,* which also includes such subjects as the length of time allowed for payment, discounts for cash and quantity purchases, and any extra benefits that are to be included in the deal; and (6) *the time.*

Some examples of objections that are legitimate are given at the top of the next page.

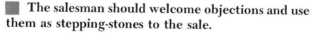

The salesman should welcome objections and use them as stepping-stones to the sale.

Need: "This old car has a lot of use in it yet. I can't see that I really need a new one."

Product: "I like the style of the chair, but the upholstery fabric is going to soil too easily."

Source: "I've always had good luck with Royal Electric appliances. I think I should stick to them."

Service: "I'm not interested in any gadget that has to be sent back to the factory for repairs."

Price: "Your price is just plain too high."

Time: "I don't see how I can take on any more insurance premiums right now."

These examples all represent real doubts that the prospect has about the wisdom of making the purchase. By contrast, the excuse is not a real doubt at all: it's simply a smoke screen behind which the prospect tries to hide the fact that he doesn't even want to hear the salesman's proposition. Excuses are really alibis that make it possible for the prospect to avoid granting the interview.

Excuses come in such terms as, "I'm too busy just now to see you," "I don't need any new brushes today," or "Just leave your brochure and I'll call you." But all excuses can be translated into the same idea: the prospect is saying, "I just don't feel like listening to a sales talk right now." So the excuse is not a *reason* for not buying, but a question of *mood.* The salesman's job is to get the prospect out of this negative mood by arousing his interest.

It can be difficult to distinguish between the objection and the excuse since sometimes they are expressed in the same terms. For example, if the prospect says, "I can't afford it," he may be trying to stall the salesman or he may be actually objecting to the price. But experienced salesmen count on three guideposts to help them to tell the difference between the excuse and the objection: the prospect's attitude, timing, and common sense.

1. *The prospect's attitude.* If the prospect's attitude is one of indifference, coupled with a casual voice and a shifting glance, the salesman can be almost certain that he is merely making an excuse. The legitimate objection carries an air of earnestness and sincerity with it.

2. *Timing.* Excuses almost always come right at the beginning of the sale, before the prospect knows enough about the sales proposition to raise a real objection. If the housewife tells the door-to-door salesman the minute she recognizes him as a salesman that she has to ask her husband before she buys anything, the chances are very good that this is a stall. But if she says it at the end of the sale, she probably means it as a valid objection.

3. *Common sense.* The guidepost common sense can be applied to that same housewife discussed under timing. The salesman can see that the woman looks bright and competent. There is nothing of the clinging vine about her, so

chances are pretty slim that she really asks her husband about every move she makes. Likewise, if a very successful businessman says, "I can't afford it," to a specialty salesman who is selling a relatively low-cost item, the salesman's common sense tells him that this can't be anything but an excuse.

In using these three guideposts, the salesman must always keep in mind that they are indeed only guideposts and not absolute rules. He must not get so brash about his ability to recognize the excuse that he forgets that sometimes what has every possible earmark of an excuse can still be a valid objection and vice versa. This is a delicate area, one that the salesman in the end has to "play by ear."

Techniques for Bypassing Excuses

The salesman must face up to one important fact on the subject of excuses: the frequency with which he meets excuses is a measure of how effective his approach is. In the approach he is supposedly *selling the interview* by gaining the favorable attention of the prospect and arousing the prospect's interest in the product. If the salesman is meeting excuse after excuse, he can only conclude that his approach methods need to be reexamined and improved. This is, of course, a matter of degree, for every salesman, even the very best, must expect to meet some excuses and must be prepared to deal with them.

The salesman should understand that when the prospect makes an excuse, he is in effect trying to get away with a half truth. He says, "I'm too busy right now," but that isn't the honest truth and he knows it. He doesn't feel like listening to the salesman, so he thinks he'll try this excuse to see if the salesman gives up. Of course, the salesman would not come right out and say, "That's not true and you know it." This would only put the prospect on the defensive. Likewise, the salesman doesn't want to make a big thing out of the excuse, because this would magnify it in the prospect's eyes and make him decide that perhaps his story is 100 percent true after all.

The correct technique for the salesman is to turn the excuse around so that it becomes a reason *for* listening to the salesman, rather than a reason for *not* listening to him. Here are some examples of this technique:

PROSPECT: Business is too poor right now. See me later.

SALESMAN: **That's exactly why I'm here, Mr. Prospect. I am selling a direct-mail campaign that will help you build business right at the time when you need it most.**

PROSPECT: I'm too well stocked with shirts already.

SALESMAN: **That could well be, Mr. Prospect, but my guess is that what you actually have are too many similar lines. Now we are offering some exclusive features that really move these shirts. With our line, you won't have more** goods on the shelf, but more sales at more profit. Every retailer is interested in that, and I'm sure you're no exception.

PROSPECT: I can't afford to buy a photocopier right now.

SALESMAN: You can't afford *not* to buy it, Mr. Prospect. If you'll just glance at this chart, you'll see how much money for typists' salaries our machine can save you in a year's time. You're losing money every day that you delay.

PROSPECT: I'm too busy to talk to you now.

SALESMAN: I only call on busy men, Mr. Prospect, because they are the only ones interested in the time- and laborsaving features of our product. May I have a moment to demonstrate them to you?

With each of these examples the salesman must, of course, be fully prepared to carry forward the momentum that he is generating for his proposition with a well-planned and absorbing sales story. The salesman's real objective is *to make a sale*, and getting past the excuse is only the beginning of this process.

Anticipating Objections

In handling objections, the salesman should remember the real key to successful selling: the good salesman is the prepared salesman. The time to think up the answer to an objection is not when the prospect brings it up. If the salesman pauses to think out a good answer, his hesitation will lose him the confidence of the prospect. If he doesn't stop to think, his talking will undoubtedly take on some "through the hat" qualities which, again, are not likely to impress the prospect. The only way out of this dilemma is for the salesman to plan for objections ahead of time, just as he plans his sales story in advance.

Courtesy International Business Machines Corporation

■ By anticipating objections ahead of time, the salesman will be ready to answer an objection as soon as his prospect brings it up. Additional information may be all that is necessary.

The Objection Analysis Sheet. When the salesman is planning his presentation, he can also anticipate objections by preparing an objection analysis sheet. To do this, he must try to look at his product through the prospect's eyes and then *predict* all the objections that the prospect could possibly make about the product. The salesman can then work out the best possible answers to these objections. If the objections in the actual sale don't come in quite the form the salesman has predicted, he nevertheless has some tools with which to work. With this system the salesman can never be caught completely off guard.

One example of an objection analysis sheet was presented in Chapter 11 on page 204. Another example is given on the following pages.

How to Use the Objection Analysis Sheet. The objection analysis sheet can be used not only to prepare the salesman to meet objections as they arise, but also to help him to forestall objections as he is making his presentation. Every virtue can become a vice when it's overdone; and while objections are generally helpful, too many of them can become a problem. The salesman wants the prospect to get the "yes" habit as the sale proceeds; constant objections introduce too much negativism.

To prevent the development of too many negative ideas, the salesman can weave the answers to the most obvious objections into his sales story, not mentioning the objection, but stating what would be the answer to it in a *positive* way. As an example, take the first and sixth objections in the objection analysis sheet illustrated. The salesman who is selling a food blender should realize that this is a relatively new item which is still considered to be a luxury. Therefore, he will make sure that the question of *immediate need* is well answered in the sales presentation itself. If the prospect is not thoroughly convinced from the salesman's presentation and brings up again the questions of need or time as objections, the salesman should welcome the chance to restate and reemphasize what he has already said. This kind of repetition can be very valuable in convincing the hesitant prospect to buy.

On the other hand, with objections such as the third and fifth in the example, the salesman should probably wait for the prospect to initiate the objection. It is usually better for the salesman to accent all the positive things about the product and not deliberately bring up questions of comparison, which might put negative thoughts in the prospect's mind.

After each sale, the salesman should revise his objection analysis sheet, adding those objections which came up unexpectedly during the sale and correcting his answers to reflect the reactions that he got from the prospect. The increased sales that will result from this kind of consistent effort to profit from experience will be well worth the time spent.

OBJECTION ANALYSIS SHEET

Product: Extramaid Food Blender

Type of Objection	Possible Expression	Suggested Answer
1. Need	"I can't believe I'll get enough use out of it. It'll just wind up taking up cabinet space."	"My wife felt the same way you do about it, but she finds she never puts the blender away. It's used on an average of six or eight times a day at our house. My wife uses it constantly to save time in cooking—from mixing the frozen juice in the morning to chopping things like onions, green peppers, and nuts; making bread or cracker crumbs; pureeing soups; and so on. Then the kids come in and make milk shakes, and I come home and make myself a cold drink with it."
2. Product	"They're starting to make blenders in colors now. I was hoping to find a [pink] one to match my kitchen."	"The blenders with the enamel bases do look very attractive when they're brand new, but I'm sure you realize how readily enamel chips. We've found that our stainless-steel base maintains its beauty for many years and looks handsome in any kitchen scheme."
3. Source	"Your company makes only blenders? I've always had the feeling that the big electric companies have the know-how when it comes to appliances."	"Bigness has its advantages, of course, but so does specialization, Mrs. Prospect. We are able to concentrate all our talents on just this one product, and we think our blender is as perfect as they come. I'm sure you realize that only a really superior product would keep us from being overcome by the big companies."

Type of Objection	Possible Expression	Suggested Answer
4. Service	"I can't count on that glass container lasting very long around my house. But I'll bet it takes months to get a replacement."	"I know that often happens with small appliances, but every dealer who handles the Extramaid Food Blender is kept well supplied with replacement parts. And each dealer, in order to get the franchise, must send a mechanic on his staff to the factory to learn how to repair the machine properly. There's none of this business of having to send the blender back to the factory for the smallest problem."
5. Price	"I'm sure you know as well as I do that your blender is the most expensive one on the market."	"Indeed we are aware of that, but we count on the fact that the buying public has gotten very sophisticated and realizes you only get what you pay for. We're so sure that our blender is the best on the market that we guarantee it for three years as against the usual one-year guarantee."
6. Time	"I can see that it's a very handy gadget and I certainly would like one some day, but I think I can get along awhile longer without it."	"There's something to be said for not rushing into things, of course. But our company has received many letters from housewives who say they don't know how they ever got along without their blenders. Here are a few sample letters, Mrs. Prospect. I think you can tell from reading them that the advice of these ladies would be to start enjoying the advantages of the blender as soon as possible."

There are nine general rules that will guide the salesman in answering objections. They are:

1. Have the right attitude toward the objection.
2. Listen carefully to the objection.
3. Get at the real problem.
4. Consider when to answer the objection.
5. Show that you understand the objection.
6. Be brief.
7. Tailor your reply.
8. Commit the prospect.
9. Remember that sometimes the objection is final.

Have the Right Attitude Toward the Objection. Perhaps the single, most important fact for the salesman to remember about any objection is that no matter how senseless, ridiculous, or unnecessary the objection may seem to the salesman, *the prospect believes it is valid.* Furthermore, the prospect believes that the thinking processes he went through in arriving at the objection were valid. It is therefore essential that the salesman treat the objection with great respect and that he make every effort to save the prospect's pride in answering the objection.

This means that the salesman must never give any indication whatsoever that he is annoyed by the objection. The salesman must also avoid any appearance of arguing. If the salesman says anything that can be directly translated into "No, you're wrong," the prospect's only line of defense is an increased determination to stick to his own opinion. The salesman must therefore be as diplomatic and conciliatory as possible. Phrases such as "I'm glad you brought that up" or "That's a good point" make the prospect feel that his opinion is being respected and that he is not being high-pressured by a smart aleck. Furthermore, such statements as these reflect a positive attitude which indicates to the prospect that the salesman is not afraid of the objection but is glad of the chance to give the prospect more information. This in turn makes the prospect more confident that the salesman is reliable, honest, and knowledgeable.

Listen Carefully to the Objection. The salesman cannot begin to answer the objection until he finds out what it is. To do this, he must listen *carefully* and *patiently* to what the prospect says. This sounds like a very elementary thought, but unfortunately it is one that is frequently forgotten. The salesman should also remember that attentive listening is one of the highest forms of flattery. The

■ In order to determine the real cause of the objection, the salesman must listen carefully to what the prospect is saying.

Courtesy Deere & Company

simplest way to convince the prospect that his opinion is respected is by the simple expedient of hearing him out.

Here is an example of what it means to the sale when the salesman will not listen and keeps interrupting the prospect:

PROSPECT: Your product doesn't wear, you see—

SALESMAN (*interrupting*): **Just a minute, Mr. Prospect. Just what do you mean, our product doesn't wear?**

PROSPECT: I mean it doesn't wear as well as—

SALESMAN (*interrupting*): **That couldn't possibly be true, why—**

PROSPECT: Are you telling me that I don't know what I'm talking about?

SALESMAN: **That's exactly what I'm telling you.**

PROSPECT: In that case, I don't think we have anything else to say to each other. Good day, sir.

Often in the process of listening to the objection and letting the prospect do all the talking, the prospect may arrive at a point in his thinking where he realizes that he really doesn't have a valid objection. Or perhaps he answers his own objection, so that all the salesman has to do is listen and tactfully agree with him.

Get at the Real Problem. Having listened carefully while the prospect stated his objection, the salesman's next job is to figure out what the objection really means. Is the prospect simply asking for more information? This is a very common cause of objections and is the one most easily answered *if* the salesman has adequate knowledge of his product. Or did the prospect misunderstand a point the salesman made? If so, the salesman has to go back over what he said, stating his point more clearly and emphatically. Perhaps the salesman has not drawn the picture of the relationship between the product and prospect clearly enough. Or perhaps the salesman has simply misunderstood what it is that the prospect wants and has been trying to sell him the wrong product. For example, a camera salesman may be trying to sell a complicated foreign camera to a man who really came in for a Brownie. Still another possibility is that the prospect is not actually raising an objection at all, but simply seeking reassurance. When the man who is lovingly stroking the fishing rod says, "I really can't afford it," he wants the salesman to play back to his conscience all the reasons why he shouldn't deprive himself of that fishing rod any longer.

The real meaning of the objection may not be immediately apparent from what the prospect says. The salesman must realize that a great many people have trouble saying what they mean, either because they are inarticulate or because they are overly polite. The prospect may phrase his objection in very veiled terms because he is embarrassed about "hurting the salesman's feelings." Sometimes this politeness goes so far that the prospect won't voice any objections at all, even though there are obviously some blocks to the sale. The salesman can handle this situation by tactfully questioning the prospect. For example, he can say, "As I hope I've demonstrated, Mr. Dickson, this calculating machine will pay off with very clear-cut savings in time and money. Now is there any point that I have not made clear?" Or the salesman can challenge the prospect by emphasizing a point that he is sure is unobjectionable. Then when the prospect commits himself favorably on this point, he may counter by naming his objection.

SALESMAN: **What is your problem, Mrs. Green? Is the pattern too conservative?**
PROSPECT: No, the pattern is just right. I was wondering about the price.

Considering When to Answer the Objection. In general, it is best to answer the objection right at the moment it is raised. If you try to put off answering the objection, you make the prospect think that you are afraid of the question and would rather evade the issue or that you don't have the answer because you don't have sufficient product knowledge. If the prospect is allowed to lose confidence in you in this manner, the sale will be doomed.

The major exceptions to this rule are objections to price. Most salesmen feel that the price of a product cannot be justified until the major advantages of the product have been set forth. Thus if objections to price are raised early in the sale, it is usually wise to postpone this subject tactfully until the prospect has enough information about the product to enable him to judge whether the product is worth the money. The how and why of this will be discussed more fully in Chapter 17, where the subject of price objections will be given special attention.

Show That You Understand the Objection. You should make sure that the prospect knows that you have understood the real point of the objection and that you are taking it seriously. The best way to do this is by restating the objection. This works very much to the salesman's advantage when the objection is a weak one; when the prospect hears the objection repeated by the salesman, he himself can often see the weakness in it. Also, some salesmen recommend that the objection be stated just a fraction more strongly in the restatement so that the answer packs more wallop. Here is an example of how this works.

PROSPECT: I don't think that I would want to go that high for a carpet.

SALESMAN: **You feel that this carpet is not worth the investment, is that right, Mrs. Bowen?**

PROSPECT: Oh, no, it's not exactly that it's an inferior carpet. It's just that it seems so high compared with other carpets.

SALESMAN: **If I could prove to you that this particular broadloom gives you more for your money than any other carpeting, you would be more willing to purchase it, wouldn't you?**

PROSPECT: Yes, I would.

Be Brief. It is just as fatal to magnify an objection in the eyes of the prospect as it is to pass over it too lightly. The wordy answer delivered in an overly digni-

It is usually best to answer the objection at the time it is raised. Otherwise the salesman gives the impression he is trying to evade the objection.

fied manner makes the objection seem much more important to the prospect than it did originally. The salesman should answer the objection with a straightforward, sincere reply that is both clear and emphatic. However, at the same time his reply should be as brief as possible.

Tailor Your Reply. The student is already well acquainted with the idea that the approach and presentation should be tailored to fit the personality, habits, and interests of the prospect. This theory also should be applied to the handling of objections. For instance, suppose that a salesman gets a price objection from a man who is very aggressive and opinionated. The salesman knows that this kind of man must be flattered, so his answer will be aimed at making the man think that the answer was his idea all along. The salesman could say, "Mr. Legrande, I know that it has already occurred to a man of your experience that the price of this machine only seems to be more than that of other models on the market, but just let me review for you why this machine is actually the cheapest one in the long run."

As another example of tailoring the reply to the objection, consider the car salesman who is trying to sell a large station wagon to a couple with five children who like to take family trips. The wife says that although she likes the car she is afraid she will have trouble parking it. The salesman reminds her briefly of the power steering and the wide windows that eliminate blind spots. He then admits that even so the car is obviously not so easy to park as the compact wagons, but he reminds the wife that parking is only a problem in local driving and that she

■ This mother likes the style of the chair, *but* she is afraid her children will soil the fabric too quickly. To overcome this objection, the salesman can use the "yes but" method to explain that the fabric is specially treated to resist soil.

must consider which car offers the most room and comfort for her family on long trips.

Commit the Prospect. The salesman should find out whether he has answered the objection satisfactorily by getting a commitment from the prospect. If the prospect does not volunteer his opinion, the salesman can say tactfully, "Have I answered your question to your complete satisfaction?" or "Is there any point that I haven't made clear?" If any small question still plagues the prospect, the salesman has to find out what it is and answer it. Otherwise it will remain as a block to the closing of the sale.

If the prospect's objection has been fully answered, the salesman should take advantage of the prospect's "yes" mood to try for a close. The moment when an important objection has been satisfactorily answered is one of the best times for a close. If the close doesn't work, the salesman can always swing back into selling.

Remember That Sometimes the Objection Is Final. The career salesman should be after long-range success rather than immediate rewards. The salesman's most important asset is the goodwill of his prospects and customers, and he should not destroy this by refusing to realize that sometimes a man means what he says. For example, the neighborhood grocer is suffering from the competition of the big new supermarket and he says, "I know I need more modern cabinets, but I can't buy them just now." The salesman realizes that the grocer cannot go out on a limb with expenses, because he doesn't know what the future holds. Therefore, the salesman says, "I can understand your position, Mr. Webb. Let me leave you my card so that you can get in touch with me if you do need anything. And if it's all right with you, I'll stop back in a few months and see if you've changed your mind." This kind of answer will not make an immediate sale, to be sure, but it will make a permanent friend and leave the door open for future sales.

Specific Methods for Answering Objections

To handle objections, experienced salesmen have worked out eight methods that are effective and yet do not offend the prospect. These methods are:

1. "Yes but" method
2. Superior-point method
3. Boomerang method
4. Explanation method
5. Question method
6. Direct-denial method
7. Demonstration method
8. Third-party method

"Yes but" Method. This is a sidestepping technique that recognizes the fact that people do not like to be flatly contradicted. Although the salesman really is going to contradict the prospect, he softens the effect by agreeing with the prospect first. This is how the "yes but" method works:

PROSPECT: I love this dress, but my little girl is a real tomboy and something as fragile as this wouldn't last two minutes on her.

SALESMAN: **Yes, this material does look very fragile. But actually it's almost as tough as denim. It's one of the newest miracle fibers, and it can really take a beating and still retain its good looks.**

Superior-Point Method. This method is used when the objection is valid. The salesman admits the truth of the objection and then offers a superior point which outweighs or compensates for the objection.

PROSPECT: The price is too high.

SALESMAN: **I admit that this is not a low-priced suit, Mrs. Stoner. Here is the reason why. Look at the label. This brand means quality to thousands of particular buyers all over the country. This is a 100 percent wool gabardine, cut on the latest pattern.**

Boomerang Method. This is often referred to as the reverse English method or translation method. The salesman turns the objection around so that it becomes a reason *for* buying and then tosses it back to the prospect, which explains the term *boomerang*.

PROSPECT: But this pan is so light.

SALESMAN: **That's exactly what you want in a cooking utensil. That is why this aluminum pan is so remarkable. This utensil is light and easy to handle, yet it is just as thick as the average iron or copper pan. This means lighter weight and no scorching of food.**

Explanation Method. The explanation should be used when the salesman feels that the objection is based on ignorance of the facts or on a false belief. The salesman asks the prospect to explain his objection. This puts the prospect on the defensive and often makes him realize that the objection is not sound. In using this method, you must be careful that you do not make the prospect feel that you are trying to show up his ignorance.

PROSPECT: I wouldn't have an aluminum pan. It causes food poisoning.

SALESMAN: **I'm interested in learning why you think that, Mrs. Weber. Would you mind explaining why?**

Question Method. In this method the salesman asks the prospect a question and then uses the prospect's own answer to prove why the objection is not valid.

PROSPECT: That's too much to pay. I can get cheaper ink erasers at the stationery store across the street.

SALESMAN: **Mr. Office Manager, you play golf, don't you?**

PROSPECT: That's right, so what?

SALESMAN: **Why don't you use those 25-cent golf balls you can buy in the dime store instead of those dollar golf balls you buy at the clubhouse?**

PROSPECT: They have a cheap cover, and they don't last.

SALESMAN: **It's the same way with rubber erasers. The cheaper eraser costs you more in the long run because it is harsh to use and causes messy-looking papers that often have to be done over. Also, they give a poor impression of your firm.**

Direct-Denial Method. The salesman can sometimes firmly deny the validity of the objection, but he must be very careful to avoid an argumentative manner. If the salesman has been generally pleasant and agreeable throughout the interview, his direct denial will carry all the more weight. This method is best used when the objection is in the form of a question. It is also best used with a smile.

PROSPECT: Won't this material shrink?

SALESMAN: **Absolutely not. This material has been preshrunk. Here is your guarantee on the label.**

Demonstration Method. Often an objection can be handled more effectively through a demonstration which disproves the prospect's claim.

■ Often the salesman can overcome an objection through the demonstration method. Here he is demonstrating that the bag is waterproof.

PROSPECT: I've heard that aluminum is a soft metal. Wouldn't that mean that this saucepan could be easily dented?

SALESMAN (*bangs saucepan against a corner of counter or some hard object*): **Look at that, Mrs. Prospect, not one dent. Does that answer your question?**

Third-Party Method. This is also called the testimonial method, because the salesman calls on the testimony of a neutral third party to prove his answer to the objection. The third-party is based on the "follow the leader" instinct that most people share to some degree.

PROSPECT: I don't think I would be interested in a three-way mirror for my bathroom. I can get along nicely with just a simple mirror.

SALESMAN: **I can understand your feeling that way, Mrs. Caldwell. That's what Mrs. Blake told me last month. However, I convinced her to try one and just this morning, while she was in the store, she made a point of coming to see me. She mentioned that she couldn't see how she managed to get along without one. Here are some of the things she said about this particular mirror.**

The Trial Sale

A device that is frequently used to overcome objections is the trial sale. The man who is looking at a color television set isn't quite convinced that the color set has that many advantages over his old black-and-white set. So the salesman says to him, "Let us send the set to your home for three days. That will give you the chance to find out for sure whether you will enjoy the extra advantages of color. If you decide to keep the set, you can pay us next month. If you don't want it, you can send it back without any obligation at all."

Because this offer obviously carries with it some inconveniences for the store, it should not be made unless the salesman knows that the prospect is almost convinced. Also, the salesman should always have the approval of his supervisor before offering a trial sale.

Tested Techniques for Handling Objections

The sales manuals of two large companies, the Hoover Company and the Dictaphone Corporation, provide the salesman with some tested techniques for handling objections. The Hoover Company instructs its salesmen to turn an objection into a definite sales advantage by the following procedure:[1]

---

[1] *The Hoover Sale*, Sales Educational Department, The Hoover Company, North Canton, Ohio.

1. Allow the prospect to state his objection. Give courteous attention, avoid interruption.
2. Ask the prospect if that is the only reason for not buying now. This informs you whether or not there may be other objections.
3. Ask for the prospect's reason for the objection. The prospect's reason will guide you in your answer. If the prospect does not know the reason for his objection, he weakens his position.
4. Repeat the objection in your own words with emphasis. State the objection more firmly than the prospect did. This assures the prospect that you understand the objection.
5. Base the sale on the objection. Have the prospect agree that if it were not for the objection he would buy immediately.
6. Prepare the prospect's mind for proof or explanation. Have the prospect agree that a test or an explanation would be sufficient proof.
7. Answer the objection. Give the prospect the needed information by demonstration, explanation, or questions.
8. Find out whether sufficient information has been given.
9. Present the sales agreement for the prospect's signature.

Here is an example of how this procedure works. The salesman is showing a floor polisher to a housewife.

PROSPECT: This is a wonderful floor polisher, but I think that it is really too heavy.

SALESMAN: **Is that your only objection to buying?**

PROSPECT: That was the reason I didn't buy it before.

SALESMAN: **Just why do you think this polisher is too heavy?**

PROSPECT: It seems big and heavy to carry.

SALESMAN: **You think our machine is made so large and heavy that it would be difficult to carry up and down stairs?**

PROSPECT: Yes, exactly.

SALESMAN: **Mrs. Andersen, if you could convince yourself that our machine is made of one of the lightest metals known and can be carried upstairs easily, you would buy it tonight, wouldn't you?**

PROSPECT: I might, if that were true.

SALESMAN: **Our experts have completely redesigned this machine. It now has a lightweight cast zinc hood with a vinyl plastic bumper all around. Notice, too, this vinyl plastic hand grip which makes this machine one of the easiest to move about. You just plug it in and guide it. The actual weight of this polisher, Mrs. Andersen, is only 14¾ pounds.**

PROSPECT: That's much lighter than I thought it could be.

SALESMAN: Our company could make it lighter if they cared to use a one-speed motor instead of the present two-speed model. Even then the machine wouldn't weigh much less and would be robbed of its efficiency and durability. Then you wouldn't want it, would you?

PROSPECT: I don't think I would.

SALESMAN: After all, you are buying this polisher for its efficiency in waxing and polishing and for its ability to continue to do so for years to come, aren't you?

PROSPECT: Yes, of course.

SALESMAN: And you are convinced that this machine will do this job more efficiently than your present one?

PROSPECT: Yes, I am.

SALESMAN: Then wouldn't you agree that every time you use your old machine you are working harder than necessary and cheating yourself of the convenience of a modern machine?

PROSPECT: I suppose that's true.

SALESMAN: Mrs. Andersen, let me suggest that you wait no longer to purchase this machine. I have a sales agreement with me, and I can make it out in either your name or your husband's name. Which one would you prefer me to use?

The Dictaphone Corporation offers its salesmen the following plan for handling objections:

The best way to answer objections is to anticipate them and dispose of them during your presentation. This method, however, has distinct limitations. If you attempted to dispose of every possible objection, you would never get into your sales story, and you would only plant in the prospect's mind doubts which had never occurred to him. Moreover, many a prospect pops objections at you before you have a chance to head them off.

By all means, plan your presentation to anticipate, and take care of, the misapprehensions you are reasonably sure are in the prospect's mind. But don't worry because you can't anticipate them all. Skillfully handled, objections are not obstacles; they are steppingstones to a sale.

Experienced salesmen recognize that objections are signs of interest, requests for information. True, they don't always sound that way, and they are not always put that way. But, nevertheless, that's what they are.

Objections tell you where your prospect needs more information.

They are welcome because they bring out into the light, where you can see them, the points about which your prospect still remains unconvinced. How much better that he voices his objections, instead of keeping them to himself, and forcing you to work in the dark. You can't change an opinion you don't know exists.

As soon as the salesman has answered an objection, he should get back to selling by pointing out additional advantages of his product.

Courtesy The Firestone Tire & Rubber Company

Experienced salesmen, therefore, welcome objections as opportunities to clarify sales points, review advantages, meet competition, and to fill unsatisfied requests for information.

Here is a simple, easy-to-use formula. An example follows the formula to illustrate how to use it in working out your answers to the objections you meet.

1. Welcome the objection, then *get the facts*. Don't stick your neck out with blind answers.

2. *Agree before you disagree.* Get in step with the prospect; don't expect him to get in step with you. Then give him some facts to clear up his misapprehension.

3. *Have third party refute.* Why risk resistance to your self-interested argument when you can cite the experience of a *dis*interested person to do the job for you?

4. *Get back to selling.* Don't let the prospect get the impression that you feel you've licked him on that one and are inviting another. Further, you make your prospect forget his objection by piling up advantages which shrink it to relative unimportance.[1]

On page 282 is an example of how the Dictaphone Corporation recommends that its four-step formula for handling objections should be used to sell an electronic Time-Master.

[1] *Dictaphone's Method of Handling Objections*, Sales Manual, VIII, A-1, Dictaphone Corporation, New York.

THE PROSPECT OBJECTS
He Says: "My Girl Wouldn't Use It"[1]

1. *Get the facts*

SALESMAN: **I'm sure she's a good secretary, and you certainly don't want to lose her.**

Where did she get her experience with dictating machines, Mr. Prospect?

PROSPECT: She used one on a previous job.

SALESMAN: **Was that some time ago?**

PROSPECT: Yes, she's been with me for three or four years.

SALESMAN: **Then she hasn't used one of our new electronic Time-Masters, has she?**

PROSPECT: No, she hasn't.

2. *Agree before you disagree*

SALESMAN: **I can understand how she feels when she bases her opinion on old-fashioned machines.**

But I think I can promise you that she'll change her mind when she sees our new Time-Master.

They're as different from the old machine she used as day is from night.

3. *Have third party refute*

SALESMAN: **You know David Brown at the Acme Company, don't you?**

PROSPECT: I know who he is.

SALESMAN: **Well, his girl felt the same way your secretary does. But when she listened to the beautiful electronic reproduction from our new Time-Master and saw how simple and easy it is to operate, she was perfectly willing to try it.**

And she is just as happy now as Mr. Brown is. I could tell you of a dozen girls like that.

4. *Get back to selling*

SALESMAN: **You'd certainly like to save an hour a day, wouldn't you, Mr. Prospect.**

PROSPECT: I'd be willing to try it out.

SALESMAN: **All right. Will you call your secretary in and ask her to give me a few minutes? I'm sure she'll change her mind when she finds out how different our new Time-Masters are.**

PROSPECT: All right. I'll get her in here.

[1] *Dictaphone's Method of Handling Objections,* Sales Manual, VIII, A-2, Dictaphone Corporation, New York.

SUMMING UP

Objections should be welcomed by the salesman. They are an essential part of the sale; and the salesman should capitalize on them, using them as tools to make his sales presentation stronger and thus win convictions.

The objection is an honest block to the sale that comes about because the prospect either does not fully understand the salesman's proposition or does not fully agree with it. Objections may be based on the need, the product, the source, the service, the price, or the time.

Excuses are not honest blocks to the sale, but smoke screens behind which the prospect tries to hide the fact that he doesn't even want to hear the salesman's proposition. The salesman can try to separate the excuses from the objections by using three guideposts: the prospect's attitude, timing, and common sense. The salesman can get past an excuse by turning it around so that it becomes a reason for listening to the salesman rather than a reason for not listening to him.

The salesman should plan for objections ahead of the actual sales time by preparing an objection analysis sheet. He can use this sheet to prepare himself to meet objections as they arise in the sale. He can also use it to help him to forestall objections as he is making his presentation by weaving the answers in a positive way into his sales story.

The nine general rules for answering objections are (1) have the right attitude toward the objection, (2) listen carefully to the objection, (3) get at the real problem, (4) consider when to answer the objection, (5) show that you understand the objection, (6) be brief, (7) tailor your reply, (8) commit the prospect, and (9) remember that sometimes the objection is final.

There are eight specific methods which experienced salesmen have worked out for handling objections. These methods are effective and yet do not offend the prospect. They are (1) the "yes but" method, (2) the superior-point method, (3) the boomerang method, (4) the explanation method, (5) the question method, (6) the direct-denial method, (7) the demonstration method, and (8) the third-party method.

Reviewing Your Reading

1. What is an objection?
2. Name the six areas in which objections may be based.

3. What is an excuse?
4. How can the salesman get past an excuse?
5. Why should the salesman revise his objection analysis sheet after each sale?
6. List the nine general rules for answering objections.
7. In general, what is the best time to answer an objection? Are there any exceptions to this rule?
8. Should a salesman ever stop trying to answer an objection?
9. List the eight specific methods for handling objections.
10. Why is the boomerang method so named?
11. When is the direct-denial method used most successfully?
12. Why do stores sometimes offer trial sales?

For Discussion

1. Why should the salesman welcome objections instead of trying to avoid them?
2. Are there any absolute rules for distinguishing between an objection and an excuse? Explain your answer.
3. Discuss the two ways in which the salesman can use the objection analysis sheet.
4. Why is product knowledge important to the salesman when he is answering objections?
5. Explain the statement, "Attentive listening is one of the highest forms of flattery."
6. If the prospect won't express his objections, what can the salesman do?
7. Early in the interview a prospect says, "This product won't save me anything." Which of the following answers would likely be the best one? Which would be the poorest answer? Explain your answers.
   a. "It may not save you a fortune, but it will save in dollars and cents. Our product is known to be the finest on the market."
   b. "Many of our most satisfied customers felt the same way until they investigated similar products."
   c. "That's where you're wrong, Mr. Prospect. If you knew as much about that machine as I do, you wouldn't say that."
8. Assume that you are selling adding machines. In checking a prospect's office staff, you observe that figures are added mentally. You happen to know that a great many errors are made. While you are demonstrating, the prospect comments that his clerks are fairly accurate and do not need adding machines. Which of the following courses of action would you take?

a. Tell the prospect that he is wrong and you can prove it.

b. Ignore the objection.

c. Treat the statement as an honest objection and proceed to answer it as if you did not know about the errors.

Sales Problem I

Assume that you are selling a tank-type vacuum cleaner. A certain department store downtown has a tank cleaner at $15 less than the price of your cleaner. Although it looks the same, it is actually inferior in construction. Your cleaner has a more powerful motor (½ horsepower against ¼ horsepower) and a better brush. Your cleaner also has a new patented dirt disposer, which means no bag to handle or container to clean or wash.

Using the eight specific methods for answering objections, as explained in this chapter, prepare eight different answers to this objection: "I can get one cheaper at a downtown department store."

Sales⁰ Problem II

A customer enters a millinery department and asks to look at some hats.

SALESPERSON: **What price would you want to consider?**

CUSTOMER: About $8.

(*The salesperson brings out a number of hats in the $8 line, but the customer does not seem to care for them.*)

SALESPERSON: **Let me show you some of our newer styles at $10 or $12. I'm sure you'll like them.**

CUSTOMER: No, thank you. Eight dollars is all I can afford.

QUESTIONS

1. What was wrong with this salesperson's technique?

2. How would you have handled this situation?

Salesmanship in Action

1. Assume that you are selling truck tires to an owner of a large truck transportation company. Prepare an objection analysis sheet that answers the following objections:

a. "I'm satisfied with the tires I have now."
b. "Tires are all the same."
c. "Your price is too high."
d. "I'm not too sure they will wear."

In preparing your answers, assume that you have made a check on the prospect's tires and on one of his trucks the tires are down to the fabric in places. In fact, the rear tires are running on the breaker strip, and the front tires are too small for the load being carried. Assume further that your product is a quality tire offered at a reasonable price, gives long mileage, and averages 20 percent more service than any other tire (proved by actual road tests). You have a sample section of your heavy-duty tire with you. The tire is guaranteed.

2. During the summer, you are going to sell door to door a line of quality bakery products priced slightly higher than store goods. You plan on covering the same territory twice a week. Prepare an objection analysis sheet, listing the possible objections that you may encounter and giving your answers to them.

Closing the Sale

WHEN SALESMEN talk about the close, they are talking about that part of the sale where the prospect agrees to buy the product or service. The closing is not a separate and distinct unit, but the logical and natural last step of the whole sales process. It is the climax toward which the salesman has been building during all his work of prospecting; of making the preapproach, the approach, and the presentation; and of handling objections.

The salesman's success in the closing will be directly dependent upon how successful he has been in the earlier parts of the sale. He cannot expect to make a favorable closing if he has not been following the principles of good salesmanship through every step of the sale. However, if the salesman has gained the prospect's attention, aroused his interest in the product, and then has not only made the prospect really *want* the product by showing him how it will benefit him but also convinced the prospect that he *needs it now,* then the fifth step of taking action should follow without any strain.

But obviously there is know-how connected with the close, as there is with the other four steps to the sale. The principles that make it possible for the salesman to stay in control of the closing are the subject of this chapter.

Closing the sale, the final step in the sales process. Having a positive attitude is an important factor in closing successfully.

Courtesy Merck Sharp & Dohme

General Principles to Observe in Closing Sales

There are three general principles which will help the salesman to close any sale. These principles are (1) have a positive attitude, (2) make it easy for the prospect to act, and (3) know when to close.

Have a Positive Attitude. In order to have the proper attitude toward the closing, the salesman must first of all realize its importance. In a football game the training, the passing, the running, and the strategy are all important; but what really counts is how many times the ball is carried over the goal line. Likewise in selling, the amount of study and preparation you have done, the number of calls you have made, the sales stories you have told, and the hours you have worked are all vital ingredients of your job; but the real measure of your success is how many *orders* you have received for your product or service. Thus closing the sale is actually the main part of your job. If you can't close, you are not a salesman and cannot continue to hold down a salesman's job.

This does not mean that the salesman should expect to close every sale. No salesman has ever made such a record and no company has ever expected it. If the salesman felt that he *had* to close every sale, he would be so tense and apprehensive that the prospect would lose all confidence in him. But there is a big difference between the salesman who brings in an occasional order and the salesman who consistently sells to a fair proportion of the prospects that he calls upon.

To be a consistent seller, you must have an attitude of positive assurance. You know that your main function is to get an order and what is more, you know that the prospect knows it. The prospect knows that you are not just making a social call; he *expects* you to try to close the sale, and if you do not, he will be convinced that you are unsure of yourself and of your product. And while you should be well aware that you cannot make a sale every time, you should nevertheless go into each sale expecting that this time you will succeed. Rather than being afraid that the prospect won't buy, you should be convinced that he will not be able to turn down the advantages that your product or service offers.

It is also important that the salesman remain calm during his attempts to close, and that he make the transition into the closing very smoothly and naturally. It should not be apparent in any way to the prospect that any change is taking place. The fact that the closing is the climax of all the salesman's efforts may tend to make him nervous or overly excited. He may heave a big sigh as he gets ready to try for a close, he may take out his handkerchief and mop his brow, or he may nervously light a cigarette. Such signs of tension over the closing will make the prospect suspicious. He will think that the salesman must not close many sales if he gets so excited over the possibility, and that there must be a reason if the salesman doesn't close many sales. The prospect will then begin searching for the reason why he shouldn't buy, which is certainly the wrong frame of mind at this point in the sale. If the salesman can act as though closing sales is a routine job, all in the day's work, the prospect will be reassured that he is doing the right thing.

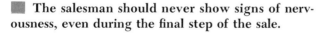 **The salesman should never show signs of nervousness, even during the final step of the sale.**

Make It Easy for the Prospect to Act. The salesman should try to make the closing as uncomplicated an act as possible. For example, a long sales contract will tend to frighten the prospect. He will be convinced that there is a "catch" somewhere in the fine print and he may be unwilling to sign it. If a long contract is necessary, the salesman should go over each provision with the prospect, being careful to point out how the contract is binding on the *seller*, as well as on the buyer, in such details as terms of delivery, guarantees of quality and service, and so on. Whenever possible, it is preferable to shorten the contract and to simplify the language, using terms that do not sound too legalistic.

Even a simple order book may seem ominous to the prospect if it is taken out too abruptly. The prospect gets the feeling that he is being trapped and he begins to wonder how he can get out of the whole thing. It is much better to keep the order book in sight throughout the sale so that the salesman can begin to fill it out without giving the impression of an abrupt transition. Incidentally, it is more reassuring to the prospect if the salesman's book is full of orders; the prospect feels that he is not alone in his decision. So the salesman should not break in a new book on a new customer.

The salesman should also make the mechanics of the sale as simple as possible. He should have a dependable pen at hand. If cash is likely to be involved, he should be prepared to make change; and he should also have a supply of blank checks with him. If the customer is going to need help with financing, as with the purchase of an automobile, the salesman should be well prepared to explain what must be done. In many sales the balance in the prospect's mind of deciding whether to buy or not to buy is a delicate one, and just a small hitch in the mechanics of the sale is enough to tip the scale on the side of not buying.

For this same reason the salesman should try to avoid interruptions at the closing stage of the sale. The entrance of another person onto the scene may make the prospect feel that he cannot act on the sale unless he stops and justifies his position to the interrupting party. The danger in this is that the interrupting party, not having gone through the first four steps of the sale, is almost certainly not going to be in sympathy with the closing and is going to throw cold water on the proposition. The prospect may thus find himself unwilling or unable to act.

Know When to Close. There used to be a theory in selling that there was a so-called "psychological moment" in every sale. This was supposed to be the exact and only point at which the prospect was ready to buy. If the salesman failed to detect this moment, he would lose all chance of selling the prospect. But most sales experts today do not agree with this theory. They believe instead that there are many times during the sales interview when the alert salesman can try for a close. The salesman must learn how to recognize these opportunities and how to deal with them.

Before the prospect will be willing to take action on the salesman's proposition, he must have gone through the first four steps to the sale—attention, interest, desire, and conviction. Since no two prospects are alike in their backgrounds, knowledge, and buying habits, no two prospects are going to go through the steps to the sale at the same rate of speed. Sometimes the salesman will find that the prospect has already gone through several steps to the sale before the interview even starts. This is especially true for products that are heavily advertised, such as television, radio, and stereo equipment; household appliances; automobiles; tobacco products; packaged foodstuff; and big-name clothing. In this case it may take very little persuasion on the salesman's part before the prospect is ready to close. In other cases, when the salesman is selling a new product or one that the prospect has not thought of in relation to himself, getting through each selling step may be a painfully slow process.

Because there is no set time for the closing, it is very important that the salesman's plans for the sales interview be flexible. The salesman must remember that his real objective is to close the sale, not to tell his full sales story just because he has prepared it. If the salesman talks on and on after the prospect has decided to buy, he could talk himself right out of the sale. And yet he can't make the sale until he has fully convinced the prospect, which poses the very real dilemma of how the salesman is to know how much talking is enough.

The answer to this problem is the multiple-close technique. The salesman can make a trial close every time he sees a favorable opportunity. If the trial close works, the salesman has accomplished his goal; if it doesn't, he can swing right back into selling. Not only will the trial close not have done any harm, but the salesman will actually be ahead. The prospect's reactions to the salesman's at-

■ Often the prospect looking at such merchandise as organs or television sets has gone through several steps of the sale before ever seeing the salesman. By keeping his sales presentation flexible, the salesman can easily make a trial close as soon as he recognizes a favorable opportunity.

tempt to close will indicate to the salesman what's going on in the prospect's mind. Perhaps the prospect needs more information or more reassurance, or perhaps he has misunderstood some points. The trial close will show the salesman what needs to be done.

The question now comes up of how the salesman can recognize a favorable opportunity for the trial close. The answer here is that the salesman must stay alert throughout the sale for things the prospect says and does that seem to show he is ready to buy. These buying signals may come at any point during the sale, but the salesman should be especially alert to the possibility of a trial close (1) after an especially strong point in his presentation, (2) after a visual demonstration of how the product works and what it can do, or (3) after he has successfully answered an objection.

Here is an example of how a salesman picks up a buying signal that comes after a strong point in his presentation:

PROSPECT: Well, that cold-wall refrigerator you put into your freezing units certainly sounds as if it would save on my electric bills.

SALESMAN: **It certainly will, Mr. Tucker. And remember that's just one of the many fine features you'll enjoy with your new Economee Freezer. But every day you delay the purchase of one of these fine units, Mr. Tucker, you are wasting money, as well as depriving yourself of the convenience of having fresh foods on hand when you want them. We can give you immediate delivery—Monday or Wednesday—whichever is more convenient for you.**

Some other examples of buying signals which show that the prospect is thinking in terms of owning the product are:

■ The alert salesman watches for buying signals. A simple remark like "I think it would look well over the fireplace" may indicate that the customer is ready to buy.

Courtesy The Du Pont Company

The appearance of an animated expression on the prospect's face may be a signal of the prospect's readiness to buy.

"I shouldn't even be thinking about buying now."

"How long does it take for delivery?"

"Is it hard to get parts for it?"

"I think it would look well over the fireplace."

"Could I have a while to pay for it?"

"I have some new shoes that match this dress exactly."

"Did you say it was guaranteed for a year?"

Sometimes the buying signal is apparent not in what the prospect says but in what he does. For example, he may:

1. Step back for a second look.
2. Scratch his chin or pull at his ear as if he's trying to make a decision.
3. Pick up the package and read the label.
4. Demonstrate the product to himself a second time.
5. Set one item aside out of a group of items.
6. Fondle the article.
7. Nod his head in an unconscious manner.

Buying signals may even be detected by watching the prospect's facial expressions and posture. His face may light up at something that you have just said or demonstrated, or he may suddenly look very thoughtful and serious. He may lean forward to listen more attentively to what you are saying, or he may suddenly relax and smile. It is the *change* of expression or posture that is the signal.

Why?
Why?
Why?
Many salesmen feel that this is the strongest closing device they use.
"Why not today?"
"Why do you hesitate?"
"Why do you say that?"
"Why do you feel that way?"

—Edward J. Hegarty, *Get the Prospect to Help You Sell,* McGraw-Hill

If the salesman is not sure that he is reading the signal correctly, there are several things that he can do to test the stage of the prospect's thinking. One good way is to treat the product roughly. The salesman of men's coats can throw the coat down on the chair without making any attempt to fold it. If the prospect picks up the coat and rearranges it, the salesman can be sure that the prospect is thinking of the coat as his own. The salesman can also try a seemingly casual remark, such as this one made by the salesman of an electric clothes dryer: "Mrs. Pierce has had her dryer only a month, but would you believe that she feels she could never get along without it again?" If the prospect says that she certainly can believe it, then the salesman knows it is time for a close.

Thirteen Methods of Closing Sales

The sales experts who advocate the multiple-close technique say that the salesman should make not less than three and even as many as seven or eight attempts to close in every sale. If all these attempts to close are done in exactly the same manner, the prospect will be too bored to say anything but the final "no" that means the end of the sale. For this reason, and also because the salesman must work with so many different types of prospects, the salesman must learn to vary his methods. He can do this through a study of the thirteen methods of closing sales that have been worked out by experienced salesmen. These methods of closing, which may be used either alone or in combination, are as follows:

1. Reviewing selling points
2. Contrasting advantages and disadvantages
3. Arousing the emotions
4. Assuming a close
5. Suggesting ownership
6. Closing on a minor point
7. Closing on an objection
8. Offering a premium
9. Cautioning on last chance to buy
10. Indicating "standing room only"
11. Narrowing the choice
12. Using the conditioned close
13. Asking for the order directly

294 **SALESMANSHIP IN ACTION**

Reviewing Selling Points. At the end of a trial, a lawyer makes a closing statement to the jury in which he sums up the evidence on which he has based his case. The salesman can also use the summary method to reemphasize and strengthen his sales story. This method is especially valuable both for the deliberative type of prospect who likes to think everything through and for the prospect who is unsure of his ability to make decisions. For both these types the salesman's review of the selling points is very reassuring. Here is an example of how this works:

SALESMAN: Mr. Travers, let's reconsider what you get with this accident policy. First, you are assured of $50 a week for fifty-two weeks in the event of sickness or accident. That's worth a great deal, isn't it?

Second, you are granted hospitalization up to $500. This means that the cost of your hospital room, medicines, anesthetic, and X rays is fully paid up to a total of $500.

Third, the provisions of this policy will cover you wherever you go. I've shown you that this is indeed a complete coverage as far as other accident policies go.

Fourth, your survivors, whoever they may be, receive a lump sum settlement of $2,000 in case of death. Don't you agree that all this is worth $60 a year, Mr. Travers?

Contrasting Advantages and Disadvantages. A second method that works well for the deliberative type of prospect is one that is based on the idea of weighing the advantages of the sales proposition against any disadvantages. This salesman uses the visual method of holding the attention of his prospect by actually taking out a pad and writing the disadvantages in a left-hand column and the advantages in a right-hand column.

SALESMAN: Now, Mr. Clark, before you make a decision, let's weigh the advantages against the disadvantages. I'll take this sheet of paper and list the disadvantages on the left-hand side and the advantages on the right-hand side. Let's start with the disadvantages first.

First, this oil-burning heating unit will cost you money—about $498.

Second, oil costs slightly more than coal to burn. Where your coal costs you about $125 a year, we estimate your oil cost will be about $140. That amounts to about $2 a month more over the heating season.

Third, there will be the slight disadvantage of dismantling your coal burner and installing this oil unit. This will take about two days.

Fourth, as you brought out, Mr. Clark, we can't afford to offer you much on a trade-in of your coal unit.

PROSPECT: That's the picture, all right.

SALESMAN: **Now, let's consider the advantages. First, you get a completely automatic heating system. No more shoveling of coal, no need for trips down to the basement to adjust the furnace. This oil-burning unit with the thermostat does all this for you automatically.**

Second, the compactness of this system enables you to have an extra room in your basement, Mr. Clark. I believe your wife told me that you were both wishing for a rumpus room. Think what an ideal place a nice dry and warm basement would be for this purpose.

Third, automatic heat as provided by your oil-burning system means a more healthful warmth. You can keep the windows open at night and still have a warm room. This means fewer colds and less sickness.

Fourth, an oil-burning system will help you maintain your beautiful home in spotless condition without a great deal of work. We've agreed on that, haven't we? And on top of that we figured your cleaning bills would be less, didn't we?

PROSPECT: I guess you've got everything there.

SALESMAN: **Now, Mr. Clark, think a moment. Do the advantages or the disadvantages weigh more?**

Some sales experts are against using the contrast close, because they feel that selling should always be positive and that it is a poor idea to introduce deliberately the negative thoughts that the list of disadvantages put into the prospect's mind. Certainly it is true that this close would be ill-advised if the prospect has not shown any sign during the interview that he is aware of or concerned with any disadvantages. But when the prospect has indicated that he knows all about the disadvantages, the salesman can gain the prospect's respect and confidence by his willingness to admit them. The prospect will feel that he is dealing with a man who believes in telling the truth, so he will be more inclined to believe the salesman when he talks about the advantages. This method allows the salesman to stay in full control of the interview when he is dealing with the very analytical type of prospect and also gives him the chance to have the last word on his own terms.

Arousing the Emotions. The two closes that have just been discussed are closes based on reason. But there is the type of prospect who will never be moved to buy through logic. He agrees with everything the salesman has said and yet he can't bring himself to say "yes." The salesman's best bet for closing a sale with this type of prospect is to appeal to his emotions—to affection, pride, self-esteem, envy, and so on.

For example, the salesman has given the prospect all the reasons why he should install a fire-alarm system in his house, but the prospect is still hesitant.

SALESMAN: **Mr. O'Brien, I'm sure you read last week about that house over on River Road that was completely gutted by fire in the middle of the night— the one where the mother, father, and three children were all burned to death. The insurance company has just found out what caused that fire. It was an electric iron that somebody forgot to unplug. Now if they'd had our fire-alarm system in that house they'd all be alive today and the house could have been saved, too. The alarm would have gone off and awakened the family as soon as the ironing board started to burn. That's the kind of tragedy that really makes you stop and think.**

When Mr. O'Brien hears this story, he thinks immediately of how much he loves his own home and family and he decides that it would certainly be foolish to turn down this fire-alarm system.

Assuming a Close. With this method, the salesman simply takes it for granted that the prospect is going to buy. When the sales interview has been proceeding well and the prospect seems to be in agreement with the salesman, the salesman takes the positive approach and implies by word or action that the prospect will buy. He says, "This is the model you like the best, isn't it?" or "You'll want to use our easy-payment plan, won't you?" If the prospect answers "yes" to these questions, then he has in effect admitted that he intends to close.

The salesman might also begin to fill out an order blank, saying, "Where do you want this delivered?" or "Is Thursday a good day for delivery?" The simple fact that the salesman so obviously expects the prospect to buy is enough to convince many prospects that they should go ahead.

Suggesting Ownership. The idea behind this method, which is similar to the assumptive method, is to keep the prospect thinking in terms of owning the product from the very beginning of the sales presentation. The salesman doesn't use any words that imply *maybe*. He says *when*, not *if*, and *will*, not *would*. And he uses the words *you* and *your* very often. For instance, the salesman says, "When you've got your new jigsaw in place in your workshop, you and your son will be doing master carpenters' jobs" or "When you put your first load of wash in your new automatic washer, you are going to feel like a new woman."

Closing on a Minor Point. Sometimes it is very difficult for prospects, even after they are completely sold, to cope with the major buying decision, which is to buy or not to buy. In such a case the salesman can steer the prospect away from

Getting the prospect to think of the product in terms of ownership is one of the methods for closing the sale successfully.

the big decision and ask him instead to decide on a minor point. The decision is no longer *whether* to buy, but *when* to buy, *which* to buy, *how* to buy. The salesman offers a choice and he can be completely impartial about the answer since either answer means a sale.

"Do you want to take this with you, or shall I send it out tomorrow?"
"Do you prefer the walnut or the mahagony finish?"
"Would you rather pay cash or use our easy-payment plan?"
"Do you want the hardtop or the convertible?"

Closing on an Objection. In order to close on an objection, the salesman has to establish the fact that the objection represents *the* block to the sale. Then when he has disposed of the objection, the prospect has no reason to refuse to buy. Here is an example of how this works:

PROSPECT: I like this sofa very much, and I'd certainly like to take advantage of the sale price, if the color of the upholstery fabric were not so light. I've got three children.

SALESMAN: **In other words, your main worry is soil; and if it weren't for that, you'd buy this sofa right now. Is that right?**

PROSPECT: Yes, that's it.

SALESMAN: **Well, this fabric is treated with silicone, which means that dirt and moisture can't penetrate the surface. All you have to do is vacuum off the surface dust about once a week and this sofa will go on looking exactly like it does right now.**

This method of closing is also called the "trap closing" because now the prospect is caught. She said she would buy *if,* and now that the *if* has been answered, she must be as good as her word.

Offering a Premium. This is a method that is as old as selling itself. If the prospect will buy *now,* he will be given a bonus—an extra benefit of some kind. For instance, if the salesman is selling an electric floor waxer, he might offer the prospect a can of wax with it for *this week only.* Offering a premium is routinely used in grocery stores. A person buys a large jar of instant coffee and gets a package of coffee-cake mix free. Or the product is offered at "10 cents off the regular price," but always for a limited time only. The idea is to make the prospect think he is getting a most enticing bargain—something for nothing.

Real estate agents make frequent use of this device. A young couple is undecided over the purchase of a house. The agent says that he will see if he can get the owner to leave the wall-to-wall carpeting and the drapes. When he goes back to the young couple and says that the owner is willing to include these items for the same price provided the deal can be closed immediately, the young couple will not hesitate any longer.

Cautioning on Last Chance to Buy. With this method the prospect is warned that if he doesn't buy the product immediately, he won't be able to buy it at all. For example, a woman seems to like very much the hat that she is trying on, but finally she hands it back to the salesperson.

PROSPECT: I'm just not sure. I think I'd better go home and think it over.
SALESPERSON: **Mrs. Martin, I wish I could hold the hat for you, but it's against store policy. It's the only one we have and I'm afraid it won't be here when you get back.**

This method is so effective with the prospect who has trouble making up his mind that it has been grossly overworked. The story is told of an antiques dealer who got so annoyed with his colleagues for constantly using the "It'll be gone when you get back" routine that he worked out a reverse technique. He would say to the hesitating prospect, "Look, that cabinet has been here for six months because it's too big for most houses. You've got the high ceilings that it needs, but why don't you go home and think it over? I want you to be completely satisfied." The customer, who had been exposed to the last-chance-to-buy method so often, would be so intrigued with the switch that he would buy on the spot.

The point is that the last-chance-to-buy method should not be used routinely or dishonestly. It should only be used when it is true. Otherwise it is nothing but a high-pressure technique.

Indicating "Standing Room Only." This method is based on the fact that people want what others want, and that one of the fastest ways to make a person desire something is to tell him he can't have it. This is an inborn trait in people. A small child will not touch a toy for an hour, but he will go into a tantrum to get the toy back if another child begins to play with it.

A woman is looking at living room furniture, and the one piece she feels she *must* have is the one marked "sold." She will ask if there are any more like it or if the sale is really all settled or if the manager couldn't do something. Real estate agents always tell their clients that if they really want a house, they had better keep quiet about their interest in it. A house may have been empty for a year, but as soon as the word gets out that one person is thinking of buying it, there are suddenly many people who want it.

It is this fact that people always want what others want or have that is behind the success of all fad items, such as the hoola hoop of a few years ago. The retail salesperson who tells the customer that "This is our most popular seller" is using the same psychology, as is the salesman who says, "Mrs. Brown has been looking at that lamp. She seems quite interested in it. It is pretty, isn't it? It's the only one we have."

Narrowing the Choice. In retail selling it is often difficult to close a sale simply because the customer can't decide which article he wants. Here the salesperson encourages a decision by narrowing the choice of items to the ones in which the customer has shown the most interest. The salesman should unobtrusively remove the items that have not impressed the customer, thus focusing the customer's attention on just a few items. The classic example of this point, which has been the subject of many cartoons and jokes, is the woman in the shoe store who is surrounded by dozens of pairs of shoes that she has tried on without being able to make a choice. But in this case it is the salesman who is at fault. It is his job to help the customer concentrate, not to confuse her hopelessly by drowning her in a sea of merchandise.

Using the Conditioned Close. When you say that a person has become conditioned, you mean that he has become used to a certain behavior pattern. Salesmen can condition their prospects to saying "yes" to the final question of whether to buy by getting agreement from the prospect throughout the sale on all the selling points. Agreeing with the salesman becomes the natural pattern. The closing decision is easy because it is not a change of any kind; it is just one more favorable decision like the many that have already been made during the sale. The prospect has said yes, she likes the tone of the piano; yes, she likes the size, the finish, and the style; and yes, she needs it now so that her young daughter can start taking piano lessons. So when the salesman asks her if he may go ahead and fill out the order, the usual answer is one more yes.

Asking for the Order Directly. With many prospects, especially ones who do a great deal of buying, such as professional purchasing agents, the best way to close the sale is simply to ask for the order: "May I have this typewriter sent over immediately?" or "Shall I draw up the contract now?" However, this method of closing should never be used for a trial closing early in the sale. It should not be used until the salesman is sure that he has presented his product as positively and favorably as possible, which usually means that it is used at the end of the sale, as the final attempt at closing.

One major reason for this is that it is harder to swing back into selling after a direct turndown—harder, but not impossible. There are many sales that have been successfully closed after the interview was apparently over. With his hand on the doorknob the salesman can say, "I don't believe I mentioned to you that the Globe Plant over in Avon has put in our machines. Mr. Roberts, the plant superintendent, told me that their output has been increased by 30 percent, and naturally they're very pleased." The door is now open for more discussion and a possible sale in spite of the turndown.

The Salesman's Departure

The manner in which the salesman makes his departure is a very important part of the sale. The discussion on this subject can be divided into three categories: (1) when the sale has been successful, (2) when another call is necessary, and (3) when the turndown is final.

The Departure When the Sale Has Been Successful. When the prospect agrees to buy the salesman's product or service, he becomes a customer; and the best time for the salesman to start building good customer relations is right then and there. First of all, the salesman must never forget to thank the customer for his order. If his thanks is overly effusive, it will make the customer think that the salesman must not get many orders. On the other hand, the thanks must be warm enough to make the customer think that the salesman really appreciates his business. This rule is often broken by retail salespeople, many of whom seem to lose all interest in the customer once the sale has been written up.

It is also important to indicate to the customer that you care whether or not he fully enjoys the product he has just bought. This is not just good psychology, for actually your future sales are tied up in this question. The satisfied customer will recommend you and your product to new prospects and he will give you more business himself. Here are two examples of how this works:

Ewing Galloway

■ After making the sale, the salesman should thank the customer for the order and then depart. He should never prolong his visit.

SALESMAN: Thank you for your order, Mr. Walt, and don't forget that our engineering department is always ready to help you with any problems connected with our line of products.

SALESMAN: I know you are going to enjoy your new automatic washer, Mrs. Murray, and I want you to know that I am grateful for your order. Our home demonstrator, Mrs. Jeffries, will call on you in the next few days to show you how to get the best use out of your machine.

Sometimes the prospect enjoys an extra touch of reassurance at the end of the sale.

SALESMAN: I know that you are going to be well pleased with your new automobile, Mr. Bates. You certainly have selected our most beautiful model. Don't forget to bring it back for your 500-mile checkup.

However, whatever the salesman says should be brief and cordial. Businessmen especially are not interested in a prolonged visit with the salesman after the sale has been completed. As the salesman, you should always be the first to arise after the sale is closed; and after a few brief comments of the type suggested above, you should take your leave. It is a good idea to stop in the reception room on your way out and thank the receptionist or secretary so that you will be remembered favorably when you call again.

The Departure When Another Call Is Necessary. The salesman must realize that there are selling situations where the sale cannot be closed in the first interview. This is especially true for products that are very technical, very expensive, or very new. The salesman should always try to close on the first call; but if he cannot, then he should concentrate on building up goodwill. This will pave the way for a successful return visit. The most important thing is that the prospect not be allowed to shut the door permanently on the sale. The following technique can be used in this situation:

SALESMAN: Mr. Andrews, I realize that I've presented my proposition to you rather suddenly, and that there are a lot of ramifications to it. May I suggest that you think over what I have told you today and then let me come back in a few days to answer your questions? Would Thursday at two o'clock be all right?

When the prospect agrees to this request, the salesman should thank him for his time and leave. The student is referred to Chapter 11 for a discussion on how the salesman should prepare himself for the return visit.

The Departure When the Turndown Is Final. The prospect has said "no" and he means it. The good salesman realizes that the turndown is all in the day's work; even the best salesmen sell only a fraction of their prospects. Therefore, this rebuff is not going to make the salesman bitter or belligerent. He remembers that he is still a salesman and departs with a final selling note. He has not sold the product, but he can sell his good reputation so that he will be welcome if he calls again in the future. Here is how this might work:

PROSPECT: I'm sorry, but I don't think that I would care to change my supply firm right now, even though you have presented quite a convincing story to me.

SALESMAN: That's all right, Mr. Evans. I can understand your desire to continue with your present supplier. You've done business with them for many years now, haven't you? We are planning some changes in our line; and when we come up with something that doesn't compete with your present supplier, I'll call again, if I may. Meanwhile, thank you very much for your time. It's been a pleasure meeting you.

The salesman should try to profit from his failure to close the sale by reviewing the presentation in his own mind and trying to figure out what mistakes he made so that he can guard against them in the future. This kind of self-analysis can only pay off with increased sales.

SUMMING UP

The close is that part of the sale where the prospect consents to take action on the salesman's proposition—that is, when the prospect agrees to buy the product or service. The close is the last step of the sales process. If the salesman has successfully led the prospect through the attention, interest, desire, and conviction stages of the sale, the closing should come easily.

The three general principles which will help the salesman to close any sale are (1) have a positive attitude, (2) make it easy for the prospect to act, and (3) know when to close. The best answer to the problem of when to close is in the multiple-close technique. The salesman should try to close no less than three times and even as many as seven or eight times in each sale. He will know when to make these trial closes if he learns to recognize the buying signals that the prospect gives him.

There are thirteen methods for closing sales, which may be used alone or in combination. These are (1) reviewing selling points, (2) contrasting advantages and disadvantages, (3) arousing the emotions, (4) assuming a close, (5) suggesting ownership, (6) closing on a minor point, (7) closing on an objection, (8) offering a premium, (9) cautioning on last chance to buy, (10) indicating "standing room only," (11) narrowing the choice, (12) using the conditioned close, and (13) asking for the order directly.

When the salesman is making his departure, whether he has closed the sale successfully or not, he should remember that he is a salesman and continue to sell the prospect goodwill.

Reviewing Your Reading

1. What do salesmen mean when they talk about the close?
2. How important is the close?
3. Is it necessary for the salesman to close every sale?
4. Why is it important that the salesman stay calm during his attempts to close?
5. Why should the order book be kept in sight throughout the sale?
6. What is the multiple-close technique?
7. What is a buying signal?
8. List the thirteen methods of closing and describe each one briefly.
9. Why is the salesman's departure technique important even though he has completed the sale successfully?
10. Why should the salesman analyze his lost sales?

1. You have demonstrated an electric mixer to Mrs. Johnson, and she has agreed, after you have made several trial closes, that she wants the machine and will purchase it on a monthly payment basis. However, she tells you that she cannot afford to begin paying on it for two weeks and to come back at that time. Which of the following procedures would you follow?

   a. Tell her that you will come back for the order in two weeks.
   b. Ask her to mail the order in.
   c. Take the order now and come back to get the down payment.
   d. Refuse the order without the down payment.
   e. Leave the machine and come back later for the order.
   f. Take the machine with you, since it is a demonstrator and you need it in your work.

2. How many trial closes should a salesman make during a sale?

3. Which of the following statements, often made by prospects, would you interpret as buying signals?

   a. "How much would that cost?"
   b. "Would you service it after it is installed?"
   c. "I have an old model that seems good enough."
   d. "I don't have the money right now."
   e. "How much would you allow me for my old model?"
   f. "I don't need one."
   g. "How does that motor work?"
   h. "When would I have to pay for it?"

4. You are selling rock-wool insulation for homes. You want to get a prospect's decision to insulate his house now rather than later. The prospect is inclined to be suspicious of salesmen in general. Which of the following courses of action would you use to get an immediate decision to buy?

   a. Imply that demand is active and delivery of the service is slow. It would be wise to sign up as soon as possible.
   b. Quote easy payments.
   c. Point out a special need that will occur soon, such as the approach of the cold season or impending scarcity of materials.
   d. Point out that you have a trained crew to handle the job now, but that you do not know how soon they will be available for work later.
   e. Explain the savings in the fuel bill as a result of insulation and the losses that will be incurred by delaying the purchase.

5. What do you think of closing a sale by making the prospect feel so obligated that it is difficult for him to say "no"?

6. If the prospect is ready to close before you have presented all your selling points, should you make an effort to complete your sales story? Explain your answer.

Sales Problem

A vacuum-cleaner salesman arrives at a house at eight o'clock in the evening.

SALESMAN: **Good evening, Mrs. Morris. I hope I'm not too early.**

MRS. MORRIS: No, not at all. Come in. This is my husband.

SALESMAN: **How do you do, Mr. Morris.**

MR. MORRIS: How are you? I'm sorry that you made the trip way out here, because it's not going to do you a bit of good. I couldn't buy oil for a vacuum cleaner—let alone buying the whole thing! Our old cleaner has satisfied us for a good many years, and I guess it'll satisfy us for a while longer.

(Mr. Morris sits down and begins to play with the baby.)

SALESMAN: **That's perfectly all right, Mr. Morris. But some day you will want a cleaner, and I want you to know about this one. So don't worry about my wasting my time! It's my job to show this cleaner to folks, and I like to do it whether they buy or not. Would it be all right for me to use the cleaner on this rug, Mrs. Morris?**

MRS. MORRIS: Yes. You can plug it into the wall here.

SALESMAN: **Thank you. Now, Mr. Morris, I'm going to show you part of what I showed Mrs. Morris in the store.**

(The salesman proceeds with the usual demonstration. Mr. Morris is not very interested and continues to play with the baby. Attracted by the whir of the cleaner and by the shining parts, the baby climbs down from the father's lap and crawls toward the machine. The salesman stops the machine and points to the child.)

SALESMAN: **Right there, folks, is one of your biggest reasons for buying this cleaner—the health of your baby!**

(Both husband and wife show immediate interest.)

SALESMAN: **I'm not telling you anything new when I tell you that dust carries disease germs. We've all known that since we were in the third grade at school. But it's just as true today as it was then. Let's take infantile paralysis, for example. Doctors have found that infantile paralysis germs enter the blood through the upper passages of the nose, carried there by** dust. There are plenty of deaths that can be blamed on dust; erysipelas and scarlet fever are two others.

MR. MORRIS: That's probably true. But our cleaner seems to do a pretty good job.

SALESMAN: I don't doubt it. But we can easily tell. How recently have you cleaned this rug, Mrs. Morris?

MRS. MORRIS: I vacuumed it this afternoon.

SALESMAN: All right, it should be still fairly clean. Now let's empty the dust that we just got from going over your rug.

MRS. MORRIS: Here, put it on this newspaper.

(*The salesman unfastens the bag and removes the dust, placing it on the newspaper. A good-sized pile of dirt is obtained.*)

MR. MORRIS: Well, what do you know about that! Guess the old cleaner is not so hot after all.

SALESMAN: At the time it came out, it was probably a pretty good cleaner. But things have changed—your cleaner suffers by comparison with the cleaner of today, just as other cleaners suffer by comparison with our new model. That's not just sales talk, Mr. Morris. You can put this cleaner alongside any cleaner made, I don't care how much they cost. Check it over point for point—the motor, the brush, the material, the workmanship—and I know you'd choose this cleaner right here!

MR. MORRIS: How about the motor—is it the universal type?

SALESMAN: Yes, it is. And it's one of the finest small motors made in the country. In fact, we claim that there is none better, at least that we have been able to find out about.

MR. MORRIS: I see that it's mounted vertically. I've always supposed the ideal way to mount a motor is horizontally.

SALESMAN: Not at all, provided the bearings and shafts are properly made. The shafts of this motor are made of the best tool steel. It's the same kind that is used in the best chisels and drills and could stand up under a motor many times the weight of this one. Both ends of the shaft are mounted in precision ball bearings, and these are packed in grease. As I told Mrs. Morris today, you'll never need to oil this cleaner. By mounting this motor vertically we have reduced the noise by a great deal—less vibration, you see, than if it were horizontal.

MR. MORRIS: Just what do you mean by precision ball bearings?

SALESMAN: They are mechanically perfect ball bearings, absolutely uniform in size, shape, and strength of metal. A less perfect ball bearing, like the kind used in roller skates or some other cleaners, would roll unevenly. They would soon wear and cause noise and, of course, would cause wear on the motor itself.

Notice this knob? That controls the adjustment for rugs of different thickness. Turning it this way raises the nozzle for thick rugs, turning it that way lowers it for thin rugs. Some cleaners do not have this adjustment, and so for thin rugs they cannot do a good job, and on thick rugs they are hard to operate.

The cord is twenty-five feet of the highest grade rubber cord. In testing cord for this machine, our laboratory found that this cord would stand up under more bending back and forth than any other we could find. Yet to make it last even longer, we have protected it here where it leaves the cleaner. That's where the strain is greatest.

Now, I think that you will agree that this machine has just about everything you could wish from a cleaner. But if you have any questions, I'll be glad to answer them.

MR. MORRIS: Looks like a good cleaner, all right, but I don't see how we can lay out $67 for one right now.

SALESMAN: You won't need to pay the whole amount now, Mr. Morris. In fact, you can make a down payment of as little as seven dollars if you want to, and we allow $6.95 on the old cleaner.

MR. MORRIS: What would the monthly payments be?

SALESMAN: Four dollars.

MR. MORRIS: This seems such a poor time for me to be buying anything.

SALESMAN: You must remember, Mr. Morris, that you buy a vacuum cleaner only once or twice in a lifetime. Now this cleaner should give perfect service for many years. Being very conservative about it, let's say that it lasts seven years. That would amount to less than four cents a day. And four cents a day is a pretty reasonable price for giving Mrs. Morris the assurance that she is keeping her rugs as clean as she could possibly keep them.

MR. MORRIS: Well, hard times or not, I guess Mrs. Morris deserves the cleaner. But we'll have to buy on payments.

SALESMAN: That's all right. But there is one thing more I want to mention. With the old-type cleaners, a set of attachments for cleaning upholstery, curtains, and such things was usually added. We have discovered that in most cases it was simply money thrown away. They were awkward to handle, and the woman simply quit using them. So instead, we have provided our junior model. This little cleaner will do all those extra jobs of cleaning, and it's very handy. Wonderful for cleaning stair carpets or the inside of your car, and easy to use. We can add it to your order for this one, and it'll mean only one dollar more down and a dollar a month.

MR. MORRIS: No siree! Nothing doing! You can't sell me another thing. Maybe some other time, but not now.

(*The salesman makes a mental memorandum to call again just before house-cleaning time. Later, he will record it on his prospect card. Together they fill in the time payment blank.*)

SALESMAN: **Good night, sir. Good night, Mrs. Morris. Thank you both very much. I'm sure you'll like the cleaner.**

—From Sears, Roebuck training materials

QUESTIONS

1. What objections were made by the prospect during the sale?
2. Discuss the salesman's method of handling them.
3. What buying signals occurred during this sale?
4. At what point did the salesman attempt to close? What type of trial close did he use?
5. Write another close for this sale, using the method of reviewing the selling points.

Salesmanship in Action

Select from a magazine or newspaper an advertisement that provides ample selling information, preferably one that actually lists its selling points. Prepare six different closes to a sale of the product, using this information.

Imagination in Selling

If there is one word that best describes America's greatest salesmen, that word is probably imagination. *The good salesman is always searching for new ideas, for new ways of appealing to his customers' buying motives. He summons his imagination to sell more to his customers, to answer their "I'm not buying" excuses. He makes the telephone and direct mail work to his advantage. The good salesman is never satisfied, because he knows there is always a better way to sell if he can only find it.*

Selling More to Your Customers

THE AMBITIOUS SALESMAN realizes that he must be constantly looking for ways to increase his sales volume. By always trying to sell *more*, he increases his value to his company as well as his own income. Also, increased sales mean more satisfaction for the salesman's customers, as long as the salesman makes sure that the added volume answers the customer's *needs*.

The salesman can increase his sales volume in three ways. They are (1) closing more sales successfully, (2) suggestion selling, and (3) selling more on call-backs.

Closing More Sales Successfully

The clue to real success in selling is never to be satisfied. The progressive salesman is always trying to beat his own record. Each month he tries to find more prospects, make more calls, obtain more interviews, and close more sales than he did the previous month. The result of this constant attempt to sell more people will obviously be a substantial increase in the salesman's sales volume.

The salesman can effect this increase through a continuing program of self-analysis and self-improvement. After each sale, whether the sale was successful or not, the salesman should analyze what he did and said, using as a yardstick the principles of good salesmanship that have been discussed throughout this book. In this way the salesman can make steady improvements in his approach, presentation, methods of handling objections and excuses, and closing techniques.

The salesman should also constantly try to learn more about his product and the field in which he is selling and about human motivation and behavior, so that he can become more adept at bringing his product and his prospects together. He should make a habit of reexamining his prospecting and preapproach methods so that he does not waste his time in calling on people who have no use for the product or can't afford it.

These are just the highlights of the subject of how the salesman can improve his methods and hence close more sales. The student will be able to explore the subject more fully in Chapter 20, which is concerned with methods for improving the salesman's use of his time.

Suggestion Selling

The second effective way of increasing total sales volume is to increase the amount sold to each customer through suggestion selling. The salesman tries to influence the customer to increase the size of his order by purchasing a larger quantity of the product, a higher-priced product, or additional items.

For example, the grocer suggests the large family size of soap powder instead of the regular size. The salesman in a garden supply shop suggests that a more expensive grade of grass seed will bring better results. The sporting goods salesman suggests bowling shoes to the man who has just bought a bowling ball.

There is no high-pressure quality to this kind of suggestion selling. Of course, it does mean increased sales and profits for the store or company, and it does mean increased income for the salesman. But it also represents better service to the customer. The salesman's suggestions remind the customer of items that he will ultimately need or that will make his life more enjoyable, so that the customer receives more satisfaction out of this one shopping session than he would otherwise get.

Suggestion Selling Versus Order Taking. To point up the value of suggestion selling to the customer, let's consider two paint salesmen. The first one simply gives the customer the can of paint that he has requested. The man takes his paint home, fully expecting to get his painting done that evening. But when he

■ By suggesting other items that the customer needed in addition to house paint, this salesman not only increased his sales but gave the customer better service as well.

gets ready to paint, he finds that he has no turpentine or sandpaper. In addition, the only brush in the house is hopelessly clogged with old paint. The paint store is of course closed; and since he has no way of getting the proper supplies, he has to postpone his project.

The salesman who merely gives the customer his paint is only an order taker. He does not have either the customer's or the store's best interests at heart. Contrast his attitude with that of the salesman in the following example:

The customer was looking at a house paint display, so I didn't waste any time. I just smiled, pointed at the label, and said, "That's our best house paint, sir. About nine out of ten customers buy that kind. It does a fine-looking job. It spreads fast and even. And a gallon covers a lot of space."

Then I asked him, "Do you have a painting job coming up soon?"

The customer explained he'd be on vacation in a week and figured he would paint his house and save some money. I agreed that was a fine idea.

Size Up the Whole Job

Next, I asked him a few questions about the house . . . its size . . . what style home . . . when it was last painted . . . if it held the last paint well . . . color of walls, roof, trim, and so on. I also asked him if there was anything—a gable or some other feature—he wanted to make stand out or to seem smaller.

He described his home. He mentioned that the large outside chimney made the house look small and added that he hadn't definitely decided on what colors to use.

Sell from Your Customer's Point of View

"Naturally," I said to the customer, "you take a lot of pride in your house. You want it to look as good as any in the block. Or better! And you want the job to last a long time after you've spent your time and money on it."

Advise Your Customer

"For your New England colonial-type home, solid white with the right green for the roof, shutters, and other trim would be very attractive and in good taste. And I'd suggest using solid white on that chimney to make it blend with the wall. Our paints lasts for years. And it's very easy to clean."

Show Products That Will Best Satisfy

"That is all the paint you'll need to do the job right."

Quickly estimating the area of the house, I set out the pails of undercoat and finish coats of each kind of paint. Then I showed him the wall demonstration panels to explain how the paint would look. I told him how well it covered and explained the reason for its smooth, even texture.

Demonstrate

Next, I showed the customer how to apply the paint for best results. I used two widths of brushes—a 4½-inch for outside boards, a 2½-inch for windows and trim.

"You'll want good brushes to do a good job," I pointed out. "Brushes like these, when carefully cleaned after they're used, will last for years."

Sell Extra Items

"This liquid brush cleaner is worth many times over what it costs because it saves the brushes. Shall we include it with the brushes now?"

"O.K.," said my customer, "but how much is all this going to cost me?"

"All the paint you'll need, the brushes, and brush cleaner will come to only $45.30. And you'll have the brushes, and possibly a little paint left over for odd jobs around the house later."

The customer wanted to know how soon he could get delivery. That was easy. And my original sale was in the bag!

Sell Related Items

Then as I wrote the sales ticket, I said, "A strong, safe ladder is a pretty important part of a painter's equipment, Mr. Anderson. Do you have one you can depend on?"

"Well, I figured I'd borrow one," he said.

"Yes, that would be a smart thing to do," I answered, "if you were only going to need a ladder for this one job. But around a home like yours, a man uses a ladder for dozens of jobs—like putting up screens, trimming shade trees, washing windows, and so on. Saves a lot of time and inconvenience to have your own. And here's one that will last a lifetime if it's kept in a dry place after using."

"Oh?" he said, kind of doubtful. Then I showed him how it was made with tough straight-grain sides, hickory rungs, and so on.

"How much?" he asked.

"Only $10.65," I told him.

"That's quite a lot to add to a paint bill!" he said.

"It would be if it were for just this one job. But you'll be doing other painting repairs, year after year," I reminded him. "And what you save this time when you paint will more than pay for it."

"Guess you're right. Might as well send the ladder along," he agreed.

The ladder was added to the order, increasing the sale by approximately 25 percent.

Help Your Customer Do a Good Job

As I thanked him and handed him his receipt, I said, "And here's a free booklet written by our paint experts. Tells you just what to do to get the best possible results. You'll find directions on the label of the pails, too."

Pave the Way for Future Sales

And I added, "By the way, Mr. Anderson, if you'll give me your telephone number before you go, I'll make a note of it. Every season we have specials on inside paints and supplies. I can often save you money by calling to let you know."

Invite Your Customer Back

No other customers were waiting, so I walked a few steps to the door with him. As he left, I said, "I hope you'll be in again soon. Good-by, Mr. Anderson."

There were some good breaks for the salesman in that sale. But he deserves a lot of the credit himself. He did a first-class selling job and made a *complete* sale![1]

Suggestion Selling and the Store or Company. Every retail store is anxious to have its salespeople increase their sales per customer, because this greatly increases the store's profits. Here is a simplified example of how this works:

Average Sale		Increased Average Sale	
1 pair hose at $1.50	$1.50	2 pair hose at $1.50	$3.00
Cost (60% of selling price)	.90	Cost (60% of selling price)	1.80
Store's gross profit	$ .60	Store's gross profit	$1.20
Operating expense	.52	Operating expense	.56
Net profit	$ .08	Net profit	$ .64

Eight times as much profit has been made by selling twice as much merchandise. This is because fixed expenses, such as rent, salesmen's wages, office staff

[1] *Sears Paint and How to Sell It*, Sears, Roebuck and Company.

■ The person who buys a new camera will need film, too.

Courtesy Eastman Kodak Company

salaries, heat, and light, remain the same regardless of the amount of the sale. The only increase in the store's expenses is the salesman's extra commission and the handling expenses.

The same kind of economics holds true in industrial and specialty selling. There is a fixed amount of expense involved in a salesman's call on a prospect— not only the cost of his transportation, but also the cost of his time if he is on salary and the cost of the time of the office personnel who make his call possible. Thus when the salesman sells the customer a larger quantity or higher-priced goods or additional goods, he is effecting a substantial increase in the company's profits.

Seven Methods of Suggestion Selling. There are seven methods that the salesman can use when he is trying to make suggestion selling work. Since each method does not apply to every selling situation, the salesman will have to choose the right ones for the kind of product he is selling. The seven methods are:

1. Suggest related items.
2. Suggest a larger quantity.
3. Suggest higher-priced, better-quality merchandise.
4. Suggest newly arrived stock.
5. Suggest specially advertised items.
6. Suggest new or additional uses for merchandise.
7. Suggest merchandise for special occasions.

Suggest Related Items. This form of suggestion selling is based on the idea of trying to sell the customer an item that he can use with the item he has

316   IMAGINATION IN SELLING

just bought. For instance, when a woman buys a skirt, the salesgirl suggests some blouses to go with it. The salesman picks out a suitable tie and suggests it to the customer who has just bought a suit. The salesman asks the man who has just bought a tennis racket whether he needs any tennis balls. The woman who has picked out a pair of shoes is shown a matching handbag. The door-to-door salesman of brushes and cleaning supplies sells a new solvent for cleaning stoves and then suggests that some steel sponges will make the job easier yet. The office furniture salesman, having sold a desk, suggests a chair and a pull-up table for extra work space.

This type of suggestion selling usually represents a real service to the customer, because the second item that he buys greatly increases his enjoyment of the first item. The salesman can do an even better job of suggesting related items if he will learn to think beyond the obvious. To help him, the salesman must really know the stock in a retail store or the whole line of merchandise in industrial and specialty selling. For example, a woman goes into an accessories shop. She asks for a scarf to wear with a beige dress and finally picks out an orange one. The alert salesgirl remembers that some bone bracelets have just come in that are exactly the same shade of orange; the result is an added sale for the store and a very pleased customer. Likewise, a salesman who sells specialty foods wholesale to grocery stores has just received an order that includes canned liver paste and deviled ham, so he suggests a special new cracker. In this case the grocer in turn will use suggestion selling by placing these items on a shelf close together. When the housewife picks up the liver paste, she will thus be reminded that she also can use the crackers.

Suggest a Larger Quantity. It can be a real service to the customer to suggest a larger quantity of the item he is buying. By buying the larger quantity, the customer almost always saves money. He is also saved the inconvenience of running out of the item too soon or of having to remember to go back for more. The drugstore clerk says, "With a family the size of yours, Mrs. Holmes, you'd be a lot better off with this large-size tube of toothpaste." The salesgirl who is selling nylon stockings says, "These stockings are $1.35 a pair, or three for $3.50. I'm sure you'll find that three pairs in the same color will give you a lot more wear. When you get a snag, you've only lost one stocking instead of a whole pair." The salesman who is selling tires to a trucking company suggests a larger-sized order on the basis that the discount allowed by his company on quantity sales will substantially reduce the price per tire.

Suggest Higher-Priced, Better-Quality Merchandise. The attempt to sell higher-priced, better-quality goods is known as "trading up" the sale. For the salesman to make the customer prefer the higher-priced goods without degrading the lower-priced goods requires tact. If he implies in any way that the lower-priced goods are "cheap" or "inferior" or of "poor quality," he may wind up losing the sale completely, because that may be all the money the customer is willing to spend. He should describe the lower-priced goods with the positive word *good;* then he can speak of the medium-priced goods as *better* and the high-priced goods as *best.*

Here are some examples which illustrate how this method can be handled successfully:

> "They're both good hinges, Mr. Adams, but see how much more strongly this one is made."
> "He'll like either one, Mrs. Stone, but this one will provide longer wear."
> "It costs a few dollars more, but its appeal to your wife will be worth much more than the small additional cost."
> "This is good; but for only 70 cents more, you can have our best model."
> "This paint will give your kitchen such a shining appearance that it is well worth the few cents' difference."

Suggest Newly Arrived Stock. The retail salesperson should routinely inform his customers of the arrival of new merchandise. Most shoppers consider this a real service, since it gives them the chance to see the merchandise while the inventory of the item is still complete. For example, a salesgirl who has just sold a customer a spring dress says, "Mrs. Williams, our bathing suits came in yesterday, and I think you ought to look at them. This really is the best time of year to buy a bathing suit. In another month they'll be so picked over that you won't be able to get what you want."

The salesman who suggests newly arrived merchandise also is doing the customer a favor because the suggestion reminds the customer of needs that will soon have to be answered. For instance, the hardware store clerk says, "Well, Mr. Morgan, I guess winter's really coming. Our rock-salt shipment arrived yesterday. Would you like me to have our delivery boy put a 100-pound bag in your garage so you're ready for the first snow?"

Suggest Specially Advertised Items. When the store has advertised an item in the newspaper or is featuring it as a "special," the salesperson is obligated to the store and to the customer to let the customer know that the merchandise is available. When a store lowers the price on an item, it does so because the item is overstocked or because selling a large number of an item for a lower price can mean a higher profit than selling a smaller number of the same item at a high price. In either case, the store advertises because it wants to move the goods; and it is the salesperson's duty to cooperate by suggesting the goods to the customer. The customer benefits because of the simple fact that everyone loves a bargain. The salesperson benefits because he makes additional sales.

Courtesy "Views & Reviews," Retail Reporting Bureau, New York City

■ Suggesting merchandise that is on display for special occasions can increase sales.

Suggest New or Additional Uses for Merchandise. The housewares clerk has just sold a large rectangular plastic wastebasket and he says, "Mrs. Egan, one of my customers just told me an interesting story about these wastebaskets. It seems she uses them all over the house. She's got one fastened to the bottom half of the inside of the door to her first-floor coat closet and one fastened just above it. Her children put their rubbers and boots in the lower one and their mittens and caps in the upper one. She says she can now get them off to school in the morning without any scenes over lost mittens and boots. And then she's got one on the inside of the linen-closet door to use as a clothes hamper, and one on the closet door in her little boy's room to use as a catchall for his small toys. Who would ever think you could do all that with a wastebasket?"

The hardware store salesman has just sold one of the metal containers with a dozen or so small plastic drawers that are used in home workshops to hold nails, screws, and other small items. The salesman says, "These things are great around the house, Mr. Murray. My wife uses one on her closet shelf to hold her costume jewelry. She thinks it's handy—says she can find everything in just a second and the pieces don't get scratched from being all jumbled together in a big box."

In each of these examples the new idea that the salesman has given the customer about how to use the product may very well lead to the purchase of an additional unit.

Suggest Merchandise for Special Occasions. It is a well-known fact that sales are greatly increased by such holidays as Christmas, Easter, Mother's Day, Father's Day, Thanksgiving, and Valentine's Day. The individual salesman should take advantage of this fact by suggesting items that make appropriate gifts for these holidays. For example, the door-to-door brush salesman has sold the housewife some cleaning supplies and then he says, "Mrs. White, Father's Day is coming up shortly. May I suggest this pair of military brushes for the children to give their father?"

Salespeople can also take advantage of birthdays and anniversaries to suggest merchandise. For instance, a salesgirl knows that Mrs. Rogers' daughter has a birthday in June; so when Mrs. Rogers is in the store in late May, the salesgirl suggests some items that would make appropriate birthday presents.

Five Rules for Suggestion Selling. Here are five rules to follow in making suggestions:

1. Satisfy the customer's request first.
2. Make the suggestion from the customer's point of view.
3. Make a specific suggestion.
4. Make the suggestion positive.
5. Show the suggested item.

Satisfy the Customer's Request First. When your customer is deciding on some shirts, it would be a mistake to say, "While you are looking at those shirts, let me show you some ties." You should complete the sale of the shirts first, and then suggest and show the ties. Don't wait too long, however. Make the suggestion before the original purchase is wrapped and paid for, while the customer is still considering his needs.

■ Make your suggestion specific, as this salesman is doing. Rather than simply suggest a new tie, show the customer how well the tie goes with the shirt he has just purchased.

Make the Suggestion from the Customer's Point of View. When you make a suggestion, the customer should get the impression that you are trying to be of service to him. You don't want him to feel that you are simply trying to make additional sales and that you don't really care whether he needs the items or not. Your suggestions should be realistically

Dealers like to buy from the salesman who not only explains *what* the merchandise will bring in (in terms of profits) but also shows the dealer *how* to display and sell the merchandise to the ultimate consumer.

—Mel S. Hattwick, *The New Psychology of Selling*, McGraw-Hill

aimed at the particular customer. For example, there's no use in the grocer trying to sell a whole case of frozen orange juice, even though it's a real bargain, to a woman without a freezer.

Make a Specific Suggestion. After selling a shirt, don't say, "Would you be interested in any of these ties?" You should say instead, "Our new line of spring ties has just come in. Look how nicely this one goes with your new shirt." While you are saying this, you should place the tie on the shirt so the customer can see exactly how it will look.

Make the Suggestion Positive. Such questions as "You wouldn't be interested in a scarf, too, would you?" or even "Will that be all?" should be avoided because they are too negative. Nor is there anything positive about such a question as "Could you use a new hat with that coat?" Instead the salesman should show the customer a hat that goes well with the coat and say, "Here's a hat I'm sure you'll like. This is the new brim that just came in this season, and our customers have really taken to it."

Show the Suggested Item. Just talking about a product is not going to sell it. The retail salesperson should get the suggested item into his customer's hands as soon as possible so that the customer can see it, handle it, and begin thinking in terms of owning it. In specialty and industrial selling, the salesman should have a sample of the product, or at least a picture of it if he can't have the product itself. The point is that the customer must be able to think of the product concretely.

Often it is best for the salesman to bring out the item before he even mentions it. If his selection has been a good one, it will sell itself.

Selling More on Call-Backs

A specialty or industrial salesman can build up his total sales volume by increasing the amount of sales that he makes to his regular customers. By regular customers we mean those customers on whom he calls periodically to get additional orders for his product or line of merchandise.

The first problem here is to figure out what the proper interval should be between calls. If the salesman postpones his call too long, he may find that the customer has become "unsold." Either he has lost his desire for the product or a competitor has taken over the business. On the other hand, too frequent calls may make the prospect feel overly pressured. As in so many other areas of selling, the answer to this problem lies in finding a happy medium through shrewd observation and common sense.

The salesman must call back often enough to convince the customer that he is genuinely interested in rendering the customer the best possible service. The call-back should not seem like a "duty," something that the salesman is trying to finish quickly so that he can get on to more important things. The salesman should make the call seem friendly, and he should show a real interest in the customer's problems. Perhaps he can advise the customer on better display methods or instruct the customer's salespeople on how to sell the line of merchandise. Perhaps he will need to report back to his company about an adjustment that is necessary on some item he has previously sold the customer. In any event, if the salesman expects to hold this customer, he must spend whatever time is necessary to make the customer feel that his business is appreciated.

If the salesman continually works to maintain a good relationship with the customer, it will be easy for him to do more on his call-backs than just refill the same order. By using the principles of suggestion selling discussed above, he can capitalize on the goodwill that he has built up and substantially increase the size of the order. This will mean more satisfaction for the customer, a larger profit for the company, and an increase in the salesman's commissions.

■ The salesman who is genuinely interested in helping his customers solve their problems will very likely increase his sales as well as build goodwill. Here the salesman is reviewing the cutting techniques at the customer's plant.

SUMMING UP

The salesman can increase his sales volume in three ways. They are (1) closing more sales successfully, (2) suggestion selling, and (3) selling more on call-backs.

To close more sales successfully, the salesman should have a continuous program of self-analysis and self-improvement so that he can constantly beat his own selling record.

In suggestion selling, the salesman tries to influence the customer to increase the size of his order by purchasing a larger quantity of the product, a higher-priced product, or additional items. Suggestion selling is not high-pressure selling; at the same time it is the exact opposite of order taking. Suggestion selling, besides meaning more profit for the store or company and higher commissions for the salesman, represents real service to the customer.

The seven methods of suggestion selling are (1) suggest related items, (2) suggest a larger quantity, (3) suggest higher-priced, better-quality merchandise, (4) suggest newly arrived stock, (5) suggest specially advertised items, (6) suggest new or additional uses for merchandise, and (7) suggest merchandise for special occasions.

The five rules for suggestion selling are (1) satisfy the customer's request first, (2) make the suggestion from the customer's point of view, (3) make a specific suggestion, (4) make the suggestion positive, and (5) show the suggested item.

The salesman's ability to sell more on call-backs depends directly on the relationship that he has been able to build up with the customer. If the customer believes that his welfare is of direct concern to the salesman, then additional sales should come easily.

Reviewing Your Reading

1. Why does the progressive salesman always try to beat his own sales record?
2. What is suggestion selling?
3. How does suggestion selling benefit the company or store, the salesman, and the customer?
4. Why does a store make more profit from selling a larger quantity of the same item?

5. List the seven methods of suggestion selling.
6. Why does the salesperson really have to know the stock in a retail store or the whole line of merchandise in specialty or industrial selling in order to be successful at selling related items?
7. What does "trading up" the sale mean?
8. Why is it important not to use the words "cheap" or "inferior" when you are trying to "trade up" a sale?
9. Why do customers like to know about newly arrived stock?
10. Why is it a good idea to suggest new or additional uses for products?
11. List the five rules for suggestion selling and explain each briefly.
12. How can the salesman tell how often he should call back on his regular customers?
13. Why is the regular customer's goodwill important to the salesman who wants to increase his sales volume?

For Discussion

1. Is suggestion selling high-pressure selling? Defend your answer.
2. What is the difference between suggestion selling and order taking?
3. Review the case of the salesman who started with a sale of house paint and ended with the sale of a ladder. Name all the points of good selling procedure involved in this sale.
4. If you were a salesman of men's shoes, what other items could you suggest after selling a pair of shoes? Write out what you would say in introducing the items.
5. On page 317 it was said that the grocer's display would do his suggestion selling for him. List three other displays you have seen that are examples of suggestion selling.

Sales Problem

You are selling in a notions department. A customer asks for white cotton thread. Your department carries a 100-yard spool for 10 cents and a 250-yard spool for 20 cents. Here is the situation at the beginning of a sale:

CUSTOMER: I'd like to have five spools of white cotton thread number 50.
SALESMAN: **Do you wish the 100-yard spools or the 250-yard spools?**
CUSTOMER: I'll take the 100-yard spools. I've always bought thread that way.

QUESTION
How would you suggest the purchase of five spools at 20 cents each?

1. Using the principles learned in this chapter, write a related-item suggestion for each of the following purchases:
   a. Cup of coffee in restaurant
   b. Bottle of mouthwash
   c. Umbrella
   d. New automobile
   e. Five gallons of gasoline
   f. Handbook on grammar in bookstore
2. Study the following sales situations and indicate how you could have improved on them:
   a. A customer asks to see the suits advertised at $35. The salesperson says, "I can show you those suits, but I'm sure that you'd like these suits at $50 better. They're a real value."
   b. A customer purchases a shirt. The salesperson says, "May I show you a tie to match the shirt?"
   c. A wholesale hardware salesman has just completed a sale of a line of tools to a retail dealer. He remarks, "I suppose you have plenty of nails in assorted sizes."
   d. A customer asks for a certain brand of toothpaste. The salesman says, "We have that brand, but our private brand is a lot better."
   e. A customer asks to look at tents. Before showing the tents, the salesman says, "Certainly, but first let me show you a new line of sleeping bags that just came in."
   f. A customer has purchased 10 gallons of gasoline. The salesman says, "How are you fixed for tires, tubes, batteries, and auto polish?"

Common Sales Problems

THERE ARE four problems that merit special attention both because of the frequency with which the salesman meets them and because of the special techniques that are required to handle them. These problems, which will be discussed in this chapter, are (1) price, (2) trade-ins, (3) competition, and (4) selling to groups.

Meeting the Problem of Price

The problem of price is a large one in selling, because everyone wants to feel that he is getting his money's worth when he makes a purchase. A man who is about to part with his money suddenly remembers how hard it was to come by and wants extra assurance that he is not being "gypped." It is therefore up to the salesman to convince the prospect that the benefits and satisfactions of owning the product will make the product well worth the amount of money being asked.

The ability to handle the problem of price satisfactorily depends on a consideration of the following points: (1) the salesman's attitude toward price,

(2) recommendations for a positive presentation of price, and (3) six suggestions for handling price objections.

The Salesman's Attitude Toward Price. The prospect cannot possibly be made to feel that he is getting a good buy unless the salesman sincerely believes that this is so. If the salesman himself feels that the price of his product is too high, then he is going to pass this feeling along to the prospect and meet with sales resistance that otherwise might never come up.

Many salesmen, especially beginners, automatically assume that when the prospect asks about price, it is because he wants something cheaper. When the prospect says, "Ten dollars sounds like a lot," the salesman forgets everything that he knows about his duties as a salesman and retreats from the field without firing a shot. He gulps unhappily and says, "Well, we have another line that sells for $6." Such salesmen have a price complex. They are so afraid that their prospects will object to the price that they spend half of their sales life thinking up excuses and apologies for it.

Here is a story that will illustrate this point: A salesman named Bill Adams sold advertising brochures for a printing company. Often he would have to quote prices of $1,000 to $2,000 for a job. Every time he got to the point of quoting the price, fear would take hold and he would state the price as though he

■ The price of the frame is too high. By emphasizing the need for a frame that does the painting justice, the salesman can overcome this objection.

couldn't be more ashamed of it. One day a stove manufacturer asked Bill the price of a printing job involving 10,000 booklets. Bill, in his usual apologetic manner, stammered, "Well, it's—it's $1,500, Mr. Rawlings." The prospect, with no hesitation whatsoever, said, "I don't think that price is bad at all, considering the service you're giving us. Where do I sign?" From that day on, Bill stopped worrying about price and began instead to develop confidence and pride in the service he was selling.

Recommendations for a Positive Presentation of Price. The best way to handle the price objection in any sales interview is *to never let it arise.* The salesman's basic tool for forestalling it is a positive presentation that makes the quality and benefits of the product stand out so emphatically that price seems relatively unimportant. It will help you as the salesman if you will think of the sales process as a pair of scales. When you start the sales interview, the scales are tipped in favor of the lowest possible price. As you show the prospect how the various selling features of your product provide him with something he needs or wants, you add weight to the value side of the scale. The customer will be ready to close when you have piled up so much value that the price is completely outweighed.

It is important to remember that the prospect usually cannot do the weighing of the product values and the money without your help. There are very few products whose values are completely self-evident; your prospect won't see or understand the hidden values unless you open his eyes. But you must not only point out the advantages of the product. You must also prove that these advantages will add so much to the comfort, safety, health, welfare, happiness, or satisfaction of the prospect that the amount of money being asked for the product actually seems low.

If the prospect is left with the feeling that the price is too high, you have not done a complete job of building value. A sales manager for an electrical firm sums it up this way:

We teach our men to anticipate the price objection. While the salesman is making his presentation, the question in the mind of the buyer is: How much will it cost? If this question is not answered satisfactorily during the salesman's presentation, the buyer will raise the objection: Your price is too high. If this anticipated objection is actually spoken, our salesmen know that they have missed in their presentation. Somewhere in the presentation, they have left this question incompletely answered. The prospect is still thinking more about what our product will cost him rather than what he will get out of it by buying and using it.

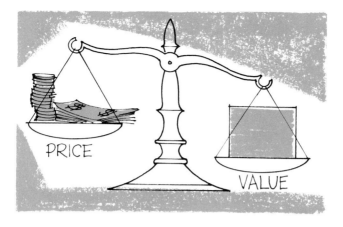

■ Tip the scales to the side of value, and the salesman will outweigh the customer's objection to price.

The salesman should try to get the scales tipped on the value side before he
mentions the price. If the prospect asks what the price is before the salesman
feels he has built enough value, the salesman is justified in trying to postpone the
price discussion. This is the approach that the salesman for an oil burner might
use:

SALESMAN: The price of this burner is important to you, of course. But first, Mr.
    Wayman, may I demonstrate that you can actually buy this burner and
    save money. I think I can prove to you that the cost of operating this
    burner is so much less than the system you now have that the savings will
    pay for the new burner in just a few years.

A water-softener salesman might use this method to postpone the discussion
of price:

SALESMAN: We have several models, Mr. Reston, depending upon the size of
    your family and the amount of water used. But before we go into the price
    of these various models, let's determine first whether or not you could ac-
    tually benefit from owning a water softener. If this is something that you
    couldn't use, it wouldn't be worth the money no matter what the price.
    Don't you agree?

If the prospect will not be put off, the salesman should go ahead and quote
the price; but he should do so in such a way as to keep the prospect's attention

focused on *value*. He should use very positive words in discussing the benefits derived from the product; but he should use such words as *only, low,* and *mere* when giving the price. For example, he might say, "The price of the jungle gym is only $65, Mrs. Danielson, and my company is proud to be able to offer such a well-made piece of equipment at this low price. With the welded tubular steel framework, you are buying freedom from maintenance for your husband and absolute safety for your children."

Another method that the salesman can use to make value sound more important when he is quoting the price is to quote a higher price. The salesman says, "Wouldn't you think that you'd have to pay at least $200 for such quality? Well, you'll be surprised to hear that this couch is priced at only $150."

Six Suggestions for Handling Price Objections. There are times when the price objection will come up in spite of all the salesman's precautions. Here are six practical suggestions that will help the salesman to handle the price objection when it does arise: (1) postpone the price objection as long as you can, (2) define the price objection, (3) prove why your price is right, (4) break down the price into small units, (5) offer easy terms of payment, and (6) consider when price adjustment is necessary.

Postpone the Price Objection as Long as You Can. It has already been said that when the prospect asks what the price is early in the sale, the answer should be postponed until the advantages of the product have been sufficiently explained. If the salesman must give the price early in the interview, he should try to keep the prospect's mind on value. But even so, the prospect may say flatly, "That's too much" or "What makes you think I've got that kind of money?" These are not simple statements or questions about price, but loaded objections.

As you will recall from Chapter 14, the general rule for the best time to answer objections is to answer them immediately. But the price objection is the exception to this rule. When the prospect says, "Your price is too high," the salesman can say, "I am sure you realize, Mr. Whitney, that with the American economic system it actually would be impossible for a company to go on selling a product that is priced too high. Competition would force the company to either lower its price or go out of business. If you will allow me to tell you a little more about my product, I am sure you will understand why it is priced as it is." The point about postponing the price objection is that the only possible answer to price objection is *value,* and the salesman must have time to build up this value in the eyes of the prospect.

Define the Price Objection. In order to handle the price objection satisfactorily, the salesman will have to figure out exactly what the prospect means by his

■ Pointing out the hidden extras shows the customer why your price is right.

Courtesy The Du Pont Company

objection. When he says, "Your price is too high," he may mean any one of three things. He may mean that the product is not worth the price being asked and that it is therefore not a good buy. Or he may mean that the price is too high *for him*—that is, he doesn't have that much money. Then again, he may mean that he needs the product and is ready to buy it but is convinced he can get either the same product or one exactly like it for less elsewhere.

It is obvious that the methods of handling these three meanings of the same objection would be quite different. These methods will be discussed in detail below.

Prove Why Your Price Is Right. If the prospect feels that the product is not worth the price in spite of the salesman's positive presentation, the salesman's first job is to remain good-natured and pleasant. The salesman may be tempted to feel that the prospect is either stubborn or stupid, but the simple fact is that this is immaterial. The prospect is not taking an examination to prove how quickly he can think. On the contrary, it is the salesman who is on trial, and the test is whether he can sell his product to all kinds of people. If the prospect needs the mental comfort of repetition before he can understand the point, then the salesman must be prepared to give it to him.

This means that the salesman must be ready to say all over again what he has already said in his presentation, using different words and examples, but making the same basic point that the product is worth the price because of the value inherent in it. The salesman must prove that the product is priced right in terms of quality, performance, style, durability, and other factors.

The salesman must be sure to point out every hidden extra. Is installation free? Then say so. Does your product have a longer guarantee? Then make this absolutely clear. Does your product have a high initial cost but such low maintenance

■ If the prospective customer feels that he cannot afford the appliance, offering him easy terms of payment may be the answer.

costs that it will soon pay for itself? Prove this with charts, graphs, or testimonials. Does your product have exclusive features that other makes of the same product don't have? Point these out. Is your product really superior in materials and construction? Demonstrate this with cross sections, parts, or working models. The point is that there is a way to reach the prospect and *prove* to him that the product is worth the price, and the salesman must find it.

Break Down the Price into Small Units. Breaking down the price into small units is a good device for minimizing the cost in the prospect's mind. When the salesman talks about 20 cents per week or 5 cents per mile, the prospect gets the impression that the cost is not so high after all. For example, the salesman for a boys' magazine may say to the housewife, "Mrs. Holden, a subscription to this magazine costs $7.50 a year because it is a weekly magazine of the highest quality. But you know, that amounts to just about 2 cents a day. Two cents a day does not sound like much to spend on your boy's mental health, does it? I'm sure that if you give him a vitamin pill every day it costs more than that."

Offer Easy Terms of Payment. The best way to handle the prospect who feels that he cannot afford the product is to offer him a long period of time in which to pay for it. In such cases the prospect usually makes a small down payment and spreads the rest of the payments out over several months or years. This is known as *buying on time.* Because time buying is inconvenient for the seller, many companies give a discount to customers who are willing to pay cash, or a surcharge may be placed on the time accounts. Even considering the surcharge, sometimes the fact that the new car can be had for only $50 a month is the deciding factor in the sale.

Consider When Price Adjustment Is Necessary. If the prospect refuses to buy because he feels that he can get the same product for less elsewhere, the salesman must first of all figure out whether it is the exact same product. If it is only a *similar* product, then the salesman must point out to the prospect that his product costs more because it is made better, more durable, and so on. In order to be able to make a comparison, the salesman must know his own product and he must be well acquainted with the competition. Here is an example of how this can work when the salesperson has not actually seen the specific product that the customer saw in another store. However, the salesperson does know the store where the customer claims to have seen the same dress for less, and she knows that the other store's whole line of merchandise is of an inferior quality.

SALESPERSON: **Madam, often dresses that look alike are really quite different in workmanship. Are you certain they were the same in every part?**

CUSTOMER: Quite certain.

SALESPERSON (*pointing to the shoulder and waist of the garment*): **Did the other garment have darts at these points to provide a better fit? Did the placket closings have one continuous lengthwise seam? That's the earmark of a better-made garment, you know. Were the pleats full like these? Notice how they hang straight and don't spread out like a fan. And notice how deep the underfold of the pleat is. Did the other garment have these features?**

CUSTOMER: Well, I don't know.

SALESPERSON: **Also, examine the reinforcement of these pockets. And notice how this dress is finished with a seam binding and hemmed with a long stitch by hand.**

CUSTOMER: I guess I really can't say that these dresses are identical.

In this case the salesperson may not make an immediate sale, but the customer will certainly check the lower-priced dress with a more critical attitude. If she finds that the dress is indeed inferior, she will return for the better dress.

Sometimes, however, the prospect is talking about the very same product which can be bought for less in another store or from another dealer. When this can be proved (many stores have comparison shoppers for this purpose), the customer is usually given the benefit of the lower price. But of course this is a decision for management and not for the individual salesman. The new importance of discount stores in the retail picture has complicated this policy for many stores; in this case the regular retail store must make the customer appreciate those services it offers that the discount house does not.

The retail salesman is not the only salesman who meets demands for price concessions. Industrial and specialty salesmen sometimes have to cope with prospects who claim that they should be given special price favors beyond the allowable quantity or cash discounts. Also, men who are in a position to "throw"

■ Handling the trade-in problem calls for tact. To help avoid excessive argument, the prospect should not be present while his old car is being appraised. Having it done by a third party is better yet.

Courtesy Ford Motor Company

additional business to the salesman feel that they should be rewarded with a "kickback" of the price or a split of the salesman's commissions, regardless of the unethical nature of such transactions.

The old adage "If you can't beat them, join them" does not apply here. The salesman must realize that giving in to such price chiselers has a far-reaching effect on the national economy when multiplied by the large number of cases that take place every day. When special discounts are given to one customer, then other customers must pay in some way for that concession. The best policy in dealing with the price chiseler is to discuss the matter straight from the shoulder, like this:

SALESMAN: Mr. Prospect, I don't believe that you mean exactly what you say when you ask for a lower price than we give to our other customers. You're a businessman. You know that no organization in the world can stay in business if it operates on a basis that causes loss or insufficient margin of profit. Our price is competitive. I don't want you to pay more than others do, and you won't if you help us to stay within our price structure.

Handling the Trade-in Problem

The trade-in problem arises when the prospect wishes to turn in a used article as part payment for the new one. This happens routinely with such products as large and small appliances, automobiles, trucks, boats, office furniture and equipment, and so on. The question of the trade-in deserves special consideration because it involves two selling problems. You must not only sell the prospect on the new article but also sell him on accepting your estimate of the value of the article that he wishes to trade in.

It is very important that the salesman sell the new article *first*. If the prospect has been fully sold on the new article so that he *really wants to own it*, he will be less likely to quibble about the value placed on the trade-in. But in presenting his estimate of the old article, the salesman must remember that the prospect almost surely places a higher value on it than it actually possesses in terms of the market. The salesman must therefore never openly talk down the used article. People who have owned something for a number of years attach a sentimental value to it. The paradox here is that the prospect knows perfectly well that the article is battered and doesn't work right. He knows it so well that he wants to replace it. And yet if the salesman comes right out and says so, the prospect suddenly remembers only the good things about his possession and feels that the salesman is being very unfair.

This situation obviously calls for great tact. To avoid as much argument as possible, the used article should never be appraised in front of the prospect. In fact, it is best to have the appraisal done by a third party, so that the salesman isn't even involved. Then the salesman can act as though he is on the prospect's side. The salesman can say, "I know you've taken wonderful care of your car, Mr. Jordan, and I'm sure our appraiser will be impressed by that. He's a professional, you know, and his job is to help us make the sale by giving you all that he possibly can for your car." This prepares the prospect for accepting the appraiser's estimate and usually precludes any argument. However, if the prospect should try to argue after he has heard the estimate, the salesman can show the prospect the classified ads in the daily newspaper to prove to him what cars such as his are selling for. Or he can take the prospect back to the used-car lot and show him how much the dealer gets for cars like his, explaining also what the dealer has to put into the car in labor and materials before he can sell it.

To illustrate the importance of tact in handling the trade-in problem, a car dealer tells his salesmen the story of a prospect who parked an old jalopy in front of a used-car dealer's place of business:

"Looking for an automobile?" asked the salesman who met him out front.

"Yep," replied the prospect.

"Of course, your old car here isn't worth much," replied the salesman. "The paint is worn thin, and it's been touched up in a lot of places. Looks like it has been in some accidents. The motor sounds rough, too. I think this car will need an awful lot of work on it before we can hope to resell it. Tell you what I'll do. I'll give you $50 for it."

"It's not my car and never will be," replied the man. "Your boss was showing it to me and let me drive it around the block to test it, but I guess you convinced me of its worth. Good-bye."

Meeting Your Competition

Competition has been at the center of the economic system of the United States ever since this country's founding. It is basic to the idea of free enterprise, which offers everyone the opportunity to follow a business or a trade of his own choosing. The business or trade can only be as successful as the ability of the businessman or tradesman to develop a product or service that people want and to get it distributed to those who are willing to pay for it. Since the customer can choose the product or service that he will buy, the man who makes the better product or renders the superior service will obviously be more successful than a less-accomplished competitor.

Business firms throughout the United States feel that this system is a source of strength for all businesses and one of the direct causes of the high level of life in the United States today, which is the highest level ever attained in the history of the world. Business firms try to pass this philosophy along to their salesmen as may be seen in this statement of the Pittsburgh Plate Glass Company in its *Handbook of General Sales Procedure:*

> Competition is a business stimulant and a challenge to the members of a right-thinking organization. Pittsburgh Plate Glass Company is an aggressively keen and worthy contender for its share of available business and wishes to merit and maintain the respect of its competitors as to its high ethical standards.

But the question is, How does the salesman handle this competition? After all, he wants to be the one who succeeds in selling the prospect, so what does he do about such statements as the following?

"What makes you think your product is as good as Hotspot?"

"I can get it for less by buying Kelley's brand."

"The salesman for the Biltmore Company said his products wear four years longer than any other type on the market."

"Your machine doesn't have the features that the Bluestone has."

There are seven rules which will help the salesman to answer such questions. They are:

1. Have the right attitude toward competition.
2. Know your competition.
3. Anticipate competition in your sales presentation.
4. Wait for the prospect to bring up competition.

Courtesy The Du Pont Company

■ Sometimes several competitive salesmen may be waiting in the reception room to see the same prospect. Instead of resenting the competition, each salesman should remember that competition stimulates him to do an even better job of selling.

5. Get at the prospect's motives.
6. Emphasize the positive.
7. Be scrupulously fair.

Have the Right Attitude Toward Competition. If you secretly believe that your competitor's product is superior and that your product runs only a poor second, then you are beaten before you start. You cannot sell with confidence unless you feel that you have a worthwhile product to offer. You cannot get enthusiastic about selling against competition unless you feel that your product solves the prospect's problem better than any other product does.

But thinking that your product is the best does not mean that you should consider the competition totally inferior and not worth any consideration at all. You must recognize that other brands of the product you are selling have many points to recommend them. If they did not, the companies making them would soon be out of business. So your attitude toward your competition must be one of respect. You should also realize that competition is good for you and your company. The fact that some other fellow is in there fighting for the same business stimulates you to do a better job and to render better service to your customers.

The only time when you are entitled to resent competition is when it is unethical. The story is told of a town where there were two undertakers, one named Smith and one named Jones. Mr. Smith began telephoning the families of very sick people and asking for their business when the patient died; but when he called, he identified himself as Mr. Jones. However, unethical practices in fighting competition have been so completely discouraged by the big companies that it is very improbable that you will ever meet anyone like Mr. Smith. Most salesmen realize that the world is not big enough to allow a man to have two characters—one in business and one in church on Sunday. The man who wants to be thought of as honest by his neighbors must be honest 100 percent of the time.

Know Your Competition. It has been stressed throughout this book that it is vital that the salesman have thorough knowledge not only of his own product but also of the products which compete with his. Buyers today are themselves very knowledgeable. The massive advertising campaigns that are conducted over television and in the national magazines keep even the people who live in isolated areas well aware of what is going on in the marketplace. And such special magazines as *Consumer Reports* are making the buying public very sophisticated about how products compete with each other and what to look for in a product.

You as the salesman cannot run the risk of being less knowledgeable than the prospect. You should learn all that you possibly can about your competitors—the chief selling features of their products, the prices and terms usually granted, the types of service offered with the products, and the names and methods of their salesmen in your territory. This information can be gathered (1) through material provided by your own company; (2) by your own personal use of competing products whenever feasible; (3) from trade magazines and from your competitors' publications, catalogs, price lists, and advertising; (4) by observing competing salesmen; and (5) through conversations with customers, prospects, friends, and relatives.

It is recommended that after the salesman has gathered all the information he can, he draw up a debit and credit sheet for his own product and for the competing ones so that he can compare what is good and bad about each product. If the salesman will do this, he will not be surprised by any of the questions that the prospect may ask.

Anticipate Competition in Your Sales Presentation. The student is already acquainted with the idea of weaving the answers to anticipated objections into the sales story, not mentioning the objections, but giving what would be the answers to them in a very *positive* way. This same principle applies in the area of competition. The salesman will thus benefit from drawing up the credit and debit sheets for his product and the competing ones. Because the salesman knows ahead of time what features of his product are most likely to be compared with the competition, he can meet the objection before it arises. Then if the objection comes up anyhow, he will be in the always fortunate position of being able to repeat and reemphasize what he has already said instead of having to answer the question as though it were a whole new train of thought.

For example, assume that you are selling stainless-steel cooking utensils direct to the home. Your main competition is a company that makes aluminum utensils. You know that the aluminum company is building its sales on the story that aluminum is a pleasure to use because it is so light and easy to handle, and also that the aluminum utensils are inexpensive. So in your sales presentation you stress the fact that your company uses relatively heavy steel because it will outwear any of the lighter metals. It does not dent or pit, and hence it is easy to clean and will last the lifetime of the housewife. You also point out that although these utensils seem expensive, they are in fact the best buy on the market since they will never have to be replaced. You have not even mentioned your competitor or aluminum itself, and yet you have scored heavily for your own product versus the competing one.

Wait for the Prospect to Bring Up Competition. The salesman should never be the first to mention the competition. Suppose that in the above example the salesman came right out and said, "We want you to know that the aluminum utensils that the Wearite Company sells are not nearly so good as our utensils because they are too light. They sell for less, but being made of less durable material, they don't last as long." The salesman has now very successfully and quite unnecessarily focused the attention of the prospect on the competition. Whereas the housewife might have been sold on the stainless steel, once she hears that there is a competing product, she feels that she had better investigate it to be sure she is making the right choice. In this case the salesman has brought his troubles on himself.

■ During a manufacturers' exhibit, the salesman will meet all kinds of competition. However, the prepared salesman will have anticipated his competition when he planned his sales presentation.

Get at the Prospect's Motives. The prospect's remarks about the competition provide very accurate clues as to what his buying motives really are. Suppose that the prospect says, "I think the Marvelle Freezer is more convenient than yours." With this clue that one of the prospect's main buying motives is convenience, the salesman can begin to concentrate his sales story on the convenience features of the freezer he is selling. He does not have to criticize the Marvelle Freezer, but can divert the attention of the prospect by making the points about his own freezer very positively. The point is that the salesman has to know what the prospect's real buying motives are before he can prove to the prospect how his product will meet the prospect's needs.

Emphasize the Positive. The old saying "If you can't say something good about somebody, don't say anything" is very applicable to the discussion of how to handle competition. When a prospect invites criticism of your competitors, do not be led astray. The time that you spend criticizing the competition would be better spent in building up the value of your own product. The Pittsburgh Plate Glass Company has stated this principle in its sales-training material:

> It is our policy not to discuss competitors with the trade, but instead to discuss our company, its products and service. Your objective is to sell our products on their merits, not to disparage competitors' products.

The more you talk about a competitor's product, the more publicity you give it. In the end, all that you accomplish is to make the prospect curious to see the competitor's brand. By talking about the competition more than is absolutely necessary, you give the prospect the idea that the competitor's product must be a very good one and a serious threat to your business since it is so much on your mind.

Stay ahead of your competitors, not by running them down, but by giving a better demonstration of the advantages of your product. Instead of fearing the competition, keep your mind free to concentrate on new approaches and methods to win the prospect's approval and business.

Be Scrupulously Fair. The salesman must always be scrupulously fair in dealing with competitors. When a salesman does anything unfair or makes an unjust criticism of a competitor, he lowers himself and his company in the eyes of the prospect. Also, the salesman must be very sure that whatever he says is accurate. If the prospect catches him in one false statement about a competitor, the sale will be over.

But being fair works both ways. The salesman is also obligated to do justice to his own product, and sometimes this requires a frank comparison of his product with the competition. The situation obviously must be handled very tactfully. Here is an example of how an expert salesman can compare his product with a competing product without saying anything to the prospect against the other product:

PROSPECT: Well, I don't know. I guess an electric range would be nice to have; but the new gas range I was looking at in Jones's appliance store was certainly modern-looking, and gas is cheaper to use, too.

SALESMAN: **I can understand your hesitation, Mrs. Macdonald. Gas may be cheaper in some cases. Suppose we just keep score on this piece of paper and jot that down as a point for my competitor.**

(*Salesman writes "gas is cheaper" on left-hand side of paper.*)

Electricity is slightly higher than gas, so the other fellow has the edge on us there. But now, balance against that the fact that electric cooking is fast. When boiling and steaming food on an electric range, very little water need be added. This allows your cooking temperature to be reached more quickly. Flame cooking, on the other hand, requires more water to cook food. This means slower cooking.

(*Salesman writes "faster cooking" on right-hand side of paper.*)

That's pretty important to you, isn't it, Mrs. Macdonald?

PROSPECT: Well, yes, that is an advantage, but there is something else that bothers me. The gas-range man said that an electric range requires special wiring, and that's quite a bit of extra cost, isn't it, Mr. Salesman?

■ The salesman can emphasize the positive by building up the advantages of his own product. He should never criticize the competition.

SALESMAN: Yes, there is an added cost for wiring, although it is not a prohibitive amount, Mrs. Macdonald. I'll put that down as another point for my competitor.

(*Writes "extra wiring costs."*)

But now balance that against the fact that electric cooking is clean. Your pots and pans stay bright and shiny; and your walls, ceiling, woodwork, and curtains stay cleaner longer.

That's a real advantage, isn't it, Mrs. Macdonald?

PROSPECT: Oh my yes, I hadn't thought of that.

(*Salesman writes "clean cooking—clean kitchen."*)

PROSPECT: I've been using a gas range all my life. I'm not sure that I could get used to an electric range.

SALESMAN: I'm sure that you could—just as thousands of other women have. Electric cooking is really easier because it is certain and sure. But just to be fair to my competitor and to give him the benefit of the doubt, I'll put that down on the left-hand side, Mrs. Macdonald.

(*Writes "accustomed to gas."*)

Now balance that with the fact that electric cooking is automatic. It's as automatic as your electric refrigerator. Electric heat, wherever you set the switch, is identical day after day. Isn't that a big advantage, Mrs. Macdonald?

(*Writes it as he talks.*)

PROSPECT: Why, yes. It actually makes cooking seem easier, doesn't it?

■ When selling to a group, the five steps of the sale still apply. If the group is small, it is a good idea to encourage each person to talk and to ask questions.

SALESMAN: Yes, it certainly does. In fact, with the automatic time controls on this range, your cooking will seem like magic.

(*Prospect nods, and salesman continues.*)

On top of these points, let's just add:

Electric cooking is cool. No flame, no burning of fuel.

Electric cooking is healthful. Doesn't consume precious oxygen and doesn't expel any by-products of combustion into the air.

Electric cooking is certain and sure. You don't need to guess at temperatures.

Electric cooking is convenient. Your switch settings eliminate guesswork. Your automatic controls start and stop cooking with no one around.

And finally, electric cooking is modern—as modern as the electric light. You wouldn't think of using gas lamps in your home any longer, would you, Mrs. Macdonald? Of course not, and so it is with electric cooking. It's the modern way because it's fast, clean, safe, cool, healthful, automatic, and convenient. Now, don't you honestly think, as you compare the two scores, that we offer you a bigger total of advantages?

A *bigger score,* a bigger total of advantages. That's the way to beat competition.

Selling to Groups

Selling is not always a matter of trying to influence one prospect at a time. Nor is it always an activity that is carried on in the privacy of the prospect's office or home. Salesmen are frequently called upon to make a sales presentation to a group of prospects. Even as a student you may have to engage in group selling if you take part in student politics or try to persuade a student meeting to accept a new idea. Here are some situations in which the salesman is called upon to sell to whole groups of prospects at once:

1. Sales where the approval of several officials is required, as in government agencies, purchasing committees, and boards of directors
2. Purchases so large that a group of company executives must make the decision
3. Demonstrations of products in retail stores, in social and church clubs, and to groups in homes
4. Fund raising for charitable organizations, such as the Red Cross, the Community Chest, hospital drives, and so on

In selling to groups, you must carry your audience through the stages of the sale—attention, interest, desire, conviction, action—just as when selling to individuals. In addition, you must be familiar with the principles of public speaking. Although selling to groups is not necessarily the same as delivering a speech, good platform poise, a well-organized talk, and voice control and development are all important.

The group salesman must direct his message to the entire group and yet make everyone present feel that the message is addressed to him personally. With small groups, this is done by letting each member of the group talk, ask questions, and demonstrate the product for himself. In larger groups, the salesman should endeavor to maintain eye contact with all the group and should avoid giving the impression that he is talking to only one or two of the members present.

Here are some points to remember in giving a selling demonstration to a group:

1. The attention and interest span of a group is just as short as that of an individual. Plan on building interesting stories, examples, and demonstrations into your group talk.
2. Talk to an audience in the same natural way that you would talk to an individual. After all, a group is only a collection of individuals.
3. Have some strong opening remarks, just as you would in an individual sales approach.
4. Stick to your time limit if you are given one. If you announce that you are going to take only twenty minutes, then complete your presentation in that length of time. Hold a stopwatch on yourself.
5. Remember that you will not be able to personalize your talk as much as you do when you talk to an individual, but you can discuss the needs that you know the group shares. Show how your product will fill those needs.
6. Watch your vocabulary. Use words that express your ideas correctly. Use the right words for what you mean. Pronounce your words correctly.
7. Avoid distracting mannerisms, such as fidgeting with your tie, swaying back and forth, leaning on one foot, gesturing wildly, and so on.
8. Have all your material ready for use. Charts, graphs, exhibits, or handouts should be ready for use ahead of time so that you can proceed through your presentation smoothly and rapidly with no awkward or embarrassing breaks.
9. Plan for audience participation. To retain interest, give the group a chance to ask questions, handle the product or exhibits, work a problem, demonstrate your product to themselves.
10. Do not read your sales talk. Nothing is more monotonous and boring, and you will lose the interest of your audience if you read, rather than communicate your ideas.
11. Speak loudly enough for everyone to hear, including the persons in the last row.

SUMMING UP

To persuade a man that he is getting his money's worth when he makes a purchase is one of your major problems as a salesman. You cannot do this unless you yourself are convinced that your product represents a good buy. Your presentation should be aimed at building up so much value for the product that the amount of money being asked for it seems relatively unimportant. If the price objection arises in spite of your positive presentation, you should (1) postpone the price objection as long as you can, (2) define the price objection, (3) prove why your price is right, (4) break down the price into small units, (5) offer easy terms of payment, and (6) consider when price adjustment is necessary.

In handling the question of trade-ins, the salesman is faced with two selling problems, selling the prospect the new article and selling the prospect on the salesman's estimate of the value of the article that he wishes to trade in. The salesman must first sell the prospect on the new article so completely that the appraisal of the trade-in doesn't seem worth quibbling about. The appraisal should be done with great tact. It should not be done in front of the prospect, and whenever possible it should be done by a third party.

Competition is basic to the economic system of the United States and is responsible for the highest living level in the history of the world. It is a source of strength to the salesman and his company for it makes them do their best at all times. But the salesman must know how to handle competition so that he gets his share of the business. The seven rules which will guide the salesman are (1) have the right attitude toward competition, (2) know your competition, (3) anticipate competition in your sales presentation, (4) wait for the prospect to bring up competition, (5) get at the prospect's motives, (6) emphasize the positive, and (7) be scrupulously fair.

Selling to groups is a challenge to the salesman, but it can be easily handled by using all the principles of good salesmanship that have been discussed in this book and by observing all the rules of good public speaking.

Reviewing Your Reading

1. Why is the problem of price a large one in selling?
2. Why is the salesman's attitude important in the price problem?
3. What is the salesman's basic tool for forestalling the price objection?

4. When and how should the salesman quote the price of the product he is selling?
5. List six suggestions for handling the price objection.
6. How many meanings can there be to the statement, "Your price is too high"? What are they?
7. Why is it important that the salesman point out all the hidden extras of his product?
8. What purpose does it serve to break down the price into small units?
9. Is it ever wise to adjust the price of an article? Explain your answer.
10. Why is it important not to give in to price chiselers? What is the best way to deal with the price chiseler?
11. Why is it important to have a third party appraise the prospect's trade-in?
12. How does competition keep a salesman on his toes?
13. Why is it important that the salesman know all about his competitors?
14. Can competition be anticipated in your sales presentation? Explain your answer.
15. Should you run down your competition? Explain your answer.
16. Is group selling completely different from personal selling? Explain your answer.

For Discussion

1. How can you postpone answering a prospect's question about price?
2. When it is obvious that a prospect cannot afford the merchandise, what should you do?
3. How would you handle the objection, "I'm sure that I saw one just like this at Green's Department Store for only $2.95"?
4. Is it good or poor practice to greet the customer with the price, such as "This is a wonderful value—only $5.95"?
5. What would you say to a customer who comments, "That's too cheap"?
6. Assume that a customer has just said, "I imagine the store makes an outrageous profit on these." How would you reply?
7. You are a tire salesman calling on an independent tire dealer. He raises the objection, "Your company makes tires for chain stores, and they're selling them so cheap we can't even stay in business. I don't want any of your stuff." What would you do?
8. How can competition help to develop better salesmen?
9. How would you try to get a prospect's business where a competitor is firmly entrenched?

10. How would you demonstrate, without hurting your competitor's reputation, that a lower-priced product will cost more in the long run?
11. Assume that a competitor's product has more good selling features than your product. What would you do?
12. When a prospect mentions competitors, one salesman says, "I'd rather not talk about my competitors, if you don't mind." Is this an effective technique for handling competition? Give reasons for your answer.
13. Evaluate each of the following three policies:
    a. Criticizing competitors
    b. Praising competitors
    c. Ignoring competitors

Sales Problem

An office-furniture salesman has made two calls on a purchasing agent in an attempt to get his business. It is the procedure, in this case, for the sellers to submit bids for the business. On this, the third call, the salesman hopes to find out whether his bid was accepted.

SALESMAN: **Hello, Mr. Rowen. What's new?**
PROSPECT: Nothing much.
SALESMAN: **Have you reached a decision yet on those 150 desks and chairs?**
PROSPECT: Yes, I hate to tell you this. But your competitor, the Zee Company, gets the order.
SALESMAN: **Those chiselers! Why, Rowen, you know they can't make desks.**
PROSPECT: That remains to be seen.
SALESMAN: **Well, Mr. Rowen, we may not be able to underbid a concern like that, but we sure can outproduce them on quality. I wish you would consider that the next time you decide on bids.**
PROSPECT: Are you trying to tell me how to run my business?
SALESMAN: **No, not at all. Only, the next time you consider buying office furniture, I would appreciate it if you would bear in mind that quality is what counts in the long run. I'll be around to see you on the next bid.**
PROSPECT: Not if I can help it.

QUESTIONS
1. Comment on this case. What general rules of selling did the salesman violate?
2. What was his attitude regarding competition? What should it have been?
3. How could this salesman make this lost order pave the way for a future sale?

1. The prospect says, "Before I take up any of your time, let's get one thing straight. How much will an oil burner cost me?" Write what you would say to postpone quoting the price.
2. If your school is producing a play or operetta and selling tickets both to students and to people in the community, make a list of possible objections to buying tickets (*a*) by students and (*b*) by people in the community. Prepare a written answer for each objection. Your answers will be discussed in class and compared with those suggested by other members of the class.
3. Prepare a list of possible objections and answers to the objections for any other function that your school may be sponsoring, such as a paper drive, scrap drive, carnival, and the like.
4. Given the following objections, write a short answer to each one:
   a. "I have decided to buy from the Globe Company."
   b. "I want to wait and see what other firms will offer me."
   c. "We buy all office supplies from the Howland Company. The president is a friend of mine."
   d. "I have a regular firm that keeps me supplied."
5. Select a commodity that is sold by an industrial or specialty goods firm in your community. Prepare a list of competitors whose products you would need to study. Tell why briefly.
6. You have been asked to address the student council on the subject of letting the senior class sponsor a paper drive to raise money to buy band uniforms. Prepare a short written sales talk on this theme, using the principles introduced in this chapter.

The Telephone as a Sales Aid

FOR THE SALESMAN, time and energy are money. To be successful in his work, the salesman must learn how to stretch his time and energy as far as possible. One way in which the salesman can do this is by an intelligent and discriminating use of the telephone.

The telephone, which only a generation ago was considered a luxury, has now become an indispensable part of every home and business. Its many advantages as an instrument of communication are obvious. But the telephone's special advantages for the salesman merit some discussion.

The Telephone Is Quick

The salesman can reach his customer, even one that is many miles away, in seconds, and can relay his message in another few minutes. This immediacy of contact can be an invaluable asset to the salesman when he wants to notify his customers of the availability of new models, contemplated price changes, special sales, and other situations in which it would be to the buyer's advantage to act quickly. As an example, consider the salesman of stocks and bonds (called a

349

stock broker) who finds out that the price of a certain stock is going up fast. He can notify his customer of this by phone and then with authorization from the client, buy the stock at a lower price than he could if he had waited until he and the client could get together personally. The time element can also be a very important factor in real estate transactions and in the sale of scarce or rare items that tend to be sold as soon as they come on the market.

The Telephone Increases the Salesman's Productivity

The telephone allows the salesman to get more work done than he could if he had to see every prospect or customer face to face. There are jobs that he can handle quickly, easily, and efficiently on the telephone, and these will be discussed in detail later in the chapter. By saving time through the use of the telephone, the salesman will be able to concentrate his time and energy on the work that is more demanding. This obviously will increase the salesman's total productivity, which is the measure of his value to his firm and the basis of his income.

The telephone also adds to the salesman's productivity because it can be used during the hours that the salesman might otherwise be wasting. For example, if the salesman concludes a sale in less time than he had figured he would need, he may have half an hour to fill before his next appointment. He can waste this time over a cup of coffee or he can make as many as ten phone calls. During the half hour that might otherwise go unused, the salesman can talk to as many people by phone as he may see in a whole day's worth of personal calls.

■ **By using the telephone intelligently, the salesman will find it an effective sales aid.**

The Telephone Is Economical

By cutting down on the necessity for traveling, the telephone can save the salesman both time and money. For instance, suppose that a salesman has four accounts in a town that is 100 miles away from his home office. If he calls all four customers on the phone, he may spend a total of $3 in money and fifteen minutes in time for all four calls, compared with $15 for the cost of a round trip in his automobile and a whole day of his time. The savings will be even more evident where there is a single customer in an isolated area.

The example just given is actually a simplification of how the telephone saves time and money. Business firms, caught in the profit squeeze, have become much more conscious of costs in general and have begun to analyze carefully the *total* cost of each personal sales call, especially when their salesmen are on salaries. Some companies estimate this cost to be as high as $85 per prospect, and even the *average* costs runs between $17 and $21. This is the cost per call, whether the call is productive or not, so that if the number of nonproductive and unnecessary calls that the salesman makes can be reduced, a very real economy will be affected. There are many ways in which the telephone can help the salesman reduce costs. One example is that by telephoning ahead for an appointment, the salesman can be sure that he will not call on the buyer at a time when the buyer either is not in or cannot see the salesman.

Uses of the Telephone in Selling

There are ten specific ways in which the telephone can be used as a sales aid:

1. To build a strong prospect list
2. To get appointments
3. To service regular customers
4. To acknowledge orders
5. To close a sale
6. To revive old accounts
7. To notify customers of special events
8. To handle complaints
9. To take orders
10. To sell to new customers

Building a Strong Prospect List. The law of averages says that the more people the salesman can see, the more sales he will make. But the law of averages can be made to work more to the salesman's advantage if the contacts are not just names but people who are qualified prospects. The telephone can help the salesman establish the difference between suspects, possible prospects, and really strong prospects. The salesman can then make his personal calls on the most likely candidates and thus greatly increase the percentage of his successes.

The salesman who sells products with wide appeal, such as vacuum cleaners or television sets, often uses the entire telephone directory as his suspect list on the theory that anyone in the book could conceivably be a prospect. The salesman who is trying to sell swimming pools, however, would be wasting his time with such an approach. For him, anyone who lives in an apartment house, in a rented house, or in a house without the necessary land for a swimming pool would not be even a suspect. Therefore, he might turn to the local real estate directory to locate his suspects. But for either kind of salesman, the telephone can be used to build a strong prospect list from a list of suspects.

As these two examples indicate, the more restricted the appeal of the salesman's item is, the less use the telephone will be to him in sorting out his prospect list, and the less need the salesman will have for this sorting-out process. The salesman of Rolls Royces, for example, or of rare books and manuscripts, does not have so many prospects that he can't take care of them all personally.

Getting Appointments. The salesman who telephones a group of people to sort out his suspect list isn't finished when he finds out who the likely prospects are. He must also make the telephone call work for him by making a favorable impression on the prospect and arousing sufficient interest to get an affirmative answer when he asks for an appointment to demonstrate his product.

Even the salesman who does not need the telephone to establish his list of prospects will find it useful for making appointments. In a survey of 3,000 industrial executives, almost 81 percent of the executives said that they instructed their salesmen to make appointments in advance by telephone for their personal sales calls.[1] A definite appointment can save the salesman a trip to the prospect's place of business when the prospect is not in or cannot see the salesman. A definite appointment will also make it unnecessary for the salesman to waste time in a reception office waiting until the prospect can see him. Finally there is a certain psychological advantage for the salesman who has an appointment. He feels more confident knowing that he will at least be seen; and in turn the buyer, who is prepared ahead of time mentally for the salesman's visit, will probably be more receptive.

Servicing Regular Customers. The salesman whose territory is very large or who has an unusually large number of accounts can use the telephone to help him to

---

[1] "Industrial Marketing Survey," special issue of the *Sales Executive,* Sales Executives Club of New York, Inc., Sept. 5, 1958, p. 16.

WAYS TO USE THE TELEPHONE
IN SELLING

give each customer the best possible service. Even if the salesman is very well organized, he may find that it is physically impossible to get around to all his regular customers as often as he would like and still have time left over for getting new accounts.

For this salesman the telephone is an indispensable aid. He can work out some kind of alternating plan that allows him to call personally on half his customers one month, for instance, and phone the other half, and then to reverse the procedure the following month. It is a well-known fact in selling that the man on the spot gets the business. With this method of regular contact, the salesman can be the man on the spot.

The key word about this plan is *alternating*. The salesman must never get so carried away with the ease of telephoning that he lets long periods of time go by without making a personal call on a given customer. The customer, once he begins to feel neglected, will be much more susceptible to the approaches of rival salesmen.

Acknowledging Orders. A phone call acknowledging an order and thanking the customer for it can accomplish two things: (1) It can strengthen customer relations, which is an important end in itself, and (2) it can even lead to a bigger order or an additional order. Here is an example of how this can work:

SALESMAN: Mr. Buyer, this is Mark Brown of the Crown Furniture Company calling. I want to thank you for the order that you placed with me last week for the new desk and chair for your secretary. Also, I want to tell you that I've checked with the shipping department and they have verified what I told you, that the furniture will be delivered two weeks from today.

CUSTOMER: Thank you for calling, Mr. Brown. It's always nice to know that one's business is appreciated.

SALESMAN: Indeed it is, Mr. Buyer. We are very pleased to be able to serve you. And if you decide that you'd like your secretary to have that pull-up table that I showed you to increase her work space, we can send it over on short notice.

CUSTOMER: Why don't you go ahead and add that to the order right now? That will save us both trouble later on.

SALESMAN: I'll do that, Mr. Buyer, and I'm sure you won't regret your decision. Thank you very much and let me know if I can do anything else for you.

Closing a Sale. When the customer has been unable over a period of time to come to a final decision about buying, the salesman can sometimes use the telephone to force a final *positive* decision. This can backfire, of course, in that the salesman may actually get a final *negative* decision. But the important point is that a telephone call can lead the prospect to think that some significant thing is about to happen which makes an immediate decision essential. The telephone call itself, which implies that the salesman has to talk to the prospect *right away,* without wasting the time to see him personally, adds to the sense of urgency.

As an example, let us say that a salesman has been trying to persuade the owner of a retail men's store to take on a new line of sports shirts. The dealer has been unable to decide whether these shirts are worth carrying or not. The salesman telephones and says, "Mr. Dealer, I had a call from my boss this morning, and he told me that our company has decided to advertise in a big way those sports shirts you and I have been talking about. The company is sponsoring an hour-long television show on April 1. There will also be full-page ads in the April issues of *Life, Look, Esquire,* and *Sports Illustrated.* It's still possible for me to see that you have a complete inventory of the shirts before the campaign starts, but, as you can see, time is running out."

As another example, a salesman of cooking utensils calls the housewife who is still hesitating about whether or not to buy, and says, "Mrs. Prospect, we received an announcement from the home office this morning that there is to be a

10 percent increase in our prices, effective the first of the month. I wanted to let you know that this is your last chance to buy the items you wanted at the price I quoted you."

Reviving Old Accounts. The telephone can be used to discover why people who have been good customers have not made any recent purchases. A salesgirl in a women's dress shop calls a customer who used to buy more than a dozen dresses a year but who hasn't been in the store for many months. The salesgirl simply says that she has missed the pleasure of serving Mrs. Customer and wants to let Mrs. Customer know that there are several lovely new styles available that she is sure Mrs. Customer will like. The conversation turns up the fact that one of Mrs. Customer's friends had persuaded her that she should shop in the nearby larger city. But Mrs. Customer says that talking to the salesgirl makes her realize how much she always enjoyed the personal attention that she received in the local shop, so she will stop by in the next few days.

Many times the salesman who calls inactive accounts finds that some irritation had occurred which annoyed the customer so much that he stopped buying. The fact that the salesman is interested enough to call persuades the customer to state the irritation, thus giving the salesman the chance to correct the situation.

Notifying Customers of Special Events. A shoe salesman in a fashionable department store keeps a list of his regular customers so that he can telephone them to let them know when the shoe sales are going to take place.

A salesgirl calls a customer and says, "Mrs. Jones, did you ever find that beaded black sweater you asked me about last week? You didn't? Well, we have

■ This automatic answering service will let the salesman know who called while he was out of the office.

just received several really lovely ones in your size, and if you'd like, I can put one aside for you until you can get in."

An insurance salesman calls his client and says, "Mr. Stevens, I've just received word about a new homeowners' insurance policy which includes fire and other damage to the house and contents, theft, and liability all in one policy at a substantially reduced rate. Since your other policies are coming up for renewal, I'd like to see you switch to this new policy."

These are only a few examples of how the telephone can aid the salesman in notifying his customers of special events. The rewards for the salesman's efforts will be to increase good customer relations and his sales volume, both immediately and in the long run.

Handling Complaints. Even poor salesmen can sell a customer *once*, but keeping customers satisfied enough to have them buy again and again is the mark of the true salesman. To do this, the salesman must answer any complaints that the customer has to the customer's complete satisfaction. The telephone can be an excellent tool for handling complaints, because it is so immediate. In just a few minutes' conversation, the customer can be assured that all will be made right. It goes without saying that the salesman must then follow through and make sure that what he has promised is done.

While customer complaints can turn up on routine calls placed by the salesman, they are more likely to be initiated by disgruntled customers. It is very important that the salesman return calls that come in from his customers as soon as possible, for it is a psychological fact that a small irritation can assume gigantic proportions if too much time lapses before the call is returned. On the other hand, a prompt answer, a pleasant and anxious-to-please manner, and an intelligent and quick adjustment will make a lasting friend of the customer.

Taking Orders. Sometimes the customer will call the salesman, not to complain, but to give him an order. This is true in all kinds of selling and is another excellent reason why phone calls from customers should never go unreturned for long. What could he more ideal than to be able to take an unsolicited order in a few minutes over the phone? This obviously represents a tremendous saving in time and energy for the salesman and the company. To encourage telephone orders, many large companies have a "call-collect" plan, whereby the customer is encouraged to reverse the charges when he calls to place an order.

Retail stores in particular do a tremendous business in telephone orders. The importance of the telephone in retail selling is indicated in the statement of the president of the American Telephone and Telegraph Company at a national business conference to the effect that "many department stores now sell from

When taking orders by telephone, the salesperson must be sure to write down all the important details accurately.

Courtesy American Telephone and Telegraph Company

5 to 13 percent of their volume by telephone." In fact, telephone selling is so important that some very large stores maintain a staff of order clerks to take calls on Sundays, so that when people read the Sunday advertisements, they can call immediately. Also, for the big buying season at Christmastime, large stores usually have an extra staff manning the telephones.

But many of the people who like to shop by phone prefer to call their favorite salesperson. This is especially true when the purchase is not a name brand or a standard item or one that the store has advertised. For example, a busy executive calls the men's store where he deals and asks for the salesman who always waits on him. The conversation goes like this:

EXECUTIVE: Harry, this is Bill Davis calling. You know that brown pin-striped suit I bought last week? You asked me at the time if I needed any ties and I said no, but it turns out I was wrong. There's not a tie in my closet that'll go with it. Could you pick me out a couple and send them over to the house? There's no use in my coming in, because I always buy what you tell me anyhow.

SALESMAN: **Sure enough, Mr. Davis. I'm certain I can find two ties that you will like. Now how about socks? Are you sure you have some that will go with the suit?**

EXECUTIVE: I haven't looked; but I was wrong about the ties, so you might as well send a couple of pairs of brown socks, too. You know the kind I like— size 11.

SALESMAN: **Fine, Mr. Davis. I'll get the ties and socks out right away. Thanks for calling.**

This conversation illustrates another important point about taking orders by phone: the salesman can attempt to sell related items just as he can in a face-to-face sale. A woman phones for some sheets and is reminded that pillowcases are on sale, too. A do-it-yourselfer phones for some varnish, but before he hangs up, he has also bought sandpaper, pumice, and cheesecloth.

Selling to New Customers. Selling to new customers is the most difficult of all the ways that the salesman can use the telephone, and therefore it is the least successful and the least used. In fact, most companies will not even allow their salesmen to attempt to sell to new customers on the phone, because the difficulties of making a good impression and interesting the prospect in the product are so enormous and because the prospect can say "no" too easily. But because the telephone is an economical way to approach many people in a short space of time, it is used for some types of selling on the theory that the law of averages will produce a certain number of sales. For instance, there are people who are hired to go through the phone book trying to sell magazine subscriptions. This kind of impersonal, mechanized selling, however, cannot be recommended in a book on personal salesmanship.

Principles of Telephone Selling

You have seen how useful the telephone can be to the salesman. Nevertheless, you must remember that telephone selling is highly competitive. In an average week a housewife may receive as many as half a dozen phone calls from salesmen, ranging from the photographer who wants her to make an appointment to let him take her children's picture to the cleaning service that wants permission to come and shampoo her rugs. The number of telephone-selling calls that a businessman gets in a week's time can be easily imagined.

The stiffness of the competition in telephone selling means that, if the salesman expects to have any success on the telephone, he must perfect his technique for using it. He must consider (1) how to develop a telephone personality, (2) what telephone etiquette is, (3) how to plan his calls, and (4) how to get past the secretary or receptionist.

Developing a Telephone Personality. In Chapter 7 you studied how important good speech habits are to the salesman. If this is true in face-to-face selling, think how much more important it is to the salesman using the telephone. Because the recipient of the call can't see the salesman, he has to gather all his impressions from the salesman's voice and manner as to what kind of man he is. Even if the salesman is already well known to the customer, his telephone manner must reinforce the image that he has worked so hard to convey—that he is intelligent, enthusiastic, alert, eager to please, and knowledgeable about ways to solve the customer's problems. These qualities will come through from the salesman's tone of voice, the words he chooses, and the way in which he handles the conversation.

> Selling is something like hog-calling: it isn't the noise you make, it's the appeal in your voice.
>
> —*Weekly Animator*, Alexander Film Co.

Practicing Telephone Etiquette. Good manners are essential whenever you hope to deal successfully with other people, but they are especially important on the telephone. Here is a list of rules to remember:

1. *Answer the telephone as promptly as possible.* No one likes to be kept waiting. But if you are doing the calling, give the other person time to answer.

2. *Try to cultivate "the voice with the smile."* It is a good suggestion actually to smile when you pick up the phone so that you sound friendly and anxious to be of service.

3. *Identify yourself and your company*, whether you are calling or being called. The old habit of merely saying "hello" is outmoded.

4. *Get the caller's name correctly* on an incoming call. If you're doing the calling, be sure that you have the correct pronunciation of the name.

5. *Keep a pad and pencil handy*, in your pocket or on your desk, so that you can easily make whatever notes are necessary.

6. *Avoid any suggestion of hurry or exasperation.* You must not imply in any way that you begrudge the caller the time and attention you are giving him or that you feel his call is unimportant.

7. *Keep your mind on the conversation.* Don't try to do something else while you are on the phone. Just as a retail salesperson is instructed to drop whatever stock or auxiliary duties he is doing when the customer approaches, so the salesman on the telephone must give the caller his full attention. This principle can create problems in a retail store when the salesperson is waiting on a customer and is called to the telephone. If the customer in the store expresses annoyance, the salesperson should explain the situation to the customer on the phone as graciously as possible and ask if he can call back in just a few minutes. He must then return the call as soon as his other customer has been accommodated.

8. *Never carry on a conversation on the side.* To avoid this, don't be in the middle of a conversation while you are dialing or waiting for a connection. Have the coast clear before you initiate your call.

9. *Don't keep the customer hanging on the phone* while you go to look up information. If you are going to be longer than a minute, say to the caller, "I'm sorry, but it will take me a few minutes to get this information. May I call you back

In telephone selling it is just as important to plan what to say ahead of time as it is in face-to-face selling, as this stockbroker knows. The five steps of the sale apply in telephone selling, too.

Courtesy Merrill Lynch, Pierce, Fenner & Smith Inc.

so you won't have to wait?" If the caller elects to wait, be sure that there are no side conversations going on that the customer can overhear.

10. *Remember the words "thank you" and "you're welcome."*

11. *Don't be in too big a hurry to hang up.* Make it a rule to let the customer hang up first.

12. *If you are disconnected,* the proper procedure is for you to call back if you placed the call, or for you to wait for the customer to call back if he initiated the call.

Planning Telephone Calls. It is just as important to plan your telephone call as it is to plan a personal interview. If you know what you are going to say ahead of time and how you are going to say it, you will be both poised and assured and you will not blurt out an ill-advised remark while you are trying to think of the right thing to say. You should also anticipate ahead of time the responses you are likely to receive from the customer.

The necessity for planning is true for any phone calls initiated by you; however, it is most essential when you are not simply telling the customer something, but actually trying to sell him something. The something you are trying to sell him during the phone call may be the product itself; or it may be that, for the time being, you are trying to sell him on the idea of making an appointment with you so that you can demonstrate your product. In either case you have to use all the main principles of selling that you have studied in this book. You have to lead the prospect through the five steps to a sale—gaining attention, arousing interest, building desire, winning conviction, and getting action—just as you would in any face-to-face selling situation.

The difference is that here you have to be a great deal briefer, and you must get to the point more quickly. The telephone conversation must move along more rapidly than a face-to-face interview could or should move. Having introduced yourself, you should begin with a short statement and then drive through at least one short question which invites a "yes" answer before the prospect can cut you off by saying, "Thank you for calling, but I really am not interested."

Here is an example of how the telephone conversation should move. The salesman in this example works for a landscaping firm. He is calling a householder who has just moved into a barely finished house.

SALESMAN: **May I please speak to Mr. St. John? This is Richard Young of the Wayside Nurseries.**

PROSPECT: This is Mr. St. John speaking.

SALESMAN: **I just recently moved into a new house myself, Mr. St. John. Is your wife as anxious to get things done right away as mine was?**

PROSPECT: She sure is, but there are just so many hours in the day.

SALESMAN: **I have a proposition that I think will save you time and trouble and make her very happy, too.**

PROSPECT: Well, that might be worth listening to, except that it's sure to cost me money.

SALESMAN: **Money is the thing I know you have least of right now, Mr. St. John. Moving into a new house is very expensive.**

PROSPECT: Well, I must say, you sound like a very reasonable man!

SALESMAN: **What I'm trying to interest you in is a gradual plan for landscaping your house. My company has worked out a plan that allows you to do a little at a time. You get a nice effect right away, but there is no big drain on your purse at any point.**

PROSPECT: You make it *sound* good, anyhow.

SALESMAN: **I wonder if I could stop by some evening to discuss this with you and your wife? I can show you exactly how it has worked for other people.**

PROSPECT: All right, Mr. Young. I'm certainly willing to listen to you. How about Thursday evening at eight o'clock?

Getting Past the Secretary or Receptionist. Very few busy executives answer their own telephone. To speak to most of them, you have to go through a secretary or a telephone receptionist. The same principles apply for getting past the secretary or receptionist on the telephone as they do when you are in an office trying to be allowed to see the executive. You must treat the secretary with great courtesy and as though you recognize that she is a person of importance. If you sound polite, intelligent, reasonable, and sure of yourself (but not cocky or brash), you will find that the secretary will treat you accordingly.

SUMMING UP

The telephone is an effective sales aid; and it can save time, energy, and money when used effectively. The most important ways in which the telephone can work for the salesman are in building prospect lists, getting appointments, servicing regular customers, acknowledging orders, closing a sale, reviving old accounts, notifying customers of special events, handling complaints, taking orders, and selling to new customers. In order to make the telephone an effective sales aid, the salesman must be skillful in its use and practice telephone etiquette. The salesman must always remember to be courteous even when the person to whom he is talking is not. Effective telephone usage requires careful advance planning, including what the salesman is going to say and how he is going to say it. He should also anticipate the responses he is likely to receive from the person on the other end of the line. The telephone salesman must be prepared to lead the prospect through the five steps to a sale just as he would if he were facing the prospect.

Reviewing Your Reading

1. Give examples of the advantages the telephone offers to the salesman in terms of saving time, saving money, and increasing productivity.
2. How can the telephone be used as a sales aid in each of the following situations?
   a. Building a strong prospect list
   b. Getting appointments
   c. Servicing regular customers
   d. Acknowledging orders
   e. Closing a sale
   f. Reviving old accounts
3. Why do some companies caution their salesmen not to use the telephone in selling to prospects whom they have not met personally?
4. List five rules of good telephone etiquette.
5. Suppose that you have telephoned a customer and you are disconnected during the conversation. What should you do? If the customer had placed the call to you, would your answer be different?
6. Why is it important to plan telephone calls in advance?
7. What telephone manners should be observed when talking with the secretary to the prospect?

1. Explain the meaning of the first sentence in this chapter, "For the salesman, time and energy are money."
2. Do you think a customer would appreciate a telephone call notifying him of a special sale? Why or why not?
3. What are some of the delays a customer might experience in telephoning a business firm? How might the delays be lessened or avoided? What rules should be observed when the caller is required to wait?
4. What types of telephone calls received by a department store might provide an opportunity for selling?
5. Why should the person answering the telephone in a store or office always identify himself and his department? Suppose you work in the hardware department of a large retail store. How would you answer the telephone for this department?
6. It is a well-known fact that many prospective customers are lost because of the careless way in which employees of the firm use the telephone. Mention five to ten faults that are annoying to telephone callers and are likely to cause the firm to lose them as friends and customers.

Sales Problem I

Mrs. Lee purchased a refrigerator from the Rockwell Company about a month ago. The door to the freezer compartment has never closed properly. She dials the store to tell them this. A salesman answers the call.

SALESMAN: **Hello.**
MRS. LEE: Is this the Rockwell Company?
SALESMAN: **Yeah.**
MRS. LEE: Well, this is Mrs. George Lee calling. I bought a refrigerator in your store last month, but the door to the freezer compartment won't close properly and so I can't put any frozen foods in there.
SALESMAN: **Probably due to rough handling in shipping. We don't handle the delivery, you know.**
MRS. LEE: I don't care who handles the delivery. I want a refrigerator that works.
SALESMAN: **All our stuff is guaranteed. I can't understand it.**
MRS. LEE: Is your manager there?
SALESMAN: **Nope, but I can have a service mechanic take a look at it.**
MRS. LEE: I certainly wish you would.

SALESMAN: Just a minute while I get an order form. (*Leaves phone for about a minute.*) Now what is your name and address?

MRS. LEE: Mrs. George Lee, 24 Worth Street, Appletown.

SALESMAN: OK, we'll send a man out.

MRS. LEE: When will that be?

SALESMAN: Tomorrow.

QUESTIONS

1. Make a list of the things that this salesman did that were wrong.
2. Rewrite the dialogue as you think it should have taken place.
3. What effect would the salesman's replies have for his store in the first dialogue? In the rewritten one?

Sales Problem II

An encyclopedia salesman is calling names he finds in the telephone book.

SALESMAN: Mrs. Smith, because you and Mr. Smith are so highly regarded in your community as professional people, my company has selected your home in which to place a set of our new XYZ encyclopedias. We know your children will derive a great deal of benefit from them. May I see you this Thursday evening about this?

PROSPECT: We have no children and we already have a good encyclopedia.

QUESTIONS

1. What do you think of this salesman's approach?
2. Do you think that this type of selling would be very helpful to other kinds of salesmen?
3. What could the salesman have said to interest the prospect?

Salesmanship in Action

1. Imagine that you are a salesman in a retail furniture store. Give three specific examples of how you could use the telephone as a sales aid. Write out an imaginary telephone conversation in dialogue form for each of the three situations.
2. With the help of other students, enact through role-playing the following situations so as to accomplish the desired objectives. If available, use a Teletrainer to add realism to the dramatizations.

a. The owner of a radio supply house, Mr. Ellsworth, telephones Mrs. King, who recently purchased a stereophonic record player from him. Mr. Ellsworth wants to know whether Mrs. King is receiving satisfaction from the stereo, but at the same time he wants to interest her in a tape recorder (the stereo set she purchased has space for a tape recorder, and the hookup would be very simple).

b. Miss Crable is a salesperson in a retail fur salon, Broadbank Furriers. She receives a telephone call from a housewife, Mrs. Fillmore, inquiring about prices of mink stoles. Miss Crable tries to interest Mrs. Fillmore in coming to the store and seeing the furs. If this fails, she plans to try to arrange an appointment for an outside saleswoman to visit the prospect's home to display a selection of furs.

c. Clyde Jackson needs two new tires for his automobile. He telephones several tire dealers for prices. Fred Levine, a young attendant at Moser's Service Station, receives a call from Mr. Jackson and learns that he is attempting to make a buying decision on price alone. Fred believes the line of tires he carries, while a little more expensive than most of the competing brands, is the best buy for the money. He attempts to convince Mr. Jackson that he should come to the service station and see the tires for himself.

Direct Mail as a Sales Aid

THE SALESMAN'S CHANCES of getting his product in the hands of customers are greatly enhanced when he is given direct-sales support by the home office. This support takes many forms, one of the most important of which is advertising—on radio and television, in newspapers and magazines, and through direct mail. Direct mail consists of letters, circulars, postcards, advertising brochures, catalogs, and any similar written matter that is sent through the mails.

Business Firms Use Direct Mail

Direct mail is used by nearly all companies and retail stores to promote sales and goodwill. Each year these firms spend millions of dollars for direct mail. It is one of the most effective "silent salesmen" that businessmen have. There are a few firms that sell only by direct mail. Products such as neckties, books, and various items for the home are distributed effectively in this manner. In most cases, however, no form of advertising can completely take the place of the salesman. Advertising simply makes the salesman's job easier by establishing the company name, by stimulating an interest in the product or service, and by "softening up" the prospect so that he will be receptive to the salesman's sales presentation.

Business firms use direct mail in such situations as the following: (1) to locate new prospects, (2) to follow up on inquiries, (3) to woo strayed customers back, and (4) to build goodwill.

To Locate New Prospects. Firms such as magazine and book publishers, life insurance companies, and various distributors of products for the home and office often build large mailing lists for the purpose of soliciting business by direct mail. Some of these names come from their own lists of prospects, customers, and former customers. Others are purchased from outside sources, including commercial mailing-list organizations. To these mailing lists the business firms send sales letters, catalogs, and other advertising literature with the hope that the addressees will respond by making inquiry by letter, by visiting a local dealer, by telephoning, or by directly purchasing the product. Those who correspond in any way are regarded as good prospects, and their names are often turned over to the salesman for personal follow-up.

Letters and other advertisements sent through the mail must be especially good or the prospect will never read them.

Courtesy American Telephone and Telegraph Company

Following is an illustration of a letter used to locate new prospects by offering a free handbook to those who are interested.

Dear Friend:

   This is important.

   With your permission, I would like you to have a valuable handbook on life insurance . . . a handbook NOT written by a life insurance company.

   You probably are one of the more than one hundred million people in the United States who own life insurance. Therefore, you should have this handbook, for in it are many fascinating facts about your protection which are often overlooked.

   We offer this handbook, free, as a public service.

   It answers questions like these: how to retire at an earlier age . . . how your Social Security benefits may be made more valuable to you . . . how to select the proper company, the proper agent . . . and, most important, how to safeguard your present insurance benefits.

   In short, it is a guidebook you will find yourself referring to from time to time.

   To obtain your copy, simply fill in the enclosed postage-free card and drop it in the mail. There is no obligation; only a hope that you will discover how to take advantage of the many worthwhile ideas it contains.

                                        Cordially yours,

To Follow Up on Inquiries. Anyone who picks up a copy of one of the popular magazines will find dozens of advertisements containing coupons or other invitations to respond to these advertisements. If the reader responds, he will receive the booklet, sample, or catalog that he asks for. Then, on a periodic basis, the company will very likely send him follow-up letters or advertising circulars, for often one of the major purposes of such advertisements is to build a prospect list. Sometimes a company sends its salesmen to call on those who have responded.

Following is an example of the first follow-up letter a company sends to a prospect after having mailed her a free booklet that she had requested.

Dear Miss Farrow:

　　We recently mailed you a free booklet on typing tips, which you had requested after reading our advertisement about our new Model 250 Electric Typewriter in *Today's Secretary*.

　　It was a pleasure to send this material to you, and we sincerely hope that you will find it interesting and helpful.

　　We appreciate the interest you have shown in our company and its products. If we can provide you with any further information, or be of service to you in any way, please let us know.

Cordially yours,

To Woo Strayed Customers Back. Prompt-paying charge customers are prized customers of retail stores. Sometimes after a customer has established a charge account and a good credit rating at a retail store, he fails to use the account regularly. Naturally it is to the store's advantage to woo such customers back to the store, and often direct mail is used for this purpose.

　　Following is an example of an effective letter that attempts to bring back a valued charge customer "into the fold."

Dear Mr. Robinson:

　　Being able to serve you—one of our preferred charge customers—has always been a pleasure and a privilege. Thus we miss you when you fail to use your account for a while.

　　Because your goodwill and satisfaction are of primary concern to us, we would consider it as a favor if you would let us know of any occasions when our merchandise or service did not meet your expectations. Simply use the enclosed card and postage-paid business envelope for your reply.

　　We hope, meanwhile, that you will have the opportunity to come in during the next month and use your account.

Sincerely yours,

To Build Goodwill. All customers like special attention. Accordingly, many smart retailers use direct mail to give them this special attention. Following is a list of different kinds of letters that they may send to their customers to build goodwill and, at the same time, to promote sales:

1. An announcement to valued charge customers of an advance showing of newly arrived merchandise. In letters such as these, the customer is given the privilege of previewing new merchandise before it is placed on sale to the general public. A sample letter follows.

Dear Mrs. Bradley:

You are invited, as one of Lamm & Mazer's select customers, to an advance showing of Hareli evening gowns. The showing will be held on Wednesday, November 1, at three o'clock, in the Jade Room on the third floor. Either your Lamm & Mazer charge plate or this letter is your admission ticket.

The gowns you will see modeled are exquisitely made in every detail and are the very latest styles that will be worn during the coming winter season. These gowns will not be placed on sale to the general public until November 15. We want you—a preferred customer—to have first choice.

Immediately after the showing, tea and other refreshments will be served. Won't you mark the date on your calendar right now?

Sincerely yours,

---

2. A message of congratulations on some important occasion, such as the arrival of a new baby or the purchase of a new home.
3. A letter of welcome to a newcomer to the community. See the sample letter on the opposite page.
4. A letter of congratulations to a customer on his promotion, election to office, or some outstanding community achievement.
5. Holiday greetings and messages at Christmastime, New Year's, Easter, and so on; and birthday and anniversary messages.
6. Invitations to demonstrations, new branch-store openings, and special events. For example, the manager of a bookstore might invite regular customers by mail to come to the store and meet the author of a best seller.

Dear Neighbors:

Bennett's Hardware Store welcomes you to Oakdale. We are pleased to have you as residents and hope that you will enjoy living in our pleasant, friendly community.

Bennett's—the first hardware store to open in Oakdale—always has a large selection of merchandise in stock. Because of our long experience in the hardware business, we know what our customers want and are ready to serve them. Won't you, therefore, come in and look around? We shall be glad to help you with your hardware needs. Enclosed is an introductory certificate that will entitle you to a credit of $2 toward your first purchase.

We hope that we shall have the opportunity of serving you.

Sincerely yours,

The Salesman Uses Direct Mail

Direct mail is generally a sales support provided by the advertising and promotion department of a business. Rarely does the salesman himself prepare and send out advertising literature or promotion letters. However, there are many instances where the salesman himself can use the mails to save time, save money, and build goodwill. Some of the ways are discussed here.

To Save Time. While direct mail is not as quick as the telephone in reaching prospects and customers, the salesman can often save time and make friends by its use. Suppose that an appliance salesman sells fifteen refrigerators to customers who live all over the city. At the time of each sale he is unable to tell the customer exactly what day the appliance will be delivered, although each customer is very anxious to know. When the salesman gets the delivery schedule from the shipping department, he might write each customer a postcard similar to the one on page 372. Such a card may be mimeographed, with only the customer's name, the time of delivery, and the salesman's name to be filled in.

The time that the salesman spends filling in these fifteen postcards is far less than he would have spent on telephone calls or personal visits.

To Save Money. When the salesman's customer is located several miles away, the salesman can often save many dollars by using the mail instead of making a trip. Of course, this economy makes sense only some of the time; but if a letter or card will serve the purpose, the salesman should by all means use it. Advance information about a salesman's visit, price changes, special sales, and competitive information are examples of how the salesman can use the mails to save money.

To Increase Productivity. Direct mail, like the telephone, is a sales aid that can be used in the salesman's spare time and in situations where a personal visit is not possible. Some salesmen who travel a good deal carry stationery and postage with them and during transportation delays and while waiting for appointments write notes, personal letters, postcards—even birthday and anniversary greetings —to their customers.

To Build a Prospect List. Direct mail can also be used by the salesman in a small firm to build a prospect list. As an example, let's say that a salesman is the representative for a small firm selling gourmet foods in a Midwestern city. In a sense, everyone in the city is his prospect because everyone eats; but, as the salesman knows, not everyone is willing to pay the prices for, or has the interest in, the kind of specialized foods his company sells. The salesman also has discovered that this interest in special food cannot be predicted by economic strata, since every family has a different way of spending its money.

So how is this salesman to find his prospects? He sends out a brochure of his company's products, accompanied by a personal letter from him, to people whose names he gets from the telephone directory. This is necessarily a form letter; but he can fill in the prospect's name in the salutation of his letter so that it reads "Dear Mrs. Daly" instead of "Dear Friend," and he can put something of his own enthusiasm and personality into the letter when he is writing it. Besides giving his telephone number in the letter, he will also enclose a postcard that the prospect can return if he is interested in a demonstration of the product.

This system of direct mail has an advantage over the telephone in this particular case because the brochure, which is colorfully illustrated, literally makes the recipient's mouth water as no words of the salesman could do.

As with the telephone, the hit-or-miss quality involved in prospecting by direct mail means that the system should only be used when the salesman has so many possibilities as suspects that he could not get around to everyone unless he sorted them out in some way.

To Obtain Appointments. The salesman whose territory is widely scattered will find that he will be wise to write well ahead for appointments. This allows him to schedule his work intelligently and assures him that he will not schedule his visit to an important buyer when that buyer is on a trip of his own.

When the salesman cannot judge his time quite so definitely, he can use letters to announce that he is going to be in the prospect's area at such and such a time and that he is planning to call on the prospect. The salesman can then telephone when he arrives in the prospect's town and ask for a definite appointment. He will find that the letter has smoothed the way. Following is an illustration of a letter asking for an appointment.

> **Dear Mr. Kane:**
>
> I expect to be in Oskaloosa all day on November 2, when I will be calling on a number of our customers. Would you have time to see me sometime during the day concerning the refinishing of your office furniture that we discussed in August? Since I have not made any definite appointments as yet, I can be at your office whenever it is convenient for you.
>
> I shall bring with me some samples of new hard finishes that we have just received. I believe I have the solution to your decorating problem, and I hope you can spare a few minutes for me to show you what I mean.
>
> **Sincerely yours,**

To Service Regular Customers. A salesman whose territory is spread out or who has a very large number of customers can sometimes use direct mail to keep in touch with his regular customers. For instance, the salesman for a fabric manufacturer who calls on decorating shops can mail swatches of material to his customers between trips with a return order form; or he can send new brochures as they come out, with a short note that simply says:

Dear Mr. Leonard:

 The sample enclosed looks like the kind of material that would go well in your store. It's a brand new pattern, and I thought you might like to see it right away. Let me know if you can use any of it and I'll have it shipped immediately. It's $2.40 a yard less your usual discount. I'll see you next month as usual.

Best wishes,

To Acknowledge Orders. Direct mail can be used effectively by the salesman to cement good customer relations by acknowledging orders and expressing appreciation for them. It is even possible by direct mail to increase the size of the order when acknowledging it. The salesman writes to his customer and thanks him for his order. In addition, he encloses a stamped, addressed envelope, with an order form so that the customer can easily order other items he may have forgotten.

To Close Sales. A letter summarizing the salesman's presentation can sometimes help greatly to clinch a sale. Even if it doesn't finally close the sale, at least it can be used to add "fuel to the fire." This type of letter can be especially helpful when the prospect is the slow, deliberative type who likes to feel that he is studying all the angles and being very wise.

To Take Orders. Although ordering by catalog (mail order) is a real factor in the merchandising picture today, it has little to do with the individual salesman. The individual salesman, however, may receive orders in the mail from his own customers, and he should make sure that these orders are promptly acknowledged. For instance, the owner of a hardware store that is serviced by a salesman in a regional office writes to the salesman that several of the items he ordered are not going to last through the month; therefore he would like an additional shipment. The salesman not only should see that the exact goods asked for are sent out as soon as possible, but should write to the store owner, thanking him for the order and explaining when the goods can be expected to arrive.

Guides to Good Letter Writing

The use of direct mail is even more competitive than the use of the telephone. In a week's time, the average householder receives a wastebasket's worth of announcements, circulars, letters, pamphlets, brochures, and catalogs, all trying to sell him something, so that a letter has to be carefully prepared if it is to get the proper amount of attention. Here are a few pointers for writing good letters:

Make the Letter Attractive. Because the letter is a personal representative of the firm sending it, it should be written on good-quality stationery (with a smart letterhead design), attractively arranged, and neatly typed. Letters are costly, yet the stationery on which they are written represents only a fraction of that cost; therefore, it is false economy to skimp on paper quality. The way the letter looks will go a long way in establishing confidence in the firm—and in the salesman who represents the firm.

Personalize the Letter. People who receive letters respond to them much more favorably when the message is addressed to them personally. Therefore, find out the customer's name (and title if he is an executive) and use it correctly in the salutation. "Dear Miss Fuller" or "Dear Pamela" (depending on how well you know the addressee) is an appropriate salutation. Letters addressed to "Occupant," "Purchasing Agent," or "Director of Public Relations" will not be taken very seriously.

Courtesy Royal McBee Corporation

Automatic typewriters are very useful for sending out individually typed form letters to various prospects. The operator simply inserts the date, name, and address, and the machine finishes the letter automatically.

> Writing, after all, is nothing but speaking on paper, speaking is nothing but thinking out loud, and thinking is nothing but silent speech. You cannot help thinking in words; you write—or should write—the way you talk; and talk according to the way ideas come to your mind and spring to your lips.
>
> —Rudolf Flesch, *How to Write, Speak and Think More Effectively*, Harper & Row

Personal pronouns like *I, you, we,* and *your* are always appropriate in a sales letter. For example, it is better to say, "I think you will be interested, Miss Fuller, in . . ." than, "It is believed that the reader will be interested in. . . ." End with a closing such as "Sincerely yours" or "Cordially yours." "Yours truly" and "Respectfully yours" are considered too formal.

Personalizing the letter also means wording it in such a way that it applies to the reader's problems and interests. Knowing that your reader is a homeowner, is interested in golf or stereo recordings or reading as a hobby, is active in community affairs, or is a proud parent who takes great pride in his family will permit you to slant your message so that it has more direct appeal.

Write Clearly. No one likes to read long-winded messages that never quite come to the point. Make the letter as brief as possible, yet give all the essential facts. Use familiar, everyday words, rather than fancy ones. In this regard, *house* is usually better than *residence; fire* is better than *conflagration; car* is better than *automobile; question* is better than *inquiry;* and so on. Avoid trite (worn-out) expressions. Say "I am pleased to answer your question concerning . . ." instead of "I am in receipt of your inquiry"; say "Thank you for giving me the chance to help you" instead of "Thanking you in advance, I remain"; and so on. In addition, boil your message down by removing all "dead wood." Experts have estimated that three out of every ten words in a letter could be eliminated.

Time Your Letter Properly. If possible, try to time your sales message so that it reaches the reader at an appropriate moment. A jeweler who sold a couple their wedding rings sends the husband a letter to his office before the first wedding anniversary, suggesting some appropriate gifts. A salesman for a fire-alarm system sends out letters asking for appointments after a dry spell in which the possibility of fire was on everyone's mind in a particular area. The owner of a children's clothing shop sends out brochures in August, suggesting in the accompanying letter that he is ready to help outfit the children for school.

Make It Easy for the Reader to Act. Most people are lazy about answering mail; they simply don't like to sit down and compose a letter. But if the letter writer has included something in the letter that makes it easy for the reader to act, the chances for a response are increased. A telephone number with the invitation to call collect, a return postcard that requires only a signature, an order form with a stamped envelope, all are inducements to the reader to take action.

Direct mail is an effective sales medium for a business organization and a useful aid for the salesman. It is used by the businessman to locate new prospects, to follow up on inquiries, to woo strayed customers back to the store, and to build goodwill. It is used by the salesman to save time, to save money, to increase productivity, to build a prospect list, to make appointments, to service regular customers, to acknowledge orders, to close sales, and to take orders. To attract attention and get results, letters should be attractive, personalized, clear, well-timed, and written so that it is easy for the prospect to act.

Reviewing Your Reading

1. How is direct mail used by business organizations in each of the following situations?
   a. To locate new prospects
   b. To follow up on inquiries
   c. To woo back strayed customers
   d. To build goodwill
2. Give examples of how direct mail can be used by the salesman in each of the following situations:
   a. To save time
   b. To save money
   c. To obtain appointments
   d. To service regular customers
   e. To acknowledge orders
3. Give an example of how direct mail, used intelligently, can increase the salesman's productivity.
4. List five guides to good letter writing and discuss each.
5. What should the salesman do when he receives a letter with an order from one of his regular customers?
6. Why is it important to make it easy for the prospect to act after he receives a sales letter?

1. Marilyn Freeman, a cosmetics saleswoman, made the remark, "I write letters to my customers rather than make a call. It saves me time and money." What do you think of this statement? Do you think direct mail can do the complete selling job?
2. Where might an appliance salesman obtain a good mailing list for sending out announcements of a new product?
3. If you were selling life insurance, would you be more effective if you used the "fear" approach in your sales letters and attempted to frighten prospects into action, or would you be better off if you used a positive appeal such as the safety, savings, and so on? Discuss.
4. What is meant by this statement: "The use of direct mail is even more competitive than the use of the telephone"?
5. A large percentage of the sales literature received by the typical homeowner lands in the wastebasket. Business organizations know this, of course. Why do you think they continue to use this medium when the chances of the mail's being read are so slim?
6. One business organization follows up every salesman's call with a letter, signed by the sales manager, thanking the customer for the courtesy showed the salesman and expressing a desire to be of service. How do you think such a letter might support the salesman's efforts?
7. A business firm that receives thousands of orders every day obviously cannot afford to acknowledge each order with a personal letter. Discuss some effective ways in which these orders might be acknowledged inexpensively.

Sales Problems

1. Criticize the following note a salesman wrote on a postcard to one of his customers to acknowledge an order:

> Dear Sir:
>
> Your order rec'd. Will ship the
> goods when possible.
>
> Joe Phillips

2. What is wrong with the following as the final paragraph of a sales letter? How would you rewrite the paragraph so that it is more effective?

> I hope you will take advantage of this offer and that you will place your order soon.

378 **IMAGINATION IN SELLING**

3. Criticize the following letter that was written to valued charge customers to get them to use their charge accounts:

Dear Charge Account Customer:

   Why haven't you used your charge account lately? We went to the trouble of setting it up for you, but you have not made as much use of it as we think you should.
   Surely you don't want us to cancel your account. Unless you make more use of it, it is doing you no good or us either. I hope to hear from you soon.

                         Respectfully yours,
                         DOWNTOWN DEPARTMENT STORE

Salesmanship in Action

1. Bring to class examples of sales literature you or your family have received in the mail. Prepare a display of these materials. Discuss the probable success and the shortcomings of these direct-mail pieces.
2. Assume that you are a salesman of office equipment. One of your prospects in a city several miles away, on whom you have been calling for about a year, has finally placed an order for twelve Fireguard Filing Cabinets. As soon as you see the order, you go to the shipping room to learn when the filing cabinets can be shipped. You are told that they will be shipped within two days and that the customer should have them within a week. Write a letter acknowledging the order and giving other details you think necessary.
3. You work for a large manufacturer of truck tires. For several months you have been trying to sell the Peerless Transportation Company in a distant city your Mile King Tires for its fleet of trucks. Today the order arrived for sixty tires—a large order that runs into thousands of dollars. When you check up on the availability of the tires, you are told by the shipping department that the Mile King is out of stock and that shipment cannot be made for another month. There is nothing you can do except to explain the problem to the customer and convince him that he should not cancel his order. Write the letter. (Hint: The Mile King Tire is so popular that the tire is difficult to keep in stock, but it is well worth waiting for.)

Succeeding in Your Selling Career

Part Five

"Show me a good salesman and I'll show you a good manager" is an old saying that rings true. The successful salesman manages his own time so that every minute counts. He knows his obligations to his employer, and he never lets his employer down. The same is true of his fellow workers; a man can't very well be loyal to his company and disloyal to those who work with him—they are the company! The salesman has a responsibility to his customers, too; they depend on him to be fair, reasonable, and honest.

380

Managing Your Sales Time

THE OUTSIDE SALESMAN has as much freedom of action and direct supervision as he would have if he were in business for himself. This is one of the strongest appeals of a selling job for many people, especially those who have so much energy and imagination that they would not be happy in a job where they are told exactly what to do and when to do it. Even the store salesperson has more freedom than those who work in offices and factories.

For the person in business for himself, freedom carries a heavy responsibility: to be successful, he has to learn how to manage. This means using the assets, equipment, and personnel of the business so that every dollar and every minute counts. The salesman's most important asset is *time;* and the price of his freedom from supervision is learning how to manage his time.

Successful Time Management—Planning

Successful time management does not mean simply putting in a given number of hours on the job. The idea is not to work harder physically, but to work more *efficiently;* and this means using your head, because you want to get the most *value* out of your time. You have to learn to make every minute count. And you can only do this by planning your time wisely.

Defining Time Planning for the Salesman. For the salesman, time planning means thinking ahead about what he is to do and how and when he is going to do it. To accomplish this, he must analyze his duties, decide on his goals, and then come up with a schedule for using his time so that his duties will be done and his goals will be met. What he is seeking is a way of investing his time to make it pay the biggest dividends.

Sometimes the best way to come to an understanding of what to do is to consider what not to do. As an illustration of the meaning of time planning for the salesman, let's look at the way that a nonplanner called Salesman Sam works.

Salesman Sam was having a hard time making his sales quota, although he spent eight to ten hours a day at his job. The sales manager decided to accompany Sam on his rounds one day in an effort to find the source of the trouble. Let's hear the rest of the story in the sales manager's own words:

> Sam's first call was a success. The prospect listened attentively as Sam gave a convincing presentation. This call took approximately half an hour. After his first call, and with his first sale of the day under his belt, Sam suggested that we have a cup of coffee.
>
> "Don't you have another appointment?" I asked. Sam said that he didn't, but that he would work up the rest of his calls for that morning while we were having coffee. So we had coffee. After that we got into Sam's car and drove across town to see prospect No. 2 Our prospect was not in, so we started back across town to see Sam's third prospect of the morning. The receptionist informed us that our man was in conference and would not be able to see us for another hour. Sam suggested another cup of coffee.
>
> "Don't you have anyone you could see to fill in this time?" I asked Sam. He said, "No, but we might try to see prospect No. 4." He had an appointment with him for after lunch, but Sam thought that the prospect might see us earlier. So we got into Sam's car and drove across town to see prospect No. 4. When we arrived, we were informed that the prospect was out to lunch and that he would not be able to see us until the appointed hour, which was 2 P.M. So we went to lunch.
>
> The remainder of the day we saw three prospects, which made a total of four prospects that day. The other men on the sales force were seeing ten prospects a day.

It will be no surprise to you that Sam was 40 percent as efficient as the other salesmen in the company, who were seeing ten prospects a day. Sam was a nonplanner, a hit-or-miss sort of fellow. From this story you can see that he "missed" more than he "hit."

Getting at the Facts. The salesman can come up with all kinds of plans for managing his time, but the only plan that will have any value is the one that is based on facts. A salesman who is just beginning may say to himself, "I will make

■ With proper planning and scheduling, the salesman can reduce the time he spends in waiting rooms.

twenty-five calls a day." This is a laudable ambition, except that when he gets
down to finding the twenty-five prospects, scheduling the twenty-five calls, getting himself from one call to another, waiting to see the prospects, making his
presentation, servicing his other customers, and doing all his paper work, his
ambition turns out to be highly impractical and unrealistic.

The only way for a salesman to figure out a time-allocation program that will
work is to keep an accurate set of records. These records may be listed under
the following headings: (1) customer records, (2) prospect records, (3) daily activity records, (4) summary records, and (5) self-analysis records.

Customer Records. The salesman should keep a 3- by 5-inch card file of his
customers in alphabetical order, with guide cards from A to Z. On each card he
can list the customer's name, address, and phone number, the dates and types
of contact (personal interview, telephone, or letter), and the dates and amounts
of purchases. The cards can also provide a description of the customer, notes
about the type of business, preferred hours for calling, and any other background information that the salesman may want to remember. See page 384.

A second set of cards with just the customer's name can be set up with guide
cards divided by week or month. Such a card file will indicate at a glance which
customers are due for a call. Each card should be marked with a colored tab
to indicate the frequency of the call. A red tab, for instance, could mean that the
customer should be checked every week, green every two weeks, yellow once

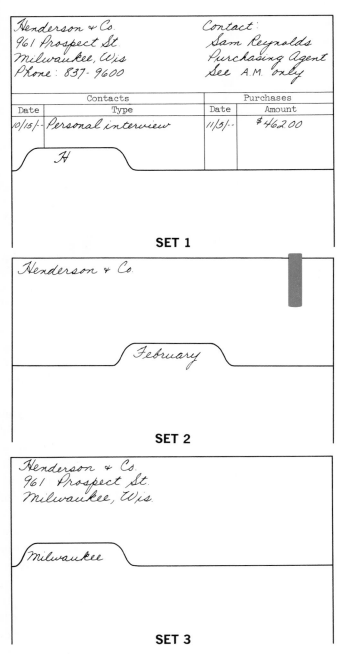

SET 1

Henderson & Co
961 Prospect St.
Milwaukee, Wis
Phone: 837- 9600

Contact:
Sam Reynolds
Purchasing Agent
See A.M. only

Contacts		Purchases	
Date	Type	Date	Amount
10/15/-	Personal interview	11/5/--	$462.00

H

SET 2

Henderson & Co.

February

SET 3

Henderson & Co.
961 Prospect St.
Milwaukee, Wis.

Milwaukee

Customer records.

Riddick, Arthur
86 Garland Rd.
New Orleans, La.
Phone: 325-6143

Metalworker   Age 34
Married   3 children (7-5-3)
Likes bowling, fishing
Prospect for family policy. Maybe
health policy later.

Date of call	Remarks
11/16/-	Prefers to wait until anniversary date of present policy.

Prospect records.

a month, blue every two months, and so on. When the file is set up originally, the salesman can date guide cards, by week or month, and then he can place each card according to the date when the customer must be checked. As he sees each customer, he can move the card ahead in the file to the appropriate date for the next visit. This system allows the salesman always to know exactly when he must call on which customers.

A third set of cards, this time with both the customer's name and address, can be set up with guide cards divided according to geographical location. The guide cards could be listed by towns, counties, or sections in the salesman's territory. This set of cards will aid the salesman in planning his travel time to save time, energy, and repeat motion.

Prospect Records. Prospect records should also be on 3- by 5-inch cards. Besides the name, address, and telephone number of each prospect, the cards should indicate occupation, age, marital status (and, if married, number of children), hobbies, and every other helpful piece of information that the salesman can discover about the prospect, including why he is a prospect. The color-tab system might be adapted here so that each color represents a degree of probability of success with the prospect—red for excellent chances, green for good, yellow for fair, and so on. This allows the salesman to concentrate his efforts first where his possibilities of success are greatest.

On the back of the card the salesman should make note of each interview. If he is unable to sell the prospect at the present time, he should move the prospect's card to an inactive section of the file and consider the prospect again after a period of time. When the prospect has been sold, his card can be removed from the prospect file and a new one made out for the customer file.

The most important point to be made about the prospect file is that the salesman must add to it constantly. The salesman's chances for success are only as good as the quantity and quality of his prospect file.

The salesman with a large geographic area should have a duplicate set of cards giving just the prospect's name and address so that he can set up a geographic file of his territory, such as by city, county, and so on. Such a file will allow the salesman to coordinate easily the servicing of his regular customers and the interviewing of new prospects when he is in a particular area.

Daily Activity Records. Many companies supply their salesmen with forms for recording what they do each day, and the forms are also available in office supply stores. But here is an example of a record that the salesman can keep by simply ruling three columns on the sheets of a pocket-sized loose-leaf notebook— loose-leaf so that the pages can be removed and filed.

■ Daily activity records.

Time	Activity	Comments
9:00-9:15	Checked in at office for mail. Put through reorder for Collins Co.	Note order in customer file.
9:15-9:30	Drove to see Joseph Reed of Howell & Co.	
9:30-9:35	Waited to see Reed.	
9:35-9:55	First interview. Reed not convinced. Made appt. for Thurs., 2 P.M.	Reed's block is price. Get exact info. from factory on costs of production before Thurs.

This kind of notation takes only a few seconds to record and should be continued throughout the day. The salesman should always note the time *exactly*—not approximate it. In the Activity column he should always note the specific activity in which he engaged. In the Comments column he should make notes to himself for future reference in planning the next call.

By keeping a daily activity record, the salesman will be able to figure out how long his various jobs are taking him. He should keep an exact record of what he does and how long each job takes for at least one or two weeks but preferably for a month. These figures can serve as a guide when he makes his first schedule, which is discussed on page 389. After that, he should continue to record the time that his activities are taking so that he can refine and improve his schedule as he gets more information and more experience.

Summary Records. The salesman's day-by-day time expenditures should be summarized on a weekly and monthly basis. The daily activity records, supplemented by the customer and prospect records, will provide the basis for the summary. The salesman's strong and weak points will be easier to see in a summary than they are day by day.

Summary records should include the total amount of time spent on each activity; the number of new prospects located; the number of first, second, third, and additional interviews made; the number of sales closed; the number of service calls to regular customers and the number of resulting orders; the number of sales lost; and the total sales volume.

Self-Analysis Records. The most successful salesmen are the men who realize that there is always room for improvement. At the end of each day, the salesman should make a practice of noting what he feels he could have done better that day—a travel route that could be shortened, a telephone call that could have been worded better, and so on. He should conscientiously go over each sales interview—even the successful ones—and evaluate his approach, demonstration, and closing techniques. The self-analysis record will indicate to the salesman where his efforts have gone wrong. By making an honest judgment as to how he handled each sale, he can learn how to improve his future sales.

Setting Goals. The salesman's records provide a ready reference that will enable him to establish his goals realistically. Realistic goals are very important to the salesman. If his goals are not practicable, he will experience only frustration and a sense of failure. On the other hand, if his goals are feasible and sensibly determined, the salesman will be encouraged to do his best work in trying to meet and then beat the standards that have been set. This is true whether the goals have been set by the salesman's company or by the salesman himself.

The salesman's goals may be expressed in such terms as the number of interviews he will aim for in a given time period, the number of sales he will try to close, the amount by which he will try to increase his orders from his regular customers, and the total sales volume he will try to reach. But no matter how the goals are expressed, they all add up to the same thing—sales. Selling is the salesman's primary function. This sounds like an obvious statement, but the fact is that it is the very essence of the problem of time management. What the salesman is trying to figure out with all his records and analyses is how to get his nonselling jobs done in the fastest and most efficient way so as to release the most possible time for actual selling.

The Maintenance Quota. The salesman's first step toward arriving at the goal which is right for him is to figure out what his maintenance quota is—that is, what does he have to do to maintain his present level of performance? The answer to this question is in the salesman's *efficiency ratio.* As the salesman studies his records, he will discover a mathematical ratio between the number of prospects he contacts, the number of interviews he is able to obtain, and the number of sales he closes. For example, he may have a 5:2:1 ratio, which means that for every five prospects contacted, the salesman will obtain two interviews, and make one sale. If the salesman's present level of performance is ten sales a week, he knows that he will have to find and contact fifty prospects and obtain twenty interviews every week to go on making the ten sales.

The Incentive Quota. The ambitious salesman will immediately understand that the maintenance quota is self-limiting; and he will want to add a second step, the incentive factor, to his goal. How much better could he be doing? A careful study of his daily activity records and his summary records will show him where he has been wasting time and where he could have used it to better advantage. The minutes that he saves will add up to more time for finding, interviewing, and selling prospects. Also, the salesman can study his self-analysis records to see how he could better his efficiency ratio and make more sales per prospect. When he puts all this information together, he will have an idea of how much more selling he could reasonably be doing. He can then raise his maintenance quota by that much. What he now has is a goal that he himself realizes is possible if he will work a foreseeable amount more efficiently.

If the process of adding an incentive factor to the maintenance quota is repeated week after week and month after month, the salesman will gradually reach the ultimate goal of top performance, top income, and top value to his company.

Courtesy Sears, Roebuck and Co.

■ **Many companies provide their salesmen with prospect cards.**

Preparing a Schedule. Now that the salesman has established *what* he has to do, the next logical question is, *How* is he going to do it? The only way that the salesman can make his plans work is by preparing an advance schedule. While this schedule will necessarily have to be flexible, it can provide the salesman with the key to how to fit his many varied jobs into his working day.

The salesman should keep an appointment book with all his advance appointments noted in it. At the beginning of each week, he can check his records and apportion to the working days the jobs that he sees must be done that week. Then each night the salesman should write out a time schedule for the following day's work, using his appointment book as a guide. The schedule should be as specific as possible about the exact time when each job is to be done. The heart of the schedule should be the time that the salesman intends to spend in calling on buyers; the other jobs, in the order of their importance, should be planned around those hours.

General Principles for Increasing Sales Time

There are five general principles that the salesman who is interested in making his working day more productive should consider. These principles are (1) stretch the working day, (2) stick to your schedule, (3) use all your time, (4) use supplementary sales aids, and (5) don't trust your memory.

Stretch the Working Day. The salesman can gain extra hours by stretching the working day from the 9-to-5 concept in any direction that will help him. For instance, the hour from 8 to 9 may be a good time for making customer service calls. Many factories and stores are open at this hour, and the salesman can soon learn which of his customers like to do business early in the day. The hour from 5 to 6 might also be put to use, because many businessmen make a habit of staying late at their offices. And there are many specialty salesmen who can benefit greatly from using the early evening hours for calling on prospects in their homes.

Shortening the lunch hour is another way of stretching the hours in the day. Many salesmen feel that they should never try to see prospects from noon to 2 P.M. It is true that it is risky to call on prospects directly during those hours, since they will probably be out to lunch. But the salesman can make a point of scheduling definite appointments for these doubtful time periods.

These are also times when the salesman can use his lunch hour to entertain prospects. Although this may mean an extra expenditure of time, it will be worth the price if the sale is important enough.

Stick to Your Schedule. As the outside salesman makes out his schedule for each day, he will have to decide how many hours he will work. When the estimate is made, he should then stick to it and not be tempted to borrow any of his working hours for pleasure. Since the salesman often has no boss looking over his shoulder, he can decide to celebrate a big order with an afternoon off for golf, or he may decide after several rebuffs that it's just not his day and he might as well go to a ball game. The really successful salesmen are able to discipline themselves so that they do not give in to this kind of temptation.

The salesman should try to do all the jobs he has scheduled for each day. Sometimes he simply cannot do the exact job that he has planned, but he should do an *equivalent* job so that his time budget will stay balanced. For example, suppose that the salesman calls on a buyer with whom he had a definite appointment. The secretary says that the buyer was suddenly taken ill and went home for the day. The salesman should have an emergency list of prospects on whom he can call without an appointment so that he can still make his planned number of calls for the day.

Use All Your Time. Sometimes the salesman will find that he has been too cautious in scheduling his day's work. Because he has allowed more time than needed in several places, he is left with odd bits of time on his hands. It is very tempting to fill up these odd moments with coffee breaks or lengthy social discussions. But the experienced salesman, realizing that there are days when the

■ The salesman can easily call ahead or do some extra prospecting from conveniently located telephones.

reverse can happen and there won't be enough time to go around, uses any leftover time in each day to the best possible advantage. In an odd half hour he can do some extra prospecting, make some extra phone calls, get ahead on his paper work, read about the latest developments in his field, make a service call on a customer, or make a call from his emergency list.

In other words, the salesman should not do less than his schedule indicates if he can possibly help it; he should even do more every time he gets the chance.

Use Supplementary Sales Aids. The salesman should take full advantage of the telephone and direct mail as sales aids. The salesman who uses them intelligently can ease his scheduling problems and free many hours a week for extra interviewing. A complete discussion of how the telephone and direct mail can help the salesman stretch his time is found in Chapters 18 and 19.

Don't Trust Your Memory. The busier the salesman is the more careful he should be to write everything down. When the salesman writes out his schedule, he should note all the special things that he must remember in connection with his appointments; then he should consult his notebook frequently throughout the day. This can save the salesman a great deal of time and trouble. For example, a salesman makes a service call on a customer whom he supplies with business forms. The customer is very busy, so after a brief visit, the salesman leaves. When he is miles away, he remembers that the customer had sent him a postcard asking about a new kind of form. The postcard is in his briefcase along with the information for the customer. He realizes that the busy customer had forgotten his request for the moment but will very likely remember when he stops for lunch and will be annoyed at the salesman for forgetting. The salesman is now faced with having to retrace his steps, a time-wasting procedure that could easily have been avoided.

Timesaving Principles for the Salesman's Nine Jobs

With the general principles of time management in mind, the salesman should turn to a consideration of how he can save time in the performance of each of his specific duties. The salesman must provide time in his schedule for the nine different functions that will be outlined here. Every minute that he can save in any of the nine areas is money in his pocket.

Selecting Prospects. One of the most obvious ways in which the salesman can waste time is by calling on prospects who do not have the authority, the purchasing power, or the inclination to buy the salesman's product. So-called prospects of this type are known as "china eggs." These are artificial glass eggs that are used to induce nesting for hens; the hens sit on them, but the eggs never hatch. It is false economy for the salesman to try to save time by cutting down on his pre-approach work. By spending a little extra time with his suspect list, the salesman can save hours of useless interviewing time on "china egg" prospects and thus improve his efficiency ratio.

The job of choosing quality prospects must be a continuing process, scheduled on a daily basis, so that the salesman will never be short of names. It would be a ridiculous situation for the salesman to find the precious time for more interviewing only to discover that he was fresh out of prospects.

■ **By studying a road map and planning his route ahead of time, the salesman will avoid the risk of getting lost.**

Traveling. The principles of saving travel time are the same whether the salesman services a large geographic territory or a limited midtown area. The salesman should plan each day's activities in such a way that he will eliminate criss-crossing and backtracking either when driving or when walking. The idea is to plan maximum coverage of each area *while he is there.* He should try to think of *all* the jobs that he can possibly do while he is on his way to, in, or leaving a particular area, whether it is a city block or a part of a large territory.

The salesman should decide as far in advance as possible what areas he wants to cover in the coming weeks. He can tell this by studying his customer and prospect records and a good map. Then he can make advance appointments according to his general travel plans. Using his definite appointments as his focal point, he can decide what other prospects he can see in the same area and which customers he can service. When he makes out his daily schedule, he should place the other calls around the definite appointments according to their geographic location, trying to plan for an orderly progression throughout the day, without repeat motion.

The salesman should use the method of transportation which is best suited to the area to be covered. In congested metropolitan areas, the salesman can usually save time by walking, not only because traffic moves slowly but because parking is so difficult. If the salesman's territory is very large, he may find that the best system is to fly between cities and then rent a car. This is expensive, of course; but while the salesman has an obligation to his company to keep his expenses down, he may find that the extra expense involved in flying turns out to be an economy when weighed against the additional orders that he brings in.

The way, then, to cut down on travel time is to *think ahead* by planning your schedule in an orderly manner. Cutting down on travel time is definitely not a matter of trying to nip off minutes by driving fast or by scheduling calls with a hair-breadth margin. When the salesman has made a definite appointment, he must allow adequate travel time so that he will not arrive twenty minutes late because he was held up in a traffic jam. This could be considered a disadvantage to the salesman who is trying to make every minute count, but again it is a question of real and false economy. The whole point of saving time is to make more sales; and if more sales can be made with definite appointments, then the extra minutes necessary for getting to the appointment on time are well spent.

Securing Interviews with Prospects. Either the salesman can obtain interviews with his prospects in advance by telephone or letter, or he can call directly at the prospect's office or home. In both cases he must be fully prepared with an approach that will sell the prospect on the idea of listening to what the salesman has to say.

Courtesy Bulova Watch Company, Inc.

■ The salesman who is conscious of taking too much time to make a call should reexamine his self-analysis record and his sales presentation.

Making advance appointments by telephone or letter has many advantages in that the salesman is more assured, knowing that he can definitely see the prospect, and the prospect in turn is set mentally for listening to the salesman's presentation. Also, the time spent in making calls that do not result in interviews is saved. But very few salesmen can sell only by definite appointment because of the difficulties of scheduling them. For example, suppose the salesman decides that he can make a 10 and a 10:30 A.M. appointment in two offices that are close together. But the first prospect turns out to be the slow, deliberative type who asks many questions and ponders the answers; and also, he gets a long distance call in the middle of the interview that lasts for ten minutes. The salesman finds that he is so worried about getting to his next appointment on time that he cannot present his product with his usual enthusiasm. Or suppose that the salesman is more cautious and makes one appointment for 10 A.M. and the next one for 11. In this case the first prospect is easily sold; and fifteen minutes later the salesman is finished, with forty-five minutes on his hands.

The answer to this problem is that most salesmen would do well to plan their days to include both definite appointments and direct calls. However, the direct calls should not be *cold* calls. The salesman should plan them ahead of time as carefully as the calls for which he has appointments. His purpose in making the direct call is to secure an interview right then and there. Statistically he knows that every call does not result in an interview for even the most accomplished salesmen, but he should always take the positive approach and assume that he is going to get the chance to demonstrate his product.

The salesman should always be prepared with an emergency list of prospects, besides the list that he has scheduled, so that he can fill all his selling time to the best advantage.

Waiting to See Prospects. The salesman is inevitably going to have to spend some time waiting in outer offices before his prospects can see him. This is the easiest time of all to waste. The salesman is told that Mr. Prospect will see him in a few minutes, so he sits down without knowing how long he must wait. It seems easier just to sit there and thumb through magazines than to try to do anything constructive. But these few quiet minutes in the salesman's day make an excellent time to plan new ideas for sales presentations, to do paper work, to think about new routes to cut travel time, and so on. These are all jobs that the salesman must eventually do. Obviously it is much more to his advantage to fit them in while he is waiting to see a prospect than to have to take time to do them at the end of the day, for example.

Interviewing Prospects. The time that the salesman spends interviewing prospects is the most important part of his day, but unfortunately his actual selling time is quite short. A recent study has indicated that "Out of 2,500 working hours each year, the average salesman spends about 650 hours face-to-face with buyers. This means . . . only two-and-one-half hours a day."[1] The hours the salesman must spend traveling, waiting to see prospects, and performing other time-consuming activities all help to shorten his actual selling time.

Realizing the value of his interviewing time, the salesman should be aware of ways to spend it more carefully. First of all, he should try to make a sale in the first interview. Obviously this is not always possible, especially for very expensive or very new products. But the salesman should plan his sales presentation as carefully and thoroughly as he can to at least try to lead the prospect through the five steps to a sale, including the closing, during the first interview.

Second, the salesman should take advantage of his self-analysis records and his preapproach planning time to consider how he can shorten his presentation. Has he been using some words, sentences, or ideas that are just "fat" and can be trimmed off the "meat" of the presentation? Has he been wasting time with irrelevant conversation beyond the limits of courtesy? Could he get to the closing any sooner?

---

[1] Robert F. Vizza, *Improving Salesmen's Use of Time*, A Research Report, Sales Executives Club of New York, Inc., 1962, p. 58.

Third, once the sale has been completed, the salesman should be the first to arise, express his thanks, and be on his way. The buyer will appreciate the fact that the salesman is not dragging out the call, and the salesman will have added several minutes to his day.

Servicing Regular Customers. The time that the salesman spends servicing his regular customers is also a very important part of his day and should be given full consideration. The salesman should think of each call on a regular customer as a selling situation. He may be simply trying to sell the customer satisfaction; but satisfaction is a very worthwhile commodity in itself, directly translatable into future sales to this customer and to the people to whom he recommends the salesman. The salesman may also be trying to get a reorder, which is an important part of his sales quota. If spending a half hour helping the customer set up a new display or giving him marketing advice is the way to get the reorder, then the salesman must consider the time well spent.

There is another way to gain extra benefits from the time spent on customer service calls, however, and that is by selling the customer more items. By studying the customer's record card before he makes his call, the salesman can often figure out new uses for his product that will benefit the customer or he may think of products in his line that he never thought of before in connection with this customer. The salesman who can do this successfully is the one who consistently beats his sales quota.

Keeping Up with the Paper Work. The salesman must allow himself enough time in his daily schedule to complete his order blanks, keep his own records, report to his company, and write and answer sales correspondence. These very necessary jobs will not be as burdensome if the salesman keeps them up on a daily basis. The key to getting them done painlessly is to use them as fillers between appointments as much as possible. This will lighten the burden considerably, so that completing the leftover paper work at the end of the day will be a simple matter.

Planning and Scheduling. It should already be clear to the salesman that any time that he spends in planning his methods of working and his schedule will repay him many times over. The point to be made here is that the salesman should make a definite time for planning a part of his daily schedule. Perhaps the salesman can think best in the early morning just before he starts his day, or perhaps he likes to think through the next day's activities the evening before. But the time for planning should be a quiet and uninterrupted time when the salesman can really concentrate. The time in which the planning process can be

■ Keeping up with the paper work is part of the salesman's daily schedule. There will be less to do at the end of the day if he has used spare moments between appointments to fill out records also.

completed depends entirely upon how well the salesman has kept up his various records.

Allowing for Self-Improvement. The modern salesman is a marketing consultant rather than just a huckster. The gift of gab, which was once all one needed to be a successful salesman, has been replaced in importance by knowledge. In to-day's complex and sophisticated society, even the smoothest talk will not hide ignorance very long. The salesman must know what he is talking about if he expects to be taken seriously.

This explains why the salesman must take time in his daily routine for study and self-improvement. He has to keep well informed about his own product and company, which means that he must read *all* the literature that his company sends him. He must also find out all he can about what the competition is doing and about other developments in the field in which he sells.

The salesman should always be looking for new ideas in selling, which involves reading the periodicals that are published specifically for salesmen, such as *Sales Management* and *Industrial Marketing.* Reading such general business magazines as *Business Week, Fortune,* and *Nation's Business* and the daily news-paper will give the salesman the picture of the total economy that he needs. He can also turn for this economic picture to the many excellent books that are published each year on salesmanship, economics, labor, and management.

Each day the salesman needs to set aside a definite time for planning and scheduling. He will find a local map an effective aid in scheduling the calls he will make.

Courtesy Hilton Hotels

In addition, the salesman can increase his knowledge by attending company sales meetings, trade or professional association meetings, meetings of salesmen's organizations, and adult-education courses in such subjects as selling, public speaking, economic theory, and so on.

Time for reading can be found in many places—on a bus, train, or plane; in a restaurant while the salesman is having lunch; in a prospect's waiting room; or during a quiet hour at home after dinner. Time for attending meetings is harder to find, but it should be taken whenever the salesman feels that what he will learn will be worth the sacrifice. It should also be remembered that such meetings as the Chamber of Commerce, the Rotary, and church and school groups can be an excellent source of prospects. Again the salesman must use common sense in figuring out whether the gain balances the time that must be spent.

Management's Role in Time Planning

No matter whether a company is large or small, its management is faced to-day with a problem shared by businesses all over the country. How can costs be kept from spiraling to a point where they eliminate all profit? This basic problem has made *efficiency* management's biggest headache. Every motion that wastes either time or money must be eliminated and replaced with a system that gives the most value in the overall picture.

Therefore, companies everywhere are beginning to take a careful look at what they expect from their salesmen. It is becoming apparent that some of the salesman's routine duties can and should be taken over by lower-paid clerical help or even by computers. The fact that there are not enough good salesmen to go around makes the salesman's time all the more valuable. He has to be released for as much selling as possible.

Clerical workers are therefore taking over such duties as completing order forms, handling reorders that come in by telephone or letter, notifying customers of shipping dates, typing the salesman's correspondence, and making routine telephone calls. Clerical workers can also assist the salesman with his records. This is the area where computers are beginning to be used a great deal. Customer and prospect records can be put on cards and fed to electronic business machines. The salesman can then get almost immediate answers to such questions as which customers and prospects are in Toledo, Ohio, and which of them are due for a call.

Management is also trying more and more to help the salesman with the setting of realistic goals; with the routing and coverage of his territory; and with all kinds of aids to selling, from audio-visual aids to training in the new techniques of selling.

This assistance obviously cannot solve the salesman's time-control problems for him, but certainly it will greatly increase his chances of success.

Time Management in Retail Selling

The retail salesperson reports to his store at a definite hour, leaves at a definite hour, and has a set time for lunch. This pattern automatically eliminates most of the time-management problems of the other types of salesmen. But the retail salesperson also must realize that time is money and must therefore use it thriftily. Long, purely social conversations on the telephone or with the other salesclerks, several trips to the stock room when a few seconds' thinking ahead would have made one trip sufficient, and insufficient knowledge of what the stock is and where it is kept are examples of the many ways in which the retail salesperson can waste time. It may seem to the unthinking beginner that being physically there from 9:30 to 5:30 is enough to earn his pay. The wiser salesman, however, realizes that, by making careful use of his time, he can increase his sales and hence receive a bigger income through his commissions and through a faster promotion.

SUMMING UP

Because the salesman's greatest asset is time, his success depends upon learning to control its use. He has to find a system for getting the most *value* out of his time. The only way that he can do this is by planning how he is going to spend his time.

In order to plan ahead, the salesman must keep accurate records of what his job involves and set realistic goals for what he hopes to accomplish. Then he must use this information to set up a definite time schedule that allows his jobs to be done and his goals to be met.

The fact that selling is the salesman's most important function is the single most important consideration in the study of time management. The salesman's purpose is to get all his other jobs done as quickly and efficiently as possible to release more time for actual selling. Five general principles for increasing his sales time are as follows: (1) stretch the working day, (2) stick to your schedule, (3) use all your time, (4) use supplementary sales aids, and (5) don't trust your memory.

Also, the salesman should study each of his duties specifically to see how he can save time in the performance of each one. These nine jobs are (1) selecting prospects, (2) traveling, (3) securing interviews with prospects, (4) waiting to see prospects, (5) interviewing prospects, (6) servicing regular customers, (7) keeping up with the paper work, (8) planning and scheduling, and (9) allowing for self-improvement. Management is becoming increasingly interested in relieving the salesman of the routine parts of these jobs.

The retail salesperson's time-management problem is much simpler since his working hours are set, but he must still realize that time should be spent as carefully as money.

Reviewing Your Reading

1. Why is it that energetic and imaginative men are attracted to the selling field?
2. Give a one-sentence definition of time planning for the salesman.
3. Why is it important that the salesman get the facts before he tries to plan his time?
4. List the five kinds of records that the salesman should keep and explain what purpose each one serves.
5. Why is it important that the salesman's goals be realistic?

6. What is the salesman's primary function? How is it related to the problem of time management?
7. What job should be at the heart of the salesman's schedule?
8. Is it true that a salesman should never try to see a prospect from noon to 2 P.M.? Explain your answer.
9. Is it safe for the salesman to trust his memory? Explain.
10. Why is it important that the names of new prospects be added constantly to the salesman's prospect file?
11. Why does the salesman need an emergency list of prospects for each day's work?
12. List three ways in which the salesman can save time in interviewing prospects.
13. How can the salesman make customer service time pay off?
14. How can the salesman tell whether it is worth his time to join community organizations?
15. Why is management interested in helping the salesman save his time?
16. What does the retail salesperson have to gain by using time carefully?

For Discussion

1. Read the story about Salesman Sam again (page 382) and list all the things that Sam did that were time wasters.
2. Define what is meant by the term *efficiency ratio*. How does being more selective about prospects improve the salesman's efficiency ratio?
3. Since the salesman is really his own boss, what would be the matter with his decision to go to a ball game during the working day?
4. What is meant by the statement, "The salesman's schedule must be flexible"? Name four things that could happen to upset the salesman's plans and state how he could adjust his schedule to allow for these upsets.
5. Explain why the salesman should plan maximum coverage of each geographic area while he is there.
6. Why does the salesman have to be concerned about self-improvement?

Sales Problem

The Wellworth Printing Ink Company is a small firm located in Los Angeles. It makes a complete line of high-grade printing inks for the printing trade. The company's products are sold only in California and Arizona. However, the northern part of California has been handled through mail orders.

The company employs four regular salesmen who confine their efforts to southern California and Arizona. The amount of mail-order business from the northern part of California, especially San Francisco, Oakland, and Fresno, is increasing; and the owner of the company feels that another salesman should be hired and assigned to this territory. This new man, like the other salesmen, would be paid a salary plus commission. Assume that you are to be the new salesman.

QUESTIONS

1. How would you go about setting up customer records for your territory?
2. How would you get a prospect file started?
3. Describe the steps that you would take after you had worked in the area a month to get a time schedule in operation.

Salesmanship in Action

1. Good supervision of salesmen requires that the sales manager:
   a. Know what is expected of each salesman
   b. Let each salesman know what is expected of him
   c. Follow up to see that each salesman is doing what is expected of him
   d. Let each salesman know his efforts are appreciated
   From the material you have read in this chapter, prepare a list of specific ideas you could use to see that each of the four objectives mentioned above is realized. You may also list ideas, which you may have, that were not mentioned in this chapter. Be sure to indicate which ideas are your own, so your instructor will recognize them.
2. Design a system, including a time schedule, that will enable you to make the most effective use of your day as a student. Use the full twenty-four-hour day.

You and Your Company

THE SALESMAN'S RELATION to his company is such a close one that his prospects and customers tend to think that the salesman *is* the company. The company knows when it hires the salesman that this will happen. The fact that it does hire him shows that the company is willing to be represented by the salesman and identified with him. But in return for this trust, the salesman must assume certain obligations to the company. These obligations are the subject of this chapter and will be discussed under seven headings: (1) the salesman's public relations role, (2) the importance of cooperation, (3) rules and regulations, (4) sales records and reports, (5) the measure of the salesman's worth, (6) non-selling duties of retail salespeople, and (7) business law and the salesman.

The Salesman's Public Relations Role

The salesman's company expects the salesman to understand the simple fact that as long as he works for the company his own welfare and the company's welfare are one and the same thing. This means that the salesman must keep the company's interests in mind at all times. He has to recognize that he has a major

403

■ Sometimes a mistake occurs, and when it does, the adjustment must be made in a friendly manner. The salesman is expected to maintain a positive image of his company at all times.

role in the firm's public relations. If the company or store that the salesman works for is to stay in business, it must keep the public believing that it is well run, reliable, stable, and popular. This is what public relations men call a *positive image*. The salesman can either foster the positive image of his firm or he can destroy it.

Most salesmen realize the importance of establishing a positive image when they are dealing with prospects, for in this case the reliability and stability of the company are important points in the salesman's sales talk. But in dealing with their regular customers over a period of time, some salesmen tend to forget the importance of never putting the company in a bad light. For example, suppose that a salesman is faced with an irate customer who has received a damaged shipment. The salesman feels that his personal relations with this customer, which have always been excellent, must not be allowed to suffer if he is to get further business. So he assures the customer that he himself is absolutely blameless and that he is very shocked at the disgraceful way in which the customer received the goods. He then goes on to explain that the company is having a hard time getting its shipping department organized. The salesman is very shortsighted in believing that this answer will soothe the customer. The customer will feel that if the company can't organize its business any better than that, he had better take his business elsewhere. But the salesman could keep the customer's business if he simply expressed his own regret *and that of his company* for the unfortunate incident and promised an immediate remedy.

The salesman also owes it to his company to watch what he says to his friends. He may be tempted to entertain a gathering of the neighbors one night with a supposedly hilarious story of some mistakes that were made in the credit department of his company. But he must realize that the funnier the story is, the faster it will get around and the more it will be built up. Eventually the story that his company is inefficiently run will come back to him through a prospect.

To sum up this point, the salesman must never say or do anything that would destroy the public's respect for or confidence in his firm. If he does, he is only making things harder for himself.

The Importance of Cooperation

In selecting a salesman, the company or store says in effect, "We believe you have the ability to make good with us. Therefore, we are going to spend our time and money to train and supervise you. In return, we expect you to justify our faith in you by giving us your full cooperation in trying to sell our products or merchandise."

What is it that the company expects of you when it asks for your full cooperation? It expects that you will:

1. Work hard.
2. Manage your time efficiently.
3. Develop a keen sense of responsibility.
4. Develop a determination to do a thorough and efficient job. Never be satisfied with halfhearted, incomplete selling.
5. Use your initiative.
6. Keep right on learning something new about your industry every day.

■ One way the salesman can learn something new about his industry is to read a trade journal in his field during his spare time.

7. Constantly strive to increase the value of your service to the firm's customers.
8. Increase your production every year.
9. Work with the other departments of the firm to ensure complete customer satisfaction.

Rules and Regulations

The new salesman must learn to appreciate the aims and objectives of the company's policies and accept the company's methods of doing business. Any organization for which you will work has definite rules, regulations, and policies that are planned to benefit the business, the employees, and the customers. You will become a valuable and reliable employee when you understand and apply these rules intelligently during your daily work.

The salesman should always keep the rules of his firm in mind when he is quoting prices, arranging credit and delivery terms, and making adjustments so that he does not compromise the company by making promises that are against company policy. The retail salesman, whether he works in a large department store or in a small specialty shop, should strictly follow the store rules in regard to:

1. Store hours
2. Employee entrances and elevators
3. Lunch and relief periods
4. Proper dress for employees
5. Personal shopping procedures and discounts allowed
6. How and when wages are paid
7. Vacation rules
8. How to record working time
9. How to write sales checks

Sales Reports and Records

Business firms require their salesmen to prepare and submit reports on their daily work. In the case of the retail salesperson, these reports may be merely keeping a tally of daily sales. In specialty and industrial selling, it may involve the preparation of daily, weekly, and monthly sales summaries. The salesman will find that he must be accurate and conscientious in preparing any and all reports.

Large companies require more record keeping by their salesmen than small companies. In large companies it is difficult for the management to keep in close touch with the daily work of their salesmen. Therefore, the reports that the

Courtesy The Goodyear Tire & Rubber Company

Keeping personal records of various expenses while traveling will help the salesman in preparing his expense account report later. He should be careful to obtain receipts of his expenses whenever possible.

salesman turns in to the company form the chief link in the chain that ties the sales force to the home office. Sales managers cannot constantly be with their men in the field. Consequently, the salesman's reports help the sales manager to determine how his men are doing and may indicate just where guidance or additional training will be needed to convert a mediocre salesman into an expert salesman.

For example, you may be asked to submit a weekly report of the communities that you expect to cover each day during the following week and the customers and prospects on whom you expect to call. In the hands of a good sales manager, such a report can be of great help to you. You may not be covering your sales territory in the most efficient manner. The sales manager may point out that you are spending too much time on unimportant customers or that a certain area will not provide enough business to warrant the time you are spending on it.

It is also important to bear in mind that the preparation of such a report forces you to plan your work. You thereby benefit through planning a schedule that will save time and provide the most profitable coverage of your territory.

Good salesmen go further than just turning in the required reports. They maintain various personal records to help them do a better job, such as records of customers, prospects, personal expenses, sales volume, and self-analysis.

The expense account report should be prepared honestly and accurately. Most companies plan to reimburse their salesmen for money spent on hotels, meals, car expenses, necessary entertainment, and other pertinent expenses while salesmen are traveling in the field. The expense account report will be used in calculating the salesman's worth to the company, as will be described in the next section. It is to the salesman's advantage to make an accurate and complete report.

The most common types of reports that salesmen are required to submit to their companies are as follows:

1. *Daily sales report.* This report gives the major facts about each call made during the day and its results. It may be mailed to the firm each night or turned in at the end of the day.

2. *Weekly sales report.* This report summarizes a week's sales. It shows number of calls, amount of sales, prospects called on, customers serviced, results obtained in all cases, and usually the expense incurred.

3. *Expense report.* This report lists all expenses by categories on a daily, weekly, or monthly basis. The weekly basis is favored by most companies.

4. *Customer record.* This report provides for information on each customer which will help the salesman make sales. It generally includes a record of calls made, purchases, and lines of merchandise stocked.

The Measure of the Salesman's Worth

The worth of a salesman to his company is measured by his wage ratio, which is the ratio of his salary plus his expenses to his sales volume. This is commonly referred to as the *selling cost percentage.* The formula is expressed as follows:

$$\text{Selling cost percentage} = \frac{\text{salary plus expenses}}{\text{sales volume}}$$

For example, if a salesman earns $500 a month, incurs an expense account of $240 for a certain month, and turns in sales of $3,700 for that month, his selling cost percentage would be computed as follows:

$$\text{Selling cost percentage} = \frac{\$500 \text{ plus } \$240}{\$3,700} = .20, \text{ or } 20\%$$

If a salesman works on commission only, his commission *rate* is the selling cost percentage. If a salesman has an expense account as well as his commission, then the selling cost percentage is derived from the *total amount* of his commission plus his expenses, divided by his sales volume.

It is possible for salesmen earning different salaries to operate at the same selling cost percentage. Also, a salesman with twice the income of another salesman can have a lower selling cost percentage. What is important from the company's viewpoint is that its salesmen maintain a selling cost percentage that allows the company to make a profit. As an illustration of this point, consider the following table, which shows the record of six salesmen who sell for the Dobbs Paper Company:

Salesman	Sales	Salary	Selling Cost Percentage
A	$100,000	$20,000	20%
B	100,000	10,000	10%
C	60,000	9,000	15%
D	40,000	6,000	15%
E	30,000	6,000	20%
F	20,000	5,000	25%
	$350,000	$56,000	16.0%

Note that the average selling cost percentage is 16 percent, obtained by dividing the total salaries ($56,000) by the total sales volume ($350,000). This average is satisfactory for this particular company, but if the average were to go as high as 20 percent, the company would begin to lose money. To prevent this from happening, the company must watch the men who have selling cost percentages above the average. The company will investigate why it costs so much more for Salesman A to produce the same sales volume as Salesman B. Also, the company will note that Salesmen E and F are not producing enough sales to justify their salaries. In this case, Salesmen A, E, and F will have to increase their sales volume or take a cut in pay to bring their individual selling cost percentages in line with the average desired by the company.

This reasoning is usually not applied to beginning salesmen. Progressive companies do not expect a new salesman to be in line with the average selling cost percentage until he has completed the company's training program and has had some well-supervised field experience.

Nonselling Duties of Retail Salespeople

Besides their selling duties, retail salespeople are expected by the store's management to take on duties in two other areas: (1) handling stock and (2) handling emergencies.

Courtesy Sport Spot, New York

■ When the retail salesperson is not busy selling, she may be asked to help with the inventory or perform certain other stockkeeping duties.

Handling Stock. The stockkeeping duties of the retail salesperson require neatness, orderliness, and a willingness to do some physical work. In both small and large stores, the retail salesperson handles stock as it comes into the store or into his department as well as after it has been placed on the shelves. The merchandise must be received and marked. In large stores this is performed by a special department set up for this purpose. In small stores the salespeople are required to perform the task. Generally this consists of checking incoming shipments to determine whether they are in good condition and are the same as ordered. The goods are then price-marked and distributed to either reserve stock or the sales floor.

The retail salesperson may be expected to replenish stock on the counters or shelves as it is sold, to arrange goods on counters and shelves, and to set up inside displays as well as help with inventory.

Every salesperson must be on guard against careless handling of merchandise, which may result in soiling or damaging the goods. Items shown to customers should be replaced neatly on the shelves so that they will look clean and fresh to other customers.

Handling Emergencies. The retail salesperson must be prepared to meet common store emergencies that will arise from time to time, such as accidents and shoplifting. In the case of store accidents, the salesperson is expected to protect the store's interest. A store official should be called as quickly as possible, and the injured person should be given aid and comfort. First aid should be of the simplest type. All facts concerning the accident should be noted and names of witnesses secured, if possible.

The salesperson should avoid making any statement that the injured party might be able to use later in a suit against the store. Until all possible facts are known, no one can be sure of where the fault lies. For example, avoid a statement similar to the one made in this situation: A customer was threading her way through a crowd in the basement section of a large department store. Suddenly she was shoved against the edge of a table as she tried to pass through an aisle. The salesgirl who rushed up to her said, "It's a wonder that more people aren't hurt, the way this table sticks out in the aisle."

In regard to theft, the salesperson must remember that he is not authorized to make arrests. If he observes someone stealing, he should call a store executive immediately without attracting attention. The thief then may be followed until the police arrive to make the arrest. In no case should the salesperson accuse a person of theft, no matter how obvious it may be, nor should he attempt to detain the person in the store. Even if caught with stolen goods in a store, an apparent thief may claim that he was taking the goods to a salesperson.

The salesperson who suspects a shoplifter should call a store executive, who will have the person watched. If it becomes apparent that the person is a shoplifter, he will be followed until he leaves the store, and then a policeman will be called to make the arrest. Large stores usually employ detectives to handle such situations.

Business Law and the Salesman

The salesman cannot properly fulfill his obligation to his company unless he has some knowledge of business law. This knowledge may be acquired while the salesman is still in school or in the sales-training programs that are given by most companies. The most important legal facts for the salesman to know are (1) the law of agency, (2) the law of contracts, (3) the law of sales, and (4) the warranty.

The Law of Agency. Legally the salesman is considered to be the *agent* of the company for which he works. An agent may be defined as a person who acts for and in behalf of another in dealing with third persons. The agent is subject to the control of the person for whom he is acting.

The agency relationship requires three things: (1) a principal, (2) an agent, and (3) one or more third parties. In selling, the company is the principal, the salesman is the agent, and the customer is the third party. As the principal, the company has the legal capacity to enter into valid contracts. When the company hires the salesman, it empowers him theoretically to take the place of the company and to deal with third persons *in the company's name.* The contract that results from the salesman's actions as an agent is binding on the principal and the third party. The agent is just the go-between who brings the contracting parties together.

The agreement between the company and the salesman may be either written or implied, but in either case the salesman binds the company by his acts. The company is responsible for what the salesman does as long as the salesman is acting within the limits of the power that the company has given him. When the salesman acts beyond the limits of his power, that is, when he exceeds his authority, the third party may hold him personally liable for any injury that results.

The meaning of the law of agency for the salesman is clear. He must know what the limits of his authority are and stay within those limits. He should also know that he cannot delegate or assign his authority to another person without specific permission from the company.

The Law of Contracts. The salesman is constantly negotiating contracts between his company and his customers. Every time he writes an order, he is engaged in the process of preparing a contract. It is important, therefore, that he understands what constitutes a contract. With this knowledge, the salesman is in a better position to make a valid contract, that will hold up legally. Here are the essential elements of a contract:

1. Every contract must have agreement, which involves an offer by one party and acceptance by the other party.
2. The agreement must be supported by consideration—something must be exchanged for something.
3. The parties to the agreement must have capacity to contract. Certain parties do not have full capacity to contract, such as minors, insane or intoxicated persons, and in some states, married women and aliens.
4. The objective of the agreement must be legal.

The Law of Sales. Knowledge of the law of sales will help the salesman to determine what constitutes a sale and to follow the title to the goods. The rights of the parties in a sales transaction are determined primarily by applying the law of contracts and the law of personal property. However, the variety of business transactions has resulted in the development of special rules that conform to established practices of merchants. These rules have been set down in the Uniform Sales Act, which has been passed by three-quarters of the fifty states.

The rest of the states either have similar statutes of their own or follow the common law on which the Uniform Sales Act is based.

It is important for the salesman to distinguish between a sale and a contract to sell. According to the Uniform Sales Act, *a sale* occurs when title is immediately transferred from the seller to the buyer. A *contract to sell* is an agreement in which the seller agrees to transfer title to the buyer some time in the future.

Sometimes merchandise is lost, damaged, or destroyed. In such cases it is important to know when title has passed from seller to buyer. Ordinarily title will pass when the parties agree that title shall pass, and this is generally contained in the contract of sale. If the contract of sale is silent on the subject of when title shall pass, then the law steps in to provide an answer. The salesman will find it exceedingly helpful to study the law of sales in the state in which he is selling.

The Warranty. The salesman should make certain that he is representing the product as accurately and fairly as possible. Selling is persuasion, but in attempting to persuade the customer to act on his proposition, the salesman should not make any statements that do not reflect the truth. Such statements may make the company and the salesman liable on a charge of breach of warranty.

Almost any statement that the salesman makes could be construed to be a warranty, depending on the particular state in which he is selling. In most states a warranty is considered to be any statement of fact made by the seller that logically leads the buyer to rely on it and to act accordingly.

A salesman's opinion as to the value of the goods cannot be considered to be a warranty. The salesman may praise or "puff" the goods in an attempt to sell

■ Writing up contracts between his company and his customers is part of the salesman's job. Therefore, it is important that he have a knowledge of the law of contracts and the law of sales.

them. Legally the buyer is at fault if he places absolute reliance on such trade talk. Of course, most modern progressive business organizations want their salesmen to refrain from practices that would tend to misrepresent their goods. To illustrate the difference between a statement of fact that could constitute a warranty and a mere statement of opinion, consider the following examples:

Warranty
SALESMAN: **Mr. Customer, bearings in this motor are machined to a tolerance of 0.0001 inches and will not break down under ordinary use for a period of two years.**

Statement of Opinion
SALESMAN: **Mr. Customer, this motor is the finest on the market.**

SUMMING UP

The company's willingness to be represented by the salesman and identified with him obligates the salesman to the company in seven ways:

1. The salesman has a major public relations role in the company or store for which he works. He must never say or do anything that would destroy the public's respect for or confidence in his firm.
2. The company or store expects the salesman's full cooperation in trying to sell its products or merchandise.
3. The salesman must strictly follow the rules and regulations of the company or store, since they are planned to give maximum benefit to the business, the employees, and the customers.
4. The salesman should carefully and honestly prepare the sales reports and records which are required by the company or store.
5. The salesman must try to keep his selling costs down and his sales volume up so that his selling cost percentage will be in line with the average that the company expects.
6. Retail salespeople are expected to perform stock duties when they are not selling. They should also be prepared to handle such emergencies as accidents and shoplifting.
7. The salesman should have some knowledge of business law in order to fulfill his obligations to his company. He should be familiar with (*a*) the law of agency, (*b*) the law of contracts, (*c*) the law of sales, and (*d*) the warranty.

1. What is a positive image?
2. How does the salesman hurt his company when he criticizes one of the other departments?
3. List the nine ways in which the salesman can cooperate with his company.
4. What are the nine kinds of store rules that the retail salesperson should know?
5. Why do large companies require more record keeping than small companies?
6. What is the formula for finding the selling cost percentage?
7. Why is it important for the retail salesperson to handle merchandise carefully?
8. Why shouldn't a retail salesperson hold a suspected thief in a store?
9. What four legal questions should the salesman study?
10. Who are the principal, the agent, and the third party in a selling situation?
11. What is the meaning of the law of agency for the salesman?
12. When the salesman writes an order, is that a contract?
13. What are the four essential elements of a contract?
14. What is the Uniform Sales Act?

For Discussion

1. Discuss this statement: "As long as the salesman works for the company, his own welfare and the company's welfare are one and the same thing."
2. Why is it important that the salesman should not make promises that compromise company rules?
3. If you go to the grocery store for your mother, are you an agent? Explain your answer.
4. If a retail salesperson is arranging stock, is he an agent? Explain your answer.
5. Explain the difference between a warranty and a statement of opinion. Give an example of each for the following items:
   a. Television set   d. Man's suit
   b. Automobile   e. Football
   c. Dishwasher

Sales Problem

The Astor Company, a large candy manufacturer with distribution throughout the East and Middle West markets, found that sales in the Middle West market were falling off. The company decided to launch a big merchandising campaign, involving special store displays and distribution of free samples on a door-to-door basis. The salesmen were briefed on the campaign through the district offices and were asked to promote the use of the displays by all the dealers on whom they called. In addition, the salesmen were asked to leave a supply of leaflets near the displays.

Sam Benson had the Chicago territory. Sam complained that he could not use all the display material, that he was hired as a salesman, not as an express-man. Besides, his customers were besieged with requests by other salesmen to put up displays, and it made no difference whether his company's displays were more attractive.

Sam's technique in making a sales call consisted of dropping in on a dealer and asking, "Need any candy today?" The answer was generally "no." Sam might then pull a small display card out of his brief case and ask, "Would you mind setting up this display for me? The company is asking us to get them up in all our clients' stores." The dealer would take the display card and whatever else Sam had and would throw them away after Sam left.

A sales supervisor from company headquarters was assigned to check up on Sam. His recommendation, after spending two days with Sam in the field, was to relieve this salesman of his duties in the sales field and offer him a position in the stock room of the plant.

The new man who took Sam's place was George Whitcomb. George found a lot of display material in Sam's old office, so he decided to put it to use. His tech-nique was to show to store managers copies of his company's advertising, set up a display on the counter, and then tell how the display was building sales and making money for other stores. After George set up a display, he would talk to the employees about how to keep the display looking fresh and attractive, what to tell customers about the new candy, and the importance of keeping the dis-play well stocked. He passed samples around and had the store manager and his employees taste the candy.

George also made a point of always having a selling idea every time he called on the dealer. Often he would take off his coat and work an hour or more in the store to help the dealer set up a special display or get a promotion under way. Sales in the Chicago territory increased 25 percent one month after George took over.

QUESTIONS

1. What do you think of Sam's attitude? Discuss it from the point of view of the material in this chapter.
2. Essentially what was the difference between these two men?

1. A small firm employs four salesmen, all of whom receive a salary plus an expense account. Below are the sales and cost figures for the sales force of this company:

Salesman	Salary	Selling Expense	Sales
A	$4,000	$200	$22,000
B	8,000	500	46,000
C	7,000	600	38,000
D	6,000	300	27,000

   a. What is the selling cost percentage for each man?
   b. Which salesmen are above the company's average selling cost?
2. As assigned by your instructor, ask for an interview with a sales manager on "What the Company Expects of Its Salesmen." Prepare a written report on your interview and be prepared to discuss it in class.
3. Prepare a sample daily sales report for a company that makes and sells a line of paints, varnishes, and lacquers.
4. Prepare a sample sales report for a company that makes and sells men's and women's hosiery (*a*) on a door-to-door basis and (*b*) to retailers.

22

You and Your Fellow Workers

AS A SALESMAN, you must make a constant effort to get along well with your customers and prospects. But you must remember that it is equally important for you to maintain good relations with your fellow workers in your company or store. Your fellow workers are an important factor in whether or not you succeed as a salesman.

Being a Part of the Team

The employees in the company or store that you work for are not just a collection of individuals, with each person doing his own separate job. The job of each individual worker is dependent on all the other jobs, so that what you have is a team. You as the salesman are an especially important member of the team, because the prosperity of the company or store depends directly on the amount of goods being sold. If you are not doing a good job of selling, everyone who works with you will suffer.

But on the other hand, you cannot sell alone. The other members of your team must give their support. These people may be in your same company, or they may be employed by various middlemen involved in the marketing process. For example, the production workers meet the production schedule that your sales demand. The workers in the shipping department fill your sales orders quickly and wrap them so that they will reach your customers in good condition. The workers in the accounting department keep your customers' accounts accurately and bill them correctly. The workers in the research department strive to develop better products for you to sell. The advertising and sales promotion department builds customer acceptance of the products that you are presenting, which in turn makes your selling job easier. This department is also responsible for providing you with all kinds of excellent tools to help you sell—sales kits, visual aids, dealers' display kits, sales letters, and so on. The management of the company is ready to talk over your problems with you and to help you in any other way that it can. The management also arranges sales conferences so that you can even get assistance from your fellow salesmen and share experiences together.

The salesman in a retail store is equally dependent on his fellow workers. He cannot do his job without the management, the buyers, the workers at the wrapping desk, the stock-room clerks, the shipping clerks, the people in charge of display, the advertising and public relations staffs, and the other salesmen. Each job is important in the total picture of customer satisfaction and increased sales.

■ **The salesman and other workers in a company are members of a team—all working for the same goal.**

Getting Along with Others

To have each worker consider himself and his fellow workers as all part of the same team is, of course, the ideal situation. Unfortunately it is not always the actual situation. The salesman who is starting on a new job may find that he must overcome a certain amount of resentment before he is accepted as a member of the team. The young salesman must remember that he represents competition to the older men. There are only so many top jobs in an organization and the older men, especially if they have not advanced very far or very rapidly, may be afraid that any chances they did have for promotion will be ruined by an ambitious young newcomer. Also, many people have an innate opposition to change. They want things to stay just as they are, and they see a new man as a threat to the established order.

The young salesman should make a real effort to overcome this kind of resentment. Here are eight rules which will guide him in winning the support and respect of his fellow workers:

1. *Remember that you have a lot to learn.* No matter how much education you have had or how highly trained you are, you will still have a lot to learn about your new job. Your immediate superiors and your fellow salesmen are not going to be very sympathetic to you if you have a brash, "know-it-all" attitude. They will be much more willing to help you if you show that you respect their experience and that you are anxious to learn from them.

As an example, consider the case of John Garland, who was hired by an appliance firm and given the position of salesman for the upper New York State territory. When John was introduced at his first sales meeting, he announced in no uncertain terms that he intended to build his new territory into the biggest sales area of the company. Needless to say, the other salesmen did not appreciate this display of tactlessness and conceit. John would have done better if he had simply said that he was happy to join the company and that he hoped for the support and guidance of the other salesmen in establishing his new territory.

2. *Don't try to reform the company.* You may feel that you have many new, fresh, and original ideas about how the company or store could improve its procedures. However, you should observe the procedures carefully over a period of time before you start telling the men who were running things before you arrived what you think they are doing wrong. When you have had more chance to observe the company's operations, you may realize that there are very sensible reasons for the procedures which seemed wrong to you at first. This does not mean that you should not present your ideas to your superior if you still feel, after

a period of careful observation, that you have thought of legitimate improvements. But you should be humble and tactful about stating your ideas, and you should have a sense of proportion about the right time and the right place.

3. *Observe the rules of sales etiquette.* You should also have a sense of proportion about how aggressive you should be. You were hired as a salesman and you are certainly expected to sell. But don't let this lead you into being a sales grabber—that is, someone who steals sales that should rightfully go to another salesman.

4. *Never criticize or embarrass the other departments.* If the salesman expects to maintain the respect and cooperation of his fellow workers, he must never criticize or embarrass the other departments in any way. For example, if production is behind schedule and the salesman continues to promise immediate delivery, he is putting the production department, the shipping department, and the whole company in an embarrassing position. Also, the salesman should not complain about the credit department because it will not allow a shipment to be made to a customer whose credit is unsound.

It is especially important that the salesman should not try to pass the blame along to another department when he is handling a customer's complaint. For

■ It is important for the salesman to get along with his fellow workers in the home office.

instance, if a shipment has been damaged in transit, the salesman should not blame the packers. His sales depend on making his prospects and customers think that his company is efficiently run and reliable. Thus it is a very shortsighted policy for him ever to criticize publicly any individual or department in the company or store.

5. *Stay away from cliques.* Every office or store has its little cliques, but the new salesman should be very wary of getting himself involved. The petty jealousies that go along with cliques will only hamper the salesman who hopes for eventual promotion.

6. *Prove that you can take it.* Accept cheerfully every job given you no matter how menial it may seem. Many training programs require that the salesman have a knowledge of all phases of the company's operation. Sometimes the salesman is required to do what seem like small, unimportant jobs in the various departments of the company for several months. He may be asked to spend time in the plant itself, in the shipping department, accounting department, and so on. The salesman must accept these jobs cheerfully and not act as though he is "too good" for them. The training program has proved valuable or the company would not be accepting the expense and trouble involved in it. Therefore, the

Courtesy Hertz Corporation

■ In his selling job the salesman is supported by many behind-the-scene workers.

■ Those in the research department are working on the development of new products for the salesman to sell.

Courtesy Monsanto Company

salesman should try to learn all that he can instead of wasting his time in resentment. Also, he should see this training period as a good opportunity to make friends in the other departments. These people can be of help to him when he starts his actual selling.

7. *Let your work speak for you.* It isn't ever necessary for you to "toot your own horn." Your abilities and talents will be very obvious to your superiors and fellow workers through the work that you do. If you constantly brag about how clever and indispensable you are, you will make everyone else in the company or store resent you.

8. *Learn to be a leader.* If you are able to win the respect and confidence of the people with whom you work, you are on your way to being a leader. Your company or store is looking for people who have enough enthusiasm and drive to inspire other people.

You can work on developing these qualities while you are still in school. Take part in your school's student government and athletic activities, join worthwhile community organizations, or take part in Community Chest or Red Cross drives. Such activities will give you confidence in making decisions, help you to cooperate with others, and make it easy for you to meet and get along well with various kinds of people. They are also a means of developing ideas and working them out successfully.

SUMMING UP

While the salesman has to make a constant effort to get along well with his customers and prospects, he should not forget the importance of maintaining good relations with the other workers in his company or store. The salesman cannot succeed without the goodwill and cooperation of these fellow workers.

The salesman is an important member of the team, because the prosperity of the store or company depends directly on the amount of goods being sold. But the salesman cannot do his job without the people who work in research, production, shipping, accounting, advertising, sales promotion, and display, as well as the management and his fellow salesmen.

The eight rules which will guide the salesman in winning the support and respect of his fellow workers are:

1. Remember that you have a lot to learn.
2. Don't try to reform the company.
3. Observe the rules of sales etiquette.
4. Never criticize or embarrass the other departments.
5. Stay away from cliques.
6. Prove that you can take it.
7. Let your work speak for you.
8. Learn to be a leader.

Reviewing Your Reading

1. Why is the salesman especially important to the company or store?
2. How does the shipping department help the salesman?
3. What does the advertising and sales promotion department do for the salesman?
4. How is the salesman's job in a retail store affected by the work done by the display department?
5. Why is the new salesman sometimes resented by the older employees?
6. What is a sales grabber?
7. What is wrong with "tooting your own horn" when you are working with other people?

1. How can the new salesman avoid a "know-it-all" attitude?
2. How can you recognize teamwork in any organization?
3. Why should the salesman avoid criticizing his fellow workers?
4. Why is it important that the salesman cooperate in the training program?
5. Why should the salesman avoid becoming a part of a clique in his office or store?

Sales Problem

You are a student in retailing who is getting practical experience in the Universal Department Store. While putting some stock away, you overhear two of the older salespeople talking. One says, "It just doesn't seem right. These students get all the special training and attention both in school and in the store. We never had a break like that."

QUESTION

How would you strengthen relations with your co-workers under such circumstances?

Salesmanship in Action

It has been said that manners in store work are very poor compared with those in other kinds of business. Visit some retail stores in your community and report your opinion concerning this statement to the class.

You and Your Customers

THE SUCCESSFUL SALESMAN is the one who has learned that if he merely sells the customer the product, he will only sell the customer *once*. The smart salesman knows that he must sell *satisfaction* along with the product, for only the satisfied customer will buy again from the salesman and recommend the salesman to his friends.

The idea of selling satisfaction is the essence of modern salesmanship and has been repeated again and again throughout this book. Because the subject is so important to the salesman, it will be reviewed in this chapter under five main headings: (1) understanding the ethics of selling, (2) building goodwill through service, (3) maintaining a spirit of friendship, (4) adjusting complaints and claims, and (5) avoiding high-pressure methods.

Understanding the Ethics of Selling

In ancient times the buyer did not expect to be treated ethically. In Greek writings there is frequent mention of the thievery, lying, dishonesty, and greed of the Phoenician traders; and Greek merchants themselves indulged in such

426

practices as watering the wine. The Roman word for salesman meant "cheater"; even the law for dealing with merchants was *caveat emptor*, which translates into "let the buyer beware." This rule meant the buyer had to look the goods over carefully to be sure he was not being cheated, because once he had handed over his money, that was the end of the matter for he could not make any claims against the seller.

The principle of *caveat emptor* has governed buying and selling for centuries. Today there are many Federal, state, and local laws which protect the consumer. Federal laws include the Federal Food, Drug, and Cosmetic Act; the Wool Products Labeling Act; and the Fur Products Labeling Act. But in the areas outside such specific laws, *caveat emptor* is still the legal rule. It is not the system under which most modern business firms operate, however. In modern selling there is no room for the idea of making a fast dollar by selling inferior merchandise to a "sucker." Modern salesmanship is based instead on the idea of selling the customer a product which is everything it has been made out to be and which will give the customer full value for his money and complete satisfaction.

In short, modern business leaders believe that honesty is the only policy that will work in the long run. Customers do not want to feel that they have to be constantly on the alert for defects in the merchandise they buy or for traps in the terms offered. They will give their business to the store or firm that consistently demonstrates its integrity and reliability, and the dishonest firm will ultimately be driven out of business. Many businesses are so anxious to deal fairly with their customers that they have adopted the policy that "the customer is king" or "the customer is always right." Such businesses bend over backward to adjust all complaints to the complete satisfaction of their customers. In any case,

■ **The successful salesman on his way to call on a prospect. In the prospect's eyes he *is* the company.**

it is standard policy in modern selling for the store or firm to stand behind its products, whether they are actually guaranteed or not.

The business firms and retail stores which operate on this reputable basis obviously do not want to be represented by salesmen who are unscrupulous or shady in character. They want their salesmen to be open, honest, and above suspicion in all dealings with customers, so that the customers can have every confidence in their salesmen and in the store or firm. This confidence is known as *goodwill,* and it is an asset that is essential to every kind of business. The customer's goodwill is won when the customer sees that the salesman is interested in satisfying the customer's needs rather than in just making a sale. Furthermore, as long as the salesman continues to demonstrate that he is thinking in terms of the customer's interests, this goodwill will be maintained.

There are four specific danger areas that should be avoided by the salesman who is trying to maintain a reputation for being ethical. These danger areas are as follows:

1. *Getting business through bribes.* A purchasing agent may make it clear to a salesman that he expects a financial reward for giving his company's business to the salesman. He may expect the salesman to split the commission with him

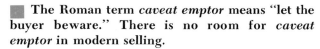 The Roman term *caveat emptor* means "let the buyer beware." There is no room for *caveat emptor* in modern selling.

The customer will look upon the salesman who consistently avoids unethical practices as a person of integrity and reliability.

Courtesy Genesco

or offer him a "kickback" on the price. Reputable businesses will not allow their salesmen to indulge in such practices, which open the door to graft and corruption of the worst kind. If a salesman is selling the customer real satisfaction of his needs, there is no need for bribery.

2. *Giving gifts and entertaining.* There is nothing unethical about taking a prospect or customer out for lunch or dinner or giving him a small gift to interest him in your product. But when the entertainment becomes very lavish and the gifts become very expensive, the line into the area of bribery has been crossed. Reputable business firms do not want to sell the buyer by placing him under obligation in this manner. Instead they prefer to sell their products on the basis of utility, service, and satisfaction.

3. *Disclosing confidential information.* In selling to a customer, a salesman may acquire information of a confidential nature which the customer does not wish the general public or his competitors to know. The experienced salesman realizes that he must never repeat such information to anyone. If the salesman also sells to the customer's competitor, the situation can become very difficult for the salesman, especially since the competitor may ask direct questions and imply that he will withdraw his business if the questions are not answered. There is only one way to handle this situation and that is to say, "If your competitor asked me to give him this information about you, you wouldn't want me to do it, would you? If I gave you this information, how could you be sure that I wouldn't tell your competitors your secrets? It is because I want you to be certain that I can be trusted with confidential information that I cannot answer your question." This kind of direct statement of the salesman's intention to be completely ethical with all his customers can only work to the salesman's advantage.

4. *Making misleading statements.* Sometimes in his anxiety to complete the sale, the salesman is tempted to make misleading or deceptive statements that seem to make his case stronger. This may close the particular sale, but it will not enhance the salesman's reputation for integrity. The customer is bound to learn the truth when he begins using the product, and he will never be willing to trust the salesman again. No one who plans to make a career of selling can afford to have this happen.

Building Goodwill Through Service

A wholesale toy salesman named George Mead took over the territory of another salesman, Bill Stokes, and within a very short time George was able to triple the volume of the orders that Bill had been getting. The reason was that whereas Bill had concentrated on selling the toys, George concentrated on service to the customer. George spent a whole afternoon helping one customer set up a window display, which resulted in a large reorder for George. George spent several hours helping another customer check his inventory and suggesting items that would complement and round out the retailer's current stock. In another instance, George worked with a customer's salesclerks to teach them how suggestion selling can be used to sell more toys. He was also always prepared to help his customers plan advertising campaigns and develop special promotional ideas. George went to all this trouble because he realized that his toys were not really that different from the toys other salesmen were offering and that the difference between keeping the customer and losing him to a competitor was simply a matter of winning the customer's goodwill by offering him the plus of service.

George's thinking represents the best of modern salesmanship. With so many products on the market and so many variations of the same product, customers find it difficult and complicated to make buying decisions. And so they naturally turn to the salesmen that make their buying decisions easier by giving extra service. This is as true in retail selling as it is in industrial and specialty selling. The salesgirl in the dress department cannot simply sell the customer the dress; she is also expected to act as a fashion consultant. The customer may ask what color shoes or what jewelry she would wear with the dress and whether the dress would be appropriate for her to wear to her son's graduation. The salesman in the furniture department must be prepared to give decorating advice whenever he sells a piece of furniture. And the salesman in a men's specialty store holds his customers because he calls them on the telephone to tell them about special sales and new shipments of merchandise. The extra effort involved in rendering these services to the customers will pay off many times over in goodwill and future sales.

It is interesting that one of the largest chain-store organizations in the world was built on the idea of friendly service. James Cash Penney, who was born in 1875, decided early in life that he wanted to be a merchant. As a young man, he worked as a salesclerk in a dry-goods store and then in 1902 he opened his first store in the little coal-mining town of Kemmerer, Wyoming. He later opened one store after another throughout the West until today the J. C. Penney Company has more than 1,600 stores. The reason for this phenomenal success is that from the beginning Mr. Penney believed in winning the goodwill of his customers by concentrating on satisfying their needs and problems.

Here is a three-point code for salesmen:

1. The customer is a human being. As such, he deserves and will get my respect and courtesy whether he buys anything or not.
2. The customer is an individual. He has his own special needs and feelings. I will seek to understand his feelings, just as I hope he will try to understand mine.
3. The customer has a right to information and the salesman an obligation to provide it. As a salesman who takes pride in his job, I will make it a point to learn all there is to know about my merchandise.

—Luther H. Hodges, U.S. Secretary of Commerce, "How to Start Things Booming Again," *This Week Magazine*

Maintaining a Spirit of Friendship

A spirit of friendship, which means mutual liking and trust, is the ideal background for successful selling. When the salesman and the customer are friends, they do not have to waste time and energy suspecting each other's motives but can get right down to the business of trying to solve the customer's buying problem *together.*

How can the salesman develop this spirit of friendship? The answer is that he must be courteous, considerate, tactful, cheerful, sincere, and honest, and he must demonstrate that he is more interested in the customer's overall welfare than in an immediate sale. As an example of this point, Jim Fisher, a truck salesman, called on Tom Mills, the owner of a hardware store that had been open for only a few months. Jim said that he thought Tom could save money by buying a truck to make his own deliveries instead of paying a delivery service. But after making a survey of Tom's business, Jim realized that at the present volume of business, the delivery service was actually cheaper. He explained his findings to Tom and suggested that Tom wait a while before purchasing the truck. When Tom's business increased, Tom called Jim back and announced that he would buy any truck that Jim recommended.

The salesman can also demonstrate his friendly interest in the prospect's welfare when the prospect turns down the salesman's proposition. The salesman can say, "I can well understand your feeling that this is not the best time for you to buy a new car, Mr. Kelly. I hope that when you decide you're ready, you will let me help you find a car that will satisfy your needs." This kind of answer makes the prospect feel that the salesman is very understanding and really anxious to be of service.

Adjusting Complaints and Claims

Every company or store, even if its products or merchandise are of the highest quality, inevitably gets some complaints and claims. Some companies set up special claim departments to handle this problem, and many stores handle all exchanges and refunds at a central adjustment desk. But very often it is the salesman who is required to settle the claim, because he is in the best position to do so. He knows the customer and the circumstances of the sale, and he has the selling ability to make the adjustment satisfy the customer.

Actually, the settling of claims is an excellent tool for building up the customer's goodwill toward the company or store. The customer whose claim is handled in a tactful, fair, and friendly manner will tell his friends of his satisfaction, which is the best kind of advertising that the firm can get. Also, the customer will return again to the salesman who has treated him so well. This is important to the salesman, because in most businesses it is easier to hold on to old customers than it is to get new ones.

What should be the salesman's attitude in handling the customer's complaint? The customer should be made to feel that the salesman is sincerely interested in his claim. Rather than being afraid of the claim, the salesman should feel grateful that the customer is voicing the complaint. It is the unexpressed grievance that hurts the firm most, since there is no chance of making it right. The salesman should feel confident that he can use the settling of the claim to strengthen the relation between the customer and himself and between the customer and the firm. Obviously the salesman cannot do this if he adopts a weak and apologetic tone and keeps trying to lay blame and make excuses. He wants to leave a positive image with the customer, not a negative one.

Sometimes, of course, an unscrupulous customer presents a completely unwarranted claim, which must be handled according to the policies of the company or store. But in most cases, the customer believes that his claim is valid and expects to be taken seriously.

Each company or store has its own specific rules for handling claims, which the salesman is expected to learn. However, the six general principles for handling claims that follow can serve as a guide for the salesman:

1. *Listen attentively and courteously.* By treating the customer courteously and showing a sincere interest in his problem, you can create goodwill even though you may have to refuse the claim. Often just letting the customer talk out his grievances makes him realize how weak his claim is. Also, listening to the customer gives the salesman more time to plan his own course of action.

Many customers are expecting a fight when they make a claim. They begin telling their story in an angry tone of voice; but when they find that the salesman is listening in a courteous and sympathetic manner, they decide to be more

■ Sometimes a customer's complaint is obviously unreasonable. Even so, the salesman should remain attentive and courteous.

reasonable themselves. This makes it possible for the merits of the claim to be discussed in a calm and friendly atmosphere.

2. *Examine and verify the trouble.* If the item is not readily transportable, the customer may have to explain to you what is wrong and you will have to be certain that you get the facts accurately. But usually you will be able to examine the goods yourself. You should examine the goods tactfully so that the customer does not get the impression that you are doubting his word. Actually this is not a large problem, because the customer generally likes the feeling that he can prove what he is saying. He is happy when you can see the trouble with your own eyes.

3. *Determine who is at fault and explain the facts.* You should determine whether the claim is the fault of the seller, the delivery agent, or the customer. If the customer received the wrong goods or defective merchandise, the seller is to blame and must make good. If the goods were damaged or lost in transit, the delivery agent is to blame and the seller must see that the customer gets satisfaction. However, it is also possible that the customer has misused the goods, in which case the seller is excused from any guarantees. For example, if a woman buys a sweater which is clearly marked "Hand wash only," she cannot make a claim against the store because the sweater shrank when it was put in the washing machine.

No matter who is at fault, the customer is entitled to a full explanation of the facts so that he can fully understand how the adjustment is to be made or why it cannot be made.

4. *Never tell a customer that he is wrong.* As you learned in Chapter 14 on handling objections, it never pays to come right out and say to a customer, "You are wrong." When a man is flatly contradicted, he feels that he has to fight to save his self-respect. If you let the claim turn into a major quarrel, an irreparable breach may be opened between the customer and the firm. You must indicate to the customer that you appreciate his viewpoint and then bring him around to your way of thinking tactfully. This calls for real salesmanship.

5. *Take action promptly.* The sooner you can handle a complaint, the better chance you have of winning the customer's goodwill. Delays and the shifting of the claim from one department to another only increase the customer's irritation and convince him that the company is not reliable.

6. *Resell.* When a claim has been settled, you have an excellent chance to re-sell the customer on your company's products or services. Obviously this is easier when the claim has been settled in favor of the customer. But even when the buyer is at fault because he has misused the product, the salesman can make him understand the advantages of the product when it is used correctly.

Avoiding High-Pressure Methods

You have seen how the good salesman builds up his customer relations by thinking always in terms of service to the customer. On the other hand, there are salesmen who do not consider the customer's needs at all, but think only of making the sale and getting the commission. They do not worry about the permanent goodwill of the customer, but employ every dishonest trick they can think of to get the customer to buy immediately. This attempt on the part of salesmen to force a customer to buy regardless of need is called high-pressure selling. Here is a typical example of how a high-pressure salesman works:

■ By handling an adjustment in a tactful, friendly manner, the salesgirl can often build goodwill that will help to increase future sales.

SALESMAN (*rings doorbell*): How do you do, madam. I'm Mr. Cole from the Wormwood Book Company. I'm bringing you your copy of *The Child's Shakespeare.*

CUSTOMER: Oh, I didn't think anyone would call on me when I mailed that coupon. I thought it would come through the mail.

SALESMAN: We feel that it is better to present this little giftbook in person. Also, it gives us a chance to talk to you about the education of your children. You are interested in seeing that they get the finest education available, aren't you?

CUSTOMER: Yes, but—

SALESMAN: Here is your free book. May I come in and show you our Junior Encyclopedia? It will take only a moment.

CUSTOMER: Well, I don't know. I was just doing my—

SALESMAN (*entering house*): Thank you. My, what a lovely living room. A set of our books in their beautiful morocco bindings would add importance to this beauty. See what I mean?

(*Places sample copy on a nearby end table.*)

CUSTOMER: It does look nice, but—

SALESMAN: Let me show you what you get, and all for a dollar down and a dollar a week. And you have a whole year and a half to pay.

(*Opens his books and proceeds with sales talk.*)

CUSTOMER (*after sales talk*): Well, I don't know. We really can't afford a set of these now, and we already have an encyclopedia.

SALESMAN: But those books are ages old, madam. And the schools today are emphasizing accurate, up-to-date knowledge. You wouldn't want your child to make failing grades, would you? Of course you wouldn't. Now I'll tell you what I'm going to do. I'll leave a set of these books with you for a few days. No obligation. You let the children look them over. They'll love them.

CUSTOMER (*wearily*): Well, all right, if that will make you happy.

SALESMAN: No trouble at all. And now, if you will sign this blank, I'll be back in a few days to hear your decision.

CUSTOMER: But this is an order blank!

SALESMAN: That's right. But it's only a routine way of sending our merchandise on approval. You can send the books back without obligation if you want.

This kind of salesman obviously has more in common with the Phoenician traders than he does with the successful modern salesman. Today's salesman considers himself a professional man and has his own ethical code of service, which demands that he be considerate of the needs, time, convenience, and financial position of his prospects and customers.

SUMMING UP

Although the rule of *caveat emptor* has governed buying and selling for centuries and is still a recognized principle of law, it is not the system under which most modern business firms operate. Reputable firms feel that the only policy that works in the long run for winning and maintaining the customer's goodwill is complete honesty. These firms want their salesmen to reflect this attitude so that the customer's confidence can be won. In addition, these firms expect their salesmen to sell the customer complete satisfaction of his needs rather than just the product.

The four danger areas that should be avoided by the salesman who is trying to be ethical are (1) getting business through bribes, (2) giving gifts and entertaining, (3) disclosing confidential information, and (4) making misleading statements.

The salesman can build up the goodwill of his customers by offering them related services that will help them to enjoy the product more. The salesman should also strive to maintain a spirit of friendship with his customers. The important thing is that the customers should be convinced the salesman is genuinely trying to help them. The salesman can build up goodwill for himself and his firm by handling his customers' complaints and claims in a tactful, fair, and friendly manner.

The successful modern salesman is the opposite of the high-pressure type of salesman who is only concerned with the immediate sale.

Reviewing Your Reading

1. What does *caveat emptor* mean in English? Explain this rule.
2. Why do reputable modern businesses not operate under the system of *caveat emptor?*
3. Why are dishonest firms ultimately driven out of business?
4. What is goodwill?
5. List four danger areas that the ethical salesman should avoid. Explain why each one is unethical.
6. How did James Cash Penney benefit from the principle of giving friendly service?

7. Why is the salesman in a good position to handle complaints and claims?
8. Describe how the salesman should feel about complaints and claims.
9. What are the six general rules for handling complaints and claims?
10. Why is high-pressure selling a shortsighted policy?

For Discussion

1. Why does service to the customer build goodwill?
2. Describe the extra service that would be appreciated by the customer of each of the following:
   a. Gas station attendant
   b. Salesgirl of women's suits
   c. Bread salesman selling to grocers
   d. Lamp salesman
3. In the story on page 431, why was Tom Mills impressed by Jim Fisher's advice not to buy a truck at the present time?
4. Why is it important to have a friendly attitude toward the man who refuses to buy your product?
5. A shoe salesman made this statement: "If I'm out of a woman's size, I just sell her the next nearest size. Women care more about style than they do about fit anyhow." Criticize this statement.
6. Why should a salesman avoid discussing the confidential aspects of a customer's business with other customers?
7. If you were a salesman and were notified by your firm to refuse a customer's claim, and your customer was at fault, how would you handle the situation?

Sales Problem

Bill Simons was one of twelve salesmen employed by a paint company. He had been given brief factory training to learn how the firm's paints and varnishes were made. However, Bill did not possess the technical knowledge needed to diagnose industrial paint problems. The company held the goodwill of its customers in high esteem, but preferred having its salesmen refer all troubles to the factory.

While Bill was calling on one of his customers, a contracting firm, a foreman came over to him and said, "You're just the guy I want to see. We've been having all kinds of trouble with that last batch of paint your company sent us. The paint hardens in the can, and we can't get it to mix."

Bill replied, "I don't see why it should. We haven't had a complaint like that in years."

QUESTIONS

1. Criticize Bill's handling of this matter.
2. How would you have handled it?

Salesmanship in Action

1. List and describe a number of ways in which salesmen may misrepresent goods. Suggest how to avoid these misrepresentations.
2. You are selling in the men's shoe department, and a customer angrily demands to see the salesman that sold him "these blankety-blank shoes." The customer is in a belligerent mood and apparently expects to have an argument. You are the salesman who sold him the shoes. How will you handle this case? Write your answer.

The Techniques of Getting
a Selling Job

IN STUDYING the principles of salesmanship in this book, you have learned how to sell a product or service to a customer. You can put these same principles to work when you go to get a selling job, only in this case the product that you are going to sell is yourself. The techniques of the salesman and the job hunter are very much the same, as the comparison at the bottom of page 440 will show.

Knowing Your Salable Qualities

Just as a salesman must have complete knowledge of his product, so you must know yourself before you can convince an employer that you are worth hiring. Examine yourself from a prospective employer's point of view.

First of all, you must know why you want to go into selling. What qualities do you have that make you think you would be a success at selling? Are you convinced that you will enjoy selling? No one should choose a career just because

■ The job hunter seeks success as his goal. The techniques he uses to get a selling job are much like those the salesman uses to sell his products.

of the money that he thinks he can earn. You are going to spend *at least* one-third of your life at whatever job you choose, and so it should be something that gives you a real sense of satisfaction.

Ask yourself also whether you are willing to learn, because if you are not, selling is not the right career for you. You may have a very winning personality and be a very persuasive talker; but today's salesman is a professional man, and like

---

THE SALESMAN VERSUS THE JOB HUNTER

Salesman	Job Hunter
1. Knows his product	1. Knows his salable qualities
2. Finds likely prospects	2. Finds prospective employers
3. Studies the best way to make the sale in the preapproach stage	3. Studies the best way to present himself in the preapproach stage
4. Tries to get appointments for interviews	4. Tries to get appointments for interviews
5. Makes an effective approach	5. Makes an effective approach
6. Presents his product	6. Sells himself
7. Overcomes objections	7. Overcomes objections
8. Gets action	8. Gets the job
9. Analyzes lost sales	9. Analyzes job turndowns
10. Gives the customer good service on the product	10. Works hard to please his employer

---

the doctor and the lawyer, he must be constantly learning more about his work. You must be sure that you can be patient through whatever training program you will be required to take, and you must be prepared to go on learning. Companies are well aware that men who are individualists make great salesmen; but while it is good to be independently resourceful, it is wrong to be an unyielding know-it-all.

As you are examining yourself from a prospective employer's point of view, think about what kind of selling you would like to do. Do you have a special interest that would help you to sell better in one field than another? If music is your hobby, perhaps you should think of selling in a music store. Or perhaps you are mechanically inclined or have a special interest in gardening, sports-car racing, fashion, or athletics. The point is that your hobbies and extra interests will be highly salable to the right employer and you should be prepared to capitalize on them.

If you feel unsure about your own self-analysis of your qualifications as a salesman, you might consider taking an aptitude test. Many large companies administer such tests to all prospective employees; but before you are even out of school, you can take one of the tests given by various counseling services or private personnel agencies. And, of course, another method of testing your conclusions about your selling ability is to take a part-time selling job while you are still in school. In this way you can find out whether you are qualified for selling before you choose the field for a permanent career.

Courtesy John H. Patterson Cooperative High School, Dayton, Ohio

Do you like to sell? Taking a part-time selling job while you are still in school will help you to answer this question.

Finding Prospective Employers

Once you have decided what your qualifications are and what field of selling is most interesting to you, you should begin compiling a list of firms which might have job openings that you would like to fill. There are seven ways of finding out about job openings: (1) suggestions from friends and relatives, (2) contacts with former employers, (3) the school placement bureau, (4) employment agencies, (5) help-wanted advertisements, (6) sales executives clubs, and (7) detective work.

Suggestions from Friends and Relatives. It is a good idea to let as many people as possible know what kind of job you are looking for, because they may know personally of some job openings and may even be in a position to recommend you for a job.

Contacts with Former Employers. If you have had jobs after school or during the summer, you should let your former employers know what kind of job you want. Businessmen belong to all kinds of organizations, such as the Chamber of Commerce, the Rotary, the Kiwanis Club, and so on. Through his contacts with these organizations, your former employer may know of some job openings.

The School Placement Bureau. Many employers make a habit of letting the guidance counselors in the high schools know about job openings. The school placement bureau, knowing your record, is in a good position to steer you to the right job.

Employment Agencies. Private and government employment agencies are, of course, an excellent way to find out about job openings. The people in these agencies are specially trained to find the right man for the right job.

Help-Wanted Advertisements. The help-wanted advertisements in current newspapers and trade magazines should be systematically checked by anyone who is looking for a job. These ads are a guide to working conditions and salaries in the selling field, as well as a way of finding a job.

Sales Executives Clubs. There are many sales executives clubs throughout the country that are very interested in helping young people to find jobs in selling. They work with students in high schools and colleges to interest them in selling. They also have current data on available selling jobs. Ask your guidance counselor for the address of the sales executives club nearest you.

■ You can find the names of different firms and get information about them by consulting various publications in your library.

Detective Work. By consulting trade directories such as *Sweet's Catalog Service* and investments manuals such as *Moody's Industrials*, you can get the names of firms whose products you would like to sell. You can also read the financial section of your daily newspaper, general business magazines such as *Business Week* and *Nation's Business*, and specific magazines for salesmen such as *Sales Management* and *Opportunities in Selling* for information about what various companies are doing. You may read that a certain company is expanding into a new field of operations or that a branch store of a national company is going to be opened in your area. You may read an article by a sales manager explaining what kind of salesmen his company likes to hire or an article about how salesmen are desperately needed in a certain field. All this information adds up to "clues" that tell you where to go for a job.

Using the Principles of the Preapproach

The success of any salesman is directly dependent upon how much thought and effort he puts into the preapproach stage of the sale. This is equally true when you are trying to find a job. The four things that you must consider in the preapproach stage of job hunting are (1) your appearance and speech, (2) your attitude, (3) your knowledge of the prospective employer, and (4) the organization of your self-presentation.

Your Appearance and Speech. It should be obvious to you that you should give a great deal of thought to your appearance when you are ready to apply for a job. The man who is going to hire you has to figure out what kind of impression you are going to make on other people. He will not be willing to hire you as a representative of the company if you have a stained, rumpled suit or dress, unpolished shoes, and unkempt fingernails or if you wear extreme clothes and have a faddish hair style. You are asking to be considered for a business position, so you must have a businesslike appearance.

You should also check your speech habits before you call on a prospective employer. Bad grammer and a halting, unsure way of speaking that is full of "uhs" and "ers" will indicate to your interviewer that you will not be able to speak well to a prospect either.

Your Attitude. All that has been said in this book about the necessity for the salesman to have a positive attitude is especially applicable to the job hunter. You must have confidence in yourself if you expect the interviewer to have enough confidence in you to hire you. If you act as though you don't expect to get the job, then you won't. Of course, you don't have to carry this self-confidence so far that you give the impression of being conceited and cocky. You must strive for the happy medium that makes the interviewer feel you have what it takes to make good if you are given the chance and yet you are modest enough to be willing to learn and pleasant to work with.

Your Knowledge of the Prospective Employer. Before you apply for an interview with a given company, you should make every effort to find out all pertinent facts about the company, its products, and its policies. You should try to get the answers to such questions as these:

1. What is the product or service of the company?
2. What and where is the market for the product?
3. To what type of customer does the product appeal?
4. Is the company growing?
5. What is the status of the company in the industry?
6. Does the company have a training program?
7. What are the company's relations with its employees?

One of the best ways to find out the answers to such questions is to ask someone who works for the company. You can also ask local businessmen who are usually familiar with all the businesses in the community. In the case of a large company, try to get hold of the printed annual report that the company's directors prepare for its stockholders.

The Organization of Your Self-Presentation. To get ready for the interview, you should organize all the information about yourself into a portfolio. The most important part of this portfolio will be a personal data sheet (also known as a résumé) which will include a brief summary of your background, education, extracurricular activities and interests, job experience, and references. The portfolio might also include any merit certificates which you have received and any newspaper clippings describing those activities with which you have been connected.

The portfolio makes its best appearance when in the form of an attractive leather or plastic binder containing 8½- by 11-inch pages. Such binders are now obtainable with cellophane pocket pages into which pertinent letters, clippings, or photographs can be inserted and viewed without becoming marred by use.

How does a portfolio help? It is a sales tool that illustrates the selling points about yourself that you give orally in the interview. It is used as a visual aid and should be arranged so that, as you turn the pages, you are demonstrating the selling points of your personal presentation in the most effective manner possible.

Once you have prepared the portfolio, you should try to anticipate the questions that the interviewer will ask you and think through your answers to them. For instance, he will surely ask you either directly or indirectly why you want to sell in the first place and why you want to sell for his company in particular. The importance of being prepared for these two questions is illustrated by the following story:

Jimmy Bates was one of Baker's best scholars. His grades were exceptionally high, he was an outstanding athlete, and he was very popular. His classmates and teachers voted him as the boy most likely to succeed. A few days after graduation, the salesmanship instructor arranged an interview for Jimmy with Mr. Charles, a sales manager for a large paper company. Everyone felt that Jimmy's future was assured. However, after the interview, Jimmy told the instructor that he had failed to get the position. The instructor was surprised and telephoned to ask the sales manager what was wrong.

"Jimmy's a fine young man, and has a lot of fine qualities," said the sales manager. "But during the entire forty minutes that we talked, Jimmy did not once tell me what he could offer our firm nor did he present a single reason for wanting to work in this field."

You must also be prepared for questions about your personal life. With the modern knowledge of and interest in psychology, business firms have come to feel that they must consider the whole man when they hire someone. They have found that if a man is discontented and unhappy at home, this will have an effect on his business life. You should also be ready to describe your school and previous job experiences, as well as your long-range objectives.

Getting Appointments for Interviews

Now you are ready to apply for the job, and the question is how to go about getting an interview. There are three methods of doing this: (1) applying directly to the personnel office, (2) sending a letter of application, and (3) telephoning for an appointment.

Applying Directly to the Personnel Office. The salesman who is trying to get an interview frequently does best if he goes directly to the prospect and requests the interview on the spot. This is also true of the job hunter, who may find that his pleasant looks and manner will say more for him than any letter could. But even if the interview is granted immediately, the applicant will probably be asked to fill out an application blank as a follow-up, so that the interviewer will have some written information to which he can refer. And sometimes the applicant is not given an interview immediately but is simply asked to fill out an application blank and then is told that he will be called for an interview after the blank has been studied. There may also be certain tests that the applicant must take before the interview, such as the sales aptitude test mentioned earlier in the chapter.

Actually the application blank is in itself a test. The company wants to know how well you can understand questions and how you approach the problem of answering them. You are also being tested on your neatness. Thus, you should be very careful about how you fill out the blank. Don't dash ahead blindly, giving too quick an answer to each question. Always read the entire application blank before beginning to answer the first question. Think out each answer before you attempt to write it. Remember that neatness, legibility, and your choice of words will tell your prospective employer almost as much about you as your answers to the questions. You should answer every question, briefly but completely. Be sure to account for all dates and periods of education and employment so that the employer can get a consecutive picture of your background.

Sending a Letter of Application. Sometimes it is best to send a letter of application before making a personal call. Many employers who are advertising in newspapers or trade journals request such letters so that they can weed out the applicants to save interviewing time. Also, if you have more prospective employers on your list than you can handle, you can write letters to help you to sort out the ones that would be interested in hiring you.

You should make a real effort to have your letter of application as businesslike as possible. Type it on good-quality paper and see that it is nicely spaced, clean, and generally attractive-looking. Be sure that you mail the original and not a carbon copy. The grammar and the spelling must be correct, and the letter must give evidence that you can think and write clearly.

Try to address your letter to a specific person, by name, rather than just to the firm. And be sure that you are spelling the name correctly. You can always verify the spelling by calling the man's secretary on the telephone.

Remember that your letter must catch the attention of the prospective employer and that it must stand out among all the others that he receives if you are to be granted an interview. The letter should be brief, but precise. Start it by stating exactly what type of position you are seeking. Then tell why you are interested in the particular firm and give your major qualifications. Don't go into any more detail in the letter itself, but enclose a copy of your personal résumé with the letter. Close your letter by saying that you will be glad to appear for an interview at the prospective employer's convenience. Examples of a letter of application and a personal résumé are given on pages 448 and 449, respectively.

■ **Some companies require their applicants to take aptitude and intelligence tests. Here the applicants have been sent by different companies to an aptitude testing firm for these tests.**

Courtesy The Klein Institute for Aptitude Testing, Inc.

```
                                               359 Beaumont Road
                                               Lakewood, Indiana    76102
                                               June 7, 19--



        Mr. Jerome Cramer
        Personnel Manager
        Kaufman's Department Store
        200 Center Avenue
        Lakewood, Indiana    76102

        Dear Mr. Cramer:

             Mr. Harrison, principal of Lakewood High School, has informed me
        that you have an opening for a salesman in your store.  Please consider
        me an applicant for the position.

             The enclosed personal data sheet describes my qualifications.  On
        June 21, I shall graduate from Lakewood High School.  My two favorite
        subjects in high school have been salesmanship and retailing.  In addi-
        tion, I have been working as a part-time salesclerk at Brown's Station-
        ery Store during my senior year, and I was employed as a salesclerk at
        the Lakewood Hardware Company last summer.  The opening in your depart-
        ment store sounds exactly like the type of work I would like to do and
        for which I believe I am best qualified.  You will also find me eager
        to learn and to improve myself.

             I shall be glad to come for an interview when it is convenient for
        you.  School is over at 3 p.m. each day, so I could arrange to come to
        your office any day after that time; or I could come to see you on a
        Saturday if you prefer.  You may telephone me at my home (463-7391).

                                               Sincerely yours,

                                               Harold Thompson
                                               Harold Thompson

        Enclosure
```

■ The letter of application should be brief, but it must catch the prospective employer's attention.

```
                        PERSONAL DATA SHEET


       NAME:            Harold Thompson

       ADDRESS:         359 Beaumont Road
                        Lakewood, Indiana   76102

       TELEPHONE:       463-7391

       POSITION SOUGHT: Salesman

       DATE:            June 6, 19--


       PERSONAL INFORMATION

           Age:     18                 Date of Birth:  February 3, 1947
           Height:  5 feet 10 inches
           Weight:  156 pounds
           Health:  Excellent

       EDUCATION

           Will graduate from Lakewood High School on June 21, 1965, with a
             major in business education
           Business subjects studied:
             General business, salesmanship, retailing, bookkeeping, and
             typing
           Member of Lakewood High School Honor Society
           Class treasurer in junior year
           Member of Student Council
           Played clarinet in school orchestra
           Reporter on Lakewood High School Echo

       EXPERIENCE

           Part-time salesclerk at Brown's Stationery Store during senior
             year in high school
           Salesclerk at Lakewood Hardware Company, summer of 1964
           Part-time assistant in office of principal during junior year in
             high school

       ACTIVITIES AND INTERESTS

           Member of church choir
           Amateur radio operator
           Hobbies include swimming, sailing, and woodworking

       REFERENCES

           Mr. Richard Harrison, principal, Lakewood High School
           Mr. Carl McGuire, Lakewood Hardware Company, 45 Center Avenue
           Mr. Raymond Brown, Brown's Stationery Store, 137 Clifton Street
           Rev. James L. Taylor, Congregational Church, 29 Hooker Avenue
```

■ A personal data sheet, or résumé, is enclosed with the letter of application.

Telephoning for an Appointment. Sometimes it is a real courtesy to the prospective employer for you to telephone him and ask for an appointment. This is especially true in small companies where the person in charge of hiring is apt to have many other duties and must find a convenient time to see you. It is also a good idea to save yourself a wasted trip if the company is at a distance from your home.

The telephone call should follow the principles for using the telephone successfully that were described in Chapter 18. Remember that your telephone call is only for the purpose of securing the interview. Don't try to go into lengthy details that may irritate or bore the prospective employer. Be brief, businesslike, confident, and polite.

Making an Effective Approach

As in any selling situation, the first few minutes that you spend with your prospective employer are in many ways the most important part of the interview. You must use these few minutes to gain the favorable attention of your interviewer and to arouse his interest in you. Much of this depends on how you look and on your manner. The interviewer is looking for a man who not only can sell but also is willing to work hard and be loyal to the company. If he doesn't see some signs of these qualities during the approach, the interview is not going to go well.

If the interviewer offers his hand, shake it cordially and briefly. Don't try to crush his knuckles, and likewise don't let your hand be limp and lifeless. But take the cue from him—don't try to force a handshake if he doesn't extend his hand first. Wait for him to offer you a seat, and when he does, sit down in a natural manner that is relaxed but respectful. Don't slouch or lie back in your chair, but sit forward and state the purpose of your visit: "Mr. Gilmore, I would like to apply for a position as a salesman."

If you have to see a secretary or receptionist before you see your interviewer, be courteous and businesslike with her. Don't take up her time with unnecessary conversation and don't get too chummy or familiar. You can be sure that her boss will hear about it if you make a bad impression on her.

Selling Yourself

There is one big difference between selling a product to a customer and selling yourself to an employer. When you are working with a customer, you try to stay in control of the interview, but when you are selling yourself, you have to let the interviewer take the lead. Answer his questions promptly and directly. Be definite and truthful. Show enthusiasm for being a salesman *for the products of his company.* Let him see that you are more interested in the opportunity to start your career in selling and to develop and learn with a reputable company than you are in how much money you will make and how quickly you can make it. Don't ask questions with a negative quality to them, such as:

"Do I have to take all that special training?"
"Will I have to work on Saturdays?"
"Do I have to put up a bond?"
"Will I have to pay for my demonstrator kit?"

Remember that the prospective employer's purpose in interviewing you is to find out whether you will be a trustworthy employee and a good representative of the company. He wants to know about:

1. Your home background
2. Your education and training
3. Your work experience
4. Your manners and appearance

■ **During the interview be sure to let the interviewer take the lead.**

5. Your social adjustment
6. Your personality qualifications
7. Your motivation for selling
8. Your objectives and ambitions

You can give the interviewer the information about many of these points by showing him your job portfolio, which will work in the same way as any visual aid in a regular selling situation.

When you go into the interview, you must be prepared for an interviewer who is an individual with his own personality and his own moods. You may find that he is hostile, cool, and abrupt, or he may be friendly and cordial. He may be easygoing or obstinate. He may be cheerful and talkative, or he may be silent and sullen. These moods may be natural, or they may be assumed. He may be testing you to determine how you stand up "under fire." His overfriendly attitude may be put on to see if you will become overfamiliar or confidential under such circumstances. His stubborn, irritable manner may be assumed to see if you will wilt in the face of obstacles. The interviewer may also try to get you into an argument, but you must not fall for this. Keep an even temper and remember that winning the argument will lose the job.

No matter what the interviewer's procedure is, you must show him that you can take it and still stay enthusiastic and interested.

Overcoming Objections

Sometimes the interviewer will test your confidence in yourself by posing objections to how well you can do the job. Here are two examples:

INTERVIEWER: Being captain of the football team is a pretty important job. But the only job I could offer you is at the bottom. I don't think a boy like you would like that.

APPLICANT: **Mr. Barnes, my friends, and even my father, told me not to go out for football in the first place because I was so light. But it was something that I really wanted to do even though it meant I would have to work that much harder than everyone else. I was willing to start at the bottom on the squad and I'm willing to start at the bottom here.**

INTERVIEWER: I see that you haven't done any extracurricular work at school. Shall I take that to mean that you weren't interested enough to bother?

APPLICANT: **No, sir. I would have liked very much to have joined some of the clubs at school. But that would have meant staying after regular school** hours, and I couldn't do that because of my job. I needed the job, Mr. Swann, to be able to get through school at all. But I feel that the experience I gained in my job is going to be more valuable to me now than any extracurricular activities might have been.

Getting the Job

When the interviewer has all the information that he needs, he will terminate the interview. Usually he will give the cue that it is time for you to leave by rising. When this time comes, don't linger and keep talking. Arise, shake hands if that is indicated, thank him, and leave. Don't remain standing at the door, and don't desperately try to crowd in some last-minute points.

If the interview has not resulted in a definite offer of a job, do not show any disappointment. The interviewer may want to check your references or review the material about you or just think over your qualifications. However, it is permissible to ask about the next step. You may ask whether you should telephone the interviewer for a decision or whether he will telephone or write you. The interviewer will think more of you if you show that you expect not to be forgotten.

When you get home, you should send the interviewer a letter of appreciation, thanking him for his kind consideration and reaffirming your interest in the company, its products, and the kind of work involved. You may restate your strongest qualifications, emphasizing those in which you feel the interviewer was most interested. An example of a letter of appreciation is given on page 454.

Then make out a card on which you record the name of the company, the names of the people you met, the date of the interview, the type of job, a summary of the interview, and the date that you should call back or can expect to hear from the interviewer. This system will keep your various interviews straight in your mind, and you will be where you should be on the right date.

Analyzing Turndowns

You are familiar with the principle of analyzing the reasons for your failure to make a sale. This is also important when you have been turned down for a job. You should go back over all the steps with a very critical attitude to see what you did wrong or what you could have done better. You should attempt to learn from your mistakes rather than becoming discouraged by them. You should feel that there is a job for you, and you should be prepared to keep going until you find it.

```
                                    359 Beaumont Road
                                    Lakewood, Indiana    76102
                                    June 14, 19--



        Mr. Jerome Cramer
        Personnel Manager
        Kaufman's Department Store
        200 Center Avenue
        Lakewood, Indiana    76102

        Dear Mr. Cramer:

            I enjoyed very much meeting you yesterday and
        discussing with you the opening for a salesman at
        Kaufman's Department Store.  The work sounds exciting
        and challenging, and I am now more convinced than
        ever that I would like to work at Kaufman's.  My
        past sales experience, together with my courses in
        salesmanship and retailing, has proved to me that
        selling is the type of work in which I know I can
        succeed.

            Thank you for your time and the consideration
        you have shown me.

                                    Sincerely yours,

                                    Harold Thompson
                                    Harold Thompson
```

■ It is appropriate to send the interviewer a letter of appreciation when you get home.

Giving Your Employer His Money's Worth

The good salesman does not simply make the sale and then forget about the customer. He tries to win the customer's goodwill by continuing to offer the customer service. Likewise the newly hired salesman has an obligation to do a good job for his employer and to prove to the employer that he made a wise choice.

SUMMING UP

Selling yourself to a prospective employer is so much like selling a product or service to a customer that the job hunter can use many of the same techniques as the salesman.

The man who is looking for a job must first of all know his salable qualities. Then he must find out about job openings which he can do through (1) suggestions from friends and relatives, (2) contacts with former employers, (3) the school placement bureau, (4) employment agencies, (5) help-wanted advertisements, (6) sales executives clubs, and (7) detective work.

The job applicant, using the principles of the preapproach, should consider his appearance, his speech, and his attitude. He should check all pertinent facts about the prospective employers that he plans to contact. He should also organize the information about himself into a portfolio and then should try to anticipate the interviewer's questions and be prepared to answer them.

To get appointments for interviews, the job hunter can apply directly to the personnel office, send a letter of application, or telephone.

The applicant should be confident and positive in the interview, so that the interviewer will feel that the applicant will be a trustworthy employee and a good representative of the company. The interview should be followed up with a letter of appreciation.

If you do not get the job, you should analyze the reasons for your failure and try to learn by your mistakes. If you do get it, you should work hard so that your new employer will be completely satisfied with your service.

Reviewing Your Reading

1. Why is a willingness to learn important for a salesman?
2. When are aptitude tests helpful to the young person who is choosing a career?
3. List the seven ways of finding out about job openings.
4. Explain what is meant by "detective work" to find job openings.
5. Why is your appearance important when you are applying for a job?
6. Give seven examples of the kinds of questions you will want answered about each company to which you plan to apply for an interview.
7. How can you find out the answers to your questions about the pertinent facts of each company?

8. Explain what a job portfolio is, how it should be prepared, and how it can be used.
9. List three ways of getting interviews.
10. When would it be wise to telephone a prospective employer for an appointment?
11. Should you always try to shake hands with your interviewer? Explain your answer.
12. List the eight things that the interviewer wants to know about you.
13. Why would the interviewer pretend to you that he is very friendly?
14. Why is it a good idea to write a letter of appreciation after the interview?
15. What can you gain by analyzing your job turndowns?

For Discussion

1. List the qualities that a man should have to be a success in selling. Think about everything you have read in this book when you give your answer.
2. Why do employers want to know about a man's personal life before they hire him?
3. Discuss the best way to go about filling out an application blank.
4. Why does a company want to know whether you can be enthusiastic about selling its products?
5. How do you think the interviewer would feel about the negative questions on page 451?
6. How do you think the interviewer would feel about the answers to the objections on pages 452 and 453?

Salesmanship in Action

1. Write a letter of application to a firm for which you would like to work. Follow the principles for such letters given in this chapter.
2. Arrange for job interviews to take place in class. The instructor or a member of the class may act as the interviewer, and other members of the class may take turns as job applicants. After each interview, analyze the way the applicant behaved.
3. Do you think that the principles discussed here for getting a selling job would apply to any job applicant? Write out your answer.

Appendix 1

(*To be assigned at the option of the instructor*)

Successful salesmen devote a great deal of time to study and research in order to discover new ideas, fresh approaches, and creative methods to make their sales presentations more effective. These top salesmen write their ideas down on paper and then attempt to organize them into a plan they can use in their work. Many fine company sales manuals have been built around the groundwork laid down by the salesmen of the firm.

You will be given an opportunity to make a complete product study and prepare a sales manual built around a product (or line of products) of your selection. Your sales manual will be a project that you will work on during the entire term. Although your instructor will provide you with a complete timetable, here are some of the things you will be called upon to do:

1. **Selection of product.** Hand in to your instructor, on a 3- by 5-inch card, your selection of a product (or line of products) for your project.

2. **Availability.** Make a list of a few places in your community where your product can be purchased. Prepare this list on a standard 8½- by 11-inch sheet of paper. State whether there is a wholesaler or special distributor in your area.

3. **Distribution.** Draw a chart showing the channels of distribution for your product as discussed in Chapter 2. Show how the product gets from the manufacturer to the ultimate consumer.

4. **Objectives.** Prepare a list of objectives you can attain as a salesman selling the product you have selected.

5. **Personal characteristics.** List the personal characteristics needed for success in selling the product and the training required.

457

6. **Buying motives.** Prepare a list of buying motives for the product you have selected. Classify the motives as (*a*) emotional, (*b*) rational, (*c*) dominant, (*d*) secondary, and (*e*) patronage.

7. **History of product.** Use the encyclopedia to obtain information about the history and background of the product—when it was first manufactured, when it was first used, and how it was developed to its present stage.

8. **History of company.** Find out when the company who manufactured your product was founded, how it has grown to its present status, and how it stands in the industry today. (Most of the information can be obtained by writing a letter to the company. Additional information may be secured from magazine and newspaper articles.)

9. **Selling features.** Prepare a list of selling features about your product. These will come primarily from sales literature that you can obtain by writing to the company that makes and sells your product. Of course, you should also plan on using magazine and newspaper advertisements regarding your chosen product, which you can find in the school library or public library.

   Classify your information into selling features and prepare a product analysis sheet similar to the one shown in Chapter 11. Make it as complete as you can, using every possible product fact that will help you sell your product. If you have selected a line of products as your project, analyze only one main item of your line.

10. **Selling adjectives.** List twenty-five adjectives that might be used in "putting over" your product.

11. **Competition.** Name three competing products. Obtain two advertisements from the competitors. Draw up three reasons for buying your product over that of a competitor.

12. **General information.** Read at least one magazine article about your product and write a brief report summarizing this article. A suggested start might be *Consumer Reports, The Reader's Digest, Business Week,* or *Fortune.*

13. **Advertising.** Obtain three advertisements for your product. State the basic buying motives appealed to in each ad. Describe what you believe to be the best advertising media for your product—radio, TV, magazines, and so on.

    Prepare an original advertisement for your product. Write your copy around the basic buying motives you listed in No. 6.

14. **The approach.** Now begin to work on the approach that you will use in your sales presentation of the product that you selected. First decide on the type of approach. Then state how you will create a favorable impression, how you will establish a friendly atmosphere, and how you will handle all the other factors discussed in Chapter 12.

    Prepare a list of at least fifteen effective single selling sentences that you could use as an opening remark.

15. **List of demonstrations.** Prepare a list of the different ways in which the product that you selected may be demonstrated. Refer to your list of sales appeals or "sizzles," and plan a demonstration for each one. The following form is suggested for planning each demonstration:

Product _____

Selling feature _____

What to Do	What to Say

The following questions will help you to build each demonstration:
a. What testimonials, facts, analogies, and so on, will you use?
b. What visual material will you use?
c. What senses will you appeal to? How? (Try to appeal to all if possible.)
d. How are you going to get the customer to participate?

16. **Objection analysis sheet.** Prepare an objection analysis sheet, listing possible objections to the product that you selected. Give your answers to each objection, following the principles discussed in Chapter 14, and name the method that you used for each.

17. **Short product stories.** You are now ready to write a planned sales presentation for your product. Prepare a series of short product stories dramatizing each of the sales appeals. End each story with a suggestion that the customer place his order.

18. **List of closing procedures.** Prepare a series of closing procedures that could be used in the sale of your product. Label each one according to its type, and insert it in the sales manual that you are preparing.

19. **List of related suggestions.** Prepare a list of related items that could be suggested to a customer who has purchased your product. Write the statements that you would make for each item. Follow the principles for suggestion selling described in Chapter 16.

If the product or line of products that you selected for your term project requires a multi-call procedure, write a plan for selling more on each call. Include at least three calls in your plan.

20. **Systematizing your efforts.** Design a timesaving system for yourself as a salesman of the product that you have chosen. Include in this system (*a*) a time schedule showing the apportionment of your day, (*b*) a set of rules guiding principles that will give you the most effective coverage of your territory, and (*c*) a series of record forms that you feel would provide you with the necessary information on your prospects and selling activities.

21. **Critical analysis of your product.** Criticize your product and provide at least one suggestion as to how your product or its distribution could be improved.

Appendix 2

Here are the answers that indicate interests or characteristics favorable to success in sales work. To obtain your score, add the number of your answers that agree with these. If your score is 16 or above, your chances of success in the selling field are favorable. A score below 16 indicates that you probably would have better chances of success in some other field.

1. — No	6. — No	11. Yes —	16. — No	21. — No
2. — No	7. Yes —	12. — No	17. Yes —	22. — No
3. Yes —	8. — No	13. Yes —	18. — No	23. — No
4. — No	9. Yes —	14. — No	19. Yes —	24. Yes —
5. Yes —	10. — No	15. Yes —	20. Yes —	25. Yes —

Key to Personality Rating Scale

A perfect score is 177 points. Needless to say, a perfect score is seldom attained. The typical personality score ranges between 65 and 100. For girls, the average is approximately 85; for boys, approximately 80.

If you score between 100 and 135, you are certain to be a well-liked person. However, there is obviously still room for improvement even though you are above average.

If you score between 135 and 177, you are exceptionally well adjusted and very personable and you possess a great deal of strength in those qualities that people generally admire and respect in others. However, don't be content to rest on your laurels. Remember, there is no perfect person. Plan on further improvement. Let your strong characteristics work for you and concentrate on those qualities on which the rating scale indicates you need improvement.

460

	KEY					SCORE
1. Confidence	25	16	10	2	0	_____
2. Perseverance	16	12	8	3	0	_____
3. Comprehension	20	15	7	3	0	_____
4. Reliability	15	10	5	2	0	_____
5. Tact	7	5	3	2	0	_____
6. Loyalty	16	12	6	3	0	_____
7. Enthusiasm	15	12	9	5	0	_____
8. Leadership	23	18	10	4	0	_____
9. Conversational ability	10	7	4	2	0	_____
10. Oral Expression	10	7	5	2	0	_____
11. Poise	12	8	4	2	0	_____
12. Grooming	8	6	4	2	0	_____
					Total score	_____

Negative Voice Score

If your answer to a question is "yes," put down 5. If your answer is "sometimes," put down 2. If your answer is "no," put down 0. Notice that the lower the numerical score, the fewer voice faults of the student.

0 to 10	Excellent
11 to 20	Good
21 to 30	Fair
Above 30	Unsatisfactory

Positive Voice Score

If your answer to a question is "yes," put down 5. If your answer is "sometimes," put down 2. If your answer is "no," put down 0.

90 to 100	Excellent—a rare score
80 to 89	Good
70 to 79	Fair
Below 70	Unsatisfactory

Index

462